Political Ideas in Mode

Political thinking in the western world has undergone dramatic changes in the late stages of the twentieth century, particularly with the recent rise of the New Right and the collapse of state communism in 1989. The world of the old orthodoxies of conservatism and socialism has come to an end and new concepts and titles, different labels, and different explanatory patterns are needed for new times.

Rodney Barker's *Political Ideas in Modern Britain: In and After the Twentieth Century* is a provocative and stimulating guide to political thinking in the United Kingdom since the 1880s. Spanning the development of political thought from Morris to market socialism, from communism to communitarianism, from fascism to feminism, this study shows how contemporary political thinking is both rooted in traditional political thought and a radical transformation of it.

Whether the future is liberal, communitarian, pluralist or simply uncertain, this fully revised and extended edition of Rodney Barker's bestselling textbook is an essential guide to the changing intellectual landscape of political thinking.

Rodney Barker is a Senior Lecturer in Government at the London School of Economics and Political Science.

Political Ideas in Modern Britain

In and After the Twentieth Century
Second edition

Rodney Barker

London and New York

First published 1978
by Routledge
11 New Fetter Lane, London EC4P 4EE

Second and improved edition published 1997
by Routledge

Simultaneously published in the USA and Canada by
Routledge 29 West 35th Street, New York, NY 10001

© 1997 Rodney Barker

Typeset in Times by Routledge
Printed and bound in Great Britain by T. J. International,
Padstow, Cornwall

All rights reserved. No part of this book may be reprinted or
reproduced or utilized in any form or by any electronic,
mechanical, or other means, now known or hereafter
invented, including photocopying and recording, or in any
information storage or retrieval system, without permission in
writing from the publishers.

British Library Cataloguing in Publication Data
A catalogue record for this book is available from the British Library

Library of Congress Cataloguing in Publication Data
A catalogue record for this book has been requested

ISBN 0–415–16166–5 (hbk)
ISBN 0–415–07121–6 (pbk)

For Ben

Contents

Acknowledgements

I have benefited from the criticism and questions, seldom innocent, of students in my lectures and seminars at the London School of Economics and Political Science. Sharon Thompson carried out onerous transcriptions for the bibliography. Helen Roberts, as always, provided support and irony in matchless combination.

1   Two introductions

INTRODUCTION 1996

Less than a year after the publication of the first edition of this book, a Conservative government under the premiership of Margaret Thatcher took office. Mrs Thatcher was to remain premier and party leader for another eleven years, and the government was to survive for a further eighteen. During that time not only did a Conservative Party converted to what was swiftly labelled 'Thatcherism' make major changes to the structure of government and the provision of public services, but the broad network of thinking which had already been termed the 'New Right' enjoyed increasingly substantial intellectual influence. Those years had a dramatic effect on political thinking in Britain, even more so than did the careers of similarly 'New Right' governments and the advance of New Right ideas in the United States under Ronald Reagan, in France under Jacques Chirac, or in what was still then West Germany under Helmut Kohl. But it was not the New Right alone which transformed the agenda. The 1980s came to a close with the even more dramatic abdication of the state socialist regimes of Eastern Europe in the 1989 revolutions, and the replacement of managerial communist despotism with a variety of regimes mixing democracy, capitalism, democratic socialism, and nationalist authoritarianism.

Both domestically and internationally the reference points had been moved out of all recognition, so that the old maps no longer referred to any recognizable terrain. The framework of politics was shaken twice, and the course of political thinking reflects on and shapes that fact. One account describes our contemporary location as post-modernism. The old universals of human nature, rights and needs have been replaced by a series of historically specific or contingent values, identities and conventions. Postmodernism thus becomes a theory to explain why no single theory will do any more, and why the best we can do is expect variety, change and uncertainty. Another way of describing where we now are and how we have got there is to speak, as Eric Hobsbawm has done, of a 'short twentieth century' which came to a close around 1989. If Hobsbawm's periodization is accepted, we are now not nearing the end of an era, but moving forwards from the start of one (Hobsbawm 1994). The chronological millennium is still to come but, in terms of a calendar shaped by significant events and historical change, we are already at the beginning of a new century, rather than at the end of an old one.

Whichever view is taken – although they are not incompatible with each other – that we face either an unpredictable twenty-first century or an equally unpredictable postmodernity, everything that defined the previous era, not just in Britain but at the very least in the whole of the western/northern/industrial world, has changed. The world of social- ism and conservatism has come to an end, and new concepts and titles, different labels, different explanatory patterns are needed for new times. Because the things we consider to be important now will shape the accounts we give, the categories inherited from the past are not so much incorrect for understanding the fluid and transitional present, as simply less helpful. The old categories no longer fit, or rather they may not be the categories which are most illuminating for present, as opposed to past, concerns. Much of the discussion of Hobsbawm's periodization has thus been not a matter of criticizing its accuracy or cogency, or his use of evidence, but simply of proposing alternative perspectives which throw different events into both light and shade (Therborn 1995; Mann 1995; Nairn 1995). None of this is to say that an account of political thinking or of any other activity can only be and should only be a working out of contemporary intellectual concerns. There is a real task in recovering the differences between the thought of the present investigator and the past, however recently past, object of her account, but at the same time the constraining, and enabling structure within which the observer operates can never be escaped. There is a dialogue between the two, and the shifting of analytical and descriptive perspectives does not simply subordinate data to the present.

But whatever the uncertainties about the application of a new vocabulary to the past, it is clearly necessary to develop new terms, or at least to recover and refurbish some underused old terms, for the present and future. The choice of left and right as, albeit vague, more serviceable terms than conservative, liberal, and socialist is a tentative attempt to refurbish old terms without being didactic in either an empirical or theoretical sense about either of them.

But the implications for the understanding of political thought before the end of the short twentieth century, or before the emergence of postmodernity, cannot be avoided. Old categories may not be the best for understanding even old events. When the intellectual and political landscape is transformed, as it has been since the beginning of the 1980s, it is not only the politics that follow that have to be written about in a new way: the politics that preceded the upheavals of the 1980s must themselves be reassessed. There is a clear relationship between the declining importance accorded to class in the analysis of contemporary politics at the close of the short twentieth century, and the usefulness accorded to it as a conceptual category by historians. At a time when ethnic, religious and national identity are increasingly prominent, an account of the earlier twentieth century which gave priority to class is being rewritten. An active debate is now going on over the relative appropriateness of class and political aspirations as vantage points for giving an account of the popular politics of the nineteenth and early twentieth centuries and of the arguments over social and economic, and political, reform and preservation (Joyce 1994; Biagini and Reid 1991; Belchem 1996; Barrow and Bullock 1996). This does not mean that history has to be reworked with the benefit of hindsight, or in the light of the ideas that eventually 'won'. Quite apart from anything else, 'eventually' is a constantly moving vantage point. It is rather a matter of different arguments seeming important or interesting from different perspectives, which is in part a matter of looking for the roots of the present, but also simply of creating a different account of the past.

One aspect of the change that has taken place in political thinking in Britain lies not in the aspirations of political thinkers, but in their aversions. Political argument, like other forms of politics, is shaped in part by the enemies it identifies for itself just as much as by the friends with which it allies itself. The 1990s saw the disappearance of traditional enemies, and a search for new ones. The polarities of the Cold War, of communist totalitarianism or western imperialism, of collective economic tyranny or market exploitation, of the denial of politics or their manipulation under the threat of nuclear war, all these faded away with the collapse of the Soviet Union and its East European satellite states, and the achievement of a settlement in the nuclear arms race. E.P. Thompson observed that after 1989 'Western commentators are bemoaning the loss of a convenient enemy' (Thompson 1990: 142). The irony of the events of 1989 in Eastern

Europe was that at the very moment at which they seemed to vindicate the analyses of New Right economics, they deprived the right of its traditional, defining antagonist. We knew who the old enemies were. It is still far from clear who the new ones are or will be, though there are many candidates.

But whilst the absence of clear enemies for either the right or the left has meant that political thinking remains more fluid and more unpredictable than over the previous hundred years, for the 'short twentieth century' running from around 1917 to around 1989, the enemies do not necessarily have to be re-written, even if they have now departed. An observer beginning her account with the year 1990 and with no knowledge of what had gone before, and unfamiliar with the words 'socialism' and 'conservatism', would not find it necessary to invent them, nor would she be likely to construct images of socialism and capitalism with which to arrange or represent the contemporary political debate. As soon as the preceding period is examined, however, both those two giants are very evidently present both as protagonists and as demons.

But there is more to the change at the beginning of the new 'long century' than a shift of dramatis personae. The very nature of the drama and its location have changed. Religion and community, in both their benign and malevolent forms, have reasserted themselves. And as they have taken up new positions in the present, so too have they assumed growing importance in the lenses through which we look at our constructed narrative of the past (Collini 1991; Nicholls 1989, 1994; Wolffe 1994). The old protagonists are not thereby dismissed, but they are joined by others. The politics of identity, of setting the context within which politics takes place, have become as important as the politics of detail, of arguing within a demarcated political, cultural space.

The attention which *Political Ideas in Modern Britain* received included various criticisms, including some lengthy ones from various standpoints within Marxism (Peregudov 1980). At the time, the Marxist criticisms seemed the least weighty, and the least troublesome to deal with. The close cousin of this view, that political expression is mere 'rhetoric' which should not be taken seriously, was neatly hit on the head within a year of the book's publication by Stefan Collini who, in his study of L.T. Hobhouse, commented that

> It is one mark of the cynic that he sees other people's expressions of their principles as a kind of smokescreen for their putative 'real interests', but even were he always correct it would not follow that

the study of such statements was devoid of explanatory power. Even the most disingenuous legitimation involves an appeal to existing characterisations.

(Collini 1979: 10)

A different view arises when the disagreements are considered from the vantage of the 1990s. The Marxist account which dismissed the study of ideas as merely examining the froth on the pudding of capitalism can now be seen as the simplified and distorted representative of a wider body of thinking for which the allocation of economic powers and resources, and the government and politics of that dimension of human life, was indeed the principal theme of politics. Most writers were not Marxists. But most, whether conservatives, liberals or socialists, worked within a perspective to which Marx and Marxism had been major contributors.

From a variety of directions, though principally from a scepticism about political thought very loosely and very distantly and very indirectly derived from Marxism, the relevance of political thought was called into question. The first edition set on one side the general question of the nature of political thinking, its relation to other aspects of political life, the relation between 'thought' and 'action', or the nature of ideology. The ascendancy of the New Right has demanded that new attention be given to this question. Whatever qualifications there may be about the effect of New Right campaigns, there is a sound prima facie case for accepting that ideas in politics changed other aspects of political life, that laws were passed, policies pursued, and institutions changed, transformed, introduced or abolished as the result of a vigorous exercise in political thinking and political argument.

The relative weight of thought and action has been discussed both amongst those who have studied the organized campaigns of think tanks such as the Institute of Economic Affairs, and amongst those seeking to give an adequate account of aspects of political thinking such as feminism. There has been renewed interest in the broader intellectual penumbra within which government and politics operates. Some, such as Michael Freeden, discussing the New Liberalism at the beginning of the twentieth century, make the fairly modest claim that 'at the very least, the mental climate of an age defines and constrains the options open to the politician' (Freeden 1978: 248–9). Others, such as Rosalind Delmar, have claimed a little more in arguing that an incomplete account is given of feminism if the description concentrates on movements and action, and ignores the shaping role of theory, and that it is political thinking, rather than movements and campaigns, which provide and illuminate political continuities (Delmar 1986: 23–4, 13–18). But it is possible, and beneficial, to pursue the argument further, and to insist that political thinking is itself a major form, perhaps the major form, of political activity, that politics 'is, amongst other things, an essentially linguistic activity' (Sparkes 1994: 1).

Precisely because political thinking is a major part of politics, political ideas are not found in isolation, but are associated with institutions and organizations. Ideas may cluster around parties (R. Barker 1994), but they do not follow the same paths as those pursued by party politicians. Not only are the issues which are of importance to parliamentary politicians frequently different in emphasis from those which concern voters and citizens, but the issues around which political thought takes place can equally be partly or entirely removed from those to which organized parties give priority. In the 1960s, 1970s, 1980s and 1990s the two questions of national economic management and relations with Europe frequently preoccupied and divided parties. They did not have the same place in political thinking. Nor is any relationship between party fortunes and political thinking guaranteed. The Social Democratic Party appeared to be changing the party landscape in the early 1980s; it made no similar impact, even briefly, on political thinking.

The place of political thinking in the activities of political parties is only one area where that part of politics which sets out and argues for a case is of central importance. All forms of politics involve political thought, and I have elsewhere (R. Barker 1996a) suggested that this reciprocal relationship – the 'Constantine relationship' – lies close to the heart of politics. But though it is impossible to write an account of one part of politics without touching on others, and though I have attempted in the present book to locate political thinking wherever possible in relation to other aspects of political life, the emphasis in the following pages is nonetheless principally on political thinking per se, and particularly on its written form.

The first edition of this book was written in one 'century'; the second was written in the next. Writing in 1996 there are good reasons for not adding to or revising an existing book, but for writing a new and different one. At the very least, this means that any revision will now be with such benefits as hindsight brings. A framework constructed around attitudes towards the expanding state is less adequate to encompass the political thinking of the short twentieth-century's end, and thence in retrospect may seem to have limitations for the preceding period as well. Ideas which seemed interesting but marginal at the earlier date may appear in retrospect to have been the recessive themes which, in the last decade of the chronological century, have acquired an enhanced importance as contributors to new, post-twentieth-century political thinking. The word 'theme' is more expressive of what is involved here than other familiar terms such as 'ideology', 'concept', or 'argument'. Ideology suggests either something normatively and descriptively comprehensive, or suspectly instrumental. 'Concept' suggests something precise, even academic, but lacking the penumbra of politics, rhetoric, policy, and the aversions and aspirations which characterizes the thinking described in this book. 'Argument' comes closest, and is frequently used. 'Themes' does best of all, however, for it suggests a cohering or unifying concern, form of argument, or intellectual predilection whose character is historical rather than logical, and which has a coherence which can be rhetorical or aesthetic, as much as logical. The identification of some of these themes as 'recessive' is a borrowing, for the purposes of analogy, from biology, where a gene may pass from grandparents to grandchildren via the intermediate generation in whom it has no great consequences, where it is recessive. In the same manner themes in political thinking can be dormant, subordinate, or recessive, yet become powerful components of the thinking of later generations.

Different accounts need to be given of the present, and it is necessary to avoid restricting understanding by the employment of images and categories which were developed to describe earlier, different situations. At the same time the roots of present concerns may be seen for the first time or in a new light by applying new accounts to the past. Yet if this is done in a wholesale manner, the very particularity of the past, and hence of the present, will be dissolved in an inappropriately universalized paradigm. The recessive genes of the present can be discerned in our ancestors. But they were recessive, and only now do they contribute to our characters. So change occurs by paradigmatic shifts, but not by magical transformations. The ingredients of the new, but not its outcomes, are already there in the old. The problem is a familiar one. On the one hand an account must differ sufficiently from the available accounts which people give, or gave, of their situation, beliefs, intentions and activities to be illuminating and not simply repetitious. On the other it must stand in sufficiently close relation to the culture of which it seeks to give an account to be comprehensibly about *that* culture, and not some alien culture of the writer's fancy.

One further issue, which arose in connection with *Political Ideas in Modern Britain* and is of even greater relevance today, is the question of how typical is the tradition of argument discussed in this book, how particularly 'British'? W.H. Greenleaf, in his monumental *The British Political Tradition* (1983a and b) has suggested that the character of British politics as a tension between libertarianism and collectivism is not a 'phenomenon of merely domestic occurrence but of European and even world-wide scope; any modern state is to be understood as a more or less unresolved tension between two irreconcilable dispositions of this sort' (Greenleaf 1983a: 15). Certainly the discussion about the length and character of the twentieth century, the fate and future of the working class, the role of gender divisions and of women, of intellectuals and students, of religious and national identity, of information, technology, and information technology, has been conducted with global reference, even when it reflected narrower cultural experiences, whilst the discussion of global politics has incorporated a debate over the relative position of the west, of Europe, and of the industrial north, all of which have provided a setting for more particularly British reflections. Political thought may not have become global, but it had certainly become more international. But however the account is qualified, it is still about the self conceptualization of western Europe, north America, the industrial first world. Self-conception involves the contrast of a created self with opposites, and what has changed at the beginning of the long twenty-first century is the disappearance of well-established opposites, and the fluid possibility of a variety of antagonist identities against which to create ourselves. God may not be dead, but Satan is.

Amongst the substantial amount of scholarly writing that has occurred since the publication of *Political Ideas in Modern Britain*, there are several questions which require recognition or response in the present book, and others which do not. Some new work increases knowledge and understanding, without significantly changing interpretation. I have in some small degree included references to such work in the text, but not in a way that requires any major alteration of what I have previously written. Other work, which puts forward other interpretations of significantly different narratives, clearly requires a different response. The most obvious of these is W.H. Greenleaf's *The British Political Tradition*. Studies on particular thinkers or themes, without making such broad contributions, nonetheless add valuably to the discussion both of specific areas of the subject, and of the character of political thinking as a whole. The work of Clark and Collini is an obvious example. Other work, whilst recovering neglected or ignored aspects of political thinking, at the same time questions the overall structure or balance of existing accounts. The growing body of work on feminist thinking is the clearest example of this.

One consequence is that a simple revision of the first edition of this book is no longer appropriate or sufficient. The familiar reasons for wishing to revise an existing work are of course all there. Not only has more been published about the period and the topic, inviting a discussion of the material in the light of new research and new interpretation, but even had none of that happened, strands of thought have a history of their own which is not delimited by the publication of a book, and in that history demand a different, or extended, or perhaps even reduced amount of attention from that which they were originally given. The amount of attention paid to feminism in the first edition, and the amount which in retrospect seems appropriate, is only the most glaring example of this. The relative stresses on socialism and on libertarianism would have been different had the book first been written in 1996. Although the present book contains chapters from the original book revised where necessary in the light of subsequent scholarship, I have deliberately not undertaken a complete re-writing of the sections dealing with the period up to the late 1970s, nor made any substantial changes to the original chapters. There are different ways in which they could have been written, but not necessarily more accurate or truer ways. Apart from making the necessary acknowledgements to new work as mentioned above, I have restricted myself to removing some uglier phrases and sentences, and adding relevant new information. The three chapters (8, 9 and 10) which follow these revised chapters, on the other hand, are new, and are written in the light of the changes which have taken place, both in political life and in the perspectives from which it can be viewed. So the book, like the politics it describes, is neither simply a continuation of old themes, nor simply a piece of work which owes nothing to the past. It has its own continuities, its own innovations, and its own recessive themes.

INTRODUCTION 1978

Writing in 1927 the former Conservative prime minister Lord Balfour suggested that 'our whole political machinery pre-supposes a people so fundamentally at one that they can safely afford to bicker; and so sure of their own moderation that they are not dangerously disturbed by the never-ending din of political conflict' (Balfour 1928: xxiv). But whilst it is true that compared with most of the other nations of Europe, Britain has heard little of the 'din of political conflict' over the past century, beyond the wrangles of everyday politics there has been a vast body of political writing that cannot be discounted as a tendency merely 'to bicker'. Partisan points have been made, but the issues have been neither momentary nor trivial. In the work of academics, intellectuals and politicians there has been a continuous and vigorous expression of political ideas. A great variety of alternative conclusions has been urged, and the result has been a combination of profound political differences with sustained tolerance and restraint. There may have been few points of fundamental agreement between the advocates of various principles and policies. But there has been a pervasive optimism which has led the proponents of many and various views to believe that it was worth arguing for their opinions, and that the politics of persuasion would eventually bring them success.

Sidney Webb, a prominent Fabian socialist and the principal founder of the London School of Economics and Political Science, expressed this optimism in a pure, almost an extreme form when he wrote of his expectations for the infant LSE. He was, he declared, a radical and a socialist:

> I believed that research and new discoveries would prove some, at any rate, of my views of policy to be right but that, if they proved the contrary, I should count it all the more gain to have prevented error, and should cheerfully abandon my own policy.
>
> (quoted in MacKenzie and MacKenzie 1977: 281–2)

The confidence in his own opinions which underlay Webb's willingness to risk them on the gaming table of scholarly investigation has been more characteristic of political writing than has his apparent willingness to consider the possibility that he might be wrong. But this confidence, and the variety of views which it has sustained, has meant that one part of the history of politics in Britain is the history of ideas. Socialists and laissez-faire libertarians, conservatives and radicals, anarchists and collectivists have written down their beliefs and hopes because they thought them correct and desirable, and have advocated and persuaded because they wished their own principles to inform public affairs.

The positions which have been praised and defended have been richly varied. There has been no single British political tradition unless it be everything that has ever been written, but rather a large number of competing advocacies of what we ought publicly to manage, how such management should be conducted, who should take part in it, and to what ends. This argument has been carried out in all manner of ways by all kinds of people. It is to be found primarily in what would be

considered conventionally political books and articles: Herbert
Spencer's *The Man versus the State*, R.H. Tawney's *Equality* or
F.A. Hayek's *The Road to Serfdom*. But it has not been defined with
the neatness of an academic discipline, nor always constrained within
the immediately obvious bounds of political writing. It is sometimes to
be found in the courts as it was in judgments on suffrage cases, in the
theatre with the plays of George Bernard Shaw or Arnold Wesker, in
the poetry of Auden, or Yeats, or Belloc, in novels such as Chesterton's
The Napoleon of Notting Hill or even in the cinema with films such as
The Guinea Pig, *The Angry Silence* or *Chance of a Lifetime*. I have
concentrated on those written expressions of opinion which are in the
first place and predominantly about the middle principles of politics,
the ideas which lie midway between philosophy and the hustings. The
more diluted contribution, where political ideas are expressed in what
are not principally political works, is so enormous that I have done no
more than occasionally touch upon it. Equally, I have said nothing of
the cinema, and little of the courts or the theatre, not because such an
account would not be important, but because one has to stop
somewhere and I have remained within the limits of the literary
contribution. But one need not stop there, for not only the cinema but
music, painting, sculpture or architecture may all play some part in the
expression of political ideas. But non-literary expression, whatever its
ritual or representative force – the romantic imperial benevolence of
Frank Brangwyn's Foreign Office murals or the bland municipal
confidence of Sir Giles Gilbert Scott's (and Herbert Morrison's)
Waterloo Bridge – is not in the same way an articulate and deliberate
expression of political ideas. Yet despite my concentration on political
writing, I have at times pursued the political thread through works
which appear primarily to be about other things, and particularly
about economics, in the language of which public affairs have
increasingly been discussed in the twentieth century, and in which
throughout the nineteenth century they were examined. Ideas about
land or rent were never far away in the works of socialists or social
radicals before 1900.

Political writing is by its very nature an articulate and deliberate
expression of views. But it has always had unspoken premises and been
informed by unstated perceptions. The way in which the world is seen
has provided the 'obvious' or 'common sense' starting point for
polemic and persuasion. These perceptions have not been shared by
everyone at any particular time, and what has been perceived as part of
the immutable nature of reality at one time has been seen as part of a
changeable way of arranging things at another, and attacked or

defended accordingly. So although I shall in this book deal principally with the articulated substance of political ideas, I will also pay some attention to the unarticulated premises, particularly when they break cover and are championed or contested.

There is always a danger that political scientists will write about things simply because they have just happened rather than because they are particularly interesting or important. I cannot pretend that there is nothing of this in my choice of the years after 1880, but nonetheless this period is worthy of study, and rewards study, for other reasons than near-contemporaneity. The period saw a massive extension of the functions and powers of the state, more substantial than had ever previously taken place, so that this growth came to be perhaps the single most important event in recent British history. At the same time wider and wider areas of social life were politicized and by one means or another activities which had previously seemed primarily economic, academic, or simply private, gained or were given a public and political aspect. The pale of citizenship was similarly being extended, not only in terms of simple proportions of the population by the extension of the suffrage to the male working class and to women, but in terms of the various capacities beyond the 'one person one vote' of electoral democracy in which citizens might be represented, whether as workers or as Welshmen, and the kinds of influence they might bring to bear and the manner in which they might do so.

The extension of the competence of politics and the extension of the competence of the state were clearly associated. Even so, not all those who argued for the one argued for the other, and the association was not an exact paralleling of argument. Anarchists like Kropotkin or advocates of direct functional control and responsibility like Tawney or Cole hoped that in extending or acknowledging the breadth of the public and political dimension, they would thereby augment a widely disseminated popular power. Whilst enlarging the area that was public and political, they hoped to set limits to the action of the state. On the other hand those who saw an extending role for the state did not always perceive a similar extension of politics, if by politics is understood among other things contention and publicity. There thus was frequently an antagonism between the attempt to extend politics and the attempt to extend government. But there was also a symbiotic relation between the two. The extension of government drew attention to the public nature of the newly governed activity; the claim that an activity should be considered under the aegis of politics made it seem more appropriate for oversight and regulation by government. The association between a resistance to state power and a denial of the political or public nature of a wide range of human activities was at one level more simple. To assert that the getting of a livelihood, or the ownership of property, or the education of children, or the treatment of the sick, were private and not public activities was to deny them at one and same time the attentions of both politics and the state. But it was possible to deny the competence of government without denying the relevance of politics. This was precisely what anarchists and pluralists did.

Both resistance to state collectivism and its advocacy could be either radical or conservative. The demand for an extension or reassertion of public power could be radical in so far as it envisaged a change in the distribution of power and advantage in society. But it could equally involve the imposition of uniformity to sustain old or dominant orthodoxies. In the same way the insistence on privacy could involve either the de facto defence of existing hierarchies, or the assertion of people's right to do as they wished, and to do so in a radical manner.

I have used attitudes towards the modern state as one way of organizing this book. But such attitudes constitute only one of the many themes in the political ideas which have been expressed in Britain since the end of the nineteenth century. There have been distinctions and disagreements not only between those who favoured and those who opposed the growth of the state, but between radicals and conservatives, and elitists and democrats. There were ideas on the nature and proper extent of citizenship, and or the relation of British to foreign and imperial politics. There is no single pattern which can be used to comprehend the whole variety. At the same time I have tried to show the ways in which my subjects are continually trying to escape from the categories which I have used. There are links which bind one category to another, melt their edges into one another and straddle particular thinkers across two or even three groups. Differences were not always seen in the manner in which I have described them, and political and intellectual divisions repeatedly refuse to sit neatly together. The arrangement of the book is in general historical, but does not involve ruthless or exclusive chronological narrative. The chapter which follows this one, Chapter 2, discusses the support and advocacy of the extension of state management, regulation and provision from 1880 until after the end of the First World War. Chapter 3 examines those who from an individualist or libertarian point of view opposed this extension during the same period. Chapter 4 describes the advocacy of various alternatives to both centralized state collectivism and individualist libertarianism in various forms of group, communal and pluralist theory. Chapter 5 looks at ideas of the political community and of the character and consequences of democracy. Chapter 6 considers the accommodation to the incontestable establishment of the modern state by the end of the first quarter of the twentieth century, and the reactions to this situation over the next twenty-five or so years. Chapter 7 deals with the development of political ideas in the third quarter of the century and with the continuities with, departures from and development of earlier themes. Around all these themes, ideas have been expressed. I have attempted in the following pages a brief sketch of the principal positions adopted and goals pursued.

2   Friends of the modern state

The increases and mutations by which political institutions grow are always misrepresented if chopped into neat periods and bisected by ends, beginnings and turning points. But though history is a continuous process, if it is to be understood at all then some violence must be done to its complex reality by representing it in terms of emphases, directions and prevailing characteristics. In the case of British government, some such new emphasis, and some such turning point, may be identified after 1880. After that date government did more of what it had done previously in the way of regulation and control, and it did what previously it had not done, or done very little, in the way of direct intervention and the provision of services. There was no sharp departure from previous practice, and little was done that had not in some degree been done before. But the number of state employees began to increase significantly in the 1880s whilst state expenditure as a percentage of national expenditure began to rise in the 1890s. The accelerations and changes in direction were not necessarily the result of conscious decisions to give the state a different role. But what was conscious was the reflection of contemporaries and the belief of many of them that something had changed, and that government now had a novel and distinctive character. Writing in 1881, the Liberal politician John Morley drew attention to 'the rather amazing result that in the country where Socialism has been less talked about than in any other country in Europe, its principles have been most extensively applied'. What Morley meant by 'Socialism' was simply the assumption by the state of extended powers for the regulation of life and work in the interests of the welfare of its citizens. He wrote

> We have today a complete, minute, and voluminous code for the protection of labour; buildings must be kept pure of effluvia; dangerous machinery must be fenced; children and young persons

must not clean it while in motion; their hours are not only limited but fixed; continuous employment must not exceed a given number of hours, varying with the trade, but prescribed by law in given cases; a statutable number of holidays is imposed; the children must go to school, and the employer must every week have a certificate to that effect; if an accident happens, notice must be sent to the proper authorities; special provisions are made for bakehouses, for lace-making, for collieries, and for a whole schedule of other special callings; for the due enforcement and vigilant supervision of this immense host of minute prescriptions, there is an immense host of inspectors, certifying surgeons, and other authorities, whose business it is 'to speed and post o'er land and ocean' in restless guardianship of every kind of labour, from that of the woman who plaits straw at her cottage door, to the miner who descends into the bowels of the earth, and the seaman who conveys the fruits and materials of universal industry to and fro between the remotest parts of the globe.

(Morley 1896, vol. 1: 303)

A similar listing was made three years later in amazement and horror by Herbert Spencer, who followed an enumeration of the collectivist actions of the Gladstone ministry of 1880 to 1885 with a warning of worse to come:

But we are far from forming an adequate conception if we look at the compulsory legislation which has actually been established of late years. We must look also at that which is advocated, and which threatens to be far more sweeping in range and stringent in character.... Nor does enumeration of these further measures of coercive rule, looming on us near at hand or in the distance, complete the account.... Partly for defraying the costs of carrying out these ever multiplying sets of regulations, each of which requires an additional staff of officers, and partly to meet the outlay for new public institutions, such as board-schools, free libraries, public museums, baths and washhouses, recreation grounds, etc., etc., local rates are year after year increased; as the general taxation is increased by grants for education and to the departments of science and art, etc. Every one of these involves further coercion – restricts still more the freedom of the citizen.

(Spencer [1884] 1969: 75–6)

Morley saw regulation, Spencer saw restriction. The Fabian socialist Sidney Webb, in 1889, saw the provision of services. But whilst the tone is a little different, the accumulation of examples reflects an increasingly common awareness of the new state:

> Besides our international relations and the army, navy, police and courts of justice, the community now carries on for itself, in some part or another of these islands, the post office, telegraphs, carriage of small commodities, coinage, surveys, the regulation of the currency and note issue, the provision of weights and measures, the making, sweeping, lighting and repairing of streets, roads and bridges, life insurance, the grant of annuities, shipbuilding, stock-broking, banking, farming, and money-lending. It provides for many thousands of us from birth to burial – midwifery, nursery, education, board and lodging, vaccination, medical attendance, medicine, public worship, amusements, and internment.
>
> (Webb [1889] 1962: 79)

Morley, Spencer and Webb differed in their attitude to what they saw, as they differed in what they chose to emphasize in their descriptions. But they did not disagree in believing that something important was happening, and it is this belief, as much as the changes to which it referred, that distinguishes the years after 1880. As the university teacher and philosophical idealist Sir Henry Jones observed at the beginning of the present century, 'Both those who desire and those who fear this change are prone to regard it as inevitable, and as taking place with an accelerating velocity' (H. Jones 1910: 100).

The ways in which people thought about the state, and the development of state activity, cannot easily be separated from each other. The development of state activity, what W.H. Greenleaf has called 'the great change' (Greenleaf 1983b) and Jose Harris the 'quantum leap' (Harris 1993: 216) can be seen as a set of changed working assumptions about the scope of public policy and the means appropriate to making and executing it. Arguments about the state were on the one hand partly reflections on changing practice, and on the other were the condition for new ways of thinking and hence of acting in government and politics. The tasks of government in the years between 1880 and the outbreak of the First World War were being considered in a way which involved, or was conducive to, a greater degree of direct action by local or central authority. Between 1888 and 1895, for instance, there developed the idea of unemployment as a characteristic of economic life rather than as a personal accident or the result of idleness or ignorance (Harris 1972). The very word 'unemployment' had not been current previously. The new conception did not replace the old, but it introduced a national problem where previously there had been only a private misfortune. In a similar way the 'discovery' of poverty by journalists like W.T. Stead, social investigators like Charles Booth, and evangelists like William Booth of the Salvation Army, appeared – as did unemployment – as the revelation of a threat to public order and national well-being. As the biologist T.H. Huxley put it in December 1890, 'unless this remediable misery is effectually dealt with, the hordes of vice and pauperism will destroy modern civilization as effectually as uncivilized tribes of another kind destroyed the great social organization which preceded ours' (Huxley 1898: 238). The condition of the people was imbued with national consequences for the quality of social life, the orderliness of public behaviour, the competitiveness of British industry and the military competence and might of the nation. Alarm over these matters cast the national interest in terms which appeared to place a solution in the hands of the state as the local or national agent of collective determination, and to require a greatly extended direct public responsibility for the mental and physical condition of the people.

The conception of an enlarged state was thus not caused by popular demand for greater public action – it was itself a part and a condition of that demand. The nationalization of economics, living standards and culture was accompanied by a nationalization of politics and of political organization. One contemporary foreign observer, Moisei Ostrogorski, complained that both the local and particular were all swept up into the craw of the organized parties. The growing mass of legislation was facilitated by a growing organization of parliamentary time and parliamentarians' voting, while in their propaganda and electioneering, parties began slowly to present themselves as the bearers of programmes (Ostrogorski 1902). Whereas the old conception of government had been static, the new was, if not dynamic, then at least ambulatory. The old conception had viewed government as administering laws, keeping the peace and defending the frontiers. But it was not a part of government's function to act upon society, nor was it expected that legislation would do much more than sustain clear and established customs. In contrast the new conception was of government as the instigator of movement. This conception of government was not restricted to the parties of progress or reform; the Conservative and Unionist Party at the beginning of the twentieth century was increasingly characterized, despite opposition, by a commitment to tariff reform, a programme of discriminatory trade duties designed to form a new economic community out of the empire and provide funds for new military and social expenditure at home. Government was not merely to regulate society, it was to improve it.

Though the expansion of the state was in this way related in one of its aspects to changes in conceptions of state activity, these changes of opinion did not flow in a straightforward manner from clearly articulated general principles. The general mood of state collectivism was complex and variegated, and existed both at the level of general reflection and argument and in a series of specific policy debates. Within the law as applied in the courts, for instance, there was an increasing tendency to accept or assert the rights of government. In *Board of Education v. Rice* in 1911, and *Local Government Board v. Arlidge* in 1915, the courts acknowledged that government departments under their ministerial heads were increasingly adopting judicial functions as their responsibilities grew beyond the bounds which formerly set limits to their competence. Equally, the discussion and formulation of policy could itself be the field on which theories about the proper role of government competed through the mediation of apparently more mundane and precise arguments. The work of the Royal Commission on the Poor Law between 1906 and 1909 was at the same time a minute examination of one area of social policy, and an elaborate duel between the particular form of individualism represented by the Charity Organisation Society, Helen Dendy, and Bernard Bosanquet on the one hand, and the paternalist collectivism of Beatrice and Sidney Webb on the other (McBriar 1987).

A great deal of the argument around the role of the state in these years was not cast in terms of general defences of or attacks upon increased action by local or central government, or the rights of the community and the individual. The more precise articulations which did deal with these general questions were often persuasive rationalizations which, by their very coherence, influenced more than they reflected. But to a degree they did reflect, or at least distil and render internally consistent and hence extend, ideas and perceptions which were expressed in less deliberately political form elsewhere. And in so far as they influenced this inchoate context, their refracted images can be discerned with varying clarity within it. It was the very fact that they drew on debates over particular public policies as well as on more general arguments that gave force in Britain to books like Edward Bellamy's *Looking Backwards*, written and first published in the United States in 1887. Bellamy's book was a fantasy of an urban collectivist socialist utopia in the near future which gained some of its attraction by being presented retrospectively by the narrator, a sleeper who sleeps too long and wakes in the developed future. But the future was presented as history rather than as vision.

Writing in 1905 the liberal academic lawyer A.V. Dicey spoke of a collectivist movement whose intellectual content he identified as utilitarian, and which involved an advocacy of increasing manipulative intervention by the state through inspectorates and regulations. As an accurate historical account of the rise of the modern state, Dicey's presentation has been much criticized, but as Stefan Collini has pointed out, this does not affect the value of his work as evidence of how contemporaries wrote and thought (Collini 1979: 13–14). It was a vision of governmental growth and change consistent with the qualifications to pure laissez faire which the economist W.S. Jevons was prepared to allow. Whilst writing that 'Providence is wiser than the legislator', Jevons also argued that 'Restrictions on industry are not good nor bad *per se*, but according as they are imposed wisely and with good intentions, or foolishly, and with sinister intentions' (Jevons 1910: 170). But in so far as the individual freedoms which state action was seen to be limiting were composed of rights over persons and over property, Dicey's account concentrated on the former whilst it was the latter that were being questioned by radical thinkers. When in 1898 Dicey began work on the lectures that were finally to appear in print seven years later as *Law and Public Opinion in England During the Nineteenth Century*, the idea of land nationalization and of other forms of public ownership had been prominent in radical and progressive discussion for nearly twenty years, and current there for longer. Despite his depiction of land as a Trojan horse of collectivism at a much earlier date in the Irish land reforms of the Gladstone government in 1881, Dicey did not deal with land nationalization until his second edition of 1914 when he treated it as a new invention of socialists (Dicey [1914] 1962). As Henry George was able to point in his preface to his own influential *Progress and Poverty* in 1880, even since he completed the book the question of public right to the fruits of land ownership and public right to arrange the benefits of ownership in the general interest, had become practical politics in the question of Irish land reform (George 1911: 5). Public ownership as a solution to the land problem was well-established and by the early 1890s the red vans of the English Land Restoration League and yellow vans of the Land Nationalisation Society were a familiar part of open-air politics (Barry 1965: 6–7). George's book was an important contribution to the debate, and probably achieved more publicity than any other single work. Its influence not only on radicals but on socialists as well was still being acknowledged a quarter of a century after its first publication, and Labour and Lib-Lab MPs elected to the new Parliament of 1906 cited George almost as many times as they did Carlyle, and more than they did Mill (Stead 1906). George's contribution was made at two levels: at the level of practical proposals and at that of general assumptions about justifiable public action. His contribution to policy was the proposal for a single tax based on land as a means both of assuring an equitable distribution of the burden of taxation, and of most effectively financing the beneficial works which the modern state ought to undertake on behalf of its citizens. Thus though his proposals were an alternative to land nationalization, his premises were a very serviceable basis for arguing for it. In asserting the public claim to land, George made the decision for or against public ownership a tactical one, not one of principle (Plowright 1987).

At a time when social reform was a topic of frequent public discussion, the assertion of a public right to any kind of wealth provided a possibility of linking the two notions in a policy of redistribution. The Liberal politician Joseph Chamberlain, talking of the condition of the poor during the 1885 election campaign, made sure that his hearers understood him to be advocating public beneficence without threatening public expropriation. The poor were to be raised up, without harming the rich, and though the notion of 'ransom' sounded to some like a form of public banditry, in so far as it was voluntary rather than a regular part of taxation and financial policy it carried an aspect of judicious if highly organized philanthropy (Lucy 1885).

Nonetheless a difficulty existed for those who sympathized with the call for social reform but who also as traditional political radicals believed in voluntary rather than coerced action. For them the state was an inherently oppressive institution whose activities, beyond a certain necessary minimum for the preservation of life and property, should be restricted in order to give full and free play to the life of the individual. A resolution of this difficulty could be found in the arguments of the Oxford philosopher T.H. Green. In a lecture given in 1881 entitled 'Liberal legislation and freedom of contract' (Green 1888), Green dealt with the apparent conflict between state interference with the freedom of contract and liberal views of freedom. Freedom, he argued, was not the ability to do whatever one liked, but 'a positive power or capacity of doing or enjoying something worth doing or enjoying, and that, too, something that we do or enjoy in common with others'. Freedom was in this way redefined in terms of its ends: 'freedom in all the forms of doing what one will with one's own, is valuable only as a means to an end' (Green 1888: 371–2). In order to secure the conditions of such freedom, public action was necessary to raise the condition of people who otherwise would be prevented in practice from acting freely. In an ideal world this improvement would be carried out by voluntary effort – and states could never directly promote free activity, for that was in itself a necessarily voluntary thing – but the world was not an ideal one, reformers had to take people as they found them. So in the interests of the free development of the capacities of all, a justification was presented for public regulation of the life and property of citizens: 'With a view to securing such freedom among its members it is as certainly within the province of the state to prevent children from growing up in that kind of ignorance which practically excludes them from a free career in life, as it is within its province to require the sort of building and drainage necessary for public health' (Green 1888: 374).

In so far as Green's theory of actual or real rights derived those rights from specific societies, it was an appropriate one for those who wanted to intensify current practices. The theory could be applied in a conservative manner as well, but it was more readily available in the last decades of the nineteenth century to state collectivists. But while Green's arguments made greater state action possible, they did not necessarily encourage it. His own preference was for voluntary individual effort, since such effort directed to good ends was the purpose of all public action, and could not be created by coercion. When he talked of state action Green tended to talk of the removal of obstacles to freedom. But the removal of ignorance could be expressed as the provision of education – the distinction is verbal rather than substantial, though it did provide justification for public reform which was of a restraining character. Thus whilst Green's preference was for voluntary education, in the real conditions in which children were, it was necessary, he argued, for the state both to require children to attend at least the elementary school which provided the foundations of education, and to bear the cost of their doing so (Nicholson 1990: 167). And in the crucial matter of property, Green believed that the duty of the state was to promote its proper use, not to engage directly in its control or ownership. Property was a necessary condition of freedom, and its ownership only became undesirable when it involved the prevention of like freedom in another. But this the ownership of land did, since unlike capital its amount was finite, and its concentration in a few hands necessarily involved its withdrawal from the hands of others. The state therefore should amend the law of entail so as to permit the wider distribution of land and to encourage 'the formation of that mainstay of social order and contentment, a class of small proprietors tilling their own land' (Green 1888: 378). The state 'in the interest of that public freedom which it is its business to maintain, cannot allow the individual to deal as he likes with his land to the same extent to which it allows him to deal as he likes with other commodities' (ibid.: 377).

The arguments of the philosophical idealists, particularly those of Green, were at first restricted in their impact. Where they influenced, they presented new ways of understanding politics and the state, rather than reasons for acting politically in one way or another. Socialists such as James Ramsay MacDonald were ready to cite the political philosopher (and sometime member of the Fabian Society) D.G. Ritchie as scholarly authority for their own persuasive arguments. But the views put forward by Green on state actions which offended traditional libertarian principles, whilst they might justify the land legislation of the 1880s, seemed to have less to say about the social radicalism which was developing in the following decade. Green has been attributed with a considerable influence via his pupils, though the gap which this influence is required to traverse is extensive, for despite Green's own interest in practical politics, there is some distance from philosophical reflection to parliamentary politics as conducted by men like H.H. Asquith. It is perhaps in a more diffuse manner, as variously argued by Melvin Richter and by Andrew Vincent and Raymond Plant, that Green contributed to the climate of political argument in Britain, by providing a distinctive tone of earnestness, social concern and addiction to principle (Richter 1964; Vincent and Plant 1984).

Other writers, however, gave idealist arguments a sharper twist in the direction of state action. Sir Henry Jones, who held the Chair of Moral Philosophy at the University of Glasgow, employed the conception of freedom to pursue good ends in a manner which gave further support to state collectivists. Privately he argued that workers might be – he had the miners in mind – 'as little free as an instrument is free from the manipulation of the man who plays on it' (H.J.W. Hetherington, *Life and letters of Sir Henry James*, 1924, p. 232, quoted in Nicholls 1962: 123). Jones argued publicly that private property was both a social and an individual institution, 'wherein the individual finds a rule of action in society and society a rule of action in the individual' (Jones 1910: 99). Both socialists and individualists missed this point, he argued, and failed to see that society and the individual were not antagonistic bases for social policy, but aspects of a single entity – the one did not advance only at the expense of the other. It was not the case that all collective action was for the general good, and each case had to be judged on its merits. But nor was it the case that private property occupied a morally inviolable position – its distribution was to be questioned in just the same way. The balance of the argument was clearly sympathetic to greater state collectivism as a means of extending the positive freedoms of citizens, and Jones presented the possibility 'that in appropriating industrial enterprises' the state 'has liberated the economic power of its citizens'. The distinction between what was and what was not one's property appeared to involve a diminution of individual property and individual freedom under expanding state activity. But whilst the individual share in any one collective enterprise would be small, 'common ownership and enterprise ... make us limited proprietors of indefinitely large utilities' (Jones 1910: 105, 110).

The argument was pushed a little further by D.G. Ritchie, both an academic philosopher and sometime Fabian Socialist, who provided some precise tools of political argument, if not for socialist collectivists, then certainly for liberal ones (Freeden 1990a: 177). In *The Principles of State Interference*, published in 1891, he attacked the individualism of Herbert Spencer, argued that there were no inherent connections between philosophical suppositions and political beliefs, and suggested that in the particular case of late nineteenth-century Britain there was 'a real affinity between the newer stages of radicalism and political philosophy such as that of Hegel' (Ritchie 1891: 138).

NEW LIBERALISM – L.T. HOBHOUSE, J.A. HOBSON

A more directly and deliberately persuasive attempt to reconcile traditional liberal beliefs with a commitment to extended and extending state activity was made by those who have been described as 'New Liberals'. By 1890 advocacy of land nationalization, or of a public claim upon the land exercised through such means as the single tax, had been joined in radical programmes and arguments by proposals for the provision by the community as a whole of specific services such as universal education and old age pensions. The Metropolitan Radical Federation in its programme of 1888 had proposed taxation-to-extinction of rent and interest, the taxation of land values and ground rent, the granting to local authorities of compulsory powers of land purchase, statutory minimum wages and maximum working days, municipal housing, pensions, and relief works to deal with unemployment. Three years later, as a culmination of a slow accumulative impetus of resolutions, the National Liberal Federation at its 1891 congress called for free elementary education, the taxation and compulsory acquisition by local authorities where appropriate of land and the taxation of mining royalties. Some of these demands followed from early radical views on land. The eight hours movement, however, and the various moves to regulate by law the hours and wages of certain industries reflected more than this: a departure from traditional economic assumptions about the wage fund and the naturalness of economic life, and an erosion of the instinctive exclusion of public policy from such matters. The identification not simply of the unemployed but of unemployment as a feature of certain economic conditions had at this same time two consequences. It shifted some of the responsibility for being unemployed away from the unemployed person and onto the community, and it shifted it to a community nationally rather than locally organized. These demands, far more than the policies on land, could not easily be sustained by traditional liberal arguments whilst the ideas of marginal utility or of a labour theory of value which were available to sustain them were not readily compatible with conventional liberal notions of economic life. This, together with the fact that Tories often had more suitable arguments to hand for justifying greater state action, made some reconsideration of the liberal position necessary, and a reconsideration which was cast at a political or moral rather than an economic level.

The new emphasis on the role of the state was not restricted to liberalism – the title 'progressive' was applied to thinkers of a variety of hues and it was in part in humorous recognition of this that when in 1893 a group of such people combined for discussion and for the publication of a journal, *The Progressive Review*, they called themselves the Rainbow Circle. But apart from the socialists, there were no articulate advocates of this progressive position who did not employ the language and assumptions of liberalism. This new application of liberal values was made with greatest force by L.T. Hobhouse and J.A. Hobson, the one an academic and a political journalist, the other a freelance writer and economist. Hobhouse joined together the worlds of politics and academe more vigorously than Green had done, being variously Fellow of Merton College, Oxford, a leader writer on the *Manchester Guardian*, political editor of the intellectual liberal paper *Tribune* and Martin White Professor of Sociology at the London School of Economics. But in his work in all these different positions, there recurred the intention of finding a basis for resolving the variety and discreteness of individual wills in society, in a common good which harmonized them without transcending them, and of linking doctrines of individual liberty with collective action through the central and local state. This second intention distinguished him from those philosophical idealists who employed the notion of the general will, and his attack on one of them, Bernard Bosanquet, and on Bosanquet's *The Philosophical Theory of the State* has given Hobhouse the reputation of being an opponent of the whole idealist tradition, a reputation which has been sustained, or encapsulated, in the memory of Hobhouse's outburst against the Gothas which disturbed him in his Highgate garden as excrescences of Hegelianism: 'the visible and tangible outcome of a false and wicked doctrine' (Hobhouse 1918: 6). Hobhouse's own work reflected the influence of the idealist tradition far more than it indicated dissent from it, and he drew specifically on Green for his discussion of rights and positive liberty. He was more an heir than an antagonist, and his arguments indicate not the political restrictiveness of idealism, but its breadth and fruitfulness.

His argument in favour of greater state activity began not with the individual, but with voluntary associations. As if to underline his intellectual lineage, the book in which these views appeared, *The Labour Movement*, first published in 1893, carried a preface by the Liberal politician R.B. Haldane, who had demonstrated something of the eclecticism of the progressive movement by contributing to the *Progressive Review* an article on New Liberalism which cited Green's argument on freedom of contract as a signpost to reform, and placed an avuncular arm around the socialists as propagandizing hucksters for the new direction in policy. Hobhouse began with an unflattering dismissal of unregulated individual initiative: 'competitive commercialism' born of 'individual selfishness' must give way to co-operation and a sense of communal membership and responsibility. His ultimate aim was for a condition where society would assume a responsibility for all its members and 'the ceaseless wearying roar of the great engine of competition would be still' (Hobhouse 1893: 80). His vision had the appearance of a rather sternly organized Oxford college, with regulation in the interests of comfort and security in the physical world, but freedom and opportunity in the intellectual and spiritual sphere:

> It is a small thing to order man's doings in the way of providing material needs if you leave him to roam unfettered in the larger field of mental and spiritual development ... we insist at one and the same time on perfect freedom in this direction, and perfect organisation of all the material basis of society which forms the foundation of the life.
>
> (Hobhouse 1893: 94)

This change from competition to co-operation could be achieved because the market, though pernicious, was neither natural nor inevitable. Economic laws were simply accounts of what followed from certain conditions, and under different conditions different laws would apply. By a series of gradual reforms, public ownership and progressive taxation would be extended until all unearned increment was controlled by the community for its own beneficial purposes (ibid.: 84).

The beginning of this development Hobhouse detected in trade unions and co-operative societies, the logic of whose growth led to the assumption of increasing responsibilities by the community as a whole through the agency of the state, which was no more than the largest and most rational version of the various associations which existed for the benefit of their members : 'Co-operation and Trade Unionism are growing to be modes of *national* organization, and it is only as their development in this direction grows complete that they take their true place as methods of the collective control of industry in the interests of the nation *as a whole*' (ibid.: 36). The only difference between this form of co-operation, and co-operation for universal objects like the provision of roads or drinking water, was that the latter was carried out through 'legally established machinery'. Hobhouse recognized that what he was advocating might be described as socialism, and he did not at the time dispute the description, simply commenting that 'it differs from voluntary co-operation solely in the employment of legal machinery – a difference justified by the nature of the commodities provided' (ibid.: 40). There was little that was new or strange in giving the nation command of what was national in extent, and the municipality command of what was municipal, because state activity was simply voluntary activity universalized and carried out under law. Municipal socialism, in this way, was 'simply the growth of the collective control of industry under a special form' (ibid.: 50).

Hobhouse was not only a political advocate, but one whose advocacy was committed to liberalism and to the organized liberal movement. Thus though he was prepared to accept that some of his proposals might be termed socialist, he nonetheless was careful to outline the differences between socialism and liberalism, and to do so in a manner which gave a slight advantage to the latter. This was especially so after the dispute over the Boer War of 1899–1902. Progressive liberal opinion had opposed the war as an imperialist adventure. The Webbs and Shaw, on the other hand, who were Hobhouse's closest associates on the socialist side, had supported it. Thus a rupture occurred between the New Liberals and the Fabians, the socialists with whom they had found closest sympathy. To indicate the division, Hobhouse presented the New Liberalism as a natural development and application of Cobdenite values. Cobden himself had accepted state interference in the case of factory legislation covering children under 13, and once the necessity of interference to secure freedom and equality as the basis for individual action was accepted, it was capable of extension without any violation of the original principles, so as to encompass Gladstone's Irish land legislation, collective bargaining and the responsibilities of a paternal state. That element in liberalism which had not only asserted individual freedom, but opposed state action as inherently tyrannous, was of merely temporary value. It was necessary at a time when the state was in the hands of an aristocracy, but not when it was the agent of the whole society. Thus Hobhouse arrived at a position where he described socialists and liberals approaching the same practical positions, but from different sides, the liberal in the interests of individuality, the socialist from the viewpoint of co-operation and organization: 'The two ideals, as ideals, are not conflicting but complementary' (Hobhouse 1905: 228–9). Conflict only occurred when the beliefs were perverted, when liberalism became commercial libertarianism, or when socialism became obsessed with collective effort and the role of the expert. Hobhouse did not mention Beatrice and Sidney Webb at this point, but his criticism is particularly apt as an attack on some aspects of the Fabian socialism of which they were among the chief exponents:

> In the socialistic presentment, [the expert] sometimes looks strangely like the powers that be – in education, for instance, a clergyman under a new title, in business that very captain of industry who at the outset was the Socialist's chief enemy. Be that as it may, as the 'expert' comes to the front, and 'efficiency' becomes the watchword of administration, all that was human in Socialism vanishes out of it.

> (Hobhouse 1905: 230)

When Hobhouse came to write his best-known piece of political argument, *Liberalism*, the New Liberalism had been extended into the legislative programme of a Liberal government. By 1911, when the book was published, a Liberal administration first under Campbell-Bannerman and then under Asquith had introduced a budget which included proposals for progressive taxation and a tax on land, old age pensions, school meals, medical inspection for school children and a scheme of insurance to provide cover for illness and unemployment. The need to persuade was to this extent reduced, but the need to explain and justify remained, and the book achieved one of the most subtle and sustained presentations of the case for direct state responsibility, argued from traditional liberal principles.

But as the argument became more abstract it became less assured, or alternatively suggested practical consequences more extreme than Hobhouse accepted in the actual course of his political recommendations. Thus when discussing the nature of injury and the necessary public restrictions upon it, he skirted around the difficulty of defining the term with the broad assertion: 'if we ask what is injury we are again thrown back on some general principle which will override the individual claim to do what one will' (Hobhouse 1911: 36). Frequently, his response to an explanatory problem of this kind was to imply unlimited rights of control to the public power. Thus when distinguishing between beliefs and the practical application of beliefs – a distinction which sits oddly in an argument which derives so much from Green – Hobhouse conceded only the right to the former, a conclusion which gives the citizen little more than the freedom once claimed by Sir Thomas More. Even that quiet liberty was not guaranteed, for as Collini points out, the right to liberty was for Hobhouse 'dependent upon the capacity for rational self-direction' which made it 'vulnerable to a particularly puritan interpretation' (Collini 1979: 124). James Meadowcroft has been more severe, suggesting that the 'deliberate displacement of liberty – and the positing of harmony at the core of liberalism – was the most striking formal innovation Hobhouse introduced in the course of articulating a liberal variant more sympathetic to the activist democratic state' (Meadowcroft 1994: xix).

Liberalism, perhaps more than any of Hobhouse's other writings, asserts the claims of the central state. There was no decrease in liberty for the individual in these claims, he argued, both because the purpose of control was the creation of the conditions for freedom, and because all social life involved coercion, and hence there was simply a choice between coercion exercised by individuals or groups, and coercion exercised by the state for the progressive freeing of individuals: 'It is a question not of increasing or diminishing, but of reorganising, restraint' (Hobhouse 1911: 81).

The more the collective authority of all individuals exercised through the state was asserted, the greater was Hobhouse's need as a Liberal publicist to distinguish between liberalism and socialism, and to incorporate in the former all common elements between the two. In 1911 he distinguished two main forms of socialism, the mechanical and the official. The mechanical form was economic materialism, and the official form the Fabian socialism which Hobhouse had already criticized, with the characterization extended by the addition of some Wellsian eugenics, the experts having extended their rule into the cultivation of people. It was official socialism not in the sense of being orthodox, but in the sense of being run by officials.

This need to establish the distinctive and predominant position of liberalism within progressive thinking was shared by J.A. Hobson, the other main publicist of the New Liberalism who, like Hobhouse, gave an account of liberalism which directed it into collectivist channels. But whereas Hobhouse began with the individual and the association and ended with the state, Hobson argued the necessity both of central action and of the active encouragement and recognition by the central power of the role of individuals and groups. Collective action could only effectively and justly be carried on if due place were given to the varied and free activity of citizens. Like Hobhouse, Hobson began with traditional liberalism, even applying some of its principles in a familiar way. Thus he argued for greater freedom and flexibility in politics, drawing on the work of Ostrogorski and Lowell to attack the unifying effects which a dominant cabinet and organized political parties had on the opinions and action of MPs. But he continued by describing traditional, political or constitutional reforms as by themselves inadequate to the contemporary situation. The old barriers to individual freedom had been of an entirely constitutional kind, hence their removal had involved the restraint of central power. But other barriers remained or had been erected of an economic and social kind, and these required positive state action for their demolition. Nor was the removal of obstacles the whole of liberalism – there was also the construction of opportunities both in the individuals' environment and in their abilities, through the encouragement of skills or the pursuit of reforms in health or education. Access had to be provided to land, transport, credit, law, mechanical power and education. This meant the nationalization of the railways and the public ownership and development not only of electricity but of future mineral discoveries. Credit would have to be available equally to all, and some means found of ensuring security against unemployment. The courts must provide a free and public service which neither demanded nor depended upon wealthy litigants. Education must provide a broad highway and at its higher levels must rest on public provision rather than private endowment.

At a practical level, argued Hobson, Liberals had been pursuing a constructive policy for some years. But it had been pursued in an ad hoc manner, and now needed to be articulated and consciously pursued. The crisis of liberalism, a phrase with which Hobson entitled a collection of articles which he published in 1909 was thus a crisis of identity. Could liberalism adopt a new conception of the state and of the state's responsibilities?

Hobson employed the analogy of a natural organism to describe society and its political functions, as did many other writers of the time. Employing the notion in a manner similar to that used by T.H. Huxley and unlike that used by individualists such as Spencer and Kidd, he argued that the common interests and functions which identified society had a distinctive claim, and one which was made through the central organizing intelligence represented by the state. The organic analogy was employed also to assert the rights of the community as a whole, by destroying the individual claim to property or to the sole credit for the creation of the value of property. But having established the priority of society over its individual members, Hobson then advanced a series of claims for those members, based on the needs of the community as a whole. The argument for a universal franchise stemmed not from any individual rights, but from a need to involve all those affected by government in its workings. If the state were to operate effectively, it would need constantly to be checked, spurred and informed by the opinions of its citizens – the wearer knew best whether the shoe fitted comfortably. Whilst Hobhouse justified the responsible state by the rights of the individual, Hobson justified the participation of the individual and the group by the needs of the organic community. So whilst Hobhouse argued for redistributive taxation in order to meet the economic rights of individuals, Hobson argued for them in order to promote the economic flourishing of society (Clarke 1978: 51). This contrast can be drawn too starkly. As both Freeden and Vincent and Plant have insisted, Hobhouse had plenty to say about the common good, and Hobson about the flourishing of individuals (Freeden 1978; Vincent and Plant 1984). But whilst there remained a difference of emphasis between the two, it was not one which necessarily pushed Hobson in favour of government. The collective purpose would often not be best pursued directly by public agency, and Hobson distinguished in this way between what he termed practical and theoretic socialism. Practical socialism, which he saw as appropriate to the New Liberalism, was the employment of collectivism where appropriate. Full or theoretic socialism was the indiscriminate application of collectivism without any attempt to assess its usefulness in particular cases. In distinguishing between practical and theoretic socialism, Hobson was in parodic form distinguishing, however unintentionally, between his present views and his own past and future ones. In the last decade of the nineteenth century he had been happy to present his views as socialist

Hobson

(Collini 1979: 38), and by the 1926 he was one of the co-authors of the Independent Labour Party's *Living Wage* programme and as such, whatever his reservations about socialism (Freeden 1986: 181–5, 1988: 22), advocating views which were, in terms of conventional polarities, on the left wing of the Labour Party. His understanding of society as like an organism meant, as John Allett has put it, that 'he saw capitalism not only as crippling the life-chances of many individuals' but also as 'a tumour derationalizing the "social mind"' (Allett 1981: 256). In his New Liberal phase, Hobson's 'practical' socialism enabled him to argue that in economic production, for instance, collectivism was appropriate in basic routine industries supplying standardized essential commodities. He contrasted this with specialized activity, which addressed itself to the production of goods not for general, but for particular and individual use: tailored clothes, architect-designed unique houses and the whole range of production which, because each item was distinctive and unrepeated and because of the individual care given to each item, was better described as craft than as mere production. Collectivism was appropriate when all that needed to be done was the efficient execution of an established function, as opposed to the individual creation of something new. It could be administered, whereas art, or craft, could not.

The distinction was aesthetic not economic, and drew on Morris, and on Ruskin of whom Hobson was a great admirer. The more collectivism advanced, he argued, the less would be its relative weight in the total production of society. Greater prosperity, security and opportunity – themselves the result of collectivism – would create a growing appreciation of and desire for the kinds of goods which could only be produced by art, and thus the scope of collective enterprise would continually be reduced. The aim of this practical socialism, which would express liberalism's new commitment to social radicalism, would be

> not to abolish the competitive system, to socialise all instruments of production, distribution, and exchange, and to convert all workers into public employees – but rather to supply all workers at cost with all the economic conditions requisite to the education and employment of their personal powers for their personal advantage and enjoyment.
>
> (Hobson 1909: 172–3)

Thus would art and labour combine.

The New Liberalism of Hobhouse and Hobson was both persuasive and reflective, standing back a little from the parliamentary and

partisan activities which it sought to influence. But as it was directed at
and drew inspiration from those activities, so too it found expression
there. The Liberal politicians who, particularly after the general
election of 1906, were engaged in liberal social reforms, explained and
defended their actions in terms different from those employed by
Gladstone or Rosebery or even by the Joseph Chamberlain of the
1880s. Phrases, arguments, ideas which were employed by the publicists
of the New Liberalism recur in the speeches of the politicians, with
varying degrees of coherence. Even amongst Liberals whose connection with social radicalism was slight, the new style could be found.
Stefan Collini has argued that it would be misleading to divide the
debates amongst Liberals at this time into disputes over negative and
positive freedom (Collini 1979: 46–9). Nonetheless when in 1907 H.H.
Asquith employed the language of social reform, he spoke also of
negative and positive liberty, and distinguished between good and bad
forms of socialism (H. H. Asquith, *Liberalism and Socialism*, quoted in
MacCoby 1961: 41–2). Three politicians in particular were prominent
in the parliamentary and electoral presentation of liberalism in this
new fashion: Winston Churchill, who had crossed sides from the
Conservatives to the Liberals in 1904 during the dispute over tariff
reform, David Lloyd George and Charles Masterman. Yet despite the
fact that it was the existence of just such politicians as these which gave
writers like Hobson cause to hope that liberalism might be rationalized
and given a progressive impetus, their presentation of liberal policies
and principles was more radical in tone and detail than in substance.
Lloyd George railed against landed wealth in a manner which led the
King to talk in horror of class war. But it was the intellectual simplicity
and electoral promise of a land campaign which attracted all three,
rather than the general assertion of a liberal collectivism as expounded
by either Hobson or Hobhouse. In Masterman's case a sense of
political benefit was complemented by a fear of social disaster, of a
society undermined at its disaffected roots and requiring a radical
programme of social reform stemming from an aroused consciousness
of responsibility. For Churchill, a series of reforms to promote 'the care
of the sick and the aged, and, above all, of the children' were to be
pursued within a general recognition of the importance of 'both
collective organisation and individual incentive' (Churchill 1909:
80–1).

SOCIALISM – H.M. HYNDMAN, BEATRICE AND SIDNEY WEBB, BERNARD SHAW, H.G. WELLS

In putting an argument for state collectivism, liberal publicists had frequently pointed out that they were not advocating socialism. But while the distinction may have had force, it lacked clarity because of the many ways in which the word 'socialism' was used. It was a word whose very imprecision made it useful as a description of the condition in which British people found themselves, and those who appeared to favour, even to encourage, the changes were loosely labelled socialists by others. The number who called themselves socialists was smaller. Their views represent the clearest and most vigorous advocacy of the expanding state, and if the 1880s are taken to be the occasion for the emergence of modern British socialism, then the earliest of the new thinkers and the first propagandist of the new British socialism was H.M. Hyndman, the organizer and patron of British social democracy in the form of the Social Democratic Federation and a man whose writings drew heavily if not deeply on Marx, from whom he took the conceptions of class war, economic materialism, the labour theory of value and a predominantly political theory of revolution. But the political position which Hyndman adopted was far too idiosyncratic to be labelled as Marxist; he propagated a socialism that was very much of his own making and which, with its mixture of paternalism and imperialism, led his enemies to dismiss him as a mere Tory, and which in its employment of radical arguments for collectivist ends emphasized how close many of his practical proposals were to those of progressive liberals.

Most of Hyndman's views, indeed, were already set out in his *The Text Book of Democracy: England for All*, published in 1881, three years before the formation of the Social Democratic Federation, and before he had claimed any affinity with Marx. In *England for All* Hyndman set out a line of 'stepping-stones to further development' which included a simplification of the laws of land tenure, the extension of the powers of local authorities to buy land and to lease it out in smallholdings and 'compensated expropriation' in the large cities. Land nationalization was eventually to be combined with that of railways and, somewhat disproportionately, of capital (Hyndman 1881: 30). But the demands for nationalization were the currants in a much more traditional pudding. Fighting a by-election in St Marylebone in 1880 Hyndman had expressed distaste for an extended suffrage, opposition to Irish Home Rule, a desire for a liberal policy at home and the maintenance of the empire abroad. A quarter of a century later, with many years of socialist propaganda behind him, he was still able to fight the 1906 general election on the four issues of free trade, secular education, Chinese slavery and home rule, a platform indistinguishable from that of most liberals (Tsuzuki 1961: 29–30, 158).

As a political thinker Hyndman shared many of the presuppositions of contemporaries who were in no sense socialists. When he came to the question of changing the condition of Britain for the better, he frequently envisaged the able and educated few at the top improving the condition and character of the disadvantaged and ignorant many at the bottom. Socialism would bring to an end the anarchy, as Hyndman called it, of unemployment, criminal disorder and prostitution. It was in consequence a sound and sensible policy, which it was in the interests of the better classes to pursue. The first number of *Justice*, a journal which expressed the Hyndmanite view of things, described the two sides of the paper's domestic policy as agitation amongst the workers, and the persuasion of the educated classes of the need for scientific socialism.

Hyndman's argument in favour of socialism was a mixed appeal to justice, inevitability and efficiency. By efficiency he understood the effective and ordered advance of the English nation, an understanding which led him to approve of Lassalle's nationalist version of socialism in Germany. Only by an increase in regulation by the state 'shall the England of whose past we are all proud, and of whose future all are confident, clear herself from that shortsighted system which now stunts the physical and intellectual growth of the great majority' (Hyndman 1881: 6). Social reform to raise the condition of the people was demanded not only by social justice, but in order that the nation might maintain its strength and advance its interest: 'Lack of good food, good clothes and good air in children, is the main reason why some 50 per cent of our urban working class population is unfit to bear arms' (speech of 29 October 1900 reported in the *Morning Post* and quoted in Tsuzuki 1961: 148). An enlightened policy, on the other hand, could turn the most worthless sections of the population into 'the flower of our navy' (Hyndman 1884a: 32). But national vigour, once established, was not to be employed for selfish purposes. Hyndman believed, as did all real imperialists, not in any existing military and economic hegemony but in the empire that might be. His dream of empire was of Britain as the social democracy at the head of a free and progressive Anglo-Saxon confederation, leading the world to a socialist future. His imperialism thus involved assumptions about the proper interests of the subjects of empire (or at least the non-white ones – the Anglo-Saxons were already worthy to be partners). When he changed his mind over British policy in South Africa, he did so in part because he believed that Britain was less likely to oppress the native population than were the Boers. In the matter of India, in which he took a lifelong interest, he believed both in the necessity of wise imperial rule in order to raise the condition of the country, and in the need to respect and foster native traditions and institutions (Hyndman 1881: 132–3, 151ff.; Tsuzuki 1961: 129).

This combination of paternalism with a belief in the necessity for self-help characterized Hyndman's arguments about British politics just as much as it did his reflections on imperial affairs – indeed for him the two were part of a single problem, and neither could be solved in isolation. Thus, on the one hand, he believed in the superiority of superior persons and in the necessity of improving things by state initiative and by the persuasion of the educated classes. On the other, he argued that nothing could be achieved unless the workers themselves took an active and informed part in their own improvement. His complaint on resigning from the Social Democratic Federation in 1901, that socialism had been failed by the stupidity of those whom it sought to benefit, was both an expression of upper-middle-class disdain, and a genuine complaint by someone who believed that the inferiority of the working-class supporters mattered (*Justice*, 10 August 1901, quoted in Tsuzuki 1961: 135). To a genuine elitist it might well have been a positive advantage. He paid little attention to the state to which he wished to transfer so much new responsibility. He was more interested in local than in central initiative and, by 'state', understood collective effort undertaken through public bodies with universal authority.

Hyndman's views were vigorously, often contemptuously expressed. With Marx, he understood a conversation to mean one person striding up and down the room talking in an authoritative manner, a coincidence which made meetings of the two men entertaining for observers but unprofitable for the participants. It was a style which rankled, as did his enthusiasm for the active assertion of Britain's place in the world. His early support of military action in Africa caused offence to colleagues like Harry Quelch and William Morris, and his support of the British involvement in the First World War led to a rupture with the majority of the members of the organization which he had dominated on and off since 1881. He declined to give any support to the Russian October Revolution, seeing it as damaging both to the war effort and to the prospects of British leadership of world progress towards social democracy.

Hyndman's socialist arguments contained many elements which

were later taken up by Fabian socialists such as George Bernard Shaw and Beatrice and Sidney Webb. He shared with the Webbs a conception of the state as heavily municipal, and of socialism as locally applied. But the Social Democratic Federation was both ideologically too conservative and politically too radical for other British socialists. It has been suggested by A.M. McBriar that it was allegations of Tory gold in 1885 and the riots of 1886 and 1887 which alienated the Fabians. But there were other good grounds of difference as well. Hyndman's emphasis on the distinctiveness of national cultures and on the need for a degree of communal self-help did not fit in easily with either the elitism or the utilitarianism of the Fabian socialists, whilst his vociferous socialist patriotism was not a style they cared to adopt so openly or so publicly. Shaw and Sidney Webb, moreover, who made their first great impact with the *Fabian Essays in Socialism* of 1889, were of a different generation from Hyndman and were less convinced of the futility of existing politics and politicians and more eager to see themselves as part of a natural evolution from liberalism.

Beatrice and Sidney Webb looked on the collectivizing state and saw that it was good, though 'good' was not a word they would have readily used to describe it. Had they been of a more abstract cast of mind, they might have followed Sidney's colleague Sydney Olivier who, in the *Fabian Essays* of 1889, talked of positive ethical science, the discovery of social obligations from social facts (Olivier 1889). As it was, they were happy to observe that collectivism was, and that therefore it was becoming. In Sidney Webb, this refusal to refer to general principles could often be forthright. When working with R.B. Haldane on the constitution of the University of London, he was asked what his idea of a university was, and replied, 'I haven't any idea of a university.... Here are the facts' (Hamilton 1934, p. 131, quoted in McBriar 1962: 73). The reluctance to appeal in any terms other than those of observation and common sense applied equally to what was proposed and to what was opposed. In 1920, in their *A Constitution for the Socialist Commonwealth of Great Britain*, the Webbs disdained to criticize or condemn capitalism, commenting simply that it had 'demonstrably broken down', and had thus failed in the only way that mattered (S. and B. Webb 1920: xi). The Webbs' championship of social democracy was in clear contrast to that of their German contemporary Edward Bernstein, who, whilst he was familiar with their arguments and policies, based his own proposals on grounds of principle and general theory, rather than on positivism or tradition (Bernstein 1993). For those who seek a contrast between an English empirical, positivist approach, and a continental theoretical one, these differing advocacies of democratic, gradualist socialism illustrate the point very clearly.

The historian and socialist R.H. Tawney roguishly described the Webbs' position by referring to the use made by the conservative political writer Michael Oakeshott of traditions and intimations. Just so for the Webbs, he suggested, socialism sprang from 'already vigorous roots', and from 'a new fabric of rights and obligations' which was already emerging. 'Their views on the economics of Socialism, therefore, are rarely, if ever, cast in a doctrinal mould. They emerge as a synthesis of generalizations suggested by the institutions explored in their descriptive and historical works' (Tawney 1953a: 9–10). The Webbs, however, left it to others to elucidate this element in their work, and to other Fabian essayists to justify socialism in this manner. It was thus Annie Besant, not Sidney Webb, who in the *Fabian Essays* of 1889 argued that as against the utopian approach to industrial organization under socialism, the more useful way starts 'from the present state of society' and 'seeks to discover the tendencies underlying it; to trace those tendencies to their natural outworking in institutions; and so to forecast, not the far off future, but the next social stage' (Besant 1889: 184). Prediction was not a separate element in Fabian politics, for unless one knew which way the tide was running, one could not swim with it.

And yet despite their use of a form of argument which seemed to avoid choices of principle, the Webbs could not prevent the moral assertions breaking through. Sidney Webb had not been averse to making moral and rhetorical appeals to socialism in his early days in the Fabian Society, whilst the choice of efficiency as a criterion for national policy involved an aversion to lethargy and sensuality, and an admiration for hard work, dedication, and asceticism which constituted, as Peter Beilharz has argued (1992) a rather severe kind of utopianism. The Japanese naval victory over Russia in 1905 led Beatrice to observe in her diary the 'terrible object lesson of the failure even in the struggle for existence of the race which has lacked conduct, abstinence from physical pleasures, and trained intelligence in the bulk of the people' (B. Webb 1948: 299). The jeremiad was brought nearer home in 1920 when the Webbs condemned the functionless rich 'who deliberately live by owning instead of by working, and whose futile occupations, often licentious pleasures and inherently insolent manners, undermine the intellectual and moral standards of the community' (S. and B. Webb 1920: xii).

Perhaps a part of the Webbs' difficulty with the First World War was their belief in tides of history which were inexorable yet gradual, which bore steadily on yet did so without the spectacular and intermittent fury of tidal waves. For the war was both an occasion for the advancement of state collectivism, and an aggregate of individual disasters. What the Webbs hoped for and expected was that inevitability would be blended with gradualness. But if the tide was a calm one, and thus navigable, what were those caught in it expected to contribute to their arrival? The answer was that they could navigate the current, avoid disaster and make the best use of the waterway, but in terms of general direction and eventual destination, 'One option we have, and one only' (S. Webb 1890: 15). There were no major political choices to be made, because they were pre-empted, and the human element was to supply only the requisite technical skills. Philosophers and politicians might be necessary if broad choices were open, but they were not, and so what were called for were men and women with less lofty but more useful talents. Efficiency in national affairs could be promoted by training and enquiry into the social sciences and it was to this end that Sidney Webb secured the establishment of the London School of Economics and Political Science in 1895. If enough information and skill could be disseminated, then collective efficiency would be advanced by the persuasion of both evidently sound argument and capable example – no overtly political campaign would be necessary or even appropriate. It was a belief which led straight to both public administration and social administration as university disciplines.

Being traditionalists, the Webbs took their models from society as they found it, and combined expertise with excellence rather than with equality. Sensible measures were to be carried out as they had been by Chadwick and as they were to be by Morant, by a caste small enough to be reached and encouraged by the arts and graces of the dining table and the committee room. In the 1920s, with times a little harder and aristocracy a little less fashionable, Beatrice Webb transmuted this ideal into a wish for what she described in conversation as 'a dedicated Order, something resembling the Society of Jesus, which should exact a high standard of training, discipline and self-control among its members, and which would furnish, therefore, a leadership of the *elite* to guide the mass of citizens to a Socialist State' (M. Cole 1955: 244). In a neat rephrasing of Bagehot, she called for faith at the level of politics, and expertise at the level of actual schemes and proposals (B. Webb 1926: 166).

The faith was, to begin with, the faith of the people, for though the landless labourer was described as Samson feeling for the pillars, he was to be a well-advised Samson, and his groping and gripping were to be limited to doing the right thing at elections. At least until their practical adhesion to the Labour Party after the failure of their campaign in favour of the minority report of the Poor Law Commission, the Webbs appear to have been suspicious of the trade unions whenever those organizations strayed into politics. But by 1920 they were arguing both that wide political awareness was good for efficient government, and that it was the most effectual way of advancing the self-fulfilment and human education of the citizen body.

Thus though the purpose of representative democracy was to avoid the impracticalities of direct participation and to secure the appointment of efficient representatives and skilled governors, both electors and rulers were to benefit from an active democracy. Merely to accept permanent rule by officials 'secured efficient administration at the expense of losing all the educative influences and political safeguards of democracy' (S. and B. Webb 1897: 32). Unlimited power was no more desirable than uninformed power, since 'not even the wisest of men can be trusted with that supreme authority which comes from the union of knowledge, capacity, and opportunity with the power of untrammelled and ultimate decision' (ibid.: 844–5). It was for this reason that the Webbs, at the same time as they attacked syndicalism, insisted that trade unions would continue to be necessary under socialism to ensure efficiency in that sphere of the national life where the unions were competent (S. and B. Webb 1912: 144).

The call for greater state participation in the affairs of society was not generally coupled with any precise or sustained description of what form this state participation was to take, or of what form of state it was that was to participate. Reticence on this matter, coupled with the use of terms such as 'collectivism' or 'socialism' to describe a broad range of views, can lead one to suppose that the conception of the state was generally uniform. That this was not so, and that there were differences both amongst the conceptions current at any one time, and between earlier and later conceptions, is illustrated by the views of the Webbs. They saw the socialist state as being active at both national and local levels, though Sidney Webb complained of the absence of any discussion of the distribution of increasing public responsibilities between local and national government. Nonetheless their heaviest emphasis was always placed on local government, and when Sidney Webb used his favourite demonstration of his case, the long recitation of actual collectivist responsibilities, the majority of these responsibilities were locally exercised. Arguing against syndicalism in 1912, the Webbs stressed the importance of even the smallest units of local government: 'What we now call the Parish or District Council, which the Syndicalist seems to despise, must, as it seems to us, necessarily become a very important affair – perhaps, in the aggregate, more important than the central administration itself' (S. and B. Webb 1912: 52). Having themselves remedied by their massive study of municipal government the neglect of this area of state activity of which Sidney complained in 1889 in the *Fabian Essays*, the Webbs went on in their 1920 blueprint for a socialist commonwealth to envisage local government as one of the great growth areas in their renewed Britain. Yet though the major part both of their scholarly investigations and their political argument was concerned with local rather than central institutions, the Webbs moved towards a larger expectation of the role of central power in the provision of the benefits of socialism. Beatrice's membership of the 1906–9 Royal Commission on the Poor Law involved both Webbs in the examination of problems such as unemployment which new styles of social investigation had presented as having national rather than local characteristics, and for the solution of which national rather than local initiatives seemed appropriate. The socialist commonwealth which they envisaged in 1920 was, despite the stress on the benefits of municipal enterprise and involvement, a recognizably centralized state. It was perhaps a recognition of this hypertrophy, as they called it, which led them to an increasing emphasis on the complementary checks on state power. Local government came to be justified not simply because it was efficient, but because it represented independence and variety.

When the Webbs wrote anything of substance, they collaborated; the bulk of their mere pamphleteering was done by Sidney, with a style and an argument that were often repetitious. Sidney Webb was completely different in this respect from Bernard Shaw, the major contributor to and the editor of the *Fabian Essays* of 1889. Shaw was intrigued by a good argument and fascinated by a bad one, and whereas Sidney Webb's single mindedness created some tedium in his platform writing, Shaw's prolific variety sometimes makes it difficult to decide where he stood on the endless tumble of subjects to which he addressed himself.

It is impossible to limit a study of Shaw's politics to his formally political writings. He recognized no boundaries within his work, and his views on politics appear in his plays, his novels, his essays and books. Because of this, and because of the variety of his interests and opinions, attempts to detect the Shavian essence have often been made and have seldom succeeded. There is a sense in which the only adequate account of his political opinions is an account of the whole range of his writing. With these warnings in mind, something can perhaps still be said.

By the time Shaw edited the *Fabian Essays* of 1889, he had already employed and examined ideas drawn from both Marx and anarchism (Hulse 1970; Wolfe 1975). But these two sources had become muted after years in the Fabian Society. His own contribution to the *Fabian Essays* consisted of a brief self-deprecatory editorial introduction and two essays, one on the economic basis of socialism and one on the transition to social democracy, setting out a programme involving the socialization of all forms of rent in order to achieve a just relation between labour and rewards, and the use of surplus value for the benefit of the whole community by means of state action. Progress was to be gradual in order to avoid disruption and crises, and would occur not because it was inevitable, but because it was reasonable and just, and would be seen as such by men and women of intelligence. Not that there were necessarily very many of these. Some socialists, wrote Shaw, had felt

> the right so clear, the wrong so intolerable, the gospel so convincing, that it seems to them that it *must* be possible to enlist the whole body of workers – soldiers, policemen, and all – under the banner of brotherhood and equality; and at one great stroke to set Justice on her rightful throne. Unfortunately, such an army of light is no more to be gathered from the human product of nineteenth century civilization than grapes are to be gathered from thistles.
>
> (Shaw 1889: 235)

The task of persuasion would not be an easy one, but the new society would still be reached by persuasion and the exercise of conscious choice. There was nothing inevitable in any historical process, nor anything natural or immutable about any social, political or economic arrangements: 'the source of our social misery is no eternal well-spring of confusion and evil, but only an artificial system susceptible of almost infinite modification and readjustment – nay, of practical demolition and substitution at the will of Man' (ibid.: 59).

If, unlike the Webbs, Shaw did not argue for socialism by pointing to the direction in which the current was flowing, then recommendations needed some other basis to give them force. The long elaboration of the theory of rent in his first *Fabian Essay* did not in itself establish the need for a socialist ordering of things. What it demonstrated was that capitalism was unjust, that wealth was to be judged by the condition of the community as a whole, and could not be assessed simply by adding up riches. Shaw used Ruskin's term, 'illth', for the contemporary condition, writing that 'a nation which cannot afford food and clothing for its children cannot be allowed to pass as wealthy because it has provided a pretty coffin for a dead dog'. Present society was characterized by 'luxury' and 'vice', and was condemned straightforwardly in moral terms (Shaw 1889: 55–6).

Shaw was immensely attracted to the social visions of William Morris, and regretfully rejected communistic anarchism not because it was wrong, but simply because it was, in the present state of human nature, impractical. His examination of the views of Benjamin Tucker, Kropotkin and Morris was called *The Impossibilities of Anarchism* and thus constituted a practical, conditional rejection, not an absolute moral one. Shaw employed here precisely that choice between legal and economic motives and sanctions for work, used by the individualist opponent of the growing state, Herbert Spencer, in 1884 in 'The Coming Slavery' (Spencer [1884] 1969: 83). But the immediate unlikeliness of an improvement did not mean that it ought not to be wished for, and in 1890 he complained of the apparent inability of women to free themselves from the social and moral restraints under which they lived (Hulse 1970: 131). Practicalities and desirabilities were not at all the same.

Shaw had hoped, in 1889, that social democracy would be created because the sensible and informed members of society would recognize its merits. But a Liberal government, surely more sensible than a Conservative one, came and went, an Independent Labour Party was formed and achieved little, and nothing seemed to get done. By 1897 Shaw, who had previously ignored the mass of the people as a force in politics, had begun to argue that the main hindrance to socialist advance was the 'stupidity of the working-class' ('The illusions of Socialism' in E. Carpenter, ed., *Forecasts of the Coming Century*, 1897 quoted in McBriar 1962: 84). The next seven years provided him with no encouragement, including as they did the Conservative victory in the 'Khaki' election of 1900, and in 1904 he complained that the vigour of capitalism and the irrationality of the populace had created

an irresistible proletarian bodyguard of labourers whose immediate interests are bound up with those of the capitalists, and who are, like their Roman prototypes, more rapacious, more rancorous in their Primrose partisanship, and more hardened against all the larger social considerations, than their masters, simply because they are more needy, ignorant, and irresponsible.

(*Clarion*, 30 September 1904, quoted in McBriar 1962: 83)

The problem lay in part in the powerful role of ideas, myths, and grand principles. They would always, short of utopia, be a means by which people were moved to act, and they would always simplify and distort reality. How to have myths which would move people to socialism but not to excess, which would be powerful enough to motivate them but not so rigid as to disillusion them, was the task which Shaw acknowledged might prove difficult even for him (Griffith 1993: 51–2).

The work of progress was to be carried out by those exceptional individuals who had the wit to see and the imagination to aspire, like Shaw's first hero, the aristocratic socialist Sidney Trefusis in his 1884 novel, *An Unsocial Socialist*. Trefusis was followed in *Man and Superman* in 1903 by John Tanner, the servant of a Life Force relentlessly pursuing the improvement of brain power by selective breeding – though with a nice touch of wit, the true 'superman' is shown to be not Tanner at all, but a superwoman. Eventually the whole of humanity might reach a higher plane of existence; but they would arrive because they had been led. By 1905, with *Major Barbara* and the *Preface* to it written the following year, the role of excellence in the generation of progress had become more familiar: it was money, and the use of money to create wealth, a theme restated with a renewed vigour after its first airing in *Fabian Essays*. The poor men and women in the drama were despised when they accepted their poverty, whilst the possession of refined sensibilities was presented in the *Preface* as the real cause for the pursuit of social improvement. This was an inversion of Oscar Wilde's argument that the 'chief advantage that would result from the establishment of Socialism is undoubtedly, the fact that Socialism would relieve us from that sordid necessity of living for others' (Wilde 1891: 1). It was also a less philanthropic view of the behaviour which Dicey had observed when he commented that the 'Englishman of the middle classes' inclines to benevolence because his 'own happiness is diminished by the known and felt miseries of his less wealthy neighbours' (Dicey [1914] 1962: lxii).

A degree of impatience with the ignorance and stupidity of ordinary humanity had always been a part of Shaw's view of politics. The First World War provided him with excessive evidence of human folly and of its disastrous consequences. Yet when he came to reflect upon it in *Heartbreak House*, a play begun before and written during the war and published for the first time after it in 1919, his major condemnation was of effete leadership, the cultured leisured classes who had failed to exploit their culture and their leisure either for their own improvement or for the good of mankind:

they were the only repositories of culture who had social
opportunities of contact with our politicians, administrators, and
newspaper proprietors, or any chance of sharing or influencing their
activities. But they shrank from that contact. They hated politics.
They did not wish to realize Utopia for the common people: they
wished to realize their favourite fictions and poems in their own
lives.

(Shaw [1919] 1964: 8)

But though the traditional and obvious leadership had failed, the first
years of peace saw Europe with new heroes who seemed to Shaw to be
fulfilling the expectations which the inhabitants of Heartbreak House
had destroyed. Great leaders could achieve things with otherwise
unremarkable nations like Russia and Italy, and in a lecture delivered
in November 1919, in the autumn of the year whose summer had seen
the writing of the *Preface* to *Heartbreak House*, Shaw recruited Lenin
to the select group of those who, with Dickens, Ruskin, and of course
Shaw himself, were to achieve his own particular form of socialism.

The people at large are occupied with their own special jobs; and the
reconstruction of society is a very special job indeed. To tell the
people to make their own laws is to mock them just as I should
mock you if I said, 'Gentlemen: you are the people: write your own
plays' .... All Socialists are Tories in that sense. The Tory is a man
who believes that those who are qualified by nature and training for
public work, and who are naturally a minority, have to govern the
mass of the people. That is Toryism. That is also Bolshevism.

(Shaw 1921: 15)

For Shaw, the increasingly obtrusive perversities of humanity were an
incentive to firmer and more drastic handling of poor quality or at
least raw and unworked material. For Graham Wallas, another of the
original Fabian Essayists, the only purpose of political reform was an
improvement of the quality of the citizens. Thus though if this quality
was low it might impede Fabian collectivism, the appropriate response
was to aim for the more fundamental reform: the improvement of
human character. It was quite wrong, he argued, 'to bring in a
constitution which the average man is not at present fit to work,
without first or at the same time striving ... by education and good
laws to improve the average man' (lecture on Aristotle's *Politics*,
quoted in Wiener 1971: 22). Education was thus the most fundamental
of all reforms, both because all else in the end depended on it, and
because it was directed towards the improvement of those qualities

which above all others were worth cultivating, and whose cultivation justified all other measures of improvement. 'If this generation were wise', Wallas argued in his Fabian Essay of 1889, 'it would spend on education not only more than any other generation has ever spent before, but more than any generation would ever need to spend again' (Wallas 1962: 181).

Wallas's contribution to the Fabian socialism of the late 1880s and early 1890s was of a distinctively moral kind, both concerned with the formation of character, and giving a place within a collective programme of reform to individual improvement and moral activity. On the one hand, the rights of the community as a whole against any individual or group claims on property were asserted to the exclusion of producers' co-operatives, but on the other the socialist system thus created was never to be, could never be, more than an appropriate context for better living: 'The system of property holding which we call Socialism is not in itself such a life any more than a good system of draining is health, or the invention of printing is knowledge' (Wallas 1889: 182). And even before the most fit environment for a higher and improving life had been formed, individuals could raise themselves above the 'immoral principles' with which the commercial system 'saturated' them. Personal adoption of the higher life was a matter of individual decision to 'live as simply as the equal rights of their fellows require' (ibid.: 179, 183).

The emphasis on the dependence of political development upon the character of the citizens separated Wallas increasingly from other Fabian socialists, and by 1895 he had effectively withdrawn from socialist politics (Clarke 1978: 55). In 1908 this developing conviction of the need to concentrate on the psychology of the democratic citizen and the means of acting upon it for good was articulated in *Human Nature in Politics*, a book whose argument took Wallas a long way from the concern with the role of the state which had characterized the socialists with whom he had associated twenty years earlier.

The perception of the strong thread of irrationality in political conduct which informed Wallas's writing was shared with a sharper but less permanent despair by those who viewed the electorate as suffering from insufficient civic education. The socialist and Labour politician and propagandist James Ramsay MacDonald complained in 1900 that the people 'took infinitely more interest in getting the vote than they have taken in using it' and argued that democracy 'can be made efficient only by the education of the individual citizen in civic virtues' (MacDonald 1900: 60, 73). His colleague in the Labour Party, Philip Snowden, observed twenty years later that 'the nominal government of an ignorant democracy may be a greater danger to the State than even the despotism of an autocracy' (Snowden 1921: 224). In the arguments of others who held similar views a concern with the psychological inadequacy of the citizens of the modern state became an occasion for intimations of social engineering. Social psychologists such as William McDougal and Wilfred Trotter toyed with the idea of a technically and scientifically skilled elite whose raw material would be the inferior but not quite intractable masses. Human nature was seen to pose immediate practical difficulties for progressive political thinkers because of the impossibility of applying egalitarian principles whilst securing the orderly functioning of nominally democratic regimes (Soffer 1969). But whilst these arguments were cast in terms of technicality and scientific detachment, with political conclusions stemming from scientific observation, the initial perception was as much a matter of political ideology as was the eventual recommendation. Apparently similar observations about the behaviour of the masses could lead to strikingly different conclusions in the arguments of a man such as G.K. Chesterton.

Wallas's career after *Human Nature in Politics*, and particularly after the First World War, illustrates a retreat from traditional political speculation. He sought for the great idea which would inspire and educate humanity, enabling it to pursue and approach the good life through active and unconstrained citizenship in a modern state. But the idea could not be found, the people could not be inspired and the modern state was sustained without any noble principles. Wallas's decision, after his retirement, to write neither on the civil service nor on local government but on *The Art of Thought* was both a recognition and a rejection of a separation of the development of government from one kind of political argument and civic aspiration.

Wallas's concern with the principled motive in politics was matched amongst the popularizers and propagandists of socialism. The men and women whose books sold in thousands, sometimes in millions, or who proselytized for a socialism which they advocated with religious fervour, depended on the presentation of new doctrines with old credentials, the credentials of evangelical commitment, self-denial and visionary aspiration. James Keir Hardie, who more than any other single person contributed to the initial creation of a distinct Labour Party in Parliament, first arrived at socialist arguments with a political opposition to parliamentary liberalism, and an industrial opposition to capitalism. But as he became a forceful and popular speaker for his political beliefs, he came to express them in increasingly religious tones, and to appeal to the sense of justice, fellowship and moral aspiration against the greed, selfishness and materialism of capitalism and landlordism. The solution to social disease was to be public ownership of land and capital through the agency of the state which would use the rent and interest, which had previously accrued to idle rentiers, for the public good. The details were however left vague: 'To dogmatise about the form which the Socialist State shall take ... is a matter with which we have nothing whatever to do. It belongs to the future' (Hardie 1907: 96). The drive of the argument was directed elsewhere: to a condemnation of the existing order, and a summons to something better.

> For a full rounded century the gospel of Selfishness has held sway, and under it the nation has stumbled on from one depth to another until it has reached the verge of a precipice from the void of which there can be no re-ascent should we be dragged over. Poverty, physical deterioration, insanity, are evils which no nation can suffer and yet live.
>
> (Hardie 1907: 34)

The alternative was 'a world embracing principle that knows no sect, nor creed, nor race, and which offers new life and hope to all created things – the glorious Gospel of Socialism' (ibid.: 86).

The opposition of socialism to selfishness, and the description of socialism as a religion was partly a rejection of laissez-faire individualism at a personal, psychological level. A society which was not powered by economic individualism needed citizens moved by altruism and fellowship rather than by competition. Faith and personal dedication thus became blended in a political campaign. *The Religion of Socialism* was therefore an almost fully explanatory title for a book published in 1890 by Katherine St John Conway and J. Bruce Glasier. This idea of socialism as a religion was frequently explored in the late 1880s and 1890s, and Conway and Glasier were repeating, in 1890, the title used five years previously by a more ambitious writer, E. Belfort Bax, an associate of both Hyndman and Morris who had proposed a social morality in an attack on ethical individualism. The religious analogy was given liturgical form with the foundation of the Labour Church movement in 1891. Socialism as a religion did not appeal to Graham Wallas, who found his higher values elsewhere, and when in 1895 he addressed the Fabian Society on the two contrasting methods of achieving social and political change – the religious and the scientific – the ILP provided him with his readiest example of the first type (Wiener 1971: 50). But though objections to sentimental enthusiasm might be applied to the proselytizing socialists of the 1890s, they are less appropriate to Bax. Bax drew on both positivism and German idealism to argue a case for socialism which was ethical rather than material, but which avoided what he saw as the merely personal holiness of Christianity, and achieved instead a morality which, though deriving its force from outside society, nonetheless was expressed socially rather than individually, and which led people to recognize and pursue the harmonized interest of the whole community, rather than self-interest. If this could be done, then both the ethical and psychological problems left by the destruction of individualism could be solved (Bax 1885, 1887).

One of the most important and effective of the propagandists of socialism was Robert Blatchford, who reached a popular audience through his *Clarion* newspaper which no other socialist in late Victorian Britain could equal. His appeal was not only popular but populist. One of his books was entitled *Britain for the British* (Blatchford 1902), and in it he set out the rights of the people – the British of the title – against the privileges of wealth and power guarded and coveted by a selfish minority. The rhetoric of patriotism and religion were employed in a way which based the socialist argument as firmly on tradition as on revolution. As Stanley Pierson lucidly put it, 'In place of the Marxist conception of a class-conscious proletariat, Blatchford substituted the ethical-religious category of a righteous people' (Pierson 1973: 158). And just as the claims of the British people were set against the depredations of a controlling minority, so the potential capacity for communal self-management of the people was set against the central direction carried on by the collectivist state. The state socialism to which Blatchford gave his assent was but a necessary and in part transitory instrument for the achievement of a utopia where the overpowering massiveness of both state and industrialism were transcended.

A socialist propaganda of a different kind was conducted in the writings of James Ramsay MacDonald. MacDonald was to become, in 1924, the first Labour prime minister, but before that he was one of the leading exponents of a socialism which was reformist and parliamentary, directing the enthusiasm of socialist evangelism into the channels of electoral politics. MacDonald has suffered at the hands of historians for his later political career, and for the events of 1931 when he became separated from the Labour Party and, following the resignation of the Labour government of which he was leader, remained in office at the head of a coalition cabinet largely composed of Conservatives. Asa Briggs has referred contemptuously to MacDonald's flabby argument 'in his evolutionist writings on socialist theory' (Briggs and Saville

1971: 3). But though MacDonald was not an original thinker, at the level of political writing in which he was engaged he did take the arguments of socialism and present them in a form which made them politically encouraging for socialists and politically acceptable for liberals. Where Hobhouse and Hobson had tried to give an account of social liberalism which incorporated the deserving parts of socialism and threw away the undeserving, MacDonald tried the trick in reverse (R. Barker 1974, 1976). His conception of socialism was unoriginal, involving the collective ownership of capital, the distribution of the fruits of production in the interests of all, the pursuit of the collective over the selfish interest and the incorporation of all in the life of the social, economic and political community. The argument was given a degree of intellectual weight by the employment, as persuasive devices, of organic, evolutionist, scientific or idealist analogies. Kant, Darwin, Ritchie were all drawn upon and cited when the debate appeared to need stiffening. But MacDonald's particular contribution – which his critics have subsequently condemned as woolliness or outright deviousness – was to pitch the achievement of the final aims of socialism well into the future. The socialist claim and the socialist critique were employed to condemn existing arrangements and to indicate a direction of advance. But sufficiently little was said about the pace of advance to accommodate everyone from the religious socialists who took their tone from Hardie, Conway or Glasier, to those liberal reformers who had worked with MacDonald in the Rainbow Circle of the 1890s. MacDonald represented the platform side of the arguments which involved progress through an expanding state. Others chose, as in part Shaw had done, a more literary medium.

In 1903 H.G. Wells joined the Fabian Society. He was to remain a member for four years, during which time he and the society reacted to each other like a ship and the cannon which is loose upon its deck in a high sea. The views he put forward about politics and the future of society in the years between the death of Queen Victoria and the outbreak of the Great War were a development and a doppelganger of Fabian ideas as put forward by Shaw and the Webbs, touching them sympathetically at some points, and carrying them at others to conclusions which just, but only just, placed them beyond sympathy and set them up in opposition. There had always been an element of Toryism in Fabian ideas, as Shaw himself had proudly asserted, and Wells developed it with gusto, arriving at a theory of aristocracy which broadened the Fabian notion of an administrative elite into a belief in a superior class of guardians, or as Wells sometimes called them, Samurai.

To begin with Wells's arguments envisaged something more like Cromwell's Ironsides (his own comparison) than like a traditional aristocracy. *Anticipations*, Wells's first reflection on social and political problems, which was written in 1901 and first drew the attention of the Webbs to him, envisaged a world internationally organized by an elite distinguished by intellectual ability, abstemious private lives and behaviour, and a mastery of the new technical, scientific and professional skills – a kind of caste of super-Henry Strakers. They would come to power by a combination of their own public-spirited determination ('a sort of outspoken Secret Society') and through the catastrophe which contemporary ignorance and mismanagement of human affairs would bring about. In something like an attempt to adapt Shavian solutions to Wallas's problems, the unregenerate mass of the population were to be herded, organized and coerced into a higher society by a refined scientific elite. It was as if the mythical gardener, whom Huxley had suggested – and rejected – for the cultivation of human society, had after all been found. Admiration for the new republicans was thus matched in Wells by an extreme disquiet towards the masses and their improvident breeding. Breeding should be controlled, or at least influenced, both in order to encourage quality and to discourage the procreation of unfit persons, whilst killing was not always ruled out as a last resort in a programme of social improvement. The exact character of this proposal to use public power to assist eugenic improvement has been the subject of some fairly passionate advocacy, both on Wells's side and against him (Carey 1992; Coren 1993; Foot 1995; Parrinder 1993; Parrinder 1995; Sutherland 1995). The discussion has sometimes been confused by the collapsing of two judgements into one: that Wells advocated sterilization, killing, and exile as part of a eugenicist policy, in addition ranking people racially and dismissing the mass of humanity in so doing; and that his eugenicist views were no more than the style of the times. The second point does not, even if conceded, evaporate the first. But Wells's version of eugenicism sometimes had a rational brutality that exceeded the less articulated assumptions of his contemporaries.

The books in which Wells developed these ideas between 1901 and 1911 did not greatly advance the original suggestions of *Anticipations*, though the technocratic elite broadened into a voluntary aristocracy, and the suppression of the unfit was replaced by more humane though no less ruthless methods of segregation and discouragement. The broadening into aristocracy was in part a reaction against a purely bureaucratic administrative elite, an ambition which the Webbs were satirized for holding in *The New Machiavelli*, and a development which

Wells was later to advance as the cause of the decline of civilizations in his *Outline of History*.

Wells considered one of the main problems of a society run by its best members to be that of combining stability with fruitful innovation, and he insisted on the importance of heavily endowed, continuing and easily accessible education as a means of achieving these interdependent aims. But though a kind of variety and discussion was to be deliberately cultivated in this manner, party politics and parliamentary democracy were rejected as characterized by corruption and inferiority: 'The old party fabrics are no more than dead rotting things, upon which ... a horrible rubbish thicket, maintains a saprophytic vitality.' The new republicans were hence 'the power that will finally supersede democracy and monarchy altogether' (Wells 1914: 18, 1906: 213).

CONSERVATISM

It might be expected that a discussion of liberal and socialist enthusiasms for the extension of state power would be followed by a similar discussion of the conservative response. Benjamin Disraeli on two nations, Mallock's defence of aristocracy against industrial selfishness, and some mention of *noblesse oblige* seem obvious candidates, and W.H. Greenleaf has devoted a substantial section of his *The Ideological Heritage* to just such an examination of 'Tory paternalism and the welfare state' (Greenleaf 1983b). Yet most of the evidence for conservative support of collectivism comes from what Conservative governments and politicians did, rather than from what conservative thinkers wrote or said. As Greenleaf himself argues, these actions of Conservative governments can be seen to have been taken 'because of specific political necessity, because a particular investigation and report seemed to demand action, because of the special interests of a minister or the exigencies of party politics, because, that is, of a practical – and rather confused – empiricism, and not because they saw themselves as implementing a Conservative philosophy of paternalistic concern' (Greenleaf 1983b: 214). Certainly Benjamin Disraeli gave a graphic depiction of paternalist Toryism in his novel *Sybil*, with its identification of the two nations, and in a speech of 1872, quoted by Greenleaf, he spoke of a policy of social reform, more local than national but still a matter of state initiative:

it involves the state of the dwellings of the people, the moral consequences of which are not less considerable than the physical. It involves their enjoyment of some of the chief elements of nature – air, light, and water. It involves the regulation of their industry, the inspection of their toil. It involves the purity of their provisions, and it touches upon all the means by which you may wean them from habits of excess and of brutality.

(Greenleaf 1983b: 209)

Yet for a tradition which, despite its largely false reputation for being a matter of instinct rather than of intellect, has produced a creditable amount of political thinking, conservatism has devoted remarkably little space to arguing for state involvement in either the economy or the condition of the people. Matthew Fforde, attacking the idea that conservatism, or at least the Conservative Party, had any trace of collectivism in it in this period, is forced sadly to observe that 'although the late-Victorian and Edwardian Conservative Party combatted the Left with concessions at an institutional level, it failed to devote substantial thought and effort to resistance at the level of ideas and attitudes' (Fforde 1990: 166). But if anti-collectivist advocacy was thin on the ground, collectivist advocacy was even thinner.

THE STATE AT HOME AND ABROAD

The alliance with the Webbs and Shaw took up only a phase of Wells's life, and though he at times argued for greater state ownership and control of land and capital, his collectivism was not essentially socialist, and could at times be distinctly anti-socialist. In 1901 he was more impressed by the potential of collaboration between trusts and the state, at least in the US, than by that of socialism (Wells 1905, 1914: 275–6). Wells admired the modern, and he admired the big. There was to be no place for the small, the local, the particular in his future society. Society and government would be worldwide and nations, parishes and dialects, would be absorbed and vanish into the world state and its cosmopolitan life. Sometimes this admiration for the larger unit led him, as a kind of transitional measure, to support the British empire, or a wider potential union of the English-speaking peoples. This drew him fairly naturally into the intellectual company of those who wished to use state power to secure greater human and social efficiency in the interest of imperial progress. This, at least, was a field where conservative enthusiasm for an active state, even if not for a collectivist one, could be found. With the Webbs and Shaw, Wells was a fleeting member of the fleeting dining club, the Co-efficients, which included amongst its members so-called Liberal Imperialists or Limps such as Haldane and Grey, and Tory imperialists such as Amery and Milner – 'one of the most bizarre dining clubs in modern British history' as Royden Harrison has termed it (Harrison 1987: 62).

Awareness of the politics of empire was not the monopoly of imperialists. To think of Britain at all was, by 1900, to think of the larger, imperial Britain as well as of the British Isles. The existence of the empire was something which was enwrapped in the conception of Britain and of the British state. The Queen was also the Empress, and the statesmen of Britain were also the leaders of the world not by virtue of their influence upon the world, but through their possession and control of large parts of it. The lessons of empire were far from clear, and were differently drawn by different groups.

For some, the imperial responsibility had clear domestic implications. A concern for national military capacity, and a desire to strengthen both the military and economic tissue of the empire, had been associated with a demand for social reform at least since the Boer War. There had been dismay at the physical incapacity of many of those volunteering for service in South Africa, and in consequence measures to improve the health and physical wellbeing of the population, and particularly of children, the future generation of soldiers and sailors, which previously had been advanced for philanthropic or egalitarian motives, now were advocated as a vitally necessary condition of national security.

The campaign for national efficiency was carried out primarily by politicians within the Liberal Party, and created more rhetoric than policy. Nonetheless the call for efficiency and a clean slate which was made by men such as Rosebery, Haldane and Asquith, the linking of the state's external power with the improvement of its domestic condition, and the call for twentieth-century Cromwells, created a further strengthening of the kind of view of collectivism which Wells was developing. Many of the ideas or phrases used by Wells in books such as *Anticipations* can be found in the arguments of the Liberal Imperialists, who in seeking to accommodate at a rhetorical level to collectivism, imperialism and the rise of the consciously organized working class, had strengthened the intellectual environment in which pro-state ideas could flourish.

Imperialism represented a territorial rather than a functional extension of state power, and though its advocates often spoke of the need to improve the efficiency of the race, their remedies were exhortatory and moral rather than collectivist. Intemperate imperialists such as Arnold White, the author of *Efficiency and Empire* (1901), were hostile to the proliferation of the apparatus and personnel of the state, and Liberal Imperialists often looked to reform as a means of reducing military expenditure. Those Unionist Imperialists such as Joseph Chamberlain who allied themselves with Milner were support-ing firm government rather than responsible or extensive government. Thus the comparison of Milnerism with Fabianism is misleading. The administrative contempt for politics was there, but little else. On the other hand, in so far as imperial sentiments affected the manner in which people thought about politics, it was likely that they would stress the individualist, hierarchical, service and self-help ideals vigorously described and propagated by Rudyard Kipling, and by the Boy Scout movement.

Whilst the state's action at home was limited, its actions in the extended homeland of the empire were grand and obvious. They magnified, moreover, the function of the state as a governing institution, rather than as a manager or provider. Thus imperialism could suggest both a powerful state and a limited one. The imperial state made even clearer what opponents of state activity believed: that government meant the policeman and the inspector. Functions which might be limited within the British Isles could appear grand and extensive within the empire simply by virtue of being conducted over a wider area and with a greater degree of pomp and ceremony. There were other implications. The distinction between rulers and ruled was even clearer beyond the British Isles, and even beyond Britain. The state confronted its subjects in the empire across barriers of race, religion and colour, which emphasized its distinct and dominating character. But the same state which distinguished between white rulers and non-white subjects abroad might make similar distinctions between ruling and ruled classes at home. The connection was seen, in one way or another, by Hyndman and by the Webbs, and by those who made an issue of the 'Chinese slavery' of indentured labour in South Africa during the 1906 general election. Those who saw the lessons of empire in this way might well want state powers extended, but extended under different control. For Fabians, the imperial example was one more instance of the need for professional leadership, for the liberal anti-imperialist, one more proof of its dangers.

Within the argument in favour of what some of its supporters called 'the Great State', there were numerous strands. And although all involved in some way the extension of public and lawful responsibility for the life and action of society, there was no simple agreement on the manner in which that responsibility was to be exercised, or upon the agency or agencies through which it was to be expressed. The most familiar form of the state for most people and for most of those who discussed the matter at the end of the nineteenth century was some kind of local government, whether the general municipal authority or the ad hoc school board. A state whose form was municipal rather than national and central was less of an evident threat to conceptions of individual or communal self-government. Yet the tendency of political discussion was to view the political and the governmental as national rather than local, and thus within the growth towards the collectivism of social affairs was a further tendency towards their nationalization.

Arguments in favour of a larger responsibility for the state can be divided into two kinds: those which were associated with a claim for some kind of social or political justice, and those which were associated with some kind of conception of individual or corporate wellbeing, national efficiency or imperial vigour. The experience of the First World War between 1914 and 1918 increased the impetus and impact of the second kind of argument and in the years after 1918, whilst the state continued slowly to extend its powers and responsibilities, it did so in a manner which frequently implied a choice between the two arguments, and a choice which was not usually made in favour of the appeal to social justice. But though the experience of the war was seen to advance the cause of those who believed in the Great State, more was involved than a simple recognition of necessity. In the first place there were many – the radical opponents of conscription, the trade union syndicalists and semi-syndicalists who were suspicious of the encroaching control which the state appeared to be exercising over the lives of the working class during war – who saw no such necessity. In the second place, what was believed to be necessary depended on other, prior perceptions of fact and of value. Amongst the reasons why the state seemed the appropriate and natural agency to which to turn in a national crisis was the fact that an increasingly pervasive opinion, accelerating over the previous thirty-five years, had already ascribed this role to central national authority.

In arguing this case the state collectivists were assisted by being able to present history as being, however tardily, on their side. Whether in its national or its local form the state was established and growing and even the most thoroughgoing socialists could present its ultimate and desirable shape not as an aspect of Utopia but as the outcome of history, as the result of a contemporary process which needed only to exert itself in the right manner, or be suitably encouraged, to give the desired outcome. A cartoon in the *Labour Weekly* of October 1911 depicted the damsel Labour harassed by the dragon Private Ownership whilst the State, a quizzical knight, hovered on the edge of the clearing. 'When will the state destroy this monster?' is the plea (reproduced in Winter 1974: facing p. 23). The hero was mounted and armed, and even heading in the right direction. What was needed was some tactical advice and a little cheering on.

Both the socialist argument and the social radical argument of the New Liberals were assisted by being part of a wider state collectivist ambience. There had been a change in the terms of the debate which had expanded the range of affairs which were thought of as public issues, extended the expectations of the state as competent and appropriate to deal with these issues, and broadened the scope of what was thought of as a political matter. All of this made it possible to put collectivist arguments in apparently 'common sense' terms, and made it increasingly difficult to sustain defences against them. It was for this reason that Dicey, reflecting on the currents of contemporary opinion, was able to contrast earlier Benthamite doctrines with the current arguments in favour of state action. The one was specific and relatively coherent, the other was ubiquitous and variegated. This ubiquitous and variegated opinion, particularly in the years between 1914 and 1918, became ever more firmly established not just in the arguments of articulate political contestants, but in the habits and assumptions of government and politics. Not only was an extension of state power in ways previously envisaged and resisted, in the form of conscription, seen as the ultimate resort to man the army; but a wide extension of the state's power to manage, control and own industry was made in order to ensure the swift and plentiful production of military supplies and the provision of essential services. By the closing years of the war the pacific complement of all this military collectivism was the preparation for social reconstruction with the onset of peace, carried out by the state and pursued with the assistance of its own investigative committees. Once lodged in the realm of 'common sense' and sustained by 'practical' measures, state collectivism looked less and less like contestable belief, and became increasingly the broad starting point for argument, rather than its disputed conclusion.

3   Pleas for liberty

THE INDIVIDUALIST RESISTANCE TO THE MODERN STATE – HERBERT SPENCER, AUBERON HERBERT, WORDSWORTH DONISTHORPE

Those who advocated or looked favourably upon the extension of state action and regulation were answered by others who, despite the variety of their views, were united in their opposition to the increasing presence of the state in the lives of its citizens. Their variety was such that they were in no historical sense a group. Even so they were frequently related in the problems which they perceived, the solutions they proposed, the sources on which they drew, and the personal and political alliances in which they engaged. These critics of the state believed themselves to be arguing against the drift of things, and this had common implications for the kinds of grounds on which they built their case. They could not rely on the tide-swimming arguments of Fabian positivism, nor on the exhortations to rationalize existing practices and beliefs employed by liberals such as Hobson. Their appeal had to be to principles of human character or society, or to moral or aesthetic values.

Earlier in the century the argument for laissez faire, though never wholly dominant or unqualified by the practices of the state, had enjoyed a broad acceptance. Even those such as T.H. Huxley, who attacked what they saw as an anarchic total laissez faire, sought a balance between security and initiative in a limited state. Some form of libertarianism was taken as the commonsense starting point for much political argument as well as being articulated and defended by writers as varied as Mill, Bentham, Cobden and Smiles. But by the last two decades of the century a change had taken place. The arguments against state action became more urgent and in doing so were frequently made more rigorous and uncompromising.

The most influential of the critics of the active state was Herbert Spencer. In 1884 he wrote the four essays which were published under the title *The Man versus the State*. The essays were a bitter and vigorous attack on the continued growth of state control and activity since the early nineteenth century, and on the desertion of liberal principles of liberty which this involved. But though *The Man versus the State* was one of Spencer's most effective political tracts, it was written fairly late in his intellectual career, and expressed little that had not already been argued by him in more solid works. His 'Letters on the Proper Sphere of Government' had appeared in 1842 (in *The Nonconformist*, appropriately), *Social Statics* in 1851, and his massive ten-volume *Synthetic Philosophy* between 1862 and 1896, most of this last task being completed by 1880.

A number of principles and analogies recur in Spencer's work: the conception of society as part of an evolutionary process; the concept of individuation whereby social functions become continually more specialized; and the comparison of society with a natural organism, an analogy which expressed its adaptive and evolutionary, rather than its mechanical or fixed, character. Like Darwin, Spencer employed a selective principle to explain social evolution, but he complemented natural selection with the Lamarckian notion of adaptation, and of the inheritability of a predisposition to successful adaptation. His familiar phrase, 'the survival of the fittest', can thus be misleading, in so far as it suggests an arbitrary process depending on the absence or presence of qualities over which the individual or society has no control. The fittest were those who adapted, and there was in principle no limit to the numbers who might make this accommodation. The struggle for survival was thus not of man against man, but of man against a changing environment.

Spencer employed scientific words, phrases and analogies. In the *Data of Ethics* in 1879 he announced: 'my ultimate purpose, lying behind all proximate purposes, has been that of finding for the principles of right and wrong conduct at large a scientific basis' (quoted in Murray 1929: 25–6). But science was the garb not the substance or origin of an argument which drew in the first place upon utilitarianism, radicalism and Malthusian economics and which reasserted the claims of natural individual rights. This use of science, and in particular of the idea of social evolution, was grafted onto an earlier advocacy of the minimalist state which had rested solely on a belief in rights to equal freedom (Gray 1990: 110). Spencer thus went beyond thinkers such as Bentham or James Mill, who had removed human society from the realm of the absolute by the destruction of natural right and the proposition of the felicific calculus. He destroyed the certainties of social behaviour previously supposed to reside in the immutabilities of human nature, arguing that human society was always evolving and hence that its values were related to its evolving structures. What was appropriate in one place was inappropriate in another, and this clearly created difficulties for any science of legislation such as Bentham had envisaged.

This relativism created difficulties for Spencer's own arguments too, for it made the basis for any political recommendations elusive. He employed two solutions, first a belief in natural processes, second the concept of ultimate equilibrium. Natural rights could be observed, not as immutable entitlements or features of some timeless human nature, but as observable features of the natural evolution of human society. They had developed because they were beneficial, and had done so without any deliberate engineering by government. The 'alleged creating of rights was nothing else than giving formal sanction and better definition to those assertions of claims and recognition of claims which naturally originate from the individual desires of men who have to live in presence of one another' (Spencer [1884] 1969: 167). Since man's social life was natural and not artificial, it was, he argued, best left alone. The appropriate forms of behaviour and the appropriate values would develop by themselves, provided that the state did not interfere. There was something of Bentham in this, though the self-effacing state was now justified not by a concept of human nature but by one of social evolution. The idea of equilibrium provided an eschatology for the process of evolution and individuation which would thus lead eventually to perfect adaptation, perfect equilibrium and perfect freedom. Hence because the natural process was beneficial and progressive, and because it tended towards a desired end, societies could be judged by their positions on the scale and their degree of differentiation and complexity. Thus was the jump from relativism to prescription achieved.

The specifically political aspect of these arguments involved the most vigorous and straightforward of contemporary attacks on the direction being taken by state action. A state, Spencer had written in 1842, did not exist

> to regulate commerce; not to educate the people; not to teach religion; not to administer charity; not to make roads and railways; but simply to defend the natural rights of man – to protect person and property – to prevent the aggressions of the powerful upon the weak – in a word, to administer justice. This is the natural, the

original, office of a government. It was not intended to do less: it
ought not to be allowed to do more.

(Spencer 1842: 5)

Such a state would involve a small amount of coercion, but no more
than was necessary to avoid or regulate the coercion that already
existed between citizens. Hence it should be 'a joint-stock protection-
company for mutual assurance', spreading the load of coercion and
interference on insurance principles (quoted in E. Barker 1915b: 102).
Such a purely defensive state would be a 'hindrance of hindrances', and
would only do as much as was necessary to let the natural processes of
society run their course. Thus what Spencer saw as the distressing
treason of liberalism since 1832 would be reversed, and the state would
no longer concern itself with things like education and health, which
were not its proper sphere. The interference of the state in such matters
would only retard the natural progressive forces of adaptation, for
debilitation and disease were a natural if harsh means of weeding out
both the physically and the morally inappropriate. 'Inconvenience,
suffering, and death are the penalties attached by nature to ignorance
as well as incompetence – [and] are also the means of remedying these'
(quoted in Murray 1929: 24). It was in consequence an arrogance of
divine pretensions for the state to try to break the natural bond
between 'ignorance and its penalties'. The argument was over-vigorous
at times – death could hardly remedy individual ignorance and
incompetence. The lesson might be a sharp one, but it would be
learned too late. But in general and apart from excesses of vigour such
as the remedial invocation of mortality, the argument was not about
natural selection so much as about natural correction. The natural
process was stern and harsh, but it was consistent, and it induced the
ignorant and the incompetent to reform themselves. It was thus far
from being a kind of Darwinian social war, an anarchy without co-
operation or social feeling. On the contrary, Spencer envisaged that
voluntary co-operation would be one of the marks of an advanced
society. He distinguished this society as industrial, as opposed to the
military coercive form. The industrial form of society was characterized by contract, which was flexible, rather than by status, which was
inflexible; by voluntary co-operation rather than coerced co-operation.
Coercion could characterize societies in their internal and external
affairs, and Spencer was equally hostile to both aspects. Arguing in
support of his Anti-Aggression League, founded during the Egyptian
crisis of 1887, he wrote to Auberon Herbert, an equally vigorous
opponent of the modern state, 'all future progress of a higher

civilization fundamentally depends on the diminution of inter-national hostility' (letter of 14 April 1887, quoted in Harris 1943: 243). The industrial manner of organization was, he argued, temporarily losing ground in Britain: 'just as the system of voluntary co-operation by companies, associations, unions, to achieve business ends and other ends, spreads throughout a community; so does the antagonistic system of compulsory co-operation under State agencies spread' (Spencer [1884] 1969: 91). The agency of this coercion was the public official, whose organized control, 'once passing a certain stage of growth, becomes less and less resistible' (ibid.: 94).

Spencer's prestige as the creator of the synthetic philosophy and the grand master of systematic and comprehensive social science made him a readily accepted if warily accepting patron for those who wished to oppose with the industrial virtues of individual effort, the 'slavery' as Spencer termed it of extending bureaucratic rule. It was these men who were largely responsible for rehabilitating the word 'individualism' and for giving it a combative and commendatory tone (Bristow 1975: 761–2). One of the warmest of these admirers, who claimed to owe 'directly or indirectly' most of his arguments to Spencer, was Auberon Herbert (Herbert 1880: 8). As an MP, candidate and prospective candidate, Herbert's simple individualism had brought him into conflict with Liberal Party members who wanted increased state activity as a means of improving working, earning and educational conditions. He believed in efficiency and economy, and opposed a long line of policies which offended his simple principles: the increasing organization and uniformity of politics; doctrines of majoritarianism which he associated with the broadening parliamentary franchise; overseas military adventures; competitive examination for public office; progressive taxation and death duties both in general and in their particular expression in measures like Harcourt's 1894 budget duties. The obverse of this version of radicalism was a belief in the necessity for the dissemination of wealth and power amongst all classes (but not necessarily amongst all individuals), the education of the people by instruments publicly provided but with a curriculum free from government control, the co-operative movement, the enfranchisement of women on equal terms with men and the qualification of the rule of majorities in an extended franchise by devices giving weight to superior intelligence. All of this represented an early clash between a purely political liberalism and a liberalism that was becoming increasingly social and economic. The consequence was to edge Herbert out of parliamentary politics and into propaganda, a propaganda which he carried on both in his writing and through organizations such as the

Party of Individual Liberty and the Voluntaryist Movement. He never formally associated with the Spencerian Liberty and Property Defence League, objecting to coercive elements in its constitution (Bristow 1975: 773). In the 1890s he tended through its brief life his own journal, *The Free Spirit* (Harris 1943: 368). His aversions and preferences received a unifying expression in his insistence on the superiority of persuasion and voluntary co-operation over coercion. Liberty was the end, and was absolutely preferable in itself: he wished to show, he noted, 'That progress without Liberty was very doubtful progress... That in such progress you got the results without the educational influence... That the educational influence was worth more than the results... of what use are riches, without the character to use them?' (*Journal*, quoted in Harris 1943: 248).

Herbert pursued the implications of the voluntary principle with a thoroughness which alarmed Herbert Spencer. Spencer had always been engaged in the double enterprise of making specific and apparently unqualified claims for political conduct based on a version of natural right and at the same time presenting a historical scheme of social evolution in which social forms were appropriate to the stage of development reached. The second enterprise was capable of modifying and checking the conclusions of the first, which if pursued without reference to time or place could appear utopian. Thus when in 1891 a collection of individualist essays was being written under the title *A Plea for Liberty* with a proposed foreword by him, he wrote to Herbert in some alarm, lest the latter was intending to discuss the idea of voluntary taxation, a notion with which he had been making some play. This was too much for Spencer, and he warned Herbert of the dangers of attempting social arrangements which were in advance of human nature in a particular society (Harris 1943: 310). Herbert's views on many subjects, untrammelled by the qualifying conception of relativism, were of a kind to lead to accusations of anarchism. His fellow individualist, J.H. Levy, protested at one of Herbert's arguments that it was 'in terms a defence of Individualism. In reality, it is an Anarchist attack on Individualism' (Herbert and Levy 1912: 7, 45n). Levy pointed in alarm to the warmth with which Herbert's views had been reviewed in anarchist circles. Herbert was not an anarchist, insisting on the necessity of some form of state. But it was to be a state more limited in its responsibilities than Spencer ever envisaged, an agency of individuals, rather than an authoritative government: 'The very shadow of state interference destroys the possible development of voluntary associations' (Herbert 1885: 3). The defence of the realm was a task which individualists normally reserved for the state, and though

Herbert did not challenge this reservation, he qualified it with the principle of voluntary organization wherever possible. In the debate on military efficiency which followed the Boer War, he urged the importance of volunteers: 'Has not the time come when the Volunteers should no longer be tacked on, as mere adjunct, to the War Office? They should have their own official organization: and be represented by their own Cabinet Minister' (letter to the *Standard*, 12 July 1905, quoted in Harris 1943: 361–2). This, however, was a mixed marriage between voluntarism and the state. In the summer of 1885 Herbert had gone further and, inspired by his discovery of the newly invented torpedo, had lobbied for a form of municipal military self-help. A fund should be set up to assist those ports and seaside towns which wished to provide for their own defence against naval attack, by the purchase of torpedo boats (Harris 1943: 274–5). The alien foe were to be answered by the salvoes of Hastings, of Bournemouth and of Lyme Regis.

The charge of anarchism was not only made against individualists by their critics and opponents, but was lobbed gently amongst and between them like a musical parcel. They were well aware how close they, or some of their colleagues, came to being accurately so described. Thomas Mackay, who edited *A Plea for Liberty*, looked forward to an 'anarchical millennium', and Wordsworth Donisthorpe generally extended the anarchist ascription far beyond himself: 'The late Lord Bramwell, Tolstoi, Herbert Spencer, Benjamin Tucker, Vaillart, Auberon Herbert, J.H. Levy, Kropotkin, the late Charles Bradlaugh, Yves Guyot, Caserio and thousands of smaller fry, including myself, are anarchists' (*Westminster Gazette*, 3 August 1894, quoted in Bristow 1970: 211). Donisthorpe, a barrister who in some respects took individualism further than Herbert and parted company with the Liberty and Property Defence League in 1888 over what he considered the lukewarmness of its resistance, was prepared to catch the parcel of the anarchist ascription, and even to unwrap a few layers to see what lay beneath. 'I think you will admit', he wrote in an open letter to Auberon Herbert, 'that we are both what some people would call *extreme* individualists' (Donisthorpe 1889: 383). In a lecture given to the Fabian Society he discussed what he termed the 'extreme doctrine' of individualist anarchism, partly seriously, partly in order to provoke argument. 'The difference between Anarchy and the present system', he argued, 'is just the difference between Voluntary Co-operation and Compulsory Co-operation, – between Individualism and Socialism.' A society which was wholly anarchic would immediately, he believed, set about organizing itself on a voluntary basis, thus fulfilling the expectations and preferences of libertarians like himself, and avoiding the consequences feared by Fabians and others. 'In my opinion a people which should begin *de novo* with complete anarchy would not get far wrong' (Donisthorpe 1889: 253–6).

The practical proposals which Donisthorpe made often went far beyond those of Spencer or even of Herbert. Herbert had argued that the state ought to treat marriage as a contract like any other contract, and hence as not externally enforceable on unwilling parties. Donisthorpe retorted that relations between the sexes were not properly a matter for contract at all, and that the only concern of the state was with the proper provision for the upkeep of children. His preference for and belief in voluntary arrangement thus led him to propose the virtually complete withdrawal of law and vigorously to reject fears of a consequent regime of promiscuity: 'People do not rush on to their own destruction, even when not dragooned by superior persons. On the whole, under the beneficial rule of natural selection, they make towards salvation' (Donisthorpe 1893: 11). They would be more saved under a voluntary than under a compulsory regime too, since the existing legal regulation of relations between the sexes encouraged and promoted female dependence, and thus retarded the economic and personal development of women. In this respect he was far more accurately termed an individualist than many others who shared the title but who saw the individual as both adult and male, exercising his freedom on the foundations of property and family, with an adult female if not included under property, then certainly subsumed as a dependant within the family.

Donisthorpe's political beliefs, when translated into preferences within the immediate situation of late nineteenth-century Britain, took the form of support for the private and the local, two categories which ideally would mean much the same thing: 'the highest form of local government is one of complete and unqualified private enterprise' (Donisthorpe 1889: 26). Local government was frequently supported in the nineteenth century as a barrier against growing central power (Greenleaf 1975a; Montague 1885), but its development was not simply and wholly beneficial from an individualist point of view. When Donisthorpe argued that a growth of the functions of local government was a decentralization of state power whereby that power was the more firmly entrenched, he was enthusiastically supported by W.C. Crofts, sometime secretary of the Liberty and Property Defence League, who saw municipal socialism not only as 'State Socialism writ small' but as containing within itself the collectivist growth which would eventually engulf even the local autonomy of socialist municipalities (Donisthorpe 1886; Crofts 1885, 1892: 13 and passim).

Yet whilst Donisthorpe proposed more withering of state power than many of his individualist colleagues, he disagreed with Spencer's attempt to establish individualism on a basis of natural individual rights, and criticized propagandists like Herbert who took no account of the needs of the organic social whole nor of what he himself saw as the need to fit measures to times and places. Voluntary co-operation and paternal coercion both had their place in existing society, and the recognition that government was 'the cement which binds the units together into a complete whole' was advanced to qualify the views attributed by Donisthorpe to 'the worshippers of liberty pure and simple, like Mr. Spencer and Mr. Auberon Herbert' (Donisthorpe 1889: 295). The movement towards greater and greater co-operation and less and less coercion was a historical process which could not be forced – 'A wise gardener does not open a rosebud with an oyster knife' (ibid.: 282). Total voluntarism and the complete disappearance of state coercion were unlikely, though things were continually moving in that direction, and Donisthorpe envisaged a stage when, though the state did little, it did that little with increasing thoroughness.

Donisthorpe's belief in the relative appropriateness of particular arrangements, a belief similar to that of Liberty and Property Defence League patrons such as the Earl of Pembroke (Pembroke 1885) and remarkably like that expressed by Spencer despite Donisthorpe's criticisms, was complemented by a recognition of the partisan character of much contemporary political argument, and the component of perceived group interest in much political judgement: 'Under a system of adult suffrage it is quite conceivable that on a question of family law nearly all the women might be found voting on one side, and nearly all the men on the other' (Donisthorpe 1889: 45). Like J.H. Levy, who was worried that there were 'some gentlemen who use Individualism as a cloak for privilege' (Bax and Levy 1904: 70), Donisthorpe argued that interest, working in this way, vitiated much of the public impact of individualism since many of its supporters were so clearly limited and self-interested in their proposals:

> the lovers of liberty are not without questionable allies, men who are open to the charge of protesting against State interference with the industry in which they are themselves interested, lest such interference should favour their weaker fellow-workers.... Let the poverty-stricken be defended against the rapacity of the merciless pawnbroker; but it is preposterous to tolerate the claim of the

helpless widow and children whom a railway accident has left destitute, for be it known that I am a railway king. One can hardly blame those demagogues who stigmatise individualism as self-ishness.

(Donisthorpe 1889: 76)

Despite his theoretical criticisms of other individualists, however, Donisthorpe found himself naturally allied with them at a practical level. His proposals tended in the same direction as theirs and when he differed, as he did with Herbert over voluntary taxation, it was over the details rather than the substance of the proposals, and over the foundations of debate rather than its conclusions.

The individualists had toyed with individualist anarchism, a policy whose contribution to British political argument reflected the openness of our frontiers rather than the variety of our intellectual life. Much anarchism, and most individualist anarchism, was propagated in languages other than English by refugees or immigrants who still addressed themselves to their own national communities, rather than to any English debate (Woodcock 1963; Fishman 1975; Quail 1978). Nonetheless, small though it was, some argument took place within the broader English debate. Between 1885 and 1892 a series of journals emanating from the English Anarchist Circle and edited by either Henry Seymour or Albert Tarn developed an individualist version of anarchism. Henry Seymour edited *The Anarchist* which ran from 1885 to 1888, and the *Revolutionary Review* which ran briefly in 1889, whilst Albert Tarn edited *The Herald of Anarchy* which was published from 1890 to 1892. Both Seymour and Tarn drew on the work of the American, Benjamin Tucker, and some of their followers were also members of the Liberty and Property Defence League. It was an indication of this closeness between individualism and individualist anarchism that when Seymour's paper *The Anarchist* criticized Herbert Spencer, its readership was divided on the controversy. Tarn himself at various points in his career edited the journal *Free Trade*, and was secretary of the Newcastle section of the National Free Labour Association (Bristow 1970: 178; Woodcock 1963: 419). The links and affinities with individualism were close, and were frequently disconcerting for both groups.

CHARITY AND THE STRUGGLE FOR SURVIVAL –
BERNARD BOSANQUET

The individualist resistance was organized not only across a broad political front in bodies such as the Liberty and Property Defence League, but also in associations devoted to particular objects such as the Charity Organization Society. The COS, as it was known, attempted by persuasion to regulate charity in the light of assumptions about individual nature, while conversely resisting the incursions of public activity into the field of poverty save under the strictest interpretation of the Poor Law. It identified the source and end of human progress in the development of fully realized individual consciousness and directed its efforts to securing this, by close study of individual cases, the state of mind and motive of the allegedly needy and deserving, and the likely consequences of providing them with material assistance. Whilst not averse to the state assuming responsibility for poverty, and indeed having strong arguments derived from Idealists such as Green for justifying its doing so, its stress on individual character, equally derived from Idealism, meant that it envisaged this responsibility being exercised in general by means of a wise restraint. A rejection of the kind of individualism represented by Spencer and his followers was accompanied by a belief in 'that individualism which alone is an ethical good – intellectual independence and moral robustness' (Bosanquet, *The Civilization of Christendom,* 382, quoted Vincent and Plant 1984: 101). One of the COS's most prominent propagandists was the political philosopher Bernard Bosanquet. In 1899 Bosanquet published *The Philosophical Theory of the State*, a book dedicated to C.S. Loch of the COS. Bosanquet set out an idealist case for limited state action – a case stigmatized by Hobhouse in the title and substance of his own *The Metaphysical Theory of the State.* The objection was, in part, fuelled by a feeling that Bosanquet both claimed too much authority for the state, and allowed it too few responsibilities. But it was also a part of what Peter Clarke has called Hobhouse's 'tussle with Bosanquet for the mantle of Green' (Clarke 1978: 63). Bosanquet wrote with clear practical intent, not to sustain or advance particular policies but to expound a perception of reality in terms of which policy could be developed. It was necessary to promote, as a first and overriding principle of procedure 'personal responsibility, invention, initiative, and energy. For it is these, and not self-interest ... which form the spur and the delight of what is known as private enterprise, and which ordinary bureaucracy destroys' (Bosanquet 1899: xii–xiii). It followed that there was a type of activity appropriate to the state as the final arbiter of disputes and defender against invasions, but that it was limited to the removal by force or by actions which involved force as their final sanction, of obstacles to social and individual self-realization through the free exercise of will. *The Philosophical Theory of the State*, however, though a book with a practical purpose, was not in its greater part a piece of political argument. Its attitude towards the state was closer to the philosophical reflections of Green than to the arguments of the individualists (Nicholson 1990: 211–21). The argument by Mill that a person's 'own good, either physical or moral, is not a sufficient warrant' for interference (Mill 1859: 15) was far from Bosanquet's position. Bosanquet denied the usefulness of the distinction between individuals and society and argued that public power ought to be employed not to defend individuals against invasion of their privacy, but to obstruct those factors, whether individual or social, which hampered the progress of the conscious self. These recommendations had already been set out four years previously in a collection of essays which he edited and to which he, C.S. Loch and Helen Dendy, whom Bosanquet subsequently married, contributed. In his argument there Bosanquet presented individualism as a stress on the importance of individual character and of the role of struggle between person and person as a means of perpetuating the fit through the production of children, and eliminating the unfit through their failure to raise children. It was a version of the struggle for existence more Darwinian than Spencerian, assuming as it did that humanity would improve not by adaptation and personal choice and effort, but by the encouragement of desirable qualities which, by implication, arose other than through their free cultivation by their possessors: 'Natural selection, then, is the process by which the struggle for existence determines the perpetuation of these stocks or family strains which have qualities most enabling them to conquer or to use their surroundings, especially so as to obtain success in the rearing of offspring' (Bosanquet 1895: 293). It followed that the state must never assist the survival of those who would otherwise sink into the oblivion of childlessness. It must let the natural processes do their work of perpetually improving the character of society, a process which would be checked and reversed by any interference with its consequences, however well meaning that interference. Even the Poor Law, whose rigorous application the COS favoured, could to some extent be guilty, in that it could encourage 'an element of the population for whom the family does not exist, or who preserved only to hand on to others the defects which, but for our elaborate hospitals and infirmaries, would have perished with them' (Bosanquet 1895: 302). For Spencer death, or the threat of death, had been remedial. For Bosanquet it became a form of social weeding, albeit at the remove of a generation. There was a disparity between the idea of self-realization set out in 1899 in *The Philosophical Theory of the State* and that of fit and unfit persons advanced four years earlier. The one was dynamic and allowed for personal and social progress, the other assumed personal capacity to be fixed, and social progress to be a matter not of improvement but of selection. The difference is perhaps more readily explained by the contrast between the occasions for the two books than by the passage of four years and their effect on Bosanquet's opinions. Nor did the earlier notion of social weeding perish when deserted by Bosanquet, but was preserved and developed within the eugenics movement at the beginning of the twentieth century.

A rougher, harsher version of essentially similar arguments was given by Benjamin Kidd, a writer towards whom Bosanquet allowed himself a guarded admiration. Whereas Bosanquet envisaged natural selection as acting through the encouragement or discouragement of the propagation of future generations, Kidd seemed prepared both to support more openly than Bosanquet's discretion allowed, racial, imperialist and social aggrandisement, and to recommend public measures of reform to allow the masses to enter into 'the rivalry of life' on equal terms. In the pursuit of this second aim Kidd accepted a version of Marx's account of surplus value, advocated an attack on economic and social privilege and accepted the resulting condition as a beneficial form of state socialism. Bosanquet had himself accepted that socialism as defined in this manner could be a proper use of state power, but the practical measures recommended by Kidd were of a kind not readily compatible with Bosanquet's general conclusions. Kidd with his state socialism was an unnerving ally against whom Mallock, amongst conservatives, devoted a whole book (Crook 1984: 71). His stress on equality of opportunity drew attention to the wrong side of imperialism, and his relish for the triumphs of the exceptionally talented and the wealthy (whom he equated) seemed a little vulgar. Nor was Kidd's enthusiasm for religion attractive, since it arose from an ascription to that sentiment of the necessary function of sanctioning conduct in the interests of social advancement against which a rational assessment of individual interest would rebel. Individual conscience, will or aspiration was neither here nor there in the onward march of the species – man's progress 'was beyond doubt the result of the conditions of his life, and was made under force of circumstances over which he had no control' (Kidd 1894: 45–6).

POPULAR ANTI-STATISM – STEPHEN REYNOLDS

The individualists had always argued that state provision and regulation were not in the true interests of the workers, and through labour colonies and agricultural settlements, or through the arguments of sympathetic trade unionists such as George Howell (Howell 1891), had tried to convince the working class of the benefits of libertarianism. But though they met with small success there was nonetheless a continuing popular hostility to state action which owed little or nothing to libertarian theory, and which neither affected nor was affected by it. The very success of the Poor Law as a deterrent to claiming or seeking public help had created an image of the state as punitive and interfering at times of distress. Moreover, in so far as its extending activities regulated the lives of people, rather than provided services, they employed the inspector and policeman and involved intrusion into homes, restrictions on the freedom of children and women to earn, or the compulsory submission to measures which, like vaccination, were immediately inconvenient and only indirectly and eventually beneficial. The restrictions on women's work could be and were seen as discriminatory, illiberal and defensive of vested interests. The invasion of privacy could be and was seen as at best an irritation and at worst a despotic intrusion on personal and family independence. The Personal Rights Association, originally formed to combat the compulsory medical inspection of prostitutes which had been sanctioned by the Contagious Diseases Acts, was particularly concerned with the effects of such legislation on women and on the poor. But this sentiment was far from being restricted to supporters of conventional laissez faire, individualism or libertarianism. Restrictions on women's work were opposed by feminists, whilst of the general advance of public regulation *Solidarity*, the paper of the shop stewards' movement, warned in March 1917, 'The state has become the almighty power, regulating and controlling the lives of all.... From the inception of the Insurance Act the speed has been cumulative.... We are rapidly approaching the heyday of officialdom in every department of life' (quoted in P. Thompson 1975: 277). Oscar Wilde subtly suggested another way in which the more government there was, the worse things became. Crime, he argued, arose from punishment (Wilde 1891).

Stephen Reynolds, who anticipated George Orwell by a quarter of a century in crossing class lines by living and working with manual workers, was able to report in 1910 that to those whom he knew, 'social reform means "police"' (Reynolds 1910: 422). Those who wished, for instance, to pursue temperance by legislation were interfering with the home lives of the poor by imposing upon them standards which arose from middle-class experience and which illustrated both ignorance of and contempt for the way of life of working people. Applying individualist notions of servility to the reforms of the 1905–1915 Liberal governments, Reynolds argued that it was useless to offer the race

> freedom from destitution, if, as a condition, they must knuckle under to a scheme of industrial conscription like the Webb Minority Report; or offering them National Insurance if the result is to make the master more powerfully a master, and the man more impotently a workman than ever.
>
> (Reynolds, Wooley and Wooley 1911: xxv)

The criticism was similar to that made by Hilaire Belloc in a series of articles which set out the ideas drawn together in 1912 in his book *The Servile State*. Reynolds greatly admired the articles, and writing about them to the *New Age*'s editor, A.R. Orage, he said: 'All the working men to whom I have shown them remarked almost in the same words: "Aye, that's it; that's the aim of the b-s, sure 'nuff!"' (Reynolds 1923: 130). R.H. Tawney in 1912 recorded a similar reaction not to Belloc, but to Reynolds himself. Students in his WEA class commented on the resentment felt at health inspectors, and at 'the way in which they make us ignorant people live in the way they think we ought' (Winter and Joslin 1972: 3–4).

Reynolds's own alternative to the 'blight of inspectors' which he saw covering the land and, as Spencer had argued, doing more harm than good, was a mixture of class laissez faire – leaving the working class to get on with managing their own affairs – and social reform designed to enable them to do so. Education, for instance, ought to be less dominated by middle-class conceptions and more directed towards meeting the practical requirements of the families of those actually receiving the education. At the same time working-class income should be increased in order to give the workers more real power: as Reynolds reported it in the words of others, '"We wants more money, an' they gives us more laws...What we wants is proper pay; the rivets to work out our own life according to our own ideas, not theirs"' (Reynolds, Wooley and Wooley 1911: xv–xx, 27, 28, 72, 112, 113, 310–11, 317).

CONSERVATISM AND ANTI-SOCIALISM – W.H. MALLOCK

Reynolds interpreted popular hostility to state action in terms of individualist theory, and gave that theory a unique basis in working-class resentment. In doing so he achieved a rooting of anti-statism in both popular culture and social reform. But the individualist resistance to the state, which ran both into anarchism and into an assertion of class privacy against state intrusion, merged also into conservatism. One of the Liberty and Property Defence League's most prolific and widely read members was W.H. Mallock, who between the publication of his satirical novel *The New Republic* in 1878 and the First World War, published a deluge of books and articles asserting the social necessity of individual effort and individual inequality. In his early writing Mallock defended an aristocracy which matched privileges with obligations, and attacked what he saw as the selfish and socially irresponsible radicalism of the industrial middle class. In harmony with this view socialism, though criticized, was regarded as a sincere but misguided attempt to apply altruistic principles. Mallock briefly hoped that the aristocratic virtue of *noblesse oblige* could be extended to a morally enhanced class of industrialists (Mallock 1886). But he had already placed his principal expectation not so much on the ethical calibre of the possessor of wealth, as on the social function of the wealth itself. Simply by enjoying their material good fortune, the rich provided an example to incite the ambition of the talented poor, whilst endowing through their expenditure culture and the arts (Ford 1974: 334). The insistence on the benefits of inequality and social hierarchy was in this way adapted to incorporate a defence of all kinds of wealth, and by the 1890s Mallock was as vigorous a defender of capital as of land. He opposed Marx's labour theory of value with an assertion of the primary importance of individual talent, a talent which was the characteristic of only a minority of the population at any one time. The dominant and distinguishing contribution in the creation of wealth was made not by those who carried on the varied and essential mechanical operations, but by the directive ability of the few: 'Though labour is essential to the production of wealth even in the smallest quantities, the distinguishing productivity of industry in the modern world depends not on the labour, but on the ability with which the labour is directed' (Mallock 1908: 40). There were four causes of wealth, he argued: land, labour, capital and ability. The last of these, ability, was both the creator of all capital, and the cause of 'all progress in production' (Mallock 1893: 154–5).

Directive ability, as Mallock termed it, was able to create wealth by operating under the constant test of market conditions. And it was an overwhelming objection against any economic activity by the state that these conditions would be circumvented, and the distinction which a free economy made between efficiency and inefficiency would disappear. Under private capitalism the unsuccessful were replaced by 'an automatic process' – the inefficient exhausted their capital, and were replaced. But when all individual supplies of capital were merged in the state's supply, the inefficient would survive since what would in the private sphere have been losses would simply be covered by the collective purse. The state official would have security of tenure and the only source of criticism or of dismissal would be the politician, of whom Mallock's opinion was equally low (Mallock 1908: 69ff.). But conservative thought in the writing of men such as Mallock or Hugh Cecil, though it opposed the extension of state activity, was distinct from the radical individualism of men such as Herbert or Donisthorpe. For Cecil the state was something to be regarded with suspicion, and to be associated with revolution and with socialism. Justice consisted of the restraint of injury or of breach of faith, so that it was not property, but assaults upon it through taxation, which required justification. Neither equality nor welfare were required by justice, though the state may relieve suffering as the agent of the general charitable wishes of society. Such a conservative resistance to collectivism stressed, as well as the importance of free individual action, the importance of inequality and oligarchy in politics and economics alike. Mallock criticized Spencer for allowing no role for great men in his social theory and it was the snub to excellence rather than to individuality which offended.

The vigorous and widespread assertion of libertarianism, individualism and forthright laissez-faire arguments against the arguments of state collectivism seems at first to have been brought to an end during the first quarter of the twentieth century. To many at the time it seemed that the First World War rendered the brief if intense protest futile, as transitory as the hot summer days which prefaced the thunderclap of 1914. But the war was no more than an acceleration. The force had gone out of libertarian politics before 1914 despite the seeming appropriateness of the death, in that year, of the Earl of Wemyss, the grand patron of the individualist and anti-socialist sects. While on the one hand Kidd had taken social Darwinism beyond individualism, on the other the argument had become narrower, had melted into anti-socialism, and had become increasingly a loosely attached auxiliary to a conservatism which allowed an accommodation with the state (Taylor 1992). The impossibilities of anarchism, as Shaw had termed them, were becoming increasingly evident, and in so far as pure libertarianism survived into the 1920s, it did so in an increasingly sectarian form.

But libertarianism had been an intensification of long-established sentiments of laissez faire, and these sentiments both survived its demise, and drew some sustenance from it as it merged back into them. Writers who attacked the drift of state responsibility without adopting the full apparatus of libertarianism nonetheless retained some of its force. Harold Cox could deplore the undermining of family and individual responsibility involved in Liberal legislation in his *Socialism in the House of Commons* (Cox 1907). The reforms which followed 1906 gave similar impetus to the warnings of W. Lawler Wilson, a propagandist of the Anti-Socialist Union, who depicted an irrevocable opposition between private property and its proliferation, and 'a complete revolution in our modes of production, in order to free the manual workers from wage-slavery.... There can be neither peace nor truce between the hostile forces' (Wilson 1909: 1). Wilson might criticize the individualists for being 'the impossibilists of Anti-Socialism', and a later observer has remarked that 'Even the anti-socialists had passed laissez-faire by' (Wilson 1909: 441; Bristow 1975: 789). But for thirty years radical laissez faire had made the running. Nor were less radical forms of laissez faire anywhere near being passed by.

Liberal libertarianism still survived in the midst of the First World War in the opposition to conscription, whilst adherence to free trade inspired the Liberal Party and caused deep division between Tariff Reformers and both conservative and liberal unionist free traders in the Conservative Party. A.V. Dicey, writing in 1914 an introduction to the second edition of his *Law and Public Opinion in England*, not only detected resistance to state collectivism, but in his own arguments bore witness to its continuation. Collectivism would ultimately be ruinous he argued, and there was an essential contradiction between democracy and socialism – as he now increasingly called state collectivism – which would become more and more evident. Moreover the democrat with a belief in freedom and variety and in the diffusion of property could never fully accept the methods and assumptions of the socialist state with its nationalization and central control: 'he knows and feels that the prosperity of men and nations has its source in self-help, energy, and originality. He is thus saved from that belief in formulas which has now and again wrecked the plans of enthusiastic socialists' (Dicey [1914] 1962: lxxvi, lxxviii). Similar sentiments were common and Sir Gilbert Parker, writing on land in the *Daily Express* in 1909, argued that the 'desire for possession is of all forces the most potent, and for that reason it must be called to our aid' (quoted in Bristow 1970: 268).

It was neatly appropriate that Dicey, who had characterized collectivist ideas by their diffuseness, should himself so well exemplify the continuing force of a diffuse laissez-faire libertarianism. The hostility which he expressed towards legislative interference with freedom of contract, departure from the strict principles of the Poor Law, and the creation as he saw it of a class of enfranchised state dependants was not part of a full-blooded laissez-faire position but did match a widespread group of preferences and antipathies which survived the demise of the pure doctrine.

The total case against the state might no longer be credible, but laissez faire still operated as a leavening principle, and as an element in popular argument. It was after all in much this way that Bosanquet, at least in his philosophic mood, had discussed the limitations on state action. In the discussion of social policy before the war and economic policy after it, this could be clearly discerned. The change was thus not one which involved the death of anti-state arguments, but their temporary association with conservatism rather than with liberalism or radicalism. Dicey had been able to speak of 'the *laissez-faire* of common sense' in the nineteenth century (Dicey [1914] 1962: xxix) and after 1918 laissez-faire assumptions, particularly on economic matters, were to continue as one part of the working material of debate.

4　Neither state nor individual
The defence of communal and group politics

COMMUNAL AND GROUP POLITICS –
CONSERVATIVES AND OTHERS

Some opposition to the contemporary and future shape of public regulation and provision was hostile to state intervention *per se*, or rested on a conception of human life which made state action external. The weight of the argument was either an objection to interference, or an assertion of self-help and individual initiative and creativity. There was the collective, and there was the individual.

But state collectivism and libertarian individualism in no way incorporated the whole of the debate in the last quarter of the nineteenth and the first quarter of the twentieth century. Many, whilst no less hostile to state collectivism than were the shock troops of laissez faire, asserted against the state neither a natural comprehensive social order nor the self-realization of individuals, but the values of groups, communities and associations. This assertion was made by people whose political variety was as great as, if not greater than, that of those whose main energy was directed towards attacking collectivism. Anarchists, conservatives, Christians, communists and socialists all contributed to the interest which was both practical and theoretical in forms of life which were not properly understood in terms either of the state or of the individual, and which traditional conceptions of citizenship seemed unsuited to encompass.

This concern ran throughout nineteenth-century conservatism, with its stress on traditional associations and on the importance of groups, the corporations and autonomous bodies which for many conservatives had constituted the substance of society and set limits for the proper operations of the state. There was a kind of pluralism in the arguments of men like Lord Salisbury for whom, in an ideal, balanced constitution, there was a check imposed on 'every class by another class' (quoted in Kedourie 1972: 52). This pluralism expressed itself not only in hostility to the democratic franchise, but in an enthusiasm for the local rather than the central exercise of state power as a means both of maintaining variety and freedom and of preventing national, co-ordinated governmental oppression. Local government fostered virtues as well as defending them. As Salisbury told an audience in 1885, Tory doctrine had always been that

> people in their localities should govern themselves – and that the attempt to imitate Continental plans by drawing all authority from the central power, though it might produce a more scientific, a more exact, and, for the moment, a more effective administration, yet was destitute of these two essentials of all good government. It did not provide a government that was suited to the facts and the idiosyncrasies of the particular community for whom it was designed, and it did not teach the people to take that active interest in their own government which is the only training that makes a man a true and worthy citizen.
>
> (quoted in White 1950: 72–3)

The educative, as against the expressive, function of public activity through small groups was frequently stressed by conservatives. And since a politics of groups, a politics of society, and a politics of individuals are mutually exclusive only at the most abstract and sharply delineated level of theory, the advocacy of group activity could be found in the arguments of those conservatives who, like Lord Hugh Cecil, also wrote of property in terms much the same as those used by individualists. Cecil was able to praise the activities of trade unions since by combining together, workmen 'obtain not only the wages or the hours for which they strive, but a most valuable social and political education by the way' (Cecil 1912: 191). Similarly W.H. Greenleaf is able to point to a praise of groups and their beneficial work in the writing of Bernard Bosanquet, an advocate of what could seem the most individualist version of social Darwinism (Greenleaf 1983b: 424).

This sentiment in favour of local and group life characterized champions of local government such as Toulmin Smith (Greenleaf 1975a), was articulated by the leaders of conservatism, and was employed to distinguish the conservative from the liberal position on local affairs. But it nonetheless was to be found more widely distributed than within a single party or intellectual tendency. The 'rediscovery of community' has been described as one of the outstanding features of nineteenth-century social thought (Nisbet 1967) – certainly in Britain the rediscovery was well-publicized. The economist Alfred Marshall praised the co-operative movement 'because it sets itself to develop the spontaneous energies of the individual while training him to collective action by the aid of collective resources, and for the attainment of collective ends' (*Co-operation*,1889, quoted in Dewey 1974: 75). It was an assumption of the Webbs that the expanding state would consist in large measure of local rather than central agencies, and many other socialists assumed that increasing public provision would be locally rather than nationally organized. In a more radical temper, the socialist William Morris could describe county councils as 'the germs of a revolutionary local opposition to centralised reaction' (quoted in J. Lindsay 1975: 336). This stress on the local dimension united conservatives and socialists, radical anarchists and cautious reformers. Hence in many ways the nearest to the conservatives in vigorous assertion of the benefits of the local unit as an alternative to central state power were communist anarchists like Kropotkin, and socialist communists like William Morris. At the same time the anarchism of Kropotkin was in many respects very close to the individualism of men like Donisthorpe.

COMMUNISM AND ANARCHISM – PETER KROPOTKIN AND WILLIAM MORRIS

Unlike many of the political refugees living in late nineteenth-century Britain, the Russian Prince Peter Kropotkin wrote and published in English. Whilst the anarchists of the East End (Fishman 1975) wrote for each other, Kropotkin directed his arguments to British readers, contributed frequently to British journals and was involved with indigenous political organizations such as the Freedom Group which was formed around him in the spring of 1886. Charlotte Wilson, a prominent member of this association, was also closely involved with the Fabian Society in its early years, whilst Kropotkin himself had a very wide range of acquaintances amongst British radicals of one kind and another: Keir Hardie, Cunningham Grahame, Shaw, Carpenter, Morris, Patrick Geddes, Ben Tillett, Tom Mann and John Bruce Glasier (Woodcock and Avakumovic 1950: 217).

Two of Kropotkin's major works, *Fields, Factories and Workshops* and *Mutual Aid*, were in the first place contributions to British discussions. The former, published in 1899, included a great deal of material which had first appeared as essays in *The Nineteenth Century* and was aimed at English readers. *Mutual Aid*, published in 1902, also drew on contributions to *The Nineteenth Century* and originated in a dispute with T.H. Huxley over the naturalness of social co-operation.

Kropotkin was thus not only a part of British politics, but a more prominent contributor to them than native anarchists or near-anarchists such as Joseph Lane, Morris's colleague in the Socialist League and author of the 1887 *Anti-Statist, Communist Manifesto.*

For Kropotkin as for his colleagues in the Freedom Group, government was the antithesis of freedom. 'We are Anarchists,' they declared, 'disbelievers in the government of man by man in any shape and under any pretext.' But the alternative to coercion was not unlimited individual competition, since people were by nature social and once the restraints of government were removed would be able to realize 'the positive freedom which is essentially one with social feeling' and which was expressed in 'the social impulses, now distorted and compressed by Property and its guardian Law' (*Freedom*, no. 1, quoted in Woodcock and Avakumovic 1950: 209). The belief in the naturalness of human co-operation had underlain Kropotkin's objection to what he understood to be the views of Huxley on the necessity of government. But co-operation was not only natural, but the most successful way for human, and non-human, communities to live. The most successful species were those characterized not by competition amongst their members, but by co-operative struggle of the whole group with their external circumstances (Kropotkin 1902). The commune, which would be the chief social form of an anarchist society, would be a flexible response to varied human social requirements and would form part of a free association of similar groupings, based on function rather than on area:

> For us, 'Commune' is no longer a territorial agglomeration; it is rather a generic name, a synonym for the grouping of equals, knowing neither frontiers nor walls. The social commune will soon cease to be a clearly defined whole. Each group of the commune will necessarily be drawn towards other similar groups in other communes; it will be grouped and federated with them by links as solid as those which attach it to its fellow citizens, and will constitute a commune of interests whose members are scattered in a thousand towns and villages.
>
> (*Paroles d'un révolté*, quoted in Woodcock and Avakumovic 1950: 311–12)

In such a society, organized in recognition of people's direct responsibility for the variety of functions they performed, the excessive division and specialization of labour which characterized the contemporary world would be overcome. This belief in the need to re-establish wholeness involved not only a widening of the experiences of practical life, but a greater emphasis on learning by doing, rather than in a bookish fashion: 'Far from being inferior to the "specialized" young persons manufactured by our universities, the *complete* human being, trained to use his brain and his hands, excels them, on the contrary, in all respects' (Kropotkin 1899: 268). This departure from specialization to integration would be at once individual and social, and would involve both a new stress on agricultural production, and an integration of the agricultural and the industrial, the rural and the urban. Unlike many social visions which involved criticism of industrial society, Kropotkin's assumed that technological advance would continue and would aid the improvement of life. Kropotkin could talk of 'our modern Renaissance' both in recognition of technical achievement and in expectation of the development of a new integrated completeness in human life (Kropotkin 1899: 271).

This deep concern with the quality of social experience linked Kropotkin with William Morris who, whilst describing himself as a socialist or communist rather than as an anarchist, was hostile to central direction and worked for a society that was liberated from both commercial materialism and governmental hierarchy. Whilst Morris envisaged a revolutionary supersession of capitalism and a popular conquest of public power, this was a means not an end. The end had little relation to state activity and was incompatible with any form of national state collectivism. Morris exemplified a trait which, whilst not shared by all those who had little time for the state, firmly divided them from the various kinds of collectivist. Like anarchists and like many conservatives, Morris placed the state and politics in a wholly secondary and instrumental position, for his view of the proper character of human living left little place for them. Thus paradoxically his most important 'political' writings are those that have least to say about politics as conventionally conceived, and concentrate instead on descriptions of how life might be. He and many other defenders of communal and group values differed from the individualists in this. There are affinities here with those conservative writers who regarded politics as instrumental and as an occasional necessity, but as having no place in the discussion of the true purposes of life.

Thus Morris's political arguments arose not from any opposition to the state as such, but from a view of the ultimate goals of both individual and social life which had no place for the state and little for politics. As the traveller in *News From Nowhere* was told, 'we are very well off as to politics, – because we have none' (Morris 1924: 99). In order to understand Morris as a political propagandist it is necessary to begin with him as a poet, craftsman and designer, for it was in such roles that he believed the true fulfilment of human life was to be found.

Morris's first impact on public life was as an eloquent exponent of the reaction against the quality of mid-Victorian society, and his early poems such as 'The Defence Of Guenevere' written in 1868, or 'The Earthly Paradise' written between 1868 and 1870, are works of romanticism, almost of escapism. This reaction took commercial form in the business later to become Morris and Company which he founded in 1859 as a joint enterprise of designers, architects and decorators working for the creation of a more beautiful living environment and for the re-establishment of art as a characteristic feature of everyday work.

Morris did not enter the conventionally political sphere until 1876, when he was already 42 and established as a designer with a solid and successful business – so solid and successful that in 1880 the firm was responsible for the decoration of the throne room at the Palace of St James. His public activities then took two forms, the first through the Eastern Question Association, the second through the Society for the Preservation of Ancient Buildings. The Eastern Question Association and Morris's work with it typified his approach to politics. The Association was designed to prevent British involvement in the conflict between Russia and Turkey, and its propaganda enabled Morris to engage in the politics of emotion and conscience, campaigning against militarism and appealing to working people against the selfish interests of the rich. The Society for the Preservation of Ancient Buildings had an apparently different style, opposing as it did the destruction of ancient ecclesiastical building in the course of imitative and unimaginative restoration. It was conservative and anti-modern, and involved asserting the uniqueness of each age in a way which was not compatible with simple derivative medievalism. But between the two of them the Eastern Question Association and the Society for the Preservation of Ancient Buildings epitomized and concentrated the two themes that were to run throughout Morris's political career: first the need to reassert quality of workmanship, pride in craft, and the reuniting of art with life and work against both anti-aesthetic materialism and a high culture which was parasitic on and divorced from the real world; second the injustice of a society based on divisions between rich and poor and the need to replace it with one based on fellowship and co-operation.

In 1883 Morris joined the Democratic Federation which was soon to become, under Hyndman's leadership, the Social Democratic Federation. He did not remain a member long. With others who were exasperated by Hyndman's domineering, and unable to accept the accommodations with the existing order which Hyndman's tactics seemed to imply, Morris left the SDF and took a leading part in founding a new body, the Socialist League. The break with Hyndman was a further indication of the primary importance for Morris of the world that might be and the quality of life that might be both worked for now and hoped for in the future. Conventional political methods seemed to divert attention and effort from this task – the real job for the present being not to work within the existing system but to educate and to prepare for the revolutionary break with it. Thus one could agitate in what seemed like a conventional political manner, but not with conventional ends in view. Morris later modified his views on the consequences of entanglements with the existing order to the extent of accepting the likelihood of some brief seizure of state power in order to employ that power for its own transcending. But this concession never involved a shift of emphasis or attention sufficiently significant to affect the general character of his argument.

Morris remained in the Socialist League until November 1890, during which time he increasingly held it together by his energy, his writing and his money. Work in the League involved collaboration with both anarchists such as Frank Kitz and Joseph Lane and with those such as E. Belfort Bax who could expound a form of Marxism and with whom Morris wrote *Socialism, Its Growth and Outcome* ([1893] 1908). Morris read and was impressed by *Capital*. He employed some of Marx's ideas, particularly the notion of class war and of the internal contradictions of capitalism together with, at one time, the expectation of a solution to social maladies through some kind of crisis. Marx provided Morris not with his vision of the good society, but with the link between now and then, a means of getting from an unacceptable present to a worthwhile future and an account of the causes of the present condition of things which confirmed Morris's own conclusions. Morris distinguished between '*practical* Socialism' which was part of politics and therefore 'a necessary if cumbersome and disgustful means to an end', and the socialist ideal (Morris 1894: 243). The latter grew from beliefs which he had held from the start of his interest in public affairs. He had appealed to the workers against the rich over the Eastern Question in 1877, and in 1881 had looked forward to 'the abasement of the rich and the raising up of the poor, which is of all things most to be longed for' (quoted in Mackail 1899, vol. 1: 360; vol. 2: 26–7). But it was reading Marx in 1884 which led Morris to see this conflict 'as a positive force for change' (Thompson 1967: 220), and which placed his argument in a specifically socialist context whereby he could take steps to 'hook myself on to the practical movement' (Morris [1894] 1973a: 245). He was in this sense 'an original socialist thinker whose work was complementary to Marxism' (Thompson 1977: 796).

It is unduly confining to see Morris as constrained within any single tradition, however much he may be supposed to have gained from it. Whilst he drew on Marx for historical tactics, his essential values were far closer to those of communal anarchism. His breach with the anarchists of the Socialist League, which was largely a practical matter, concerned with methods rather than ends, in no way qualifies this – indeed one of his most important works, *News From Nowhere*, was first published in the League's journal *The Commonweal* after the anarchists had driven him from the editorship.

Morris himself appeared on one occasion to refute the anarchist ascription:

> What I aim at is communism or socialism, not anarchism. Anarchism and communism, notwithstanding our friend Kropotkin, are incompatible in principle. Anarchism means, as I understand it, the doing away with, and doing without, laws and rules of all kinds, and in each person being allowed to do just as he pleases. I don't want people to do just as they please; I want them to consider and act for the good of their fellows – for the commonweal, in fact. Now what constitutes the commonweal, or common notion of what is for the common good, will and always must be expressed in the form of laws of some kind – either political laws, instituted by the citizens in public assembly, as of old by folk-moots, or if you will by real councils or parliaments of the people, or by social customs growing up from the experience of society....
>
> (quoted in Woodcock and Avakumovic 1950: 216)

But the anarchism Morris is dismissing is individualist anarchism, and the values he is advocating are in effect communist anarchism. What Kropotkin described was very like Morris's common good pursued 'by social customs growing up from the experience of society'. Both men shared the hostility, expressed by Morris in a review of Edward Bellamy's *Looking Backwards*, to 'State Communism, worked by the vast extreme of national centralization' (*Commonweal*, June 1889, quoted in Marshall 1962: 91). Morris's preferences as described in *News From Nowhere* are clear and in this book, in part envisaged as a reply to Bellamy, the quality of Morris's communism was expressed as fully and colourfully as in any of his other writings. The government of contemporary Britain, as seen from the future, is viewed as an instrument of the possessing class: 'for what other purpose than the protection of the rich from the poor, the strong from the weak, did this Government exist?' Not only was it the instrument of this class, but without the existence of rich and poor and the economic system which sustained this division, the state could have no function. Consequently in the fraternal and uncommercial world of the future, separate and distinct institutions of government did not exist (Morris [1890] 1924: 88–92). Thus state socialism could at best be a temporary measure, and in 1890 Morris was not even prepared to concede it this role. In his criticism of Bellamy, this form of collectivism had been tyrannical; in *News From Nowhere* it was futile (ibid.: 123ff.). The society of the future, if it could be achieved, would have neither state nor the 'artificial coercion' which the state embodied (ibid.: 108). Morris's argument was not that the abolition of government and coercion made free life possible, but that the destruction of commerce – he referred to it as commerce, not as capitalism – and the growth of self-management made government irrelevant and impossible.

Thus whereas some anarchists might argue that the removal of the coercive power of the state frees human social qualities and reduces or removes violence between persons, Morris argued that the end of commerce, of patriarchy, and of coercive and externally enforced marriage, removed the chief causes of both robbery and assault and thus left no place for the function formerly performed by the apparatus of the law (Morris [1890] 1924: 94–5).

In the place of the separate institution of the state, there would be a form of direct, occasional politics, communal self-management in small units which in the early phases of the transformation would emerge through a mixture of encroaching control and independent alternative organization (Morris [1890] 1924: 102–4, 123ff.). There would be a form of spontaneous self-management both in the new society and in the political events which preceded its creation. This spontaneity would be not so much a matter of unconscious reaction or instinct, as of an equally active participation of all persons in the conduct of social life, so that organization in the old sense would be redundant. The new structure of social life would arise from several causes. Partly it would be a matter of awakened rational self-interest: 'Thou shalt not steal, had to be translated into, Thou shalt work in order to live happily. Is there any need to enforce that commandment by violence?' (ibid.: 94). In the transitional period both socialist propaganda and the new understanding which came from new action would play their part, though in the fully established new society there would be fully established new habits. Such a scenario arose naturally from Morris's preferences for persuasive rather than conventionally political methods. The change, when it came, would be one of social attitudes transforming social conduct, rather than of legislation or government altering things from the outside.

The greatest positive motive in the new society would be pleasure and fulfilment in work, the reconciliation of art and labour which fascinated Morris throughout his life. Drawing on Ruskin, he argued that useful work as opposed to 'useless toil' would realize the three great hopes of humanity, for deserved rest after worthwhile labour, for work that is in itself satisfying, and for the production of goods that are valuable (Morris [1885] 1973b). How, the narrator in *News From Nowhere* asks his friend in the transformed Britain, are people made to work when without wages or prices there is no reward for labour? '"No reward of labour?" said Hammond gravely. "The reward of labour is *life*"' (Morris [1890] 1924: 106). The failure to recognize and act on this fact impoverished both rich and poor in nineteenth-century Britain – 'the ugliness and vulgarity of the rich men's dwellings was a necessary reflection from the sordidness and bareness of life which they forced upon the poor people' (ibid.: 225). The disappearance of both rich and poor, the emergence of a 'happy and lovely folk, who had cast away riches and attained to wealth' would make, for the first time, aesthetic pleasure compatible with a love of humanity (ibid.: 234, 15).

Joy in natural work would be accompanied by joy in the natural world, and a decreasing use of machinery by an end to the breach between man and nature. Thus would be ended that 'life of slavery' which had led people to 'try to make "nature" their slave, since they thought "nature" was something outside them' (Morris [1890] 1924: 209). At the same time the recolonization of the countryside and the ruralization of the town would be accompanied by a recovery by town and country dwellers 'of those arts of life which they had each lost' (ibid.: 84–5, 207). It was a vision, with its 'necessary dwellings, sheds, and workshops scattered up and down the country all trim and neat and pretty' (ibid.: 85), very like that of Kropotkin in *Fields, Factories and Workshops*. But it was one which Morris had held long before he became a socialist. In 1874 he had written in a letter: 'Suppose people lived in little communities among gardens and green fields, so that they could be in the country in five minutes' walk, and had few wants ... then I think we might hope civilization had really begun' (quoted in Clutton-Brock 1914: 98).

THE REFORM OF SOCIETY – THE ASSIMILATION OF DISSENT

Morris died in 1896. But already the change of communistic anarchism into a leavening of the quality of life within existing social and economic structures had begun. Both Kropotkin and Morris made their greatest impact not on a new society, but on the old. The reconciliation of town and country, the vision of England as a garden, the belief in the value of small social and productive units, the notion of the importance of artistic pleasure in production, all took on new and reformist shapes after the early 1890s.

Woodcock and Avakumovic have argued that from 1893 the anarchist movement centred around Kropotkin lost touch with the masses and 'declined into a neglected sect', and have commented on the paradox whereby this date marks the beginning of the growing influence of Kropotkin's writings on a wider, non-anarchist readership (Woodcock and Avakumovic 1950: 240–1). But if there is a paradox it is an illuminating and representative one, for what was happening to Kropotkin was happening to anarchism as a whole and in varying ways to most of the arguments against central power and state direction. It was a characteristic of anarchism that it was more difficult to achieve in a whole society than were the various forms of collectivism, but was capable of being realized on a small scale in a way that collectivist ideals were not. The step from the immediate, small microcosm of utopia in a commune or on a farm, to the qualitative improvement of existing society by the reform of local government or market gardening was a small one. Kropotkin's *Fields, Factories and Workshops* developed notions of increased and self-sufficient agricultural production which had appeared in a revolutionary context in *La Conquête du Pain* in 1892. But it developed them in a way that made them accessible to piecemeal reform in a most unrevolutionary England. Something of a recognition of this perhaps lay in Kropotkin's mind when he wrote to Paul Robin in 1896 that he could no longer go on living by his pen, 'whereas if I went over to market gardening and the planting of corn I could give real teaching' (quoted in Woodcock and Avakumovic 1950: 253). Certainly he was always ready to give advice to those who wanted to be taught in this way and gave both support and practical advice to a group of workmen on Tyneside who wanted to found an agricultural community (ibid.: 253–4).

Some of the possible implications of this can be seen in the work of Edward Carpenter. Carpenter's ideas stand at the point where socialism of the kind expounded by Hyndman, anarchistic communism as described by Morris and Kropotkin, and qualitative rejections of industrial life by writers as varied as Ruskin and Henry Thoreau, met to form a solution based on individual withdrawal from existing society, and alternative ways of living coupled with a broad socialist collectivism. The appeal was made as if from outside the system, from a simple life which was aimed towards self-sufficiency, recycling what was taken from nature, and assuming the possibility of work as a pleasure. It is what Dennis and Halsey have called the anti-historicist component of ethical socialism (1988: 5): 'come out of it! It may take you years to *get* out; certainly you will not shake yourself free in a week, or a month, or many months, but still – Come out!' (Carpenter [1887] 1906: 11).

Like Morris, of whose Socialist League he was a member, Carpenter saw both rich and poor as suffering under the existing order and looked forward to a society characterized by personal and social unity, by free production and exchange, by pleasure and satisfaction in work, and by a mutual co-operation which would replace systematic coercion as an instrument of social organization, and render government unnecessary (Carpenter 1889). Carpenter's reliance on individual effort and the withdrawal from conventional political action which this implied led William Morris to write to Georgina Burne-Jones in 1884 that despite the attractions of a simple private life it was 'dastardly to desert' in this manner (quoted in Henderson 1950: 223). Yet at times Carpenter combined this expectation of slow change within the general structure of the existing order, of transformation rather than either overthrow or supersession, with a belief in the necessity of conventional collectivism, albeit as a necessary first step to provide the means of fostering the growth of the 'Sentiment of the Common Life' (Carpenter 1897: 178–9, 187 and passim).

Carpenter's blend of a form of socialism with a moral and aesthetic criticism of bourgeois society and an advocacy of social regeneration through personal progress, particularly personal progress in the transformation of consciousness and sexuality, may account for some of his popularity, and for the very different response to him amongst the Fabians (Tsuzuki 1980: 79–81). For he provided both an inspiration for private life and a hope for public progress, and a suggestion that these would arise out of a transforming reconciliation between the two. On the other hand, he represented yet another instance of the assimilation of libertarian and anti-statist arguments within a collectivist framework, both by his acceptance of transitional centralization, and by his transmutation of communistic anarchism into personal, private endeavour.

In a similar way, in encouraging the establishment of agricultural settlements, or in encouraging through his writings a revival and reassimilation of agriculture, Kropotkin was moving into an area which was reformist rather than anarchistic. Farm colonies were set up under all kinds of inspirations: under the influence of Bellamy, under the aegis of General William Booth and the Salvation Army, and were a standard part of both labour and liberal collectivist solutions for unemployment. The resettlement of the land was advocated by those who saw in it an answer to unemployment, to industrialism, to the corrupting influence of the towns or to the threat of social revolution. Lord Wantage reminded the Select Committee on Small Holdings in 1889 of Thiers' assertion that every acre of land in the hands of a smallholder provides a musket for the defence of property, and he was active, with Auberon Herbert, in the Small Farms and Labourers' Holding Company in pursuit of this diffusion of sturdy yeomen (Marshall 1962: 101; Harris 1972; Bristow 1970: 264–5). It was Kropotkin's work on agriculture on which Bertrand Russell drew in *Roads to Freedom*, whilst giving a far more cautious appraisal to Kropotkin's expectation that work might be done for the enjoyment which it gave (Russell 1918).

In a similar way the notion of the reconciliation of town and country, and their disappearance as distinct and separate forms of social life, which in both Morris and Kropotkin was something to be looked for in a transformed society, was beginning to appear in the ideas of other people in the 1890s, many of whom were influenced by this form of communal anarchism, but who advanced it as a practical proposal for town planning. The polymath and pioneer urban planner Patrick Geddes knew Kropotkin and Kropotkin's ideas, but in his own arguments he drew a distinction between utopia and what he termed 'eutopia'. The former was ideal and by implication impractical, the latter, whilst inspired and informed by values and vision, built on what was practically available, transforming by improving rather than by removing: 'Eutopia, then, lies in the city around us; and it must be planned and realised, here or nowhere, by us as its citizens – each a citizen of both the actual and the ideal city seen increasingly as one' (Geddes 1915: vii). Geddes, a man of eclectic activities who eventually earned a part of a living in a specially endowed chair of botany at the University of Dundee, has been credited with a major influence on the tradition of town planning which rationalizes and exploits what is already there, rather than bulldozes and blueprints. His work in Edinburgh attracted the significant attention of Elisée Réclus, the friend and editor of Kropotkin, entwining further the interplay between communistic anarchism and qualitative piecemeal reformism (Réclus 1896).

Ebenezer Howard, whose *Tomorrow: A Peaceful Path to Real Reform* was published in 1898, proposed the garden city as a practical solution to urban problems, a proposal which was carried out in the building of Letchworth. Howard appears to have been more influenced by Bellamy than by anarchist or anti-state writers (MacFadyen 1933: 20–1), though his response to *Looking Backwards* was principally to react against it (Beevers 1987: 28), and there was much in his garden city proposal that associated it with the practical implications, rather than the ultimate hopes, of men such as Kropotkin, whose work he may have known (Beevers 1987: 17, 24). The garden city was to enjoy municipal autonomy, and the society in which it flourished was to be characterized by a dispersal of both population and power, and by some form of communal ownership of land (Howard 1898: 63–71). As soon as the proposals of the anarchist communists entered the world of immediately practical reform, they became part of a milieu where similar schemes were being proposed for very different motives, and where their own ideas became both a means of qualitative reform within an unregenerate social structure, and a bridge from alienation from that society and its political forms to acceptance of it. Proposals which seemed to arise from an initial disenchantment with the existing order, nonetheless involved those who made them in working on and within that order. This was strikingly so in the cases of Edward Carpenter and Robert Blatchford. Blatchford believed extensive government to be only a temporarily necessary evil and wrote that in 'a nation where a free, educated, and independent People really studied and took part in national and international affairs ... there would soon be very little need of legislation or of any complex machinery of government at all' (in the *Sunday Chronicle*, quoted in Thompson 1951: 135). One of his most widely read series was the essays later published as a separate volume under the title *Merrie England*. Where the town planning and garden city movements blended the insights of the communistic anarchists with reformism, Blatchford blended them with a centralized socialist state. The socialist England which he envisaged in *Merrie England* was inspired at many points of its life by Kropotkin, whom Blatchford quoted and cited. Agricultural revival and intensive cultivation would counter the effects of industrialization and urban living, while social life would be communal. Children would be fed, clothed and educated at the cost of the state, and there would be communal dining halls, wash-houses and bath-houses. Thus were Kropotkin's insights assimilated (Blatchford 1894). In a similar manner the influence of William Morris was greater upon the arts and crafts movement than it was upon radical or socialist politics. Morris was 'the father of the Modern Movement' (Pevsner 1960: 9); to left-wing political arguments he was for many years little more than a distant cousin.

DISTRIBUTISM – G.K. CHESTERTON AND HILAIRE BELLOC

The variety of group and communal arguments, and the impossibility of categorizing them in conventional terms of left or right, is well illustrated by the contribution of G.K. Chesterton. Chesterton is often seen as a right-wing thinker. His reputation has perhaps been gained or at least enhanced by his activities and by the causes he espoused after the First World War, by his Roman Catholicism and his anti-Semitism, and by his opposition to the state at a time when most of those who were considered radical or left-wing saw in the state the instrument of progress. The striking thing about his relation to contemporaries on the left, however, was how many affinities there were, not how many differences. If he is seen, as Margaret Canovan (1977) presents him, as a populist, then this transitional position is easier to grasp. Anti-Semitism, certainly in the early part of the century, was far from being a shibboleth whereby to divide left from right, and in the matter of anti-statism, Chesterton's main contribution to political argument was made at a time when his ideas were enthusiastically received by the left.

These ideas were most clearly expressed in his apparently non-political writings, in novels such as *The Napoleon of Notting Hill*, published in 1904, and *The Flying Inn*, published in 1914. Chesterton wrote prolifically in essays and journalism, often on conventionally political subjects, and many of his ideas were firmly and sometimes best expressed in this form. But much of this writing is characterized by whimsicality, a trick of those who like to be taken seriously but who do not like to be taken up. Chesterton's fiction often provides a clearer and less teasing expression of his opinions. The first of the two novels, *The Napoleon of Notting Hill*, takes place in a London sufficiently in the future for unusual things to happen, but sufficiently close to the author's time for the social and geographical context to be recognizable. London is divided into areas which are supposed to approximate to ancient boroughs, and each area is given civic rituals to sustain a sense of local identity. But what was originally intended as little more than a joke by a bored governor, begins to be taken seriously and the battles of London politics begin to be fought, eventually in a military fashion, between citizens newly aroused to local group consciousness.

The Napoleon of the title is Adam Wayne, the most enthusiastic of the new borough men and the only one at first to take the new arrangements seriously. His career follows that of Napoleon, and his downfall, like Napoleon's, comes when, from defending his own immediate community, he moves to dominate the other boroughs of London. The small and immediately knowable local community and local area is portrayed as the true and truly desirable object of people's loyalties. But its virtue is not impregnable against the charms of extending power, and it may be corrupted by them. *The Flying Inn*, published ten years later, illustrates another of Chesterton's most valued forms of social activity, the spontaneous action of the English crowd. In contrast to the crowd psychologists and those who, like Wallas, perceived a dangerous irrationality in the masses, Chesterton believed that the crowd expressed the quality of the nation in a direct way, cutting through the compromises, distortions and clear deceptions of conventional politics. The inn of the title is a mobile speakeasy whereby the increasing oppressions of a conspiratorial state are avoided, and around which the opposition to this state is centred.

In these two books several main features of Chesterton's arguments emerged. First there was the admiration for community loyalty, but hostility to large groups and organizations, a position which could make him both a patriot and a pro-Boer. Both imperialism and socialism could be rejected together from this position since both encouraged unification and centralization on a large scale (Chesterton 1936: 107). Second was a belief in popular instincts, and in public collective action as their most accurate expression. It was an English crowd, suitably armed, which toppled the repressive state of *The Flying Inn*, defeating its alien allies (Turks, as Chesterton euphemistically represented them) in pitched battle. The mob, Chesterton wrote, was one of the 'two great forms' of 'collective humanity' (Chesterton 1909: 192), and he identified with admiration 'the common soul of such a crowd, its instinctive anger at the traitor or its instinctive salutation of the flag' (ibid.: 184). Third, Chesterton whittled down the notion of immediacy into the belief that ideally there need be no social or political organization or coercion beyond the family and the land on which it lived and worked. His objection to Morris's *News from Nowhere* and Wells's *Anticipations* was that neither gave a place for the family, and more particularly that both deprived (male) people of the dignity of being heads of households (Chesterton 1910: 73). Fourth, and in this he had much in common with the tradition of Ruskin and Morris and the later contributions to that tradition by R.H. Tawney, Chesterton believed in the prior claims of the cultural and moral over the economic order. This, coupled with a general distaste for industrialism and with the agrarianism which seemed a necessary part of his family-based economy, could lead him to cavalier dismissal of the merely material advantages of modern life, especially if they arose from the energies of industrial patriarchs like Lord Leverhulme.

> If soap-boiling is really inconsistent with brotherhood, so much the worse for soap-boiling, not for brotherhood.... Certainly, we would sacrifice all our wires, wheels, systems, specialities, physical science and frenzied finance for one half-hour of happiness such as has often come to us with comrades in a common tavern.
>
> (Chesterton 1910: 109)

The force of Chesterton's argument was his assertion of the broad possibilities of human choice and his readiness to demand the apparently impractical, unrealistic solution which he believed to be right, even if this meant a simple reversal of four centuries of history. The implications of Chesterton's various preferences and aversions were that government, which was no more than a necessary evil at best, which rested on force, and which corrupted more than it cured, would have no place in a reshaped society. With it would go the fragmentation of life into distinct and exclusive spheres of expertise. The more expert someone was, the less representative he was, and what Chesterton wanted was a return to wholeness, and the recapture of unifying themes which alone could give meaning to such terms as 'efficiency': 'as far as I can make out, "efficiency" means that we ought to discover everything about a machine except what it is for' (Chesterton 1905: 11–24; 1910: 10). Chesterton was thus not in the first place concerned about the state at all, as indeed befits an opponent of the modern state. It was not hostility to the state, but attraction to something other than the state, which provided him with his starting point. Self-sufficiency and non-intervention made centralization irrelevant and unnecessary.

Chesterton is often considered in conjunction with his friend Hilaire Belloc. Had the association never been made in the public mind, it could not have resisted Shaw's designation of their political alliance as the 'Chesterbelloc'. But Shaw's observation was intended to illuminate both the political alliance and the intellectual disparities – the beast was, in his eyes, rather like an ill-coordinated pantomime horse. Though both Chesterton and Belloc disliked the modern state and looked forward to social reorganization on the basis of self-sufficient domestic units, there were important differences between them, and Belloc had closer political affinities with Chesterton's brother Cecil, with whom he collaborated in satirical political journalism and in a book attacking conventional parliamentary and party politics, than with Chesterton himself. G.K. Chesterton's dislike of experts made him a populist. Belloc's dislike of politicians made him an aristocrat.

Belloc's arguments had the appearance of being more realistically related to the world in which he wrote largely because they were more concerned with pointing out that world's deficiencies, and less with proposing alternatives in the Chestertonian manner. *The Party System* which he wrote with Cecil Chesterton in 1911, and *The Servile State*, which he wrote by himself a year later, are primarily indictments with which many of less utopian views could associate themselves. In Cecil Chesterton's case, the utopianism was almost wholly absent – his was little more than the satirical venom of the partisan journalist, attacking a variety of intrusions by the state into the liberties and territories of the family head, after he had moved, under Belloc's influence, from socialism to distributism.

Belloc began a parliamentary political career before he turned to the politics of written argument, and this career he began in the tradition of political radicalism, speaking out for working-class interests and for legal guarantees of trade union rights, but stressing also the necessity of free trade and Irish home rule. He wanted, he told his electors, to destroy the brewing monopoly, and he opposed the Education Act of 1902 because it might cause children to be educated against the religious beliefs of their parents. He made an anti-aristocratic speech in the debate on Asquith's 1907 motion on the Upper House, and described Lloyd George's 1909 budget as 'perfectly excellent'. In the first general election of 1910 he told electors that society 'is trembling with desire to produce a new and better England. But it cannot be done without raising great sums of money and without putting burdens on the rich' (Speaight 1957: 190–1, 221, 233, 279). On the other hand Belloc had the political radical's hostility to state action, and opposed proposals to provide for the indefinite detention of incorrigible recidivists in the 1908 Prevention of Crimes Bill. There came a point when the political and the social radical found themselves fundamentally opposed, and by 1911 Belloc was describing Lloyd George's National Health Insurance Bill as 'a vile enslaving measure' (Speaight 1957: 231, 314). The implications for traditional radical liberties had perhaps been emphasized for him by the reading of books like Arthur Ponsonby's *The Camel and the Needle's Eye* with its assault on the pursuit of money and its moral condemnation of the rich. But he was becoming disillusioned with what he saw as the compromises of principle and the pursuit of mean ambition and advantage. A distrust of state power as such thus combined with a belief that this power was being put to personal material advantage by politicians and business-men, a belief which slid easily into a readiness to see conspiracies behind an increasing number of the activities of an increasing number of statesmen. The book which he wrote in 1911 with Cecil Chesterton epitomized this tone. Belloc's attack on the growth and direction of state power received wide currency through the strikingness of the phrase whereby he identified the likely direction of things: 'the servile state'. The use of the word 'servile' to describe the condition of the people under a state was not original – Spencer had spoken of 'slavery' – but Belloc gave it wider currency than it had ever received before, initially in a series of articles between 1908 and 1912, mainly in *The New Age*, and then in a book, *The Servile State*, published in 1912. The contemporary form of social organization, capitalism, was unstable, Belloc argued. This instability arose both from the material insecurity which capitalism inevitably created for the majority of the population, and from the contradiction between the moral values of capitalist society and the actual condition of that society. In moving out of this phase into one of stability, society could arrive at one of three forms: socialism, slavery or property. It was in fact moving towards the second, slavery, in the sense that society would increasingly be divided into two classes, employers and masters, employed and subordinates, the former free, privileged, but with responsibilities for the material security of their inferiors, the latter legally bound in and to their work, but guaranteed in return a minimum standard of security. Measures such as the 1911 National Health Insurance Act were instalments of what was likely to come. The state by this act created Belloc's two categories of men, and 'compels the lower man to registration, to a tax, and the rest of it, and further compels the upper man to be the instrument in enforcing that registration and in collecting that tax' (Belloc [1912] 1927: 166). The introduction of unemployment benefit and of labour exchanges, whilst not in themselves immediately increasing the element of servility in the state, made its advance more likely and were an intimation of measures 'which compel a man lacking the means of production to labour, though he may have made no contract to that effect' (ibid.: 164).

All of this, Belloc argued, was distinct from socialism, even though much of it was being carried through under the influence of socialists or with their support. Socialism involved the control of property by public officials, whereas all that was happening or was envisaged in England was the purchase of private enterprises by the state, thus leaving the capitalists with their wealth intact, and the control of the citizens' incomes for the funding of purposes decided upon by the state. Belloc purported to be doing no more than indicating the likely drift of things, but his own preferences were very clear. The servile state, arising out of the action of timorous and thus false socialism on capitalism, was the easiest way out of the existing unstable conditions, because it required small transitions rather than the upheaval which would be involved in the distribution of property in such a manner as to create independent and self-sufficient economic units out of families. But Belloc was contemptuous of such practicality, and illustrated the choice by a metaphor of a patient 'whose limbs were partially atrophied from disuse'. One physician – the distributist – recommends a change in the patient's manner of life and the adoption of exercises, so that the use of the limbs will be regained. The other advises a wheel chair (Belloc [1912] 1927: 108–9).

Belloc's distributist attack on the servile state claimed traditional, conservative inspiration, and invoked the peasant and guild society of the Middle Ages as a lost experience of distributism. More recently, it echoed Chamberlain's policy of three acres and a cow, the papal bull *Rerum Novarum* of 1891, and the redistribution of land in Ireland culminating in Wyndham's Irish Land Act of 1903. Belloc specifically mentioned Ireland as a society which had chosen the distributive solution. But the appeal of his arguments was considerable not so much in Ireland as amongst socialists of one kind and another who, whilst they wanted social reform, were suspicious of the state, or who felt that the insurance principle in social reform had little to do with the redistribution of wealth. During the First World War Belloc's ideas were to have particular appeal amongst syndicalists who saw the servile state emerging in the ways in which labour, but not capital, was conscripted in the interests of direct and indirect military activity.

The rumbustious and often amusing sniping which Belloc and Chesterton conducted against the state endeared them to socialists with libertarian sympathies and to pluralists with socialist sympathies, at a time when the Chesterbelloc had not become the enemy of all decent things which it was later to seem. There is truth as well as eccentricity in Vitoux's reference, in a discussion of 'les formes différent de socialisme' to 'la persistance de la persepctive organaciste dans le *Guild Movement* et chez H. Belloc' (Vitoux 1969: 176). The arguments which went to inform *The Servile State* were first published in *The New Age*, a journal which was also a platform for guild socialist ideas, and Belloc's argument made a deep impression on many guild socialists (Glass 1966: 28, 21). Cecil Chesterton and S.G. Hobson, the latter to become a leading exponent of guild socialist ideas, considered in 1907 forming a new socialist party. Guild socialists were fascinated by *The Napoleon of Notting Hill*, and the songs in *The Flying Inn* received the compliment, political if not musical, of being provided with tunes by Maurice Reckitt and G.D.H. Cole (Glass 1966: 26; Cole 1971: 52–3, 136). Syndicalists, too, were sympathetic to Belloc's warnings (Holton 1976: 182–3), and *The Servile State* provided ammunition for contributors to the *Daily Herald* who saw liberal social reforms as encroachments by a capitalist state upon the free action of the workers (Holton 1972: 28). A contributor to the SDF's *Justice* in 1912 warned of the dangers of the servile state, and Belloc's ideas influenced the shop stewards' movement during the First World War (Tsuzuki 1961: 186; Hinton 1973).

Chesterton, Belloc and the group around them represent the end of a tradition. The very shrillness of their tone, the extravagance of their writing, is a feature of a last-ditch stand. After them, their few supporters and would-be followers retreated into the maquis of sectarianism in Croydon, religious petulance, and unsophisticated Merrie Englandism. Intimations of impossibilism are evident even in Chesterton. Like Morris, he expressed his dreams in utopian novels, but Chesterton's novels are the more fantastic by being placed in familiar surroundings. The London of *News from Nowhere* is sufficiently overgrown with verdure not to jar with the unfamiliarity of the society which occupied it. But Adam Wayne and his halberdiers fight for a Notting Hill which is immediately recognizable, and are by the same token immediately the more fantastic and improbable.

If Chesterton's romanticism seemed utopian in the years before 1914, thereafter it was merely quaint. Following the death of his brother Cecil, Chesterton took over the latter's *New Witness* and in this and the subsequent *G.K.'s Weekly* and *Weekly Review* he reiterated the views of romantic distributism already set out in *What's Wrong with the World*, drawing both on Belloc's views and on his own romantic localism. Chesterton's creative urge did not build on Belloc, though he could draw on Belloc for his polemics, as when he compared Port Sunlight to 'a slave compound' (quoted in D. Barker 1973: 215). But the disparity between those views and the world in which they were expressed was far greater in the 1920s and 1930s than it had seemed at the beginning of the century. They were not developed, nor did they excite any echo amongst other thinkers. One of the few voices making similar objections, that of Sir Ernest Benn, was dismissed by Chesterton as commending nothing more than a utopia of stock-brokers. Distributism as a political movement continued in a series of small sects into the 1950s and beyond, but its intellectual force was gone and there was no other source of protest to revive or replace it.

SYNDICALISM

Chesterton's and Belloc's group theory was uncompromising in its
hostility to the central state, and both hostility and indifference
increased as the state established its position in the early part of the
century. But the course of other arguments against central power was
often more ambivalent. In the years immediately before the outbreak
of the First World War, syndicalism appeared to offer a clear
alternative to both conventional politics and the conventional state.
But there was sufficient ambivalence in the general context within
which the syndicalist argument was put, for the end result to be a
closer engagement of the organized working class with the state, rather
than any heightened separation of the energies and aspirations of the
two. The consequence of the assertion of separate interest was a
renewed emphasis on the place of the trade unions in a process of
consultation and co-operation. By the end of the war syndicalist
agitation had been complemented and then eclipsed by what Hinton
has described as 'a new and lasting accommodation of organized
labour within the capitalist system' (Hinton 1973: 13).

The initial demand of the syndicalists had been uncompromising.
Tom Mann, who put the syndicalist case most articulately, argued that
economic rather than political power was the key to the workers'
control of their own lives. This economic power could only be directly
seized at the point of production, and could not be indirectly gained
via political action:

> True, a thorough going, fearless revolutionary group in the House of
> Commons might succeed in being a nuisance to the plutocratic
> members, even though there were no industrial organisation at all.
> But there is no possibility of achieving economic freedom, nor even
> of taking any steps towards that end, unless the workers themselves
> are conscious that what they suffer from, as a class, is economic
> subjugation and consequent exploitation by the capitalists.
>
> (Mann [1910-11] 1974: 80)

The authors of the declaration published by miners in South Wales two
years later gave this general doctrine a specific application:

> To have a vote in determining who shall be your fireman, manager,
> inspector etc., is to have a vote in determining the conditions which
> shall rule your working life. On that vote will depend in a large
> measure your safety of life and limb, and your freedom from
> oppression by petty bosses, and would give you an intelligent
> interest in, and control over, your conditions of work. To vote for a

man to represent you in Parliament, to make rules for, and assist in appointing officials to rule you, is a different proposition altogether.
(*The Miners' Next Step*, 1912, quoted by Pelling 1954: 215)

Because of its stress on action and on control at the point of production, syndicalism involved an argument for industrial unionism rather than for trade unionism. This organizational radicalism was matched by a conception of syndicalist activity as itself a radicalizing experience. Direct action and direct power were to be both means and ends: ends in that they involved the workers' control over their own economic situation, means in that whether successfully pursued or not, they developed a radical working-class consciousness of distinct identity and separate interests.

The engagement between syndicalist ideas and trade union activity had been facilitated by the high unemployment of the years 1908–10 and the bitter industrial conflicts of the years 1910–12. But the attraction of syndicalist ideas often lay in their appropriateness in the pursuit of militant collective bargaining, rather than in their being a revolutionary alternative to conventional politics or a revolutionary transformation of working-class organization. After 1914 this ambivalence became clearer. On the one hand the need to produce war materials induced the government to seek the co-operation of organized labour, which gained new status through the high importance of industrial workers both in production and through their representatives at the national level. On the other hand the unions made concessions at the expense of the privileges of their members, which whilst benefiting lower-paid and unskilled workers in particular and women in general, caused resentment amongst the organized members of the labour force because they seemed to threaten them from above in the interests of the employer and from below in the interests of the less well-organized and less well-paid. The increased militancy and the increased importance of the unions in national politics which arose from this situation had within it elements both of assimilation and of disintegration and conflict. As Hinton has put it, writing of the shop stewards' movement during the First World War: 'The "militant craftsman" and the "revolutionary engineer" certainly described categorically different states of consciousness; but both states may well have coexisted, and interacted, in the same head' (Hinton 1973: 335).

The assimilative element in syndicalism was not new, and G.D.H. Cole had argued in 1913 that the movements amongst industrial workers could be the genesis of a new and more substantial national political harmony (Cole [1913] 1973). By the end of the war increased workers' participation was being more widely discussed than ever before, but its implications were if anything even more various. R.H. Tawney remarked in 1920 that 'The formulation of a "Constitution for Industry" is conducted with something of the same energy as that which past generations have given to the discussion of a Constitution for the State' (Tawney 1921a). The shift of attention away from the conventionally political was typical of the whole drift of group theory, and appeared to involve the creation of alternatives to central state politics. But what was involved was not so much a desertion of the political for the social or the economic, as a politicization of organizations and activities which had previously not been political, or had not been so political as they now became. At the same time the shift of attention away from 'a Constitution for the State' facilitated the acceptance of newly extended and consolidated state functions, resting as they did within the competence of an institution whose fundamental and justifying principles were less and less scrutinized.

Had the unions been the only party to the debate over industrial power, the result might simply have been to direct attention away from the new role of the state. But the state was equally interested, and the improvement of industrial relations by discussion and co-operation in general and by Whitley councils in particular became a part of public policy. And as a contemporary observer remarked, 'There is no one break in the long series from Syndicalism to Whitleyism, and the widespread acceptance of the latter in middle-class thinking is a hint of the driving force of more drastic doctrines' (Goodrich 1920: 7). In France this 'driving force' had expressed itself in separate trade unions with their own distinctive 'political' line; in Britain it was matched and to some extent assimilated by a series of measures which turned assertion into participation, and conflict into collaboration.

POLITICAL PLURALISM – F.W. MAITLAND, J.N. FIGGIS, HAROLD LASKI

Just as a great deal of argument about the state in the latter part of the nineteenth century arose from reflection on the changing function of central power, so the arguments of the political thinkers described as 'pluralists' in the early part of the twentieth century arose not only from a consideration of scholarly writing, but from a knowledge both of the course of political events and of the contribution to those events of persuasive rather than descriptive ideas such as those of the syndicalists. Disestablishment, nationalism, home rule and devolution, and the legal and political role of trade unions all provided nourishment for argument and discussion at a further remove from the forum of politics.

Some pluralist argument was predominantly reflective and descriptive. The immediate roots of the work of the lawyer and historian F.W. Maitland lay in history and in German jurisprudence rather than in British politics. An association or group, argued Maitland, was 'no fiction, no symbol, no piece of the State's machinery, no collective name for individuals, but a living organism and a real person, with body and members and a will of its own'. To deny this was to threaten not only the identity of groups and associations but that of the state as well, and 'the State's possession of a real will is insecure if no other groups may have wills of their own' (Maitland 1900: xxvi, xlii). The consequences of this for political argument were implied, but they were not drawn out. As Collini has put it of Maitland's writings, 'when they were published they did not cause the stir among non-specialist readers' which, say, Maine's books had done (Collini 1991: 304). Judicial theory has not constituted a major part of the body of political ideas in modern Britain. The law has been considered to be a world neutrally detached from the contests of political ideas and argument. Particular laws and particular legal judgments may have had recognized political consequences which have been applauded or resisted, but the general character of the judicial system and the general assumptions of law have been little considered in debates about the political character and goals of the nation. Dicey had of course given an account of the basis of rights and of the rule of law which was allied to his preferences for limited and general government, and the discussions of administrative law and of delegated legislation continued to be carried on with reference to such preferences. The phrase 'the rule of law' was later in the present century employed by Hayek to express and legitimize his own political ideas and beliefs. But in general, legal ideas were invisible in the elaboration of political argument.

It was not in the work of the lawyer Maitland, but in that of an Anglican priest, J.N. Figgis, that pluralist ideas were developed as part of an argument about the position of an organized group, the church, in the public life of the nation and about the relations between that group and the public power of the state. Figgis rejected individualism as providing either an adequate account of social life or an adequate basis for freedom, since it saw social life as no more than 'a heap of sand'. It was clear, he argued, 'that the mere individual's freedom against an omnipotent State may be no better than slavery; more and more is it evident that the real question of freedom in our day is the freedom of smaller unions to live within the whole' (Figgis 1913: 49, 52). He argued that man was a social animal, but that the society in which that animal lived was not a single monolithic one encompassed by the national state, but rather a series of societies particular to the citizen, and not necessarily shared with large numbers of fellow citizens. People

> will grow to maturity and be moulded in their prejudices, their tastes, their capacities, and their moral ideals not merely by the great main stream of national life, but also, and perhaps more deeply, by their own family connections, their local communal life in village or town, their educational society (for it is of the essence of education to be in a society), and countless other collective organisms.
>
> (Figgis 1913: 72)

The social existence of the individual was thus made up of a series of societies: church, family, school, workplace, whose particular combination was a distinguishing factor rather than one making for national uniformity. Moreover,

> the State did not create the family, nor did it create the Churches; nor even in any real sense can it be said to have created the club or the trades union; ... they have all arisen out of the natural associative instincts of mankind, and should all be treated by the supreme authority as having a life original and guaranteed.
>
> (ibid.: 47)

In order, therefore, to take proper account of its citizens, the state must recognize and take account of the particular groups and societies in which their social nature was expressed. The group with which Figgis was particularly concerned was the church, and he employed his arguments about the nature of social life in the practical controversy over disestablishment.

With the syndicalists the argument about the political function of groups was a largely practical affair, with Figgis a mixture of the persuasive and descriptive, and with Maitland largely a matter of arriving at a satisfactory account of law. But this movement between the level of political argument and the level of political reflection existed not only between and within the thinking of different individuals and groups, but gave form to a change in the character of the debate during the first quarter of the century. The end of the process was a breach between wide and widely conscious argument and political persuasion, and it was related to the increasing contribution to the debate of professional scholars whose profession shaped their interests in a manner more predominantly reflective and more removed from recommendation and advocacy than had previously been the case.

An intermediary position was taken by writers such as Ernest Barker and A.D. Lindsay. Drawing on the arguments of syndicalism on the one hand and the work of academic pluralists on the other, they sought to give an account of the modern state which both took account of the operation of groups and associations and justified the tolerant and eclectic nature of the resultant political life. Barker, more than Lindsay, was aware of the difficulties which might face pluralist politics, but he had a donnish optimism about how they might be avoided. The potentially murderous conflicts of various groups and of groups with the state were after all, he argued, only conflicts between ideas since the identity of groups rested on common ideas, and 'one can deflate a bubble idea with a prick of logic' (E. Barker 1915a: 113).

Lindsay was concerned to give an account of an apparently triumphant and ascendant state challenged from above and from below, by international society on the one hand and by groups and associations on the other (Lindsay 1914). In this sense his approach was less directly related to practical conclusions than was that of Barker, who attempted to relate pluralist perspectives to the problems of nationalism and of trade unionism. But the final point in the academic progression, at which pluralist discussion left the sphere of political argument and became something different, occurred in the early work of H.J. Laski. This is paradoxical in view of the later career and reputation of Laski as a political don and a scholarly propagandist. But in his pluralist phase he represented, as perhaps only Maitland also does, the translation of political argument to the almost purely reflective and descriptive sphere.

In the years during and just after the First World War Laski's writings drew on academic pluralists such as Maitland and the French jurist Duguit, on reflective polemicists such as Figgis and on the activities of trade unionists, Ulster Unionists and suffragettes. But the purpose for which he reviewed them all was to examine in the light of contemporary experience notions of sovereignty, obligation and legitimacy (Laski 1917: 12). When trade unions were discussed, it was in order to place them in an account of political and industrial democracy, rather than to contribute to the debate in which syndicalists or socialists were engaged (Laski, review of J.R. MacDonald, *Parliament and Revolution*, in *The New Republic*, quoted in Deane 1955: 56). So whilst Laski argued more vigorously than anyone else during the first quarter of the twentieth century against the claims of the national state to a comprehensive and unlimited sovereignty, his arguments remained within the sphere of political science and law, rather than forming part of a wider political debate (Greenleaf 1981; Hirst 1989; R. Barker 1989).

Just as Laski illustrated the distillation of political philosophy in the pluralist tradition, so also he illustrated the demise of group theory as a criticism of the modern state. In 1918 he was advocating parallel parliaments, one of producers, the other the conventional parliament. In 1920 he was arguing for a single overall body, and by 1921 was advocating public control of the coal mines by nationalization. By 1922 he was rejecting any final control lying in the hands of functional groups, lest the many be overruled by the few (Deane 1955: 60–5).

GUILD SOCIALISM – S.G. HOBSON, G.D.H. COLE

But this weakening of the power of pluralism to convince was not so marked at the level of political argument. The ten years after 1914 saw not so much a disappearance of pluralism as an increasing division between the two ways in which it was articulated. Guild socialism exemplified this development. Particularly in the arguments of its main exponent, G.D.H. Cole, it drew on the wide variety of group arguments from Belloc to Figgis, and on both the practical experience of trade unions and the philosophical arguments of European political theorists. Ruskin, Rousseau and the Rhondda all went into the mincer to provide the guildsman's sausage.

But as was so often the case with the contribution of professional scholars to political argument, Cole made his entry into the debate when the general positions had already been in part established. The initial arguments were advanced with less intellectual sophistication, and not only in books but in pamphlets and in articles in journals such as *The New Age*. *The New Age* is sometimes thought of as a vehicle for guild socialist ideas. But it was much more than this: an eclectic literary and political journal which gave space to many ideas, some conflicting with each other, others closer together than in retrospect they have often been considered to be. A.J. Penty, who organized a Gilds Restoration League with the *New Age*'s editor A.R. Orage, later toyed with distributism, writing for the Distributist League formed by another *New Age* contributor, G.K. Chesterton (Penty 1937), and ended up a supporter of fascism.

Penty, whose ideas were set out in *The Restoration of The Gild*

System in 1906, drew on Morris and Ruskin, and on the attempts
which had already been made to establish guilds, often as part of the
late nineteenth-century movement to revive the arts and crafts. It is a
tradition which runs back through many sources, taking in conservatives such as Toulmin Smith on the way. The gilds of the future
(the medieval appearance of the spelling was deliberate) would develop
out of existing trade unions, but they would be the guardians of a very
different kind of production. The problems of existing society arose
from the division of labour and from machine production, and the
ideal which Penty presented was one of hand-production and the
centrality of the craftsman, an ideal which drew directly on Morris but
which had also been transmitted at times through the writings of J.A.
Hobson.

Following Penty's and Orage's interest in guild restoration, S.G.
Hobson developed the notion in a series of articles which were
published in book form in 1914. Hobson's arguments illustrated more
clearly than any others had by then done the accommodation with the
state which could be accomplished or facilitated by group theory. The
socialism of the Fabians and of the ILP was rejected by Hobson
because it made no essential changes in the wage system which was at
the basis of the oppression of the workers. It rested on the assumption
'that the State was economically a better capitalist than the private
employer' and simply presaged 'the wage system of a universal civil
service' (Hobson 1914: 8, 9). But the struggle for control at the point of
production was not, as it had seemed to be for the syndicalists, an
assault on the state. The guilds 'ought not and must not be the absolute
possessors of their land, houses, and machinery. We remain Socialists
because we believe that in the final analysis the State, as representing
the community at large, must be the final arbiter' (ibid.: 133). Thus
guild socialism was to ensure a form of second-order autonomy for
functional groups within the limits of overall public policy expressed
through the collectivist state.

The functions of this state were, however, to be limited, and the
dangers of a bureaucratic socialism avoided. The state should co-
ordinate rather than actually do, a principle which divided Hobson
from conventional contemporary Fabianism: 'The Fabian attitude
towards democracy – an arrogant and supercilious attitude – is largely
due to the reliance which it places upon the bureaucracy to administer
social reforms from above; it cannot conceive wage slavery doing it for
itself' (ibid.: 219). There is a trace here of the hostility to centralism
and officialdom expressed in the notion of a servile state, and an echo
of the populist independence asserted by Stephen Reynolds. But guild

socialism of this kind involved no radical challenge to the existence of the state, even though it seriously questioned its function. What was envisaged was a separation of what was properly economic from what was properly political, thus refining and raising politics and the character of politicians – a touch of Belloc. Hobson attempted to accommodate both the group conception of people as defined by their particular associations, and of citizens as conceived in their different ways by individualists and state collectivists. People would be both members of guilds and citizens, and would have different responsibilities in the two roles.

The guild socialist method of dispersing the exercise of public power proved attractive to many who wished to pursue a progressive public policy without creating an over-mighty central power. The philosopher Bertrand Russell described the state in 1916 as representing a principle antagonistic to creativeness. The state was becoming a threat to individuality, and whilst it had positive purposes to pursue, these should be carried out as far as possible by independent agencies: 'The positive purposes of the State, over and above the preservation of order, ought as far as possible to be carried out, not by the State itself, but by independent organizations, which should be left completely free so long as they satisfied the State that they were not falling below a necessary minimum' (Russell 1916: 72). Russell followed Belloc in seeing the great danger not as poverty, but as slavery. He followed the guild socialists in so far as they represented a practical step along the path at whose further bridge lay anarchism, a style of politics which could for the present be no more than an ideal. Workers' control in industry trained the workers, shifted political power and created restraints upon the central state (Russell 1920: 120–1; Ryan 1988). Russell quoted one guild socialist in particular with great approval. This was the young university teacher G.D.H. Cole (Russell 1918). Cole was the most consciously theoretical and widely assimilative of the guild socialists, and the writer whose work made the most sustained contribution to guild socialist argument. In Cole's work can be detected the influences of Morris and Oxford philosophy, whilst the argument of his first major contribution to the debate, *The World of Labour* of 1913, was consciously set in the context of the views of Belloc, Spencer, the Fabians, Rousseau, English syndicalism, Lagardelle, Ruskin, Morris and Kropotkin. Cole was greatly interested in the work of Chesterton and Belloc, and as an undergraduate had been briefly involved in the publication of *The Oxford Syndicalist* (Glass 1966: 36ff.) at a time when his briefly held collectivist socialism was being humanized by the earlier influence of Morris and the stronger influence of syndicalism (Wright 1976). Group theory, a belief in the decay of collectivism, a perception of class war, an advocacy of functional and regional devolution and an employment of the notion of the general will were combined in a vigorous statement of the need for producers' power. Cole did not, like some group theorists, envisage the complete atrophy of the state, and syndicalism as transmuted in his writing became the assertion of a growing producers' interest alongside the function of some kind of central responsibility by the state at the highest level. Cole assimilated earlier guild socialist concern with producers' satisfaction to syndicalist concern for producers' power: 'No doubt the ultimate power must reside in the democratic State; but it does not follow that the State should do all the work' (Cole [1913] 1973: 28).

The writings of G.D.H. Cole are of especial interest. This is not because of their volume but because they illustrate with particular force how guild socialism, which seemed such a radical rejection of the modern state, provided an intermediary position for those who wished to accept that state and get on with their business within its confines and in terms of its responsibilities. This had been evident in other guild arguments which had always been more attuned to the existence of some central co-ordinating power than had the arguments of communists, distributists or syndicalists. Guilds had even been proposed as a means of equalizing the electoral power of workers and employers (Candidus 1910). In asserting the primacy of group functions, and particularly economic functions, over the functions of the state, the guild socialists were according political status to areas of life which had not previously been considered political. This was necessary in order to make any realistic alternative assertion to the claims of the modern state. But it undermined the position taken by Morris in two ways: if it were asserted that a wide range of activities were political, then the state, as the supreme political body – some would say as the only political body – had a proper interest in them. The corollary of the trade union demand for political functions which were independent of the state was an increase in trade union legislation between 1906 and 1913, which whatever its consequences in terms of trade union strength made trade union functions more securely than ever before the consequence of public policy and state decision. Second, by insisting that a range of group functions were in themselves adequate for the full and secure life of the citizen, the guild socialists enabled those citizens to be content with whatever activities they could pursue within their groups, irrespective of the powers claimed and taken by the state over the whole political society.

Cole's earlier guild socialist writings are more strongly in the uncompromising tradition which draws on Morris. But a new emphasis is to be found with the development of his notion of encroaching control, derived in part from the experiences of wartime trades unionism. The unions were to assert themselves not through parliamentary action and legislative nationalization, but from the bottom up, through individual factories. Such national political changes as might ultimately occur would thus simply be reflections of causally prior economic changes. At a national level, and in forms which might sustain or legitimize the role of the responsible state, 'encroachment' was specifically eschewed: profit-sharing and direct co-partnership were joined with national and local Whitley councils as proscribed reformism. But there were two implications of boycotting the state in this way. For Cole, all that was involved was the application of his beliefs in a state that in the guild society would be minimal and shadowy. But if the same methods were pursued before the achievement of this society, in a nation where the state was both secure and expanding, then the consequences would be that funda-mental political questions were either ignored, or dealt with indirectly through relatively small-scale technical debates and stratagems about detailed arrangements within the unchallenged character of the modern state.

In the event, this is much what happened. Cole's first major political book after his 1920 *Guild Socialism Restated* was *The Next Ten Years*, published in 1929, which represented just such a change from radical communalism to collectivist reformism. Subsequently he was to become involved in two substantial research exercises designed to inform and render even more effective the work of the modern interventionist state: Beveridge's manpower survey in 1940, and the abortive Nuffield Reconstruction Survey of 1941 to 1943. Though unlike Laski he never entirely transferred his allegiances, remaining an often irascible dissenter to the end (Wright 1979), his intellectual career is a microcosm of the fate of the pluralism he expounded. The reasons for Cole's change of mind did not lie in any self-antagonistic logic within guild socialism: 'Cole's explanation or excuse', Beatrice Webb observed in her diary in 1928, was 'that post-war conditions do not admit of such revolutionary change ...' (quoted in M.I. Cole 1971: 161–2). But if one wanted to arrive at such conclusions, guild socialism was not a bad place to start from.

The outbreak of war in 1914 was followed by an undermining of traditional political argument. Some dispute was possible over the introduction of conscription. But the extension of central state power over the life and labour of the English people made many collectivist arguments seem superfluous, and most anti-statist ones futile. As Ernest Barker put it early in 1915, 'We have forgotten that we are anything but citizens, and the state is having its high midsummer of credit' (E. Barker 1915a: 121).

A sense of fait accompli made the whole debate seem unrelated to the realities of political life. By 1925 the old styles of political argument seemed to have moved aside, and they had been hurried on their way as a result of the experience of war. But the new forms of argument were not the creation of the war, any more than the war was the sole cause of the fading of the old. The change had been nurtured earlier and independently, and the war had only accentuated a change that was already and simultaneously occurring.

Group theory was characterized by enormous variety: for radicals, pluralism needed to be achieved; for conservatives it needed to be preserved. A reconciliation between collectivism and anti-statism had been provided by the various group and pluralist arguments of the last quarter of the nineteenth and the first quarter of the twentieth century. Pluralist arguments were advanced in opposition to central power, and commentators such as Ernest Barker and A.D. Lindsay saw them as part of a wider erosion of the centralized national state. But the conclusion of the pluralist episode was different, and in facilitating the subsiding of the clash between statist and anti-statist arguments allowed the state to slip out of political discourse and to become the greatest unstudied feature of twentieth-century British politics. Pluralism provided both a mediator between contesting opinions, and a nest for the cuckoo of the modern state.

But the legitimate offspring continued to inhabit the nest, or many of them did, albeit in an environment dominated by the usurper. The distributists were pushed off the branch and fell into the undergrowth of sectarianism. Other libertarian and communal impulses were assimilated within the state's confines, and whilst anarchism and the visions of Morris and Kropotkin might fade into ungrounded utopia, town planning and garden cities became part of the content of a directed policy of social reconstruction, and artistic revival grew out of revolutionary aestheticism. Class politics contributed to pluralism, but at the same time it made pluralism seem a means of accommodating social conflict. Activities which began as radical alternatives to the collectivizing state ended by providing improved means of pursuing existing activities within it.

This synthesis of opposing concerns on the middle ground of policy was reflected in both parliamentary politics and in political scholarship. The parties stopped arguing about the constitution or even about the right of individuals faced with conscription, and turned instead to housing, unemployment, education, health and the condition of the economy. At the same time social science – the 'new social science' as it has been called – was addressing itself to public policy and the development of middle-range normative policy studies, to utilizing the power of the state rather than to assessing or criticizing it (Soffer 1970). For pluralism involved an extension of the public and the political at the same time as it attempted a limitation of the state. The consequence was a proliferation of the state's functions accompanied both by a justification of functional devolution and of the prerogatives of the expert.

Accompanying this was a divorce between political philosophy and political science which Graham Wallas was already able to detect, and deplore, in May 1915 (Wallas 1915). The history of political argument after the first quarter of the century is not one of decline, but of transformation. In part this was a matter of the unifying themes being dissipated by proliferating specialisms. This was in part a feature of another change, the decline or disappearance of the occupationally non-aligned man of letters or intellectual, and the increasing dominance of political thinking by those whose profession it to some extent was, in particular teachers in the universities. One consequence of this was, as Collini puts it, that 'the intellectual, political, and fashionable circles of English society became less concentric by the early twentieth century' (Collini 1991: 21). Much was implied or assumed which previously had been asserted or contested. Nonetheless, argument, perception and belief, often on surprisingly traditional lines, was to remain an essential feature of English political life.

5 The pale of the constitution
The idea of citizenship

DEMOCRATS AND ELITISTS

Alarm, despair and defiance had been expressed in response to the
extensions of public power, and the growth of the state had been the
central and overshadowing fact for a vast body of political argument
throughout the latter part of the nineteenth and the early part of the
twentieth century. But there were other reasons why many people were
alarmed at the course of affairs in the half century which fell on either
side of 1900. Both the growing action of the state on the one hand, and
the extension of the franchise, the growth of popular parties, and the
proposals of social reformers, socialists and social radicals on the
other, implied a redistribution of power, wealth and status. In response
to this, criticism of the state was joined by criticism of democracy or as
it was frequently called, popular government. The two attacks, though
normally associated, were distinct.

There was nothing new in much of this criticism. The unfitness of
the masses for the exercise of power had been a theme running
throughout nineteenth-century discussion and Carlyle and Arnold,
Bagehot and James Stephen had all in their different ways contributed
to this tradition. Others too who did not reject democracy as a political
form looked to more select underlying arrangements to make the form
work. Mallock argued that 'in any great country pure democracy is
impossible' and that 'democracy is impossible unless the principle of
oligarchy is its concomitant' (Mallock 1918: 378). Despite Shaw's long
arguments with Mallock, this was not so different a principle from that
assumed by many of the early Fabians, and particularly by Shaw
himself. But these socialist elitists differed from elitists who attacked
democracy, both in their approval of the forms of popular government
and in their enthusiasm for the extension of state function which they
believed went with it. The tradition of democratic oligarchy

represented by Shaw saw most citizens as consumers of government. And just as the Webbs had dismissed producers' democracy, so Shaw rejected the possibility of citizens exercising politically productive power:

> A country governed by its people is as impossible as a theatre managed by its audience.... Government is a fine art requiring for its exercise not only certain specific talents and a taste for the business but a mental comprehensiveness and an energy which only a small percentage of people possess in the degree necessary for leadership.

(quoted in Chappelow 1969: 165)

This view, though a very Fabian one, was not limited to Fabians. It represented a form of elitism which was both diffuse and continued to flourish after the particular disquiets over the extension of the franchise had all but disappeared. For whilst it involved a low opinion of the masses, it also gave them a role in the political and electoral process. Other forms of elitism did not find even this passive role for the people.

Resistance to the extension of democracy was in some respects more specific than hostility to the state. This was because it centred around particular extensions of the franchise whereby between 1884 and 1918 Britain moved from being a nation where a minority of the adult population had the vote, to one where the majority did so. This was to undermine the arguments of opponents of democracy who increasingly did not have an existing set of arrangements to defend, but only a preference to assert. But in the meanwhile a rallying resistance to democracy was fostered by disquiet about other public policies. Amongst liberals, and particularly amongst those who became Liberal Unionists and opponents of Irish home rule after the crisis of 1886, there was a growing hostility to what was seen as the potential tyranny of the masses and the accompanying demagogy exemplified by national politicians such as the Liberal leader Gladstone. The support for home rule was seen as further proof of the follies to which a democratic electorate would commit the country. These years gave a brief intensity to criticisms of democracy. An assertion of traditional social and political hierarchies whose upper layers were characterized and distinguished by capacity and judgement was blended with a distaste for the people in the electoral mass, a conviction that this mass was unfitted by both intellectual inferiority and selfish and short-sighted materialism, for the exercise of political power or the influencing of public policy. This counter-attack involved a characterization of the citizen body and of those who were to be excluded from it and hence from the full exercise of political rights and powers. The objection was not simply to numbers, but to the inclusion within the political community of those who, it was felt, ought to be disqualified whatever the size of the citizen body. Aliens were obviously to be excluded. But the conception of what was foreign was extended to include not only those who were of foreign nationality, but those who appeared to be distinguished by race, culture or religion from what was taken as the British norm. This notion of the normal Englishman was used to draw a line not only between one race, culture or religion and another. It was also employed to exclude the poor, in a franchise with a property qualification, the dependent, when receipt of assistance from public funds carried the disenfranchising stigma of pauperism, and those who were seen as in their very social nature dependent, women. The ideal citizen was male, culturally English, and endowed with a degree of capital or income. He was neither foreign, nor poor, nor a pauper, nor a woman. But as the franchise was extended each of these barriers was in one way or another eroded. The lowering and removal of property qualifications included growing numbers of the poor. The provision of social services outside the Poor Law restricted the status of pauper. And the increasing political activity of women both within and without the conventional constitutional world of politics compelled a slow revision of the status of what William Thompson had, early in the nineteenth century, referred to as 'one half the human race'. Each of these erosions of the ramparts around the status of citizen was resisted, and none more rigidly so than that of the sexual disqualification.

The views of those who felt democracy and equality to be incompatible with liberty and quality were graphically expressed by Sir Henry Maine, who made both a conservative and a progressive case against popular government. Democracy, he argued, was an unstable form of government, and those who saw in it the way forward to a good or even a better society had no historical grounds for their optimism. This view of Maine's was in part a judgement against democracy, though it might be regarded also as a hopeful footnote to his dismay at the democratic advance. The dangerous folly could not last.

In so far as democracy worked, argued Maine, it was made to do so by party organization and by corruption. The first was a matter of wire-pulling and caucus management, a mechanization and manipulation of politics, and such motive force as it had was breathed into it by party spirit which made up in emotion and devotion what it lacked in intelligence or principle. It was in these conditions that demagogy developed, and that statesmen debased themselves in the flattery of the electorate. There was a touch of Coriolanus in much of this argument, and Maine observed that 'Democracy is Monarchy inverted, and the modes of addressing the multitude are the same as the modes of addressing Kings' (Maine 1885: 77). The second necessary prop to democracy was corruption, which was not so much a matter of individual venality (though in the United States it was) as of the bribery of the electorate through public works and policies designed to redistribute property. In consequence, democracy led to the further fault of trespass by the state beyond its principal functions of defence and the maintenance of lawful behaviour. In thus pushing government beyond its proper functions, democracy would become involved in social pillage unregulated by a consideration of the general well-being:

> If the mass of mankind were to make an attempt at redividing the common stock of good things, they would resemble, not a number of claimants insisting on the fair division of a fund, but a mutinous crew, feasting on a ship's provisions, gorging themselves on the meat and intoxicating themselves with the liquors, but refusing to navigate the vessel to port.
>
> (Maine 1885: 45–6)

The pillaging characteristic of democracy would destroy the basis of prosperity. The kinds of taxation on which a democracy would be likely to insist would kill the motive for creative work and would destroy or deaden, by taking their fruits, 'the springs of action called into activity by the strenuous and never ending struggle for existence, the beneficent private war which makes one man strive to climb on the shoulders of another and remain there through the law of the survival of the fittest' (ibid.: 50).

Popular government would stunt initiative and social progress in another way. People were not rational as supposed by the utilitarian advocates of democracy, and would not be guided by a full and intelligent perception of their interests. Worse, basing itself upon this irrational electorate, democracy would involve the ascendancy of average opinion and the chances were that 'in the long run, it would produce a mischievous form of Conservatism, and drug society with a potion compared with which Eldonine would be a salutary draught' (Maine 1885: 35). Popular opinion was reactionary and intolerant, and would stunt social and intellectual progress.

All that has made England famous, and all that has made England wealthy, has been the work of minorities, sometimes very small ones ... if for four centuries there had been a very widely extended franchise and a very large electoral body in this country, there would have been no reformation of religion, no change of dynasty, no toleration of Dissent, not even an accurate Calendar ... the gradual establishment of the masses in power is of the blackest omen for all legislation founded on scientific opinion, which requires tension of mind to understand it and self-denial to submit to it.

(ibid.: 97–8)

Maine's was thus a progressive and a conservative argument for oligarchy, and one which blended the case for limited government with an attack on democracy and a plea for innovation and tolerance.

Those who saw Irish home rule and a reckless extension of social reform without the penalties of pauperization as the fruits of democracy found a clear expression of their views in the writings of the lawyer A.V. Dicey. A part of the blame for what Dicey saw as the folly of Liberal policy towards Ireland lay, he believed, in the combination of an ignorant electorate with the operations of party machines to produce an influence on political life that was fickle, venal and tyrannical (Dicey 1913: xxviii–xxx). The harmful policies which had been pursued showed how carefully the benefits of full citizenship ought to be, and ought to have been, conferred. Citizenship and the exercise of a vote was not, Dicey argued, a right and should not be conceded in response to emotion or mere demand. It was a public function and ought not to be exercised by those who had a direct interest in its use by virtue of being dependants on the public purse. Dicey was writing at a time when the status of pauper, whereby recipients of public aid were excluded from citizenship, was being avoided by the provision of services such as old age pensions, school meals, medical inspection or publicly subsidized unemployment and health insurance, which carried no civil disabilities. To give old age pensions as they were being given after 1908 was, he argued, to extend the benefits of pauperism without extending its necessary, discouraging disadvantages.

The belief that citizenship was a responsibility which not all could or should be allowed to assume was a strong one. It was an assumption of those who defended the principles of deterrence embodied in the Poor Law, that dependence on the state should be limited by being made less attractive than the least pleasant condition normally attainable by independence and self-reliance. People in receipt of public assistance were dependent upon the citizen body and therefore must be firmly and clearly distinguished from it. This view that citizens should be independent and have no immediate personal financial interest in the state in whose government they participated was widely held. The young William Beveridge, who over thirty years later was to publish the report which bore his name on the social responsibilities of the state and the community, told the Sociological Society that the unemployed for whom, for whatever reason, work could not be found, 'must become the acknowledged dependants of the state, removed from free industry and maintained adequately in public institutions, but with the complete and permanent loss of all citizen rights – including not only the franchise but civil freedom and fatherhood' (Beveridge 1907: 327).

But though the opposition to these weakenings of the principle of citizenship as a privilege exercised and enjoyed by a minority of adults was continued by men such as Dicey well into the twentieth century and up to and beyond the outbreak of the First World War, others who shared his preferences had come to regard the advance of popular government as inevitable, and whilst not ceasing to deplore some of its consequences, no longer opposed its progress. W.E.H. Lecky in *Democracy and Liberty* in 1896 regretted the consequences of a spread of democracy which he did not believe could be resisted, yet which might in some respects both be brought under benign and improving influences, and even contribute to the quality of British political life. In this way Lecky was moving away from the oligarchy and hierarchy of men such as Maine and Dicey and towards, though not arriving at, the position of those such as Wallas who sought for ways of making democrats fit for democracy.

Unlike the oligarchic argument, the democratic argument against whose expression it reacted was muted by the end of the nineteenth century. This was not because it lacked strength or support, but rather the reverse. Its postulates had become implicit and ingrained in the assumptions of public discussion, and they provided the starting points for debates, rather than the goals of argument or the asserted, because contentious, general themes of discussion. The years after the Third Reform Act of 1884 were the tail end of the disputes and for the anti-democrats this involved a last-ditch resistance, but for the democrats it involved the quiescence which comes from satisfaction and acceptance. There was more concern, in the half century from 1875 to 1925, with the levelling down of the peaks of political power in the House of Lords, than with raising the base by extensions of the franchise.

CITIZENS, PEOPLE AND WOMEN

But there was a disjunction between the decline in the deliberate and vehement assertion of democratic principles, and the state of the franchise which still extended to less than 30 per cent of the adult population. Women were left largely out of account, and the criticism of their exclusion and the assertion of their claims to inclusion within the pale of the constitution meant that what was being vainly shored up from one side by the oligarchs, was being eroded on the other side by the feminists. Whilst attacks were being made on the extension of constitutional rights and of political participation to a larger section of the adult population, demands were being put which involved not simply a numerical extension of the franchise, but a reformulation of the notion of what constituted a citizen. Between 1905 and 1914 the movement to extend the vote to women developed a new vigour, but as was the case with the conventional democratic argument, the principles on which the feminist case rested had already been stated earlier in the nineteenth century (Lewis 1987; Caine 1992). John Stuart Mill in 1869 had put the case for equal freedom under law for men and women, and for ending the subjection of women to patriarchal domination. He had argued on the grounds both of individual and collective benefit, and of laissez-faire and self-government (Mill [1869] 1975). The force of Mill's egalitarian argument persisted in the work of other feminists, and Millicent Fawcett drew directly on Mill in her own statement of the case (in Theo Stanton, ed., *The Woman Question in Europe*, 1884, quoted in Rover 1967: 30; Fawcett 1912). Similarly W. Lyon Blease, in reply to Dicey's anti-feminism, based his argument on two points made by Mill: the need for enfranchisement in order that women's interests might be protected, and the essential function of complete citizen rights in providing people with the opportunity fully to develop their characters and capacities (Blease 1913). Keir Hardie employed the Mill argument that there were no good grounds for discriminating between women and men in the admission to the franchise (Hardie 1905, 1907: 61–70). Thus most feminist argument, like most conventional democratic argument, was by the end of the nineteenth century conducted in terms of 'common sense', arguing from existing practice or common existing assumptions. But if political conceptions about women were changing, this was accompanied by changes in other conceptions which had sustained the sexual monopoly of voting and the exclusion of women from national political life. The new 'common sense' had to displace an earlier and comprehensive perception of what was normal and central in social life, and in which women frequently had no place. What is involved in grasping the prevailing nineteenth-century notions, notions which continued into the twentieth century, is in the first place an imaginative rather than a logical leap from one world of common sense to another. Fenner Brockway wrote revealingly in 1967 'That women should vote is now so generally accepted that few of the post-war generation can appreciate the long and intense struggle before woman's right to political equality was recognised' (Rover 1967: v). As ever, the commonplace was the greatest defence against change – not what was considered essential, but what was considered obvious. There was a widespread assumption that there were citizens, who were male, adult and financially independent, and that there were also children and women, who were both deficient in the qualities which were needed for political activity and, as dependants, in a relation to male heads of family somewhat like that of paupers to the state. But women were unlike paupers, or aliens, or the unemployed, or any other group which was thought to be beyond or below the citizen body. For these groups were visible in their segregation, whereas women's exclusion was characterized by political invisibility. Their social identity was absorbed into that of their male patrons and guardians. It was this perception which Mill had in mind when he observed that the position of women 'is not felt to jar with modern civilization, any more than domestic slavery among the Greeks jarred with their notion of themselves as a free people' (Mill [1869] 1975: 434). The belief in the inferiority of women rested on more than overt argument and, as Mill pointed out, a recognition of this strengthened rather than weakened the convictions of the anti-feminists:

> For if it were accepted as a result of argument, the refutation of the argument might shake the solidity of the conviction; but when it rests solely on feeling, the worse it fares in argumentative contest, the more persuaded its adherents are that their feeling must have some deeper ground, which the arguments do not reach; and while the feeling remains, it is always throwing up fresh entrenchments of argument to repair any breach made in the old.

> (ibid.: 427)

Women were not envisaged when 'people' or 'Englishmen' of 'Britons' were spoken of. The characteristic of the prevailing conception of citizenship was not that it involved limitation by age and sex, but rather that it was given meaning by a series of specific and unquestioned assumptions about the social and economic character of the essential person. This person was taken to be male and adult, and in so far as this was not the case, then something less than a normal person was involved. This was not a matter of political preferences or values so much as of how the political world was seen.

This world was viewed with a perception of the normal member which excluded the majority of people. The smallest political unit was taken to be not the individual, nor even the person over the age of 21, but the adult male, with a subordinate and supporting family which constituted his private hinterland, was personal to him, and was cut off from the rest of society by him. As Frederic Harrison put it in 1893, 'Socially and morally considered, family groups are the smallest units into which social life can be resolved' (Harrison [1893] 1918: 34). So the adult male was the mediator between the members of his family and the larger world, and his dependants were, as James Mill had contended (Okin 1980: 201–2), fully represented for political purposes by him. The family constituted in an important sense his personality, and T.H. Green argued in his *Lectures on the Principles of Political Obligation* in 1879 that the

> formation of family life supposes ... that in the conception of his own good to which a man seeks to give reality there is included a conception of the well-being of others, connected with him by sexual relations or by relations which arise out of these. He must conceive of the well-being of these others as a permanent object bound up with his own.
>
> (Green 1886: 539)

Given such a perception of society and its components it required no argument to deny political rights to women, since women were both excluded by a common-sense view of things which saw them as something other than the individual units of which society was constructed, and included in the social existence of males and hence incapable of distinctive social action or representation. The point is not that women were accorded low status, but that they were frequently ignored. They were, in the neat terminology of sociology, socially invisible. Discussions of citizenship assumed that citizens were male, and this assumption, being an element of perception rather than of belief, was not argued but was rather the foundation on which arguments were built. There are good reasons for expecting that a different perception would have been associated with the arguments of individualism. Individualism was a doctrine which seemed capable of macerating the tissue of institutions and corporations, leaving only the solitary persons within. Certainly some individualist thought did adopt feminist positions, and the arguments of Wordsworth Donisthorpe and

Auberon Herbert in particular illustrate how close to each other individualism and feminism could come. Sir Henry Maine in 1875 had written that the diffusion of property had assisted women through encouraging 'the substitution of individual human beings for compact groups of human beings as the units of society' (*The Early History of Institutions*, 327, quoted in Roach 1957: 77). Herbert Spencer himself, in the first edition of *Social Statistics*, had envisaged the ultimate erosion of the contemporary form of the family by the establishment of equal freedom for both women and children (Spencer 1851). But even before these early indiscretions had been silently removed from the 1892 edition, Spencer's writing was reflecting the more conventional view. In 1884 he wrote of the problems which the citizen, assumed to be male, could face in his 'domestic experiences' when attempting to manage wife, children and servants. Adultery was indeed, in these terms, a form of trespass (Spencer [1884] 1969: 167).

Individualism thus became a kind of patriarchal familialism, taking its precise meanings from the prevailing tone of social perceptions. These perceptions were not particular to one view or doctrine, but informed individualists and collectivists, pamphleteers and politicians, novelists and judges. In the important suffrage case of Chorlton v. Lings in 1868, the *obiter dicta* of one of the judges, Willes J., illustrated how courteous deference set women outside what was thought of as normal adult society: 'the exemption from voting was founded upon motives of decorum and was a privilege of the sex' (quoted in Fulford 1957: 58). In Lady Sandhurst's case in 1889, and de Souza v. Cobden in 1891 the courts declined to consider women as 'persons', displaying, as Sachs has put it, 'partiality that was all the stronger for being unconscious, and that objectively assisted one side to a dispute against the other in a manner structured by the way in which the issue was classified' (Sachs 1976: 115).

The seeming deference displayed by Willes J. was part of a set of assumptions with very different practical consequences. As D.G. Ritchie observed in 1889, there was a contrast between rhetoric and function in 'a worship that professes to exalt woman – whether the Madonna or *das Ewig-Weibliche* – above man, combined with a refusal of rationality that sinks her beneath him' (Ritchie 1895: 70). But whatever the justification, women were not perceived as part of the adult world, and discussion of general humanity was assumed to refer to men. G.K. Chesterton, writing in 1910, complained that the social proposals of writers such as Morris and Wells would take away from 'the ordinary Englishman ... the little that remains of his dignity as a householder and the head of a family' (Chesterton [1910] 1912: 73).

The propagandist Horatio Bottomley attacked socialism because, amongst other things, 'in future it will not be my wife or your wife but our wife' (quoted in Fulford 1957: 93). That it might mean 'our husband' was beyond the pale of perception. And at the moment when some of the sexual discrimination in politics seemed about to be ended, at the close of the First World War, posters unwittingly delivered the fundamental insult of 'The Nation thanks the Women' (quoted in Rover 1967: 209). Women, in other words, were seen as coming to the help of a nation to which they were as external as colonial levies.

When women emerged from this perceptual blankness, they did so into a role which both distinguished and excluded them from the 'normal' concerns of the 'real world'. In so far as the family and the home were viewed as their special sphere of competence, this sphere was treated, however courteously, as something different from the essential work of the world and the business of society. Women were different and, in the important things, inferior. As T.H. Huxley put it, in 'every excellent character, whether mental or physical, the average woman is inferior to the average man, in the sense of having that character less in quantity and lower in quality' (quoted in Fulford 1957: 66). It required no special argument to believe that, as Green said, woman stood in relation to man as servant to master or child to parent (Green 1886: 536–7); it was a matter of common sense. Even when the belief in inferiority was not so baldly stated as it was by Huxley, the assumption of special spheres with all that followed from this was made in the most radical discourses. M.D. O'Brien, a vigorous individualist who had some radical things to say about the independence of women and of the equal responsibility of both male and female parents for the upbringing of children, nonetheless was convinced that 'The natural functions of women ... lie inside the family.... In proportion as she fails to perform these functions she stultifies herself and passes unperfected through this world of time' (O'Brien 1893: 215). 'No need to go to Girton College to learn what they are. Plainly, and without any gloss; they are the conception, birth and training of children, in conformity to the laws of Nature, and by means of that domestic and only natural organization; the home: the family circle: the highest and purest flower of the infinite' (ibid.: 213). It was on the question of the family, and of the conventional sexual roles of men and women, that O'Brien was led to attack, almost to harass, Edward Carpenter (Rowbotham 1977a: 88–91). Frederic Harrison, in a similar eulogy, also gave the game away in the final accolade:

What is the inspiring force – the genius of the Home? The instinct of mankind, the hearts of us all, poetry, art, the commonplaces of ordinary speech with one voice answer the question with the name of Woman! – the mother, the wife, the sister, the daughter, the serving maid.

(Harrison [1893] 1918: 42–3)

Similar assumptions occur in the work of socialists such as William Morris and Robert Blatchford. Despite his suggesting on occasion that domestic work might be shared (Thompson 1977: 707), in Morris's *News from Nowhere* the main business of work and conversation is done by the men, most of the women serving and waiting, on the periphery of the action. In the utopian society portrayed by Morris women do the housework because they are better at it than the men and because they enjoy it, and housework and the bearing of children are for the first time properly and highly valued (Morris [1890] 1924: 69–71). Similarly in Blatchford's *Merrie England*, the drudgery is taken out of cooking, cleaning, waiting and rearing children by the collective and communal performance of these tasks – by women (Blatchford 1894). Kropotkin argued that technical progress would eliminate the drudgery of housework, thus liberating women (Woodcock and Avakumovic 1950: 321). Even an ostensibly progressive ally of feminism like H.G. Wells could write in 1903 of the need to ensure that the minimum wage for a civilized adult male should be sufficient to cover the rent of the 'minimum tenement permissible with three or four children, the maintenance of himself and his wife and children ... and a certain margin for the exercise of his individual freedom' (Wells [1903] 1906: 48).

These general social conceptions gave detail and form to more abstract political values. At the same time the precise articulation of these values in developing a view of politics which left women beyond the pale strengthened women's exclusion. When discussion of political representation invoked the representation of occupations and interests, those were either the occupations and interests of men, or occupations and interests in which, though women had a part, they were socially invisible. The care of young children in the event of accident or illness was a profession and an occupation; their care in moderate health was assumed not to be. When the principle invoked was that of radical individualism, women were frequently once again defined out because though viewed necessarily as biological human units, they were not seen as social or political ones.

In the later nineteenth and early twentieth centuries, the debate over women's suffrage caused a slow change in the views which sustained women's exclusion. Eventually the concept of citizenship was to alter in order that it might include women, and this change came about not by any direct modification of the notion of citizenship itself, but by a change in the social and economic perceptions within which it was applied.

The first stage of this change was the articulation of assumptions which up until then had been largely unexpressed, and which had drawn most of their force from their status as commonplaces of perception rather than of value. But because the feminist claim involved a challenge to such fundamental conceptions, the first resistance to it was not a rational one, but the response naturally given to any statement which flies in the face of the 'obvious': dismay, ridicule, shock. As J.S. Mill observed when introducing his amendment to the 1867 Reform Bill, 'the reasons which custom is in the habit of giving for itself on this subject are usually very brief: that, indeed, is one of my difficulties' (H.C. Debates 3 ser., vol. 187, c. 819, quoted in Rover 1967: 38). The stigmatization of an argument as trivial, absurd or risible is not itself a trivial response, and should not be treated as such by those who wish to understand a political argument. An incident quoted by Strachey is illuminating here:

> Amid considerable laughter the Clerk announced that he had received a communication from the National Society for Women's Suffrage, wanting the Board to adopt a petition in favour of female enfranchisement. Mr. Bell: You must get Miss Becker to come. Mr. John Haworth: I move that all women stop at home and mind their own business (laughter). The Chairman: Can you manage to keep your own at home? (laughter). No reply was given and the subject was dropped.
>
> (*Accrington Times*, 13 April 1872, quoted in Strachey 1974: 265)

In a similar vein the title applied to the militant supporters of the suffrage, the WSPU, employed the diminutive form, 'Suffragette', and it was a favourite device of cartoonists to portray female supports of the suffrage as embittered spinsters who were simply sublimating their frustration at failing in woman's chief task: the attraction of a husband. In more sober terms, Dicey could argue as one of the objections to votes for women that it would lead to demands for wider sexual equality and to women in the cabinet and on the judicial bench. The further demand was presumed evidently ridiculous, and hence could be used to discredit the more limited proposal (Dicey 1909: 62).

At this stage of the argument the opposition to feminism consisted of a restatement, or sometimes of a statement for the first time, of the grounds on which the perceptual exclusion of women rested. Principles could be contested but they could not be sustained by argument, since they themselves constituted the grounds of the argument. But their articulation made them more vulnerable than they had been when they were dormant. Speaker Lowther's ruling in the House of Commons in 1913 that a women's suffrage amendment to the government's franchise bill would so alter the bill as to make it necessary to withdraw it and begin again, entailed the assumption that to add women to the electoral roll in however small numbers was not primarily a matter of increasing the size of the electorate, but involved a qualitative change of great constitutional significance. In general, however, the parliamentary debate which accompanied the Liberal government of 1905–15 involved an increasingly expanded expression of the perception baldly stated by Lowther. The reasons advanced by W.R. Cremer in the Commons in 1906, whilst not forming a coherent argument for withholding the vote from women, presented a fine sketch of a way of seeing adult females which disqualified them from being perceived as political persons. First, argued Cremer, women were not breadwinners and did not understand the responsibilities of life. Second, deference towards women prevented an imposition upon them of the onerous and distasteful responsibilities of the real world. Third, women were frivolous and irrational, and fourth the decorum which existed between the sexes would inhibit free political debate and controversy (Strachey 1928: 298–9). Scientific opinion was on hand to prove that women who strayed outside their natural sphere though excessive education would damage their peculiar feminine constitution. Educated women tended to madness, and both a physical and an intellectual incapacity for motherhood was the awful consequence of too much ambition (Dyhouse 1976). This argument was developed at length and with vehemence by Sir Almroth Wright in *The Unexpurgated Case Against Women Suffrage*. Women, declared Wright, were morally, intellectually and physically inferior, and even their apparent virtues often did no more than reflect male influence. There might have been an appearance of progress, but this was superficial:

> If to move about more freely, to read more freely, to speak out her mind more freely, and to have emancipated herself from traditionary beliefs – and, I would add, traditionary ethics – is to have advanced, woman has indubitably advanced.

But the educated native too has advanced in all these respects; and he also tells us that he is pulling up level with the white man.

(Wright 1913: 40)

In often similar tones and with warm words for Wright, Belfort Bax, Morris's and Hyndman's former colleague, inveighed against a tide of feminist deceit designed to preserve and increase female privileges, and lead to the subordination of the male. He appealed to sympathizers with the feminist case 'to view with contempt and abhorrence the mass of disingenuous falsehood and transparent subterfuge, which the votaries of Feminism systematically seek to palm off' (Bax 1913: 175). So great was Bax's antipathy that he could scarcely bring himself to contemplate the spectacle of women insisting on these things for themselves, and generally referred to the feminist as 'he', interposing a misguided but essentially sound patron between the author and the object of his alarm.

But the obvious did not need stating, and lost status when it was thus presented. The main obstacle to the feminist argument lay not in the reasons advanced by opponents nor in the fluctuating state of parliamentary majorities, but in the perceptual terms in which the campaign had initially to be conducted. When these terms could no longer be assumed, and when the opposition moved to arguing the case against enfranchisement, the principal obstacle had been overcome. The fact that the dangers of clerical influence, or of emotion and hysteria, or of an electorate the majority of whom were unable to sustain the empire or insist on their wishes by the ultimate sanction of force, or of the disruption of the home and of the unity of family life, were being put forward meant that women were already on the agenda, and that the principal though not the sole obstacle to their advance into electoral rights had been removed.

Thus whilst the conception of democratic citizenship was being challenged by the elitists, it was being applied from a very different point of view by the supporters of female suffrage. This was appropriate at a time when the state was recognizing and dealing with more and more of its subjects and treating more and more people as directly subject to it. Its provision of services and its role of over-parent was involving it with women and children directly as well as with families through the head of the family. Familialism was breached at a time when the state was looking beyond the paterfamilias. Such direct dealing was not possible if the social unit were assumed to be the headed family, and in this sense the modern British state would be barely conceivable without some more advanced position for women. At the same time the recognition of the importance of individual wellbeing for collective security and prosperity began the mobilization of the population as an aggregate of individuals well before the legal and deliberate conscription and recruitment of people in the military and civilian war effort after 1914. The war then involved adults and children on a spectacular scale. It came to be seen as impossible to avoid giving the vote to male service personnel and as possible to accede to some of the demands of the feminists. This individualization of the population was a consequence both of collectivism, as the state dealt with categories and persons rather than only with ordered groups through those groups' hierarchies, and of libertarian resistance to collectivism. Individualists had asked whom so-called protective legislation was protecting and W.E.H. Lecky, who did not look on the expanding state with any great enthusiasm, was a founding member of the Freedom of Labour Defence, an organization which resisted further regulation of women's work, observing that protective legislation might protect not the welfare of women but the vested interests of men (Lecky 1896). Auberon Herbert, similarly, was associated with Josephine Butler in campaigns against the regulation of women both at work and under the Contagious Diseases Acts.

THE BROADER AGENDA OF EDWARDIAN FEMINISM

Because the opposition to feminism rested on social and cultural perceptions at least as much as on political arguments, any articulation of the feminist claim needed, correspondingly, to question not only women's constitutional status but their social and cultural situation as well. The Edwardian campaign for the suffrage thus took in, in addition to the demand for the vote, an argument about the economic position of women, about marriage, about the distribution of power and responsibility within the domestic household, and about the broad range of authority and power distributed along the divide of gender. The suffrage feminism of the pre-1914 years, if for no other reason than the location and character of the opposition it aroused, involved amongst other things the depiction of men as the enemy, and an assumption that the achievement of the vote would lead to a general removal of the oppression of women. Even so moderate, in its feminism as in much else, an organization as the Fabian Society could be the source of such broad ambition for women. The modern feminist 'wants work, she wants the control of her own financial position, and she wants education and the right to take part in the human activities of the State, but at the same time she is no longer willing to be shut out from marriage and motherhood' (M.A. [Mabel Atkinson] 1914 Fabian Tract 'The Economic Foundations of the Women's Movement', quoted in Alexander 1988: 9).

So when the novelist and journalist Rebecca West said that she did not know what feminism was, but that men always accused her of it whenever she refused to behave as a doormat, she was doing more than make a political joke. She was pointing out the possible subversive ramifications of feminism for the whole distribution of status and power between the sexes (Spender 1983). And because Edwardian feminism questioned the status of women as such, and not just their constitutional position, its political methods could frequently call into question assumptions of what political action consisted of, and of what forms of protest and propaganda could, and could not, be used by citizens to pursue their causes.

Not only did the campaign for the suffrage involve a consideration of other aspects of the inequalities between men and women, but the vote itself was never the self-sufficient end of the suffrage feminists (Dyhouse 1989). Whilst full participation in the political life of citizenship was valued and sought after, membership of the political community was seen also as a means to secure or defend the economic and social, the educational and domestic, rights and interests of women.

The heritage of John Stuart Mill and his essay *On the Subjection of Women* is ambivalent here. Mill's depiction was of an essentially legal and constitutional inequality, but one which had wider social consequences, and one whose rectification would, equally, not be confined to the legal and constitutional sphere. On the other hand, as critics such as Okin and Pateman have pointed out (Okin 1980; Pateman 1983a), Mill assumed also that once legal and constitutional inequalities and privileges were brought to an end, marriage would be for most women a 'natural' choice and one involving responsibilities of a different kind from those which marriage devolved onto men. For women it would be a choice of voluntary domestic responsibility and the provision of domestic services.

The arguments of Olive Schreiner in *Woman and Labour* in 1911 (Schreiner [1911] 1978) mark a break with this tradition. Schreiner argued not only for equal treatment of males and females in the world of paid employment, but also for an equal sharing of domestic responsibilities between the sexes. She regarded inequalities in the former sphere as deriving from inequalities in the later, a carry-over, a 'remnant of a past condition of society' (ibid.: 24). For Schreiner an end to sexual inequality thus involved changes in the character of both sexes, a new woman but also a new man.

The attention paid by historians to the campaign for the vote has sometimes drawn consideration away from other aspects of Edwardian feminism, where the gradations of radicalism were not necessarily the same as the differences in campaigning tactics in pursuit of the ballot. The tactical radicalism of the WSPU, the organization led by the Pankhursts, was not necessarily matched by radicalism in the analysis of the social condition of women, which was frequently discussed in ways more subversive of the existing sexual order by those whose campaigning style was more conventional. To that extent Edwardian feminism divided over the issue of the domestic work of women, and the extent to which differences between the sexes were essential and unchangeable, and the extent to which they were cultural.

A feminist analysis of the relations between the sexes within the marital household which caused much controversy at the time of its publication, but which was relatively mild in its domestic analysis, was Christabel Pankhurst's *The Great Scourge* (Pankhurst 1913). A married woman undertook a massive portmanteau of responsibilities which far outweighed any maintenance she received from her husband, and yet was denied any financial reward.

> It is not as though a married woman does not earn her keep by the work she does. Here are some of the avocations which married women pursue: cooking, laundry work, dressmaking, marketing, mending, scrubbing and cleansing, bathing, dressing and general care of infants, house-management, sick-nursing, social entertaining, husband's career-making.
>
> (Pankhurst 1913: 115–16)

On the other hand the conception of social and domestic life put out by the WSPU tended to be conventional, if puritanical. Emmeline Pankhurst stressed both the naturalness and the importance of the conventional home (Holton 1987: 23–4) just as Christabel's argument, in *The Great Scourge*, is not for the abolition of the domestic divide, but for its proper valuation. In a similar vein Lady McLaren's *Women's Charter of Rights and Liberties* argued that wages should be paid for housework to the equivalent of what would have been earned had the services been bought on the market (Garner 1984: 15).

The more radical position was to see conventional marriage itself as a feature of women's oppression, and to argue not that the free and equal woman would be properly valued in the family home, but that she would probably choose not to accept any specially 'female' role within it in the first place. Dora Marsden, in her journal *The Freewoman*, argued in 1911 that 'though some men might be servants, all women are servants, and all the masters are men. That is the difference and distinction. The servile condition is common to all women' (Garner 1984: 65). In contrast to the demand for wages for housework, feminists on *The Freewoman* opposed the education of women in domestic tasks on the grounds that such schemes 'aim at perpetuating women's inferiority by perfecting her in a role which puts the greatest difficulties in the way of her development' (Garner 1984: 71). A more sustained analysis was set out by Cicely Hamilton, in *Marriage as a Trade*, written in 1909 (Hamilton [1909] 1981). As a trade into which their lack of economic power or opportunity forced most women, marriage, argued Hamilton, was not a relationship but a job, involving the care of husband and children and the assumption of general responsibility for a household. It was a trade, a way of making a living, but the absence of any better opportunities, in fact the absence in many cases of any opportunities at all, forced women into it. It was thus not so much unequal for men and for women, as completely different in what it involved for the two sexes. Marriage was the culmination of the unequal economic bargain whereby the subordination of women is perpetuated. It was the least bad of the various bad economic offers available to women. And because marriage had become established as the principal trade for women, they were trained and educated for little else, and thus became even more dependent upon it.

Hamilton might observe that 'I have no intention of attacking the institution of marriage in itself – the life companionship of man and woman; I merely wish to point out that there are grave disadvantages attaching to that institution as it exists to-day' (Hamilton [1909] 1981: 18) and suggest that the human male will someday 'discover that woman does not support life only in order to obtain a husband, but frequently obtains a husband only in order to support life' (Hamilton [1909] 1981: 25). But it was clear that for the foreseeable future, marriage was condemned as the quintessence of women's inequality.

The Act of 1918 marked a pause but not a conclusion in the debate over democracy and citizenship. The immediate spurs to the resistance had been enfranchisement and, less directly, Irish home rule. The one was partly completed in 1918, the other in 1922. Neither demand was met in its entirety. But despite the granting of only a limited franchise to women, Dicey's fear of an ever-broadening wedge of feminism seemed an inaccurate premonition of the following forty years. The exclusion of women from the legal perception of a 'person' was not ended until the Privy Council judgment in the Canadian Senate case of 1929. Within two years of this limited concession the socialist and historian R.H. Tawney felt able to write that whilst class remained a salient division in Britain, sex did not, for 'men and women are treated as political and economic equals' (Tawney 1931: 64). This assumption that feminism had been no more than a transient argument for the vote was given some credence by the fading away of any general discussion of democratic politics. At the same time the discussion of democracy declined, and the term became used as one of broad approval for open and popular regimes, rather than as an instrument in a particular discussion of British political arrangements (for example, Brown 1920). As Harold Laski observed in 1925, 'For Western Europe, at least, democratic government has become a commonplace beyond discussion' (Laski 1925: 16).

But whilst the limited enfranchisement of women in 1918 brought an end to the franchise campaign, the broader feminist case continued to be argued. Feminists such as Vera Brittain and Winifred Holtby continued to argue for the equal rights which they considered still to be a long way off (Banks 1993: 15). One of the most eloquent arguments for a comprehensive feminism was put in 1938 by Virginia Woolf in *Three Guineas.* The educational and employment discrimination suffered by women was all of a piece, Woolf argued, with the belligerence of international relations and the pomposity of public life. An end to sexual inequality would achieve not just the emancipation of women, but a far wider social and political transformation (Woolf [1938] 1993).

It was appropriate that women should be entering the pale of citizenship at a time when the political representation of citizens as equal and identical units was being challenged by pluralists for its abstraction from the reality of social life. For whilst on the one hand individualism could dissolve the family as the ultimate unit into which the political order could be broken down, women were a category or group for whom paternalist, familial individualism had hardly catered at all and who, more than any other group, suffered from the form of representation which pluralists like Figgis criticized. So long as it was assumed that individual interests were simply particular, but not partial, reflections of a single public interest, and that the interest of any one individual was similar in essential points to that of any other individual, a number of arguments could be sustained. It was not necessary to take particular note of groups, categories or classes in the representative or political process whilst, paradoxically it might seem, certain individuals or categories could be excluded from politics because of their unfitness to perceive, as well as could their superiors, the common good. If on the other hand people gained their social identity from their particular social position rather than in any uniform or universal manner, then the possibility of a variety of interests was introduced and it became difficult to assert that women were adequately represented, or in any sense represented, by husbands or fathers. The act of 1918 did not therefore bring feminist political argument to an end, even though the forms which it would take were not always a simple or obvious continuation of the political thinking of the pre-1914 era.

NATION, CLASS AND THE STYLE OF POLITICS

A similar argument to that which applied in the case of sexual groups applied in the case of functional or national ones. The argument for a specific trade union or industrial working-class interest which required at least a separate party in Parliament and, more radically, some form of participation in politics peculiar to itself, was parallelled by nationalist arguments in Wales and in Ireland. In one sense nationalism was no more than a proposal to alter the geographical boundaries of the state and to withdraw certain areas and their inhabitants from the competence of one state and place them under that of another. But it was also a statement about the nature of political community, and of the cultural qualifications for citizenship. To the arguments of sex and occupation was added that of national identity, advancing a principle which was absolute and uncompromising. As the Welsh nationalist Saunders Lewis put it in 1936, 'a nation, its language, its literature, its separate traditions' were amongst 'the truly sacred things in Creation' (Jones and Thomas 1973: 122). This nationalism was assertive, in the case of Ireland, and defensive, in the case of England. In England the notion of the 'ordinary' or 'normal' citizen, which had at various times left out of account women, children and paupers, was applied to exclude those who either by race or culture could be termed alien. A muted and diffuse anti-Semitism pervaded much political speaking and writing in the early part of the twentieth century. In the labour and socialist movement it could be expressed as a form of anti-capitalism, in the work of populists like Chesterton or Belloc it could be a mixture of nationalism and anti-plutocracy, in the politics of the Conservative Party it formed part of the xenophobia which issued in measures like the 1905 Aliens Act. Lord Hardwicke told Parliament in 1898 that if the 'alien element' in the poorer classes were allowed to increase, it would mean 'that these classes would become to a great extent non-English in character, and that, both in physique and in moral and social customs, they had fallen below our present by no means elevated standard' (quoted in Foot 1965: 87).

The challenge made by and on behalf of the constitutionally invisible involved more than a revision of accepted perceptions of who were and who were not political persons. It involved also, though to a lesser extent, a revision of or an addition to accepted conceptions of appropriate political actions and methods. What the female feminists did was not seen as political in terms of prevailing conceptions, because women were themselves not considered as political persons. There was no category 'women' which was seen as relevant in political discussion, and in so far as women were analysed out of the adult population, and seen as distinct, it was in order to emphasize their peripheral political position. By breaking away from expected forms of behaviour, by committing violence against property, becoming the objects of police and (male) mob violence, and by attracting violence to themselves through the hunger strike, women created a tension within the perceptions which excluded them. To this extent the novel methods of the suffragettes were an important, indeed a necessary, part of their argument, not because they added the argument of force to the force of argument, but because in a very special form of propaganda by the deed they shattered the prevailing and limiting conceptions of 'women' and 'citizens'. Far more than anarchists such as Kropotkin, who theorized about propaganda by deed, feminists developed this form of argument in the only way in which, given its own account of the activity in which it was engaged, it could be articulated or developed. Sachs has suggested that by breaching the decorum of the courts and refusing to recognize their authority, 'women declared in word and action that they would not be bound by a constitution that refused to accord to them the status of being persons in public life' (Sachs 1976: 130). But more was involved than a simple withdrawal of allegiance. An assault was being made on a view of the world which sustained the political subordination of women.

In the case of syndicalism, forms of political action such as the strike and the assertion of the identity of new groups were related. If trade unionists, or industrial workers, were not represented as such by parliamentary politics, then when they did act politically as industrial workers rather than as citizens voting in a geographical constituency, methods of political action other than representative or parliamentary methods might be appropriate. One alternative was simply representative politics with functional rather than with geographical constituencies. Another was some form of direct action which employed methods peculiarly available to people as members of a particular functional group.

For groups or classes within a national society direct action might arise out of a failure of representation which was in no way a necessary feature of the representative system, or which could be remedied. Women could be enfranchised. For groups which believed themselves to constitute a nation or the vanguard of a nation within an existing national society, representative politics within that larger society were necessarily inadequate, and the road to direct action was less escapable. In Ireland the tactic of Sinn Fein, 'ourselves alone', involved a withdrawal of consent from both the power and the authority of the larger state, and the attempt to begin the new world here and now. Such a tactic was appropriate to a group which saw its identity in communal terms.

So various forms of direct action were employed, by feminists, syndicalists and nationalists, at a time when proposals to extend the franchise were arousing expectations which representative politics could not meet. The arousal of those expectations exacerbated feminist direct action; the frustration of those expectations exacerbated industrial and nationalist direct action. So discussion of the forms of popular government was shifting away from the question of universal franchise towards the examination of those kinds of representation which might be complementary or alternative to a majoritarian form of popular government. This move towards pluralism had two aspects: pluralism as a form of representation, and pluralism as direct action, an alternative to all forms of representation and an attempt, by fragmentation, to return to the conditions of direct communal democracy. The discussion of the adequacy of the franchise thus raised not only the question of the proper limits and extension of democracy, but the additional or alternative character of group representation and of direct rather than representative politics.

Such attempts to extend or improve upon democracy were only one part of the continuing discussion, however. After the end of the First World War, discussion of the distribution of political power took two main forms: on the one hand the discussion of forms of participation beyond and/or in elaboration of representative democracy; on the other, the elaboration of political arguments which preserved or developed elitist assumptions by means other than the restriction of the franchise. One direction which this elitism took was the aristocratic rejection of popular politics and of parliamentary and democratic methods to a point where the views advanced were only incidentally political. The other was the development of elitist arguments within the structure of the popular democratic state, in the form of advocacy of elites of experts of one kind and another. The notion of expertise had already been encouraged by pluralism with its conception of specialized interests and areas of competence, whilst many collectivists had envisaged a growing role for the trained or specially skilled person. For Shaw it was either the new technician in the form of, 'Enry Straker, or the new industrialist in the form of Andrew Undershaft. Wells had his samurai, and even Kipling's empire had its engineers and pioneers.

6 Accommodations to the modern state

Political ideas in the second quarter of the twentieth century

THE PRESENCE OF THE MODERN STATE

Looking back on his youth Lord Bryce observed that the earlier generation 'busied itself with institutions; this generation is bent rather upon the purposes which institutions may be made to serve' (quoted in Fisher 1927, vol. 2: 268). It was a pertinent comment. During the second quarter of the twentieth century there was a different emphasis in political argument. Champions and opponents of the state, of libertarianism, of democracy or of oligarchy all seemed to have less to say, and to utter what they did say in ways which were both muted and indirect. There was an accommodation to state collectivism, less discussion in general terms of whether or not the responsibilities and powers of the state ought to be increased, and more argument about how the acknowledged strength of the modern state ought to be employed. The dominating political arguments of the second quarter of the century were about the character of public policy, and of how the state should use its powers, not about what powers it should have. The sheer weight of the state might have induced a sense of powerlessness amongst those who in earlier and more fluid times might have criticized or praised it, whilst those who had earlier argued for various forms of state collectivism now no longer saw the need to do so. The essential point had perhaps been won, and what was now appropriate was to pursue its implications. By the end of the Second World War these implications were overwhelming, and involved a general commitment to a degree of public responsibility for economic management and social services which would have seemed substantial to many socialists in the 1930s.

Given this commitment, extensions of state power which would previously have been controversial were now pursued as little more than practical necessities. As the Labour Party leader Clement Attlee pointed out in a letter to Harold Laski in 1944, 'the acceptance of the doctrines of abundance, of full employment and of social security require the transfer to public ownership of certain major economic forces and the planned control in the public interest of many other economic activities' (quoted in Martin 1953: 161). But whilst Attlee found this development heartening, it was not a victory for socialism. The policy of economic demand management by the state, which Keynes had developed with little impact on public policy before the war, rapidly became the new financial orthodoxy once the war had begun. But the intention of Keynes's prescriptions was to sustain and cultivate capitalism, not to overthrow or supersede it. Similarly with the ever-broadening commitment of the state in the social services, epitomized in the wartime report of William Beveridge. In terms very similar to those used by Attlee, Beveridge wrote in 1944 that full employment 'cannot be won and held without a great extension of the responsibilities and powers of the State exercised through organs of the central Government . . . . To ask for full employment while objecting to these extensions of State activity is to will the end and refuse the means' (Beveridge 1944: 36). The 1944 report recommended a rationalizing of the state services so as to provide 'a comprehensive scheme of social insurance', a policy which, whilst socialists might support it as an improvement or for tactical reasons, was neither a radical departure from existing procedures nor an attack on the existing distribution of wealth or power. Nonetheless the logic which Spencer had feared was clear. It was expressed in the practices of politics and government, and it meant that an extension of state activity which had earlier been considered a contentious breach of strongly held principles, now became simply a technical, instrumental means of seeking widely accepted goals. At the end of the nineteenth century the state could still be regarded as something external to the ordinary lives of its citizens, an institution whose actions could be seen as intrusions into an autonomous social or private sphere and one which could be resisted or even simply ignored. By the beginning of the second quarter of the twentieth century the state had already become involved in all those activities which previously had characterized the areas of life set apart from it: the provision of housing, getting a living when unemployed, the nutrition and medical care of children, the regulation of industrial relations and disputes, the securing of an income, or a part of an income, in old age.

By the end of the second quarter of the century the state had assumed a responsibility for its citizens 'from the cradle to the grave'. Life at work and life in the family were increasingly lived not only under the regulation of the state, but with its assistance. Simply to go about one's affairs involved, far from having nothing to do with the state, having everything to do with it. The very same activities which previously would have involved separateness, now involved absorption. The increasing acceptance of social service responsibilities by the state precluded traditional debates, since the state was no longer so much a restrainer, interferer or governor, as a provider, benefactor or at the very least a contractual supplier of services and goods. In the one case it was beneficent, in the other it was not a threat because citizens could be seen to stand in a contractual relationship to it and could criticize and demand its attentions, even if the contract was more like a marriage than a free bargain. But whatever the nature of the claim which citizens felt they had upon the state, it made it increasingly difficult to express the kind of resentment at the mere fact of state activity which Stephen Reynolds had sometimes recorded. When a similar attempt to Reynolds's portrait of the working class was made by George Orwell in the 1930s, the complaint was not of the interference of the state, but of its incompetence. In these circumstances overt radical anti-statism, though it persisted, did so in isolated and sectarian forms. Much of its energy had been diverted into partisan anti-socialism, and what remained was scattered and had little impact. Chesterton and the Distributist League carried on but when Father McNabb debated with John Strachey on behalf of the League in 1937, he was indicating the persistence rather than the vitality of his cause. A.M. Ludovici, a prolific propagandist for a re-established paternal elitism (Greenleaf 1983b: 218–19), who had been one of the *New Age*'s 'Nietzscheans' (Mairet 1936: 50) and whose energies, and writings, ran from before the First World War until after the Second, flailed publicly organized and provided social reform as sapping the vital energies of the populace, called for a new and enforced responsibility in the exercise of the beneficial rights of private property, and deplored 'the modern stampede in favour of Democracy and Feminism' (Ludovici 1932, 1923: 363). Ernest Benn, reasserting well-established principles of libertarianism and laissez faire, particularly in the economic world, found himself 'in a world most of which is strange and much of which is repugnant to me'. He was, he wrote, 'an unrepentant believer in private enterprise', and he vigorously and frequently defended the benefits both to the country and to himself of that system: 'I am, in fact, the sort of person against whom the whole of the Socialist propaganda seems to be launched and, when I listen to current political discussion, I find myself regarded not only as a superfluity but as a bar to progress, as one of the causes of poverty, want, and distress' (Benn 1946: 6; 1925: 19, 9). Benn's attack on state provision, and his argument that initiative was smothered by a growing desire for state provided security, was vigorous and repeated. But it set up few resonances.

In the border lands between distributism and guild socialism, the social credit ideas of Major C.H. Douglas achieved some currency. Douglas shared Belloc's apprehension of encroaching state control leading to servility, and feared that state socialism would be no more than another and grander form of monopoly. His own preference was for a society organized by function, an idea which he drew from the guild socialist Ramiro de Maeztu. A 'co-operative State' would have a 'functionally aristocratic hierarchy of producers accredited by and serving a democracy of consumers' (quoted in Finlay 1972: 105). But these ideas hardly flourished or, when they did, did so outside the United Kingdom. Other forms of political pluralism and the various arguments for the power or autonomy of groups and communities also lost their vigour or changed their character. Guild socialism had been replaced by doctrines of participation, and Cole had made reluctant accommodations to the modern state. There was some continued discussion of workers' control, but Cole, and Laski, typified the main current of argument. Cole, whilst continuing to advocate workers' control, did so in the context of a strengthened trade unionism exercising new functions in publicly-owned industry under the general and ultimate direction of the central state (Cole and Mellor 1933). During the First World War Laski had been the principal exponent at a theoretical level of political pluralism, drawing both on legal thought and practical political movements to develop a critique of existing theories of sovereignty. By 1925 he had moved away from pluralism and, whilst not denying the limited usefulness of group activity, asserted the national and central power of the state acting in the interests of consumers against the particular powers of functional groups of producers. The state was 'the ultimate source of decision within the normal environment about which my life is lived. Clearly, that attaches to its will an importance for me greater than that which belongs elsewhere' (Laski 1925: 38). Laski's massive 1925 book, *A Grammar of Politics*, opened with the sentence, 'A new political philosophy is necessary to a new world' (ibid.: 15). It was a recognition of the vastness and complexity of the modern state, and prefaced a severe qualification of pluralism as either an adequate descriptive or prescriptive notion. The arguments about the social and group rather than the individualistic character of people's identity, of the kind which had been developed by Figgis, were rejected by Laski as a sufficient account: 'To exhaust the associations to which a man belongs is not to exhaust the man himself. You do not state the total nature of Jones by saying that he is a Wesleyan barrister who belongs to the Reform Club and the Ancient Order of Oddfellows' (ibid.: 67). Laski was equally critical of proposals to give political power to functional groups, and placed, as had the Webbs, the rights of consumers above those of producers. The 'will of any single association' could never be accepted as 'the final will' and the state should thus be 'the association to protect the interests of men as citizens, not in the detail of their productive effort, but in the large outline within which that productive effort is made' (ibid.: 67, 70). A revision of constitutional arrangements to provide for the formal political representation not only of individual citizens but of functional groups, as suggested by Cole, Laski rejected, on grounds both of appropriateness and of practicality. So the man who during the war had stood at the theoretical end of the movement which provided an alternative to the centralized state socialism of the Webbs, by 1925 was repudiating even the modest proposals for constitutional reform which the Webbs, by contrast, had now come to support.

The important transition for Laski had thus been made by the mid-1920s, and was as important to his arguments as the growing attraction which he felt for the ideas of Marx. Others were similarly qualifying their earlier pluralism. When R.H. Tawney stated the case for functional control in 1920, state collectivism was asserted as a necessary corrective. When he argued for an assault on the inequalities of the class system in 1929, the role of the state was taken for granted (Tawney 1920, 1931). But not only was pluralism becoming an intellectual tame elephant, leading anti-state thinking into the collectivist stockade; collectivist arguments also were being stated in muted, almost inaudible tones as all sides of the argument began to fade from the public ear.

Yet whilst anti-statist and overtly collectivist arguments became less audible, at the level of 'common sense' a great deal not only remained but was developed as well. The articulated discussions of state and anti-state arguments had taken place within a series of assumptions which had in the process been not only expressed but stretched and challenged. State collectivism had been asserted against a body of powerful rather than necessarily articulated beliefs. These beliefs took the form of a common sense which was heavily influenced by laissez faire even though it was in no sense a direct application of pure libertarian principle. It was a matter of how things were perceived without reflection, rather than of consciously developed preferences or values. In the years after 1880, state collectivism was itself becoming one of these perceived rather than considered beliefs, a new common sense. By the 1920s both kinds of perception, state collectivist and libertarian or laissez faire, had become strands in assumptions about what was obvious, normal and right. State collectivism and libertarianism had sunk, but into the popular consciousness, not out of it. This being so, they were no longer generally asserted, even when they continued to inform debate. There was no simple victory for one side or the other. Despite the enormous extension of public activity in the war years there was widespread decontrol after 1918, whilst social reform proceeded from expediency rather than from overt principle. The 'middle way' of the 1930s, or the social reforms undertaken by inter-war Conservative governments, were ad hoc reactions to events, or attempts to give first aid to private enterprise, or administrative tidying by men like Neville Chamberlain whom Bentley Gilbert has described as having a 'passion for order and logic in public affairs' (Gilbert 1970: 219–20), and who was engaged in a rationalization of an existing body of functions and responsibilities rather than a radical attack on them. But the nature of 'practicality' and 'expedience' were a matter of how one saw the world. Much of the 'merely' practical debate which began over economic policy was informed by competing but subdued articulations of state collectivist or libertarian doctrines which still provided poles, though not articulated principles, for discussion. The articulated principles of the first quarter of the century provided the alternative taken-for-granted grounds of the practical discussions of the second quarter. To the supporters of state collectivism there were clear advantages in this, and Clement Attlee could observe with satisfaction in 1944: 'I count our progress much more by the extent to which what we cried in the wilderness five and thirty years ago has now become part of the assumptions of the ordinary man and woman. The acceptance of these assumptions has its effect both in legislation and administration, but its gradualness tends to hide our appreciation of the facts' (Attlee to Laski, May 1944, quoted in Martin 1953: 161). A similar development is evidenced by the argument used by the young Harold Macmillan in 1938 where pure, free, private enterprise capitalism and pure state collectivism were both accepted as being sincere but misguided, whilst providing the limits and contexts for discussion or the basis from which practical politics would proceed in order to create a capitalism which incorporated socialism (Macmillan 1938).

In addition to this quiet and obscured transformation of argument about the state, there was also some deliberate and articulate attempt

at a resolution of the differences between collectivism and libertarianism. The members of the Next Five Years Group, who included J.A. Hobson, Ernest Barker, A.D. Lindsay, Norman Angell and H.G. Wells, in 1935 claimed that the 'historic controversy between individualism and socialism – between the idea of a wholly competitive capitalistic system and one of State ownership, regulation and control – appears largely beside the mark, if regarded with a realistic appraisal of immediate needs' (Abercrombie et al. 1935: 5). It appeared to many such centrists that 'immediate needs' involved social and economic reforms which, whatever their desirability on other grounds, were now popularly expected and demanded. To the extent that this was an accurate perception, the progress of state collectivism had proved self-sustaining, since the provision of services had created its own demand. As the members of the Next Five Years Group saw it, the 'faith of the mass of the people in democratic methods and democratic ideals are only be maintained if they believe that the democratic State is moving, however gradually, towards the objective of Economic Justice' (Abercrombie et al. 1935: 39). Compared, however, with the reconciliation already provided by pluralism, the activities of the second quarter of the century were little more than recognition and application. The developed function of the state made this application conservative, or conserving, rather than radical, resting on a recognition that 'our actual system will in any case be a mixed one for many years to come' (ibid.: 5). Such centrism implied extremes, and the position of the centre was wholly determined by the position of the poles – the centre had no independent existence and cannot be understood as an alternative to the extremes but only as a consequence of them.

So whilst a great deal of political discussion in the second quarter of the twentieth century took place within a context set by collectivist and anti-state assumptions and employed those assumptions rather than directly challenging them, it nonetheless took place with reference to them. The discussion, in an apparently isolated, particular, or technical fashion of economic or social policy or of aspects of state machinery or constitutional practice, drew upon wider issues and applied them in specific circumstances. In this manner resistance to the power of the central state and the assertion of the rights to self-management of groups and individuals continued to be expressed. Pacifism, for instance, revived and sustained the liberal assertion of individual rights against the state. It also involved the appeal to an absolute principle beyond the competence of the state's authority in the belief that killing was, simply, wrong. But in so far as it was discretionary, as it was for many, like the editor of the *New Statesman*, Kingsley Martin (Rolph 1973), it was a complete claim to individual rights, in this case the right to decide in each particular instance whether or not to support with force – or rather with the surrender of the individual's own capacity for force – the policies of government. Similarly, the campaign in the 1930s against restrictions of speech and assembly, which were themselves a reaction by the state to the troubled politics of the time, involved in however partisan a way the championing against paternalism of the traditional rights of the free citizenry, or individual liberty against public coercion. The term 'civil liberties' which was adopted by the National Council for Civil Liberties might have been a novel one, but the principle was not.

In a similar way, arguments for a system of properly recognized and organized administrative law involved a clear application of views about the relation between individual and public rights. Lord Hewart, the Lord Chief Justice, in his *The New Despotism* in 1929 attacked this 'despotism' – 'the pretensions and encroachments of bureaucracy' – with the traditional Diceyan weapons of parliamentary sovereignty and the rule of law (Hewart 1929). When the political scientist W.A. Robson examined the problem in 1928, the basis of his specialized proposals was equally plain, an assertion of collective rights and interests against individual autonomy: 'Absolute rights of property and contract, or individual activity and personal freedom, enforceable in the courts of law regardless of urgent social needs, have given way to qualified rights conditional on the extent to which they are compatible with the common good, as interpreted by administrative authorities exercising judicial power.' This power, he suggested would 'be exercised wisely, and the results are likely to be good' (Robson 1928: 323, 324).

In the attitudes of central towards local government there was a persisting belief in the virtues of local discretion, leading Herbert Morrison, for instance, to prefer local to national, central initiatives both as a member of the 1929–31 Labour government dealing with local works schemes for the relief of unemployment, and as Home Secretary during the early phase of the blitz of provincial cities during the Second World War.

ECONOMISTS AND OTHER EXPERTS

It is not always easy with arguments of this kind to detect the differences between technical discussion and principled discussion or to determine when the principles were overt and when they were implicit. There was frequently a transition from the one to the other within a single book or article. Nonetheless there was sufficient articulation and awareness to suggest a diffusion rather than a decline of arguments about the role of the state. This was strikingly so in the debates over economic policy, in particular in the debates on planning, which were set in the context of implicit and explicit perceptions of the character and proper functions of government. In the argument of F.A. Hayek, at that time a teacher at the London School of Economics, the context was fully examined. Advocates of planning like Barbara Wootton or Evan Durbin conducted their arguments principally in terms of the tactics and techniques of planning (Wootton 1934, 1945; Durbin 1949). Hayek, however, in his *Collectivist Economic Planning* of 1935 attacked not the methods but the assumptions of planning, which he identified as a supposition, unargued, of the primary competence of the state.

> For more than half a century, the belief that deliberate regulation of all social affairs must necessarily be more successful than the apparent haphazard interplay of independent individuals has continuously gained ground until today there is hardly a political group anywhere in the world which does not want central direction of most human activities in the service of one aim or another.
>
> (Hayek 1935: 1)

Discussions of socialism had concentrated on the ethical problem of whether it was right and the psychological problem of whether and how people could be brought to carry out socialist plans. But there was no discussion of whether, even if carried out, the plans would work. The term 'socialism' was employed by Hayek in a wide sense and a narrow sense, the former to refer to 'any case of collectivist control of productive resources, no matter in whose interest this control is used' (ibid.: 16). Guild socialism and syndicalism, two forms which were not susceptible to the charge of centralized collectivism, were set aside, because 'they provide no mechanism whatever for a rational direction of economic activity' (ibid.: 19). Planning, Hayek argued, could not allocate resources in the present state of knowledge – the only possible solution – though an unlikely one given the drift of the times – was the market.

The political implications of these arguments were developed in a more openly combative manner in 1944 in *The Road to Serfdom* a book whose title recalled Spencer, and Belloc to whom Hayek admiringly referred. Hayek's reaction to totalitarianism in Germany was to assert even more firmly the liberal values which he saw being similarly eroded in Britain. The argument he put was original in that it identified the antithesis of totalitarianism not as democracy, but as laissez-faire liberalism, and in that it was stated at all. Then totalitarianism was redefined as at root economic collectivism. The substance of the argument was remarkable less for its originality than for its vigorous and articulate restatement of the libertarian anti-statist case. Minimal government, argued Hayek, was the only appropriate policy in economic affairs. This was so both because no rationality superior to that of the market could be discovered whereby to allocate goods, services and rewards, and because the consequences of actions could not readily be predicted. The proper virtue in social scientists and legislators was, thus, restraint.

These beliefs were expressed most concisely in Hayek's explanation and use of the term 'the rule of law'. A.V. Dicey had used the term; it meant that no one could be punished save for a clear breach of the law established in the courts, and that hence the state had no special discretionary powers which were above, outside of, or distinct from the execution of ordinary law. It had been argued by Hewart that the growth of delegated legislation, since it involved ministerial and departmental discretion, offended against this doctrine. Hayek went further. Both delegated legislation, and particular legislation, he argued, offended against the rule of law. Particular legislation, which was intended to achieve certain social or economic effects such as a redistribution of wealth or the regulation of agricultural production, he termed substantive rules as opposed to formal legislation, which merely set out conditions of a high level of generality.

> As soon as particular effects are foreseen at the time a law is made, it ceases to be a mere instrument to be used by the people and becomes instead an instrument used by the lawgiver upon the people and for his ends. The state ceases to be a piece of utilitarian machinery intended to help individuals in the fullest development of their individual personality and becomes a 'moral' institution.
>
> (Hayek 1944: 57)

What Hayek was doing was not talking about the rule of law as it had been understood by Dicey, but rather developing an ambiguity in Dicey's argument and the assertion of a preference for a particular kind of law which Dicey shared:

> formal equality before the law is in conflict, and in fact incompatible, with any activity of the government deliberately aiming at material or substantive equality of different people, and

... any policy aiming at a substantive ideal of distributive justice must lead to the destruction of the Rule of Law.

(Hayek ibid.: 59).

It was liberty, not democracy, which Hayek regarded as the proper end in politics. Democracy was only an instrument, and though it might be more effective than tyranny in checking state interference, 'it is by no means infallible or certain. Nor must we forget that there has often been much more cultural and spiritual freedom under an autocratic rule than under some democracies' (ibid.: 52).

The collectivist and socialist reply to this argument was not generally cast at such a broad level and rested in the first place on the advantages of economic planning and central, public management in promoting, as Barbara Wootton put it in 1934, equality, fairness and a reduction in unemployment. Evan Durbin accused Hayek of misunderstanding socialist planning which involved not one centrally imposed proposal or pattern of proposals but the wider consideration of the consequences and conditions of economic choices and the provision, under general state direction, for those consequences and conditions (Wootton 1934; Durbin 1945). Douglas Jay argued that collectivist planning was the only way to achieve generally desired and just results, since the economy did not and could not operate in the way that the exponents of laissez faire such as Hayek supposed. The distribution of privilege, which bore no relation to merit or need, meant that real needs could in no way be expressed by demands made on the market. Laissez faire was a

> process which does not even in theory take account of the differences between different people's needs or efforts; which is grossly distorted by the existence of unequal or unearned incomes; and which is even further distorted by the prevalence of monopoly and imperfect competition in all their forms, and by social privileges of which the worst is inheritance.
>
> (Jay 1938: 127)

But the collectivists showed less concern than did their opponents to assert the principles on which their case rested, and they concentrated more on particular outcomes and deficiencies of economic planning on the one hand and laissez faire on the other. More noticeable than any assertion or examination of the principles of state action was the development of the oligarchic strand within collectivism. One feature of the development of a common-sense collectivism was that problems which might previously have been seen as political came to be regarded as technical. Discussion was increasingly particular, and conducted as the Webbs had envisaged in terms of the bodies of technical knowledge and assumptions presumed to be appropriate to each area of policy. The growing stress on economics in public debate strengthened this process. Not only did individual economists begin to be accredited with special insights, but the fact of having a professional skill and of belonging to a particular functional group came to be regarded as a qualification for certain kinds of advisory and administrative power. The Economic Advisory Council of the 1930s and the various wartime boards for the management of newly controlled areas of economic life exemplified this change, while the essential contribution of experts in the management of the centralized collectivist state was clearly put in the writings of Barbara Wootton. Wootton acknowledged the charge made by Hayek that the accretion of greater economic power in the state involved a threat to freedom, but proposed that this be circumvented by an informed and critical electorate. The manner in which the electorate was to apply its power, though, involved that diminution of the scope of popular debate and oversight which had been envisaged by all those who believed that the work of modern government was increasingly the proper sphere of specialists:

> A new relationship between government and governed which is more in keeping with the contemporary ethos, will demand more attention to the quality of governing personnel than to the actual details of what potential governments propose.... Most of us are already better judges of people – even of public men – than we are of public issues; and most of us could probably improve the quality of our judgment of personalities more easily than we could equip ourselves effectively to judge these issues.
>
> (Wootton 1945: 147)

The electorate, in other words, was not to concern itself with policy, but to defer to persons of superior quality and let them get on with the tasks of governing for which their special skills qualified them. This blend of twentieth-century technocracy with a view of democratic politics with which Bagehot or Ostrogorski would have sympathized, was vividly illustrated in the arguments of Laski. He had written in *A Grammar of Politics* of the need to have experts in particular areas of public policy, leaving citizens a general role through the institutions of representative government:

> the administration of the modern State is a technical matter, and ... those who can penetrate its secrets are relatively few in

number.... Any system of government, upon the modern scale, involves a body of experts working to satisfy vast populations who judge by the result and are careless of, even uninterested in, the processes by which those results are attained.... A democracy in other words, must, if it is to work, be an aristocracy by delegation.

(Laski 1925: 17, 43)

The implications of this view were fully worked out by 1950 when, in the lectures which were to be published after his death, Laski discussed the proposals for devolution, regional parliaments and, illuminatingly, the economic claims of Scotland:

The decision, for example, whether or not to use Prestwick as a permanent alternative to London Airport, is, in essence, a technical, and not a national, question. If it can be shown that there is a good case, on economic and aeronautical grounds, for the permanent use of Prestwick as a viable alternative to London, it seems to me obvious that the recognition of Prestwick's value is beyond question.

(Laski 1951: 48)

Allowing for the fact that Laski is making a debating point against geographical pluralism and in favour of centralized state collectivism, the point still stands, and is actually given a further dimension. For Laski, as for a substantial body of political thinkers, politics in the context of state collectivism had come to mean a series of particular decisions where alternatives could only survive until the clear light of technical knowledge – economic, aeronautical, medical, as appropriate – had removed all but one of them.

One implication of this had been pointed out by Laski in 1925: there was a division of powers between the democratic and political sphere where general directions were considered, and the technical and professional where policy was formed and executed. The further the competence of the latter spread, the more oligarchy replaced democracy; the more broad political discussion was replaced by particular and technical discussion, the more fragmented and inaccessible the action of the state became. The signatories of *The Next Five Years* proposals in 1935 thought that the difficulties facing democracy demanded 'a leadership capable of evoking the co-operation and enthusiasm necessary.... In these times a special responsibility rests upon informed men of moderate opinion' (Abercrombie et al. 1935: 7). Democracy was to exercise its right not, as for earlier oligarchic revisionists like Ostrogorski by recognizing superior persons, but by appointing informed ones: 'the surest foundation for creative leadership is an educated democracy' (ibid.: 311). The traditions of Toryism and oligarchy were thus being transmuted into the doctrines of expertise and professionalism. This was to prove the main road for oligarchy in the latter part of the century and one that was to take a heavy traffic.

Appropriately, political argument was itself becoming professionalized. A growing number of those who engaged in it, or who came close to doing so, were in one way or another associated with the universities. Either the new voices were increasingly those of dons, or the owners of the old voices became dons. In part this was a simple reflection of changes in the availability of certain kinds of income. Spencer, or the Webbs, could live without salaried employment. There were wealthy people who contributed to political argument, and contributors to the argument whose contributions brought them wealth. But such writing paid less in the twentieth century, the wealthy made less of a contribution to public affairs, and contributions were made by those who could only afford to do so by earning a living first, or in the process. Hobhouse became a university teacher, Laski was never anything else. Those who could make a living from their writing paid less attention to politics, and it was rare for scholars to be able to apply their scholarly skills in non-scholarly ways to make, like the economist J.M. Keynes, the wealth which sustained and nurtured their public life. Thus amongst all the other changes, political argument was beginning to move into the universities and became more closely associated with the developing subject of political science. Political argument travelled upwards into academia, whilst at the same time academics travelled downwards into the forum. The new subject reflected from, and almost in, its origins the wider dimensions of political argument in general. On the one hand there was a breach between the normative, and the descriptive and instrumental, a division between political philosophy which was increasingly philosophical and removed from historical politics, and a study of government or of public administration which, whilst critical, was critical largely in detail only, and within the limits set by the contours of the political system or systems being examined. On the other hand, within the specialism that politics, or at least government and administration, was becoming in the arguments of the various new kinds of elite and oligarchic thinkers, political science, or a certain sector of it, was becoming the specialism of specialisms, the academic concentration on the new skills of managing human affairs piece by piece. The ambitions of the Webbs for the London School of

Economics, where social science and administration had early on been severed from the more abstract discipline of sociology, had indicated the way in which things were to go. Not only the evidently practical, but the apparently more purely academic, took on an instrumental character. Bryce's massive two-volume survey of *Modern Democracies*, published in 1921, employed comparison as the basis for recommendations and warnings for those who wished the existing political order to thrive, and by the Second World War talents as distant from each other as those of Beveridge and Cole were being employed for the tasks of planning the state's programmes of wartime mobilization or post-war reform.

There was something of the iron law of oligarchy, in its organizational aspect, in these changes. Political science came to be seen as a profession or at least an occupation, as well as a public activity of articulate citizens, and as it did so, it began to develop a professional relationship with government. Thus a discipline which in some of its parts was instrumental rather than critical, had its conservatism strengthened by association with the state. Moreover its activities contributed to the articulation and sophistication of a milieu which sustained both it and its political and administrative collaborators. Even when it was critical it was so within limits which did not spread wide enough to challenge any deep assumptions. Variety and originality were made more difficult, and the dialogue became less radical, more contingent – it is not easy to have salaried dissenters. Some of the new academic protagonists in political argument were even absorbed into the direct service of the state during the Second World War, leading Hayek to describe them as 'absorbed by the war machine, and silenced by their official positions' (Hayek 1944: v).

POWER AND CLASS – R.H. TAWNEY AND GEORGE ORWELL

Nonetheless, both within the universities and amongst those who made a living from writing, there were those who reflected in a wide and sustained manner within the limits of the prevailing character of argument. Laski discussed the application of state collectivism, Hayek attacked its very attempting. The fact that neither the general principles of public action nor the function and purpose of the state were at the centre of attention did not prevent equally fundamental issues from being dealt with. The economic historian R.H. Tawney and the writer and journalist George Orwell were both concerned with class, and with forms of power which, whilst they might not be political in immediate origin, were public in their operation and consequences. In this they were developing a strand in the socialist tradition which Hardie had invoked, which MacDonald had employed, which Morris had asserted, and which had been intimated even in that social democratic argument which had led the Fabian Essayists of 1889 to state that, after the establishment of a democratic franchise, the next step was to secure a just distribution of less directly political forms of power. The form of politics might no longer be widely contested, but the use of it was, and in this argument the aims were no less radical, the criticisms no less deep.

Tawney made clear his intention of tackling the general principles of public policy and eschewing unreflective practicality. The alternative was to follow those who 'take their philosophy so much for granted as to be unconscious of its implications' (Tawney 1920: 4). This did not involve a primary concern with political relationships, but it did lead to a general argument about both the conditions and the consequences of those relationships. Tawney detected a common disorder in the social, economic and political spheres, whereby privilege was severed from responsibility, and power and rewards were distributed with no regard for merit or social function. This disorder was reflected in a political system which was hierarchical despite its democratic forms. At the same time the resolution lay in the determined use of those democratic forms. The proper condition of things, Tawney is reported to have told friends, would be when anyone could tell anyone else to go to hell, but when no one would be obliged to take any notice of the instruction (Terrill 1973: 133).

But Tawney was far from believing, as this might suggest, in the law of equal freedom. In his earliest piece of lengthy political argument, *The Sickness of an Acquisitive Society* which was published in 1920, he attacked social orders based solely on rights. Individual rights without any corresponding duties were dismissed as no more than one-sided privileges. Society ought to be organized on the basis of functions, as Tawney called those activities which were defined and justified in terms of their contribution to some social need. With the rejection of individualism went a rejection of economic materialism. The production of material goods was not an end in itself, but a means to the enrichment of social life. It was for this reason that he had been able to argue as a member of one of the Ministry of Reconstruction's committees during the First World War that the needs of industry ought to take second place to the cultivation through continued education of the capacities of young workpeople. Production was, in other words, a function, by which in turn rights of ownership and the control of production should be judged. Right of ownership could never be absolute, but must be conditional on the performance of services. At the same time the immediate, though not the ultimate, control of the provision of those services should lie in the hands of those who were actually required to provide them. Thus on the one hand, producers should be made directly responsible to the community, whilst on the other the responsibility for 'the maintenance of the service' should be placed on 'the professional organization of those who perform it' (Tawney 1920: 84). This was a doctrine which placed him in equal measure alongside guild socialism, and the Tory *noblesse oblige* of Carlyle or the early Mallock.

Tawney thus often seemed inimical to individualism, concerned as he was with the social justification of personal conduct, the limitation of personal activity and even perhaps the restriction of private happiness. In 1920 he wrote that if 'a man has important work, and enough leisure and income to enable him to do it properly, he is in possession of as much happiness as is good for any of the children of Adam' (Tawney 1920: 83). But in the lectures published in 1931 under the title *Equality* a complementary emphasis was evident. *Equality* was an attack on the British class system, and one of the grounds of Tawney's complaint was that this system obliterated or eclipsed individual differences, capacities and needs with a rigid system of social stratification under which merits and rewards, talents and opportunities bore little relationship to one another. At one level Tawney's complaint was instrumental and economic: class was the palsy which drained productive efficiency by inappropriate recruitment, internal antagonisms and the reduction of enthusiasm and energy. At another level his complaint was cultural and moral: class was antithetical both to a common culture and to the full realization of individual capacity, whilst at the same time it offended against the conception of common humanity under divine aegis. The equality of men was a consequence of their all being children of God:

> I find it impossible to believe, with some Christians, that the love of God, whom one has not seen, is compatible with advantages snatched from the brother whom one sees every day, or that what they describe as spiritual equality, a condition which they neither created nor – happily – can alter, has as its appropriate corollary economic, social and educational inequalities which, given the will, they can abolish out of hand.
>
> (Tawney 1953b: 164)

It was not simply a matter of tempering the material world with spiritual values, but of asserting the unequivocal claims of religious principle: 'A Christianity which resigns the economic world to the devil appears to me, in short, not Christianity at all' (ibid.: 165). Thus Tawney insisted that the economic was only to be valued as instrumental to the cultural and moral: equality

> is not to be desired primarily as a means of putting more money into the pockets of those who have too little, though that result is, doubtless, to be welcomed; on the contrary, if it is desirable to put more money into their pockets, the reason is primarily that such a course may be one means, among others, to a much-needed improvement in human relations.

As a Christian Tawney wished, as Tony Wright has neatly put it, to turn 'Christians into socialists (sensibly preferring this to the task of turning socialists into Christians)' (Wright 1987: 33). In a society where not everyone held a religious faith, there had to be other albeit moral arguments for equality. So Tawney went on to argue that both economic and social goods are worthy of pursuit, and may be pursued conjointly – 'there is nothing illogical or fantastic in desiring two good objects rather than one' (Tawney 1931: 46). Yet despite Tawney's acceptance of the fact that Christianity was not a sufficient lever to convince everyone of the socialist case, and despite his dismissal by some critics as a 'mere' preacher (Arblaster 1989) or as the exponent of 'cliché ridden high mindedness' (Alastair McIntyre, *Against the Self-Images of the Age*, London, 1971: 39 quoted in Dennis and Halsey 1988: 149), his significance lies in his employment of religious faith, and in an assumption of its efficacy. W.H. Greenleaf not unreasonably entitles his own discussion 'The Christian Socialism of R.H. Tawney' (Greenleaf 1983b: 439–63).

Tawney's conception of class was wide and flexible, distinguishing class from simple occupation and asserting its cultural rather than its material aspect on the one hand, but denying on the other that an absence of class consciousness indicated an absence of class. This enabled him to conduct an examination of social justice in terms not simply of wealth or income, but of all the other opportunities, accesses and advantages which, whilst they might be sustained by or lead to monetary privilege, were not themselves simply financial: education, health, recruitment to positions of power and benefit. His conception of equality was broad enough to subsume economics, whilst his conception of economics was sufficiently generous to merge with his view of culture. A common culture, he wrote

rests upon economic foundations.... It involves, in short, a large
measure of economic equality – not necessarily, indeed, in respect of
the pecuniary incomes of individuals, but of environment, of habits
of life, of access to education and the means of civilization, of
security and independence, and of the social consideration which
equality in these matters usually carries with it.

(Tawney 1931: 41)

Perhaps more than anyone else Tawney provided for British socialism
in the second quarter of the century a view of power and of
deprivation which, whilst informed by economic insights, combined
those insights with others to give a complementary cultural
perspective.

Tawney's arguments owed something to the idealist notion of
positive liberty, in that he argued for the equal right of all to make the
best of themselves, and to do so in terms of socially rather than
individually described values. This best was seen in terms of
intellectual and spiritual experience and this gave his thinking an
anti-materialist cast which enabled him at times to subordinate
economic considerations to the beliefs about the quality of life which
made the physical arrangements of society's business no more than a
means, albeit a necessary one. The very pursuit of monetary equality
was to reveal the secondary importance of material things and was to
be an alternative to the materialism which underlay the competition
for differential financial advantage. In his rejection of the valuations
of the industrial market Tawney stood in succession to the
condemnations of Ruskin. He quoted with approval the phrase of
another heir to that tradition, J.A. Hobson, who in terms reminiscent
of Ruskin called functionless property-owning 'improperty' (Tawney
1920: 34).

Tawney's conception of socialism had other affinities: the notion of
an age of communal rather than individual conduct which had been
succeeded by industrialism linked him to Morris. His desire to
facilitate 'the restoration of the small property owner in those kinds of
industry for which small ownership is adapted' sat in line both with
liberals like Hobhouse and with the distributism of Chesterton and
Belloc, and he specifically claimed an affinity with the latter, arguing
that the abolition, for socialist reasons, of 'kinds of property which are
merely parasitic' was 'a necessary preliminary' to the distributive state
(Tawney 1920: 46). He absorbed the pluralist and guild socialist esteem
of professional and functional self-management and their suspicion of
central power – 'social and political organization, which may itself

become so arbitrary, tyrannical and corrupt as to thwart the performance of function instead of promoting it' (ibid.: 9). He also absorbed the varied and particular energies of the associations within the framework of state collectivism.

Tawney's sense of social injustice stemmed from experiences of classes other than his own – in the infantry which he joined as a private soldier during the First World War, in the Workers' Educational Association and in the settlement movement. But his conception of human possibilities was a blending of democratic sentiments with both the experience of talent and merit frustrated by the arbitrary barriers of class, and of his own privileged and cultivated upbringing. Unlike thinkers who saw culture as necessarily the concern of a minority, Tawney applied a concern for cultural and spiritual values to popular rather than to elite raw material. Moreover, since Tawney believed in the mere instrumentality of material conditions, he could never support arguments which involved hose-piping the masses to their salvation by vigorous coercive leadership, however enlightened. He was committed to persuasive and consensual open democratic methods and thus could sympathize with neither fascist corporatism nor communist revolution. Radical solutions there had to be, but they must be pursued by the application of free popular choices lest they defeat their own purposes by giving simply the shell of an empty achievement. It was possible to do things by persuasion: 'Men have given one stamp to their institutions; they can give another. They have idealized money and power; they can "choose equality".' Change could be achieved 'by deliberate organization and collective effort' (Tawney 1931: 289, 291), but since ends could be freely willed, which presented the possibility of political choice, to attempt to achieve them by coercion was a fundamental mistake. Compulsion offended against the belief in equality and missed the essential point that any social order depended on the free co-operation and support of its members. Even purely material achievements depended 'upon co-operative effort, and co-operation upon moral principles' (Tawney 1920: 5). Tawney's political beliefs were not greatly affected by the Second World War and the events preceding it, partly for these reasons. He had already firmly rejected coercion, hierarchy and the pursuit of either material domination or material salvation, and totalitarianism, though repugnant, was not the shock to him that it was to others, nor was the division of Europe after 1945 along the apparent lines of political oppression and political freedom so surprising. There was consistency and continuity in his writing before, during and after the war, and his contribution to the post-war debate was characteristically cast in terms of a historical example and an examination of the mistakes committed with the abolition of public controls after 1918 (Tawney 1943).

Whilst some political argument was increasingly taking foreign or foreign-derived terms of reference, other grounds for persuasion were being discovered which were both novel and indigenous. This both gave radicalism a new, because traditional, force and brought it into closer association with more established or dominant views. The consequences of this were both to make radicalism more compelling, and to cut it off from arguments or proposals which its new style rendered alien. This change was particularly found in socialism, and it was a change which many conservatives and socialists found equally disconcerting. For conservatives it looked like poaching, for socialists it sometimes looked like too ready a consorting with gamekeepers. The Webbs had argued on the basis of what was becoming or what government was doing, and Morris on the basis of what had been and what might be. But writers such as George Orwell based a part of their case on the existing character of the English people.

Orwell is best known for his two books, *Animal Farm* published in 1945, and *Nineteen Eighty-Four* published in 1949. The first book was a satire on the fate of the Soviet revolution under Stalin, the second an account of the life, and obliteration, of the individual under totalitarianism. The books have gained the reputation and have gained for Orwell the reputation of making a classic attack on modern socialism. That this is not what their author intended has not affected this reputation, and in a survey of the reading of Labour and Conservative MPs carried out in 1976 it was the latter who were the only ones to mention Orwell (Hall and Higgins 1976).

This reputation is doubly inappropriate, first because Orwell was both a libertarian and a socialist, and second because *Animal Farm* was generated by the example of a foreign state, while *Nineteen Eighty-Four* drew on the oppressive combination of power and orthodoxy in all its forms, foreign and domestic, left and right, public and private (Crick 1980: 391–9). Orwell's outstanding contribution to political discussion was the elaboration of a theory of socialism which rested on a specific analysis of English culture and character. Orwell's case for socialism rested not on economic analysis nor on conceptions of efficient or rational social and political organization, but rather on a sense of national character and of the justice owing to the English people. He was, to use a distinction which he made himself, not a nationalist but a patriot. These arguments run through all his writing from *The Road to Wigan Pier* published in 1937 until his death at the age of 46 in 1950. They were eloquently summed up during the Second World War in his short book, *The Lion and the Unicorn: Socialism and the English Genius*. Orwell put a case for radical policies whilst arguing that they must be grounded in practicality – it was necessary 'to try and determine what England is, before guessing what part England can play in the huge events that are happening' (Orwell [1941] 1968a: 76). What England was, apart from a nation divided by class, was a nation whose best and most essential characteristics were found amongst its working population. This working-class culture was in opposition to established, ruling-class culture: 'in all societies the common people must live to some extent against the existing order. The genuinely popular culture of England is something that goes on beneath the surface, unofficially and more or less frowned on by the authorities' (ibid.: 78).

But whilst the working class set a standard for change, their role as actors in that change was less certain. As portrayed by Orwell in *The Road to Wigan Pier* in 1937 they were honest, straightforward, kindly, 'decent' as he was fond of saying. But they were also adaptable, and adaptable in their own worst interests: 'Instead of raging against their destiny they had made things tolerable by lowering their standards' (Orwell [1937] 962: 78).

> I have been into appalling houses, houses in which I would not live a week if you paid me, and found that the tenants had been there twenty and thirty years and only hoped they might have the luck to die there. In general these conditions are taken as a matter of course, though not always. Some people hardly seem to realize that such things as decent houses exist and look on bugs and leaking roofs as acts of God; others rail bitterly against their landlords; but all cling desperately to their houses lest worse should befall.
>
> (ibid.: 46)

There was a difficulty here, because the very tolerance which Orwell found admirable was close to the adaptability which made the working class the perpetual objects, rather than subjects, of political action. Orwell was aware that in his depiction of working-class deprivation, he was, as the passage on housing illustrates, seeing working-class situations through middle-class eyes. On the other hand he argued also that 'we are mistaken when we say that "It isn't the same for them as it would be for us", and that people bred in the slums can imagine nothing but the slums' (ibid.: 16–17). There are two characteristic beliefs at work and being defended here: first that the people, though deprived of many of the benefits and refinements which constituted the dominant notion of cultivation, were nonetheless the repository of the true, and most truly valuable, English culture; second, that though one of the aspects of popular culture was tolerance and though the people adapted to their deprivations, they had a perception of a better way of life. But this better way of life consisted of a fairer distribution of material advantages, not a popular aspiration towards 'cultivated' standards. Both popular worth and popular deprivation could in this way be asserted. But how was popular dissatisfaction to lead to national reform? Orwell was convinced that there could be no revolution by middle-class leadership. His hostility to socialists who from their own socially secure and superior desks and armchairs aspired to lead the workers to socialism was greater even than that which he displayed towards the existing ruling class. There was only one way in which he could combine without moral and intellectual discomfort his own recommendation of popular culture with his role as a writer, intellectual and hence, so it would seem, leader. This was by placing himself in terms of tastes and lifestyles amongst those whom, since he was merging his public identity with theirs, he could not be accused of condescending towards by presumptions of leadership. This position was adopted not only in the attacks on middle-class Marxists who would not dream of eating their soup noisily or wearing their cap in the house, but in the populist patriotism of such essays as 'In Defence of English Cooking'. In this short piece of journalism Orwell not only defended English cooking against foreign cooking but implied an association, which had echoes of both Blatchford and Chesterton, between the upper classes and foreign tastes, and indigenous cooking and the domestic tastes of the people: 'If you want, say, a good, rich slice of Yorkshire pudding you are more likely to get it in the poorest English home than in a restaurant' (Orwell [1941] 1968b, vol. 3: 58).

The conception of working-class decency provided Orwell with a standard against which to judge other groups: the middle and upper classes, and intellectuals. In *The Lion and the Unicorn* he used his conception of Englishness both to suggest that intellectuals, particularly left-wing intellectuals, were foreign or deviant, and to portray the upper classes as acting, albeit unwittingly, in a treasonable way. The disparity between the mass of the people and the wealthy minority was employed both to give edge to his argument and, by its continuation or disappearance, as an indication as to whether or not things had been set to rights: 'At some point or another you have got to deal with the man who says "I should be no worse off under Hitler". But what answer can you give him – that is, what answer that you can expect him to listen to – while common soldiers risk their lives for two and sixpence a day, and fat women ride about in Rolls-Royce cars, nursing pekineses?' (Orwell [1941] 1968a: 109).

Salvation for the people and for England thus had to come from within. If leadership there was to be, it had to be leadership which led by participating, and by participating in a manner which involved a negation of everything normally associated with the concept, and privileges, of leading. But leadership had always been the quick way to progress and if it were to be eschewed, optimism had to be tenacious and resilient. By the end of his life Orwell's optimism was bruised and strained. Yet it would be wrong to see *Nineteen Eighty-Four* as a final confession of the death or decay of hope. The novel is a portrayal of a possible future not of a necessary one. The people – proles as they were called in the book – had been subdued but in so far as there was hope, it was founded on them. Apart from *Nineteen Eighty-Four* and the world it contained, Orwell retained his English populism. The people had not made the revolution during the war, but they had both chosen Churchill during it and rejected him after it as he pointed out in his last piece of journalism (Orwell 1968b, vol. 4: 556–7). If *Nineteen Eighty-Four* portrays a gloomy possibility, it is also an indisputable rejection of any attempt to save the people from above by the sole power of the centralized collectivist state.

There was a further problem. Orwell asserted the primacy in terms of Englishness and worth of popular culture. He also worked within a literary culture which was clearly a minority affair. His review of Eliot's *Notes Towards a Definition of Culture* in 1948 expressed this ambivalence, hoping that culture in the narrower sense might grow in a classless society, but recognizing the force of Eliot's assertion that it was only accessible to minorities (Orwell 1968b, vol. 4: 514ff.).

Orwell argued that the war gave a new urgency to the socialist claim, though the claim as he made it did not differ from that which he had advanced in the 1930s. The war, he argued, increasingly involved the arousing of expectations which would subvert the privileges of birth and wealth. Only by such a process could the war be won: 'It is only by a revolution that the native genius of the English people can be set free. Revolution does not mean red flags and street fighting, it means a fundamental shift of power' (Orwell [1941] 1968a: 108). In all of this Orwell was arguing for a redress of balance, despite his talk of revolution. His description of England as a 'family with the wrong members in control' (ibid.: 88) was a long way from the class struggle. The suggestion, rather, was that there were standards of conduct which could form the basis for national unity, and that even those who did not at the time adhere to those values, could be brought to do so. In much the same way in 1937 Orwell had suggested that one section of the middle class, what he termed 'the sinking middle class', should 'sink without further struggles into the working class where we belong' (Orwell [1937] 1962: 204).

Orwell was a socialist who argued from the character of the British people – a revolutionary patriot as George Woodcock called him. He was also a libertarian. As a journalist and man of letters he responded to events and to changed circumstances, and thus whilst his principles and preferences remained the same, the distribution of emphasis in their expression altered in response to contemporary circumstances. In 1937 he criticized the inflexible and bureaucratic suppression of individual taste on public housing estates, in *Homage to Catalonia* in 1938 the suppression of popular revolution by Stalinist communism, and in *Nineteen Eighty-Four* the repression of individuality by a world divided, in parody of the Teheran style, into three centralized states. Throughout his life Orwell's writing was characterized by an insistence on the freedom, and responsibility, of the writer to describe and analyse without consideration of party, national or class interest. In his later work the stress on freedom was greater – and the hopeful association of revolution with the English people less. The change in emphasis in Orwell's later work has led to several interpretations. On the right, he has been viewed as disillusioned with socialism. On the left, writers such as Raymond Williams have argued that Orwell's conception of England as 'a family' and his lack of a materialist analysis of class led him to an increasingly non-radical position. But Williams has also properly pointed out that the change does not involve the introduction of new ideas or the disposal of old ones, but rather a shift of the weight given (Williams 1958: 276ff.; 1971). The circumstances changed and the resistance to Stalin succeeded the resistance to fascism. The political context in which the arguments were interpreted changed too, but the context of values within which the arguments were conducted remained unaltered.

A different criticism of Orwell can be made. His depiction of ordinary people had both the strengths and the weaknesses of populism. Orwell's people were not only working class, but male and English. As Beatrix Campbell has put it, 'women do not appear as protagonists in Orwell's working class' (Campbell 1985: 129), whilst Deidre Beddoe has complained that 'Orwell was not only anti-feminist but he was totally blind to the role women were and are forced to play in the order of things' (Beddoe 1984: 140). For all his eloquent defence of English patriotism, similar sentiments in Scotland, Wales or Ireland were crushingly dismissed as 'power hunger' with 'a strong tinge of racialism' (Orwell 1968b, vol. 4: 423).

CULTURE AND POLITICS – T.S. ELIOT, D.H. LAWRENCE, PERCY WYNDHAM LEWIS, HERBERT READ

Orwell had attempted to reconcile the work and character of the intellectual with the renunciation of leadership by an elite or class. For other writers the prospect of lofty eminence was not so repugnant. This eminence was characterized by a slipping apart of actual proposals on the one hand and the visions or principles which had previously informed them on the other. The dislocation was perhaps most marked amongst those who were in the first place artists rather than political writers, and for many of whom the politics of their time were degraded or distasteful. For some an aesthetic sense led to the dramatization of politics, particularly of foreign politics. But for others, even their political views led them away from politics and towards a distant oligarchy which, unlike the old aristocracy of *noblesse oblige* or the new oligarchy of professionalism and expertise, was to lead into by-ways and dead-ends of Coriolanian pique. There had been many before the 1920s both inside and outside the world of public affairs who had advocated authoritative or despotic solutions to what they saw as society's problems. They had proposed or implied the leadership of a small group characterized by status, or capacity, or traditional position. But all from Milner to Shaw, from Wells to Mallock, directed their recommendations towards a society which, however retarded, depraved, incompetent or irrational, could in some degree be led to something better. The few were in this sense justified by the services which they could provide for the many. Cultural elitism was frequently of a different kind, and a reflection of an indifference to politics rather than of an interest in or concern with it. This might seem to link these arguments with the arguments of men like Morris. But Morris's apolitical ideals were of standards and a way of life which were intended eventually to transform the lives of all. The ideals of the later generation were something to be pursued because of their excellence, and to be enjoyed by the minority who were capable of attaining them. It was the difference between yeast and caviare.

These views, as expressed by writers such as T.S. Eliot, D.H. Lawrence, Percy Wyndham Lewis and W.B. Yeats, have in the past attracted attention because of their supposed affinity with fascism. But this affinity was symptomatic rather than essential. These writers did not adopt the views they adopted because they were fascists, which they were not though Lewis came pretty close in his adulation of Hitler (Carey 1992), rather anti-Semitism (Ricks 1988; Julius 1995), intolerance and authoritarianism drew them at times close to what seemed the promise of fascism. But their politics developed independently of fascism and suffered in reputation, rather than gained in clarity or coherence, from the association. Shaw's admiration for Lenin was of a similar kind – the detection in conduct and policy outside the United Kingdom of qualities which had long been recommended by the speaker or writer, under different forms and titles, within it. Thus though there was often a fear of Soviet Russia, or a feeling of guilt towards Germany, much more important was the impatience with democracy, the attraction to ideals of dynamism and efficiency, and a concern with culture and its preservation against dilution which confused quality with excellence and excellence with exclusiveness. Though there was a deliberate European dimension to the arguments of many of these writers, their views were also a feature of a period when grand domestic politics seemed either rare or impossible, and where expression of high and comprehensive ideas had to be sought in the sectarian, the surrogate, or the insulated and aristocratic.

None of this was without precedent or genealogy. There was a link with the romantic contempt for politics shown by Belloc and the Chestertons whilst A.R. Orage, with the assistance of Nietzsche, had made a transition from the politics of vision to a similar politics of aristocracy. There was a continuation of the tradition of anti-democratic elitism and, in the case of Wyndham Lewis at least, of anti-feminism and patriarchal familialism. The arguments of feminism had been the most subversive of all attacks on oligarchy, since they attacked the oligarchy which was the most secure, that based on sex. The resistance to it was appropriately vehement, and of a piece with a more diffuse defence and assertion of the elevated position of particular groups.

The claim to tradition was most clearly evident in the writings of the poet T.S. Eliot. Eliot was born and educated in the United States but, like Kropotkin, lived, worked and wrote in Britain. There was something of an outsider's zeal in the way in which he took the tradition in which men like Coleridge and Arnold had worked, and made it both more intense and more exclusive. At the same time he was influenced by arguments from the rest of Europe, and developed a Toryism made fierce and sectarian through familiarity with the work of the right-wing French thinker, Charles Maurras. Cultural excellence was the creation and experience of a few, by whom alone the nation could be preserved and developed: 'the intelligence of a nation must go on developing or it will deteriorate... the forces of deterioration are a large crawling mass, and the forces of development half a dozen men' (in *The Egoist*, May 1918, quoted in Kojecky 1971: 47). The problem for Eliot was thus in a wide sense an educational one, 'of how, in the lower middle class society of the future, to provide for the training of an elite of thought, conduct and taste' (Eliot 1939: 77). In a similar manner W.B. Yeats urged 'the despotic rule of the educated class' (letter of 1933, in Allen Wade, ed., *The letters of W. B. Yeats*, 1954: 811–12, quoted in Chace 1973: xv). This was a monopolist view of culture, and it led Eliot to stress homogeneity, to view deep differences as characteristic of undesirably close contact between distinct cultures which would lead them 'either to be fiercely self-conscious or both to become adulterate' (Eliot 1934: 19). In consequence, 'a spirit of excessive tolerance is to be deprecated' (ibid.: 20). This homogeneous and intolerant view was not necessarily a view of a national culture: local and particular loyalties, he argued, following Chesterton and the Scottish nationalists, took priority (ibid.: 20–1). But there was little room for either cultural miscegenation or for dissent within cultures. Eliot's conception of social order depended on hierarchy and authority, both on the large and the small scale, and he could write of the benefits of employing 'a large staff of servants, each ... profiting by the benefits of the cultured and devout atmosphere of the home in which they lived' (in *Criterion*, January 1932, quoted in Kojecky 1971: 83). This passage, when Orwell came across it three years later, led him privately to exclaim of the *Criterion* that 'for pure snootiness it beats anything I have ever seen' (letter to Brenda Salkeld, Orwell 1968b, vol. 1: 175). The reliance on authority made normal persuasion and controversy out of place: 'In a society like ours, worm-eaten with Liberalism, the only thing possible for a person with strong convictions is to state a point of view and leave it at that' (Eliot 1934: 13). Thus politics was involved only at a second remove. Principles and persons were to be improved and standards were thus to be advanced, but the reliance on authority meant that the principles had simply to be recognized, rather than accepted as the result of persuasion or argument, and hence at the moment that the political implications of the position were stated, there was a simultaneous revulsion from what was ordinarily understood as politics. For someone such as the poet W.B. Yeats this stance was made the fiercer by a disillusionment with earlier hopes.

Others who in the substance and style of their writing were very different from Eliot took a similar political stance towards the contemporary world. The novelist D.H. Lawrence believed in the disabling limitations of what he saw as the masses, and in the need for a governing elite who would be both intelligent realists capable of using the necessary instruments of rule, and culturally sensitive and capable of employing those instruments to high ends. Both Eliot and Lawrence led into a tradition within literature, and more particularly within literary criticism, which stressed elite culture, the division of society into the excellent and the mass, and a further and yet wider separation between the cultural elite and the society which, in almost monastic seclusion, they were to fructify from afar.

For Percy Wyndham Lewis the perception of decline was stronger, balancing more evenly the complementary invocation of an elite. Wyndham Lewis cannot be ascribed satisfactorily to a conventional left- or right-wing position despite the stance he took in the popular disputes of the 1930s. He favoured what he saw as the socialism of strong coherent government, but argued that democracy had been a failure, and parliamentary politics – in terms reminiscent of Belloc and Cecil Chesterton – a mixture of trickery and humbug, sustaining imperialism and large-scale private enterprise and profits at the expense of a gullible and manipulated public. But the opposition to plutocracy and traditional aristocracy, though it formed part of a form of populism, was associated with a low opinion bordering on contempt for the majority of the population who were seen as preferring to sink into a common mass and move with it, rather than to have the threatening responsibility for deciding their own affairs. Feminism was portrayed by Lewis as one more tunnel dug beneath the foundations of society, since women and feminine character would oust men and masculine character, but would then form a society lacking in creativity and vigour and even more malleable to the intrigues of those who exploited the people. Within society as a whole there would have to be 'a *separation*, limited in kind, between creative man and his backward fellow' (Lewis 1950: 184), and this separation would reflect the division between the masculine and the feminine, just as it would between 'those who decide for the active, the intelligent life, and those who decide (without any stigma attaching to the choice) for the "lower" or animal life' (Lewis 1926: 199).

For someone whose political vision was out of accord with the times, there was an understandable attractiveness in revolution and subversion on the one hand, or oligarchy and authoritative imposition of change on the other. Both were ways of trying to jump from the reality to the wish, and though the latter was the more common, the former was also to be found. Anarchism had not flourished in political argument since the beginning of the century, but it continued to receive distant support in the writings of Herbert Read. Read, a poet and critic and a colleague of Eliot and of Lewis, attempted to subvert where Eliot, Lawrence, Lewis and Yeats had hoped to command. The solution was to be found in the destruction of impediments rather than in the creation of orthodoxy:

> To make life, to insure progress, to create interest and vividness, it is necessary to break form, to distort pattern, to change the nature of our civilization. In order to create it is necessary to destroy; and the agent of destruction in society is the poet. I believe that the poet is necessarily an anarchist, and that he must oppose all organized conceptions of the State.
>
> (Read 1938: 58)

Herbert Read's arguments have affinities with the tradition of Kropotkin, Carpenter and Morris. Like Morris, Read attempted to integrate social theory, obliterating the distinctions made between art, work and politics, and like all three he believed in the possibility of transformation by the cumulative and leavening consequences of personal and small community changes in the manner of living. But unlike his predecessors, Read was little involved in public politics, arguing for the effects of gentle, persuasive, educational transformation. This distance from conventional politics set Read apart from less articulate but more engaged anarchist contemporaries, and gave him affinities with the oligarchic artistic critics of the right. It was illuminating that though he liked the work of Orwell, he had reservations about the man on grounds of taste. 'There were some aspects of his character that irritated me – his proletarian pose in dress etc., his insensitivity to his physical environment, his comparatively narrow range of interests' (letter to George Woodcock, quoted in Woodcock 1972: 239). In this respect he shared a common stance with Eliot, Lawrence and Lewis, as a man of artistic sensibilities who could only urge from afar that society order its affairs differently. George Woodcock perceptively quotes Read's statement that in 'any natural order of society *all* social activities would be aesthetic' and comments: 'In other words, art in the present is inevitably aristocratic, but aristocratic values can be universalized' (Woodcock 1972: 212).

Very little, politically, came of any of these arguments, and although there was volume, there was no corpus. The political comments might be sharp and frequent, but they were not sustained and were not only secondary to the principal concerns of their authors, but occasional and fragmentary.

The aristocratic remove was not the only stance which those who felt alienated from contemporary society and politics adopted. As the novelist and writer E.M. Forster pointed out, sensibility could lead to vacillation as well as to imperiousness. Sensitive people, as he put it in 1939,

> are having a particularly humiliating time just now.... They are vexed by messages from contradictory worlds, so that whatever they do appears to them as a betrayal of something good.... Their grasp on reality paralyses them. Paradoxically they become more and more negative and ineffective, until leadership passes to their inferiors.
>
> (Forster [1951] 1965: 34)

People of Forster's sensibilities, as Orwell pointed out three years later in the middle of the war, had they been charged with managing Britain's empire in India, 'could not have maintained themselves in power for a single week' (Orwell 1968a: 219). And there was a further response, which Forster himself epitomized, a liberalism of privacy where concern for the cultivation of perception and of art led not to the assertion of privilege either in the enjoyment, practice or dissemination of culture but to an insistence on tolerance, variety and privacy. These values Forster set out in some of the most attractive anti-Nazi broadcasts made in Britain (Forster 1951: 41–53). Freedom was asserted against authority, a freedom which was necessary in order to allow people to achieve the maturity which could come only through the making and taking of choices and responsibilities. But though the solution was to an extent a public one and had public consequences, its major characteristic was private and individual: the preservation of art through personal creativity and sensibility and the living of a life which was personally satisfying whilst at the same time being an ark of culture for both present and future.

THE FOREIGN DIMENSION: FASCISM AND COMMUNISM

Eliot and Wyndham Lewis have been accused of fascism; Forster made anti-Nazi broadcasts, and in their different ways both these things showed the creation of an external reference point for political debate within Britain. There was nothing new in British enthusiasm for political events and conflicts in other countries. The French Revolution, Bonapartism, Greek and Italian nationalism and the Bulgarian atrocities had all in their different ways attracted vigorous attention and been the occasion for vehement argument. Events in Europe, whether anarchist bombings, Tsarist pogroms, or the Russian revolutions of 1917, provided images for the hotter moments of British political imagination, and protagonists for its moral dramas. At the same time the seeming ease with which Germany or the United States rivalled Britain's industrial efficiency by the end of the nineteenth century provided examples for technical, educational and social reform. But as Britain's imperial capacity seemed less sure, as the imperial state failed to increase its vigour, the state at home extended its responsibilities, its powers and its services. The relationship was the reverse of that implied in the rhetoric of imperial social reform. The domestic issues for which foreign analogies might be sought or which might be placed in a more than insular British context were changing. But so was the world in which they were considered. The world beyond the British Isles was less and less in substantial part Britain overseas, and more and more a collection of independent states with concerns and solutions which often seemed both varied and original. The politics of other countries, by their distance, were frequently seen both as more straightforward and as more dramatic than politics in Britain. And in the 1930s and 1940s other people's revolutions provided in practical form what utopias had previously given in mere literary speculation. Conflicts and beliefs which were latent or obscure at home seemed manifest with clarity and force abroad, and as the century advanced the great political events which seized the imagination moved beyond Britain and its empire to other nations. The philosopher R.G. Collingwood reported the political phenomena which had deeply impressed him as the South African War, the pre-1914 Liberal reforms, the politics of David Lloyd George and the Spanish Civil War (Collingwood 1939). The first three directly concerned the politics of Britain – the last affected the way people thought about politics. Herbert Read, who was, in his own words, 'never ... an active politician, merely a sympathizing intellectual', described how 'for a few breathless months it became possible to transfer our hopes to Spain, where anarchism, so long oppressed and obscured, emerged as a predominant force in constructive socialism' (Read 1938: 57). For Read it was anarchism, for others democracy, communism, socialism, liberty – or nationalism, authority, and religion. As the Federation of Progressive Societies and Individuals put it, 'The Spanish workers, peasants and intellectuals are fighting our battle.' But the purpose of that battle, they continued, was 'to save Spain and Europe from the savage tyranny of a universal fascism' (quoted in Wilford 1976: 69).

British discontents received form and substance in foreign struggles, and those struggles in their turn gave a more than simply insular significance to British politics. British enthusiasms were engaged abroad, and foreign and international enthusiasms spread into Britain (R. Barker 1994: 1–8).

During the second quarter of the twentieth century, political argument in Britain became enmeshed with political arguments and conflicts in other countries with a force and consistency that was novel. This was most obviously the case with fascism and communism. The liberal dilemma described by Forster was particularly acute as the competition between communism and fascism welled in the 1930s, and it is appropriate that in much that is written on political ideas in the twentieth century great prominence is given to these 'ideologies', as they are often termed. But whether or not such an emphasis is illuminating when looking at the world or at Europe in general, it can cause distortion if applied to Britain. Certainly the 'great political debates of the century' were conducted in the British Isles, and fascism and communism had their vigorous and prolific adherents – it often seemed as if the intellectual energies of an entire generation were enmeshed in that particular international and heroic contest between left and right. 'Our thoughts have bodies', as Auden wrote when the contest was manifest in the Spanish Civil War, and political beliefs took on physical and symbolic form.

But the impact of fascism and communism, for all the apparently simple and straightforward attraction of their epic manoeuvres on the international and European field, was far from simple and straightforward in Britain. Certainly new poles were provided for political argument which complemented the existing alternatives and cut across them. Both fascists and communists hoped and intended to employ the collectivist state, though communism came to many to incorporate the enthusiasms for freedom and renewal which had in the past been more usually associated with libertarian policies. At the same time a new fierceness was given to the demarcation between left and right, and the terms frequently absorbed or at least covered a variety of notions which previously had been more distinct from one another: democracy, socialism, progress, liberty, internationalism and revolution on the left; nationalism, tradition, order, religion, property and capitalism on the right. Enthusiasm for a communism purged of the blemishes which disfigured the Russian example could lead to the belief, expressed by Stephen Spender, that liberal democracy had failed, and that the only choice was between communism and fascism (Spender 1937). This effect of the communist–fascist conflict, the conflation of political preferences and aversions and their polarization, at least for rhetorical purposes, under highly emotive labels, was perhaps the most lasting and eventually the most important. The terms of reference of political argument in Britain had never before contained such clearly external points of authority and appeal.

On the other hand the impact of fascism and communism on political debate in Britain was far less than it was on the conduct of European politics – less even than its impact on public affairs and public order in the United Kingdom. The movements made more of a splash than did the ideas, whilst those who employed the ideas either did so with little effect, or changed their minds, or secured an intellectual influence through their contribution to thinking in a broader context which was not specifically either communist or fascist. Moreover, despite their originality, both bodies of argument in Britain owed something to ideas, prejudices and forms of debate which were a well-established part of the British political tradition. Both were essentially, as they were employed in Britain, competing doctrines on the application of state power drawing on, amongst other sources, the aristocratic Tory traditions to which Shaw at times waggishly but appropriately attached himself. Communism and fascism received much of their support through elective affinity rather than through conversion.

Both fascism and communism were discussed in the light of the examples of the three foreign countries where they were taken to be practised: Germany, Italy and the Soviet Union, and both achieved their impact on British discussion in the first place because of what was happening outside the United Kingdom. For John Strachey it was the Soviet Union as a practical example, as much as communism as a nationally unattached body of arguments, which showed the way forward out of the kingdom of necessity towards the kingdom of freedom. One consequence of this was that conviction became as dependent on international events as on either argument or internal politics, and such events could be traumatic, wrenching up beliefs by their roots and leaving them dislocated and unnourished: 'my whole political position would be shattered. I should have to reconsider everything' was Strachey's reaction to the Nazi–Soviet pact of August 1939 (quoted in Thomas 1973: 184).

Fascism with its flamboyant political rituals, rather than communism, made the greater immediate domestic impact. However, the intellectual quality of fascism was more ambiguous. On the one hand it clearly drew prestige from the larger and more successful movements in Italy and Germany, whilst on the other it stressed nationalism and patriotism and presented international movements as agents of subversion and infiltration. For all the strangeness of its outward show, fascism in Britain drew on conservative traditions of patriotism and ethnicity, and persuasive comparisons have been drawn between Mosley's impatience with parliamentary politics and the similar sentiments of pre-war right-wing conservatives (Jones 1965). At the same time it had affinities with left-wing dissatisfaction with the failures of unco-ordinated and unregulated private economic enterprise to provide employment or prosperity. The intervention of the corporate state, however, was not to be in the affairs of all private economic enterprise, but only in those of large or monopolistic ones. The small shopkeeper, for instance, was to be favoured in a way that the multiple store was not, for the fascist antipathy was not so much to capitalism, as to plutocracy. Nor was all wealth presumed to be employed in incompetent, irresponsible or anti-social ways. Mosley had a Tory conception of *noblesse oblige* and a respect for landed, as against industrial, capital. As he put it 'most ownership of urban land will pass to the State, as that category of landlord is a great deal less likely than the leader of the countryside to justify his hereditary wealth by public services' (*Tomorrow We Live*, 1936, quoted in Benewick 1972: 146). There were those of many views who could identify with a stress on strong and responsible government and an impatience with the interpositions of parliamentary politics. Government, argued Mosley, 'must be given the power to act.... We must eliminate the solemn humbug of six hundred men and women indulging in detailed debate of every technical measure handled by a non-technical assembly in a vastly technical age' (Mosley 1932: 21). The advocacy of special powers was more central to British fascism than were the elaborate proposals for a corporate state and it was this advocacy, or the spirit which it seemed to imply, which brought Tories in the wider sense used by Shaw, including men like Bevan and Strachey, into initial alliance with Mosley in the early stages of his break from conventional politics. But in its admittedly subordinate role, even the corporate state was not such a novelty, for it was in an extreme form a combination of pluralism and state collectivism. The state was to recognize the distinctive variety of economic life by the creation of twenty corporations, but it was to absorb them within itself by ending conventional political activity and making the incorporated corporations the sole forum for disagreement and negotiation.

All of this eclectic side of fascism gave it an appeal, even in its European forms, which it did not enjoy by virtue of its novelty. The

Conservative politician Lord Eustace Percy wrote approvingly in 1934 that

> Mussolini has, in fact, propounded no new doctrines of government or social organization. He has shown an almost English capacity for effecting a revolution without changing the ultimate seat of social authority.... Fascist dictatorship differs, in fact, from communist dictatorship precisely to the extent to which it does not embody a struggle for power – to the extent to which it aims, not at constituting an elect body of saints, a kind of theocratic oligarchy, but at embracing the mass of the nation.
>
> (Percy 1934: 220–1)

Nonetheless communism, in its initial appearance, was less alien than fascism. The early excitement at the Russian Revolution of October 1917 arose from a belief that the hopes of socialists in England had fructified in the east of Europe. There were sceptics like Bertrand Russell who, rejecting bolshevism in 1920, wrote that the dictatorship of the proletariat was more thoroughly dictatorial and less thoroughly proletarian than most of its admirers supposed (Russell [1920] 1948: 26). But many former parliamentary gradualists joined in with the enthusiasm for revolutionary politics and for the soviet as both an instrument of radical policies and (for what had pluralism been about?) a more direct and accurate expression of democratic sentiments. J.A. Hobson, writing in 1921 of the ideals of social justice, utility and fellowship and of the abolition of parasitism which he perceived in Russia, observed: 'there is nothing new in these revolutionary ideas. They had been the common stock of socialism for all time. But hitherto they have been empty preachment. Now they come upon us with the *cachet* of achievement' (Hobson 1921: 160). There was an ambiguity here: on the one hand the Soviet Revolution provided a spur and an incentive to a radical solution developed in a British situation; on the other, it suggested that a model already existed for the goal of such action, and that what had to be emulated was not the radical spirit and the democratic methods, but the collectively organized conclusion, the Russian soviet state. The radical and libertarian enthusiasm did not last, and the emphasis increasingly shifted from admiration of Russia as an example of radical optimism, to Russia as an achieved collection of economic and political institutions. At the same time the breadth of the support for the Soviet Union narrowed and became more homogeneous, whilst the relevance of communism, as opposed to Marxism, to British politics became almost wholly dependent on external affairs. More came to be written on soviet communism in the

1930s than in the years immediately after the First World War, but it tended to draw on the soviet model as an example of a planned egalitarian society, as an indication of the substance of policy and the finished form of the state. It was at this stage, when the revolution had become frozen and given institutional form, that Beatrice and Sidney Webb became interested, an interest which resulted in the publication in 1935 of the nearly 1,200 pages of their *Soviet Communism: A New Civilisation?* The question mark was omitted from the end of the title in later editions, and the book was the major expression of the attraction which the soviet model could have for state collectivists and the adherents of technocratic oligarchy, though different Fabians could be attracted by different aspects: 'The Webbs saw a seamless tapestry of consultation, advice and discussion. Shaw saw Bolshevik Tories getting things done' (R. Barker 1984: 34). The charm of the soviet example lay thickly on the pages of the most prominent exponent of communism in the 1930s, John Strachey. In *The Coming Struggle for Power*, which was first published in 1932, Strachey argued both that the prospects of communist revolution had to be considered in the specific context of each particular country, and that communism was non-national, being inconsistent with the maintenance of separate states. Nations, like classes, would disappear in the spreading of communism: 'when the German working class obtains power, the world will not see a communist Germany and a communist Russia. There will still be one Union of Socialist Soviet Republics, but now it will extend westwards to the Rhine' (Strachey 1932: 350).

Strachey argued that the compulsion of necessity which character- ized labour under capitalism would slowly be replaced. The control of production would under communism be in the hands of the citizens of a classless society, and they would work in the main under the sole compulsion of rational communal interest. Thus the distinction between exploiters and exploited would disappear, and all would be obliged to work: 'the obligation to work which in a communist society is binding upon all its members, is not in the least a contradiction of the principle of voluntary association upon which the productive activity of such a society is based. For the obligation is self-imposed' (Strachey 1932: 347). Even the most optimistic British socialists might have cavilled at the prospect of eternal life which Strachey offered after the revolution (ibid.: 358). But apart from this breach of the Church's monopoly, there was little in his arguments to which most of them would have objected, apart perhaps from the quickness with which the hand attempted to deceive the eye in the leap from necessity to freedom. Strachey's tactical argument was less close to other forms of

British socialism. That such a communist system could only be established by some form of revolution under the inspiration of 'that indispensable instrument of the workers' will, a Communist party' (ibid.: 357) was a less familiar belief, but even this belief shared oligarchic implications with Fabianism.

The influence of communism was only one of three related strands: the soviet example, organized communism and Marxism. Organized communism in Britain had little direct impact on political ideas. Its combination of tight organization and deferential shifts of policy gave it an increasingly sectarian role. On the other hand it was important as a vehicle for the other two strands which, though encouraged by it, operated independently of it. The soviet example had by the early 1930s begun to be absorbed into the arguments for planning and rationalization. These on the one hand filtered the soviet influence, and on the other fused it with an older indigenous tradition of technocratic oligarchy. By the outbreak of war, moreover, early enthusiasms were being eroded by growing perception of the political character of Stalinism, whilst the British war effort provided the symbol and the object for an enthusiastic if critical support which previously had been sought and found abroad.

The impact of Marx, though the Russian example provided the vehicle for it, was separate and wider, and was fed into British argument both by those who were and by those who were not communists. Although it was the apparent manifestations of Marx's ideas in the Soviet Union which first gained them wide and substantial attention, those ideas had been present in the consciousness of many since the 1880s. Nor did British Marxism necessarily have the Soviet associations which communism had. Laski by the early 1930s was an example of Marxism without communism, and his work illustrates the way in which the ideas of Marx were employed in the reaction to the events of 1931, in the elaboration of a class analysis of politics, in a suspicion of the view that the state and the constitution were impartial, and in the relation of political to social and economic analysis. In Laski's writing the influence of Marx led to a stress on the economic dimension of inequality when other dimensions of class were increasingly being discussed by Tawney, by the Coles and by Orwell. It also sustained a belief in the existence of deep political conflicts and of conflicts of economic interest which the politics of constitutional agreement did not so much erase, as tilt in the permanent interest of one side.

PESSIMISM, CAUTION AND THE POSSIBILITIES OF DEMOCRACY

This was the basis of the tentative pessimism with which Laski and other left-wing intellectuals within the Labour Party, such as Cripps, regarded parliamentary democracy after 1931. In *A Grammar of Politics* in 1925 Laski had described and proposed for the state the overall reconciliation of group disagreement, and the final adjudication in the definition of the public interest. But by the early 1930s he had departed from this conception of the state as an impartial institution abstracted from its social and historical situation. In a series of essays and articles whose essence was summed up in 1938 in *Parliamentary Government in England*, Laski argued that institutions which were normally thought of as constituting the political area of life – in this case, Parliament and parliamentary government – were not in themselves the predominating feature in politics. They were themselves, rather, formed by beliefs and ambitions which arose out of the class structure of society. English parliamentary government in the twentieth century was an expression of a liberalism which ran back to Locke, which had as its primary assumption the need to defend private property, and which sustained the interests of the property-owning classes. Representative government in the British parliamentary manner rested on three conditions: a fundamental agreement on all major aspects of government activity; the absence of any feeling by any class of importance that it was permanently excluded from effective political activity; and habits of tolerance towards different opinions and dissenting judgements. These three prerequisites had been met in Britain, Laski argued, because of an underlying agreement amongst all political parties about the distribution of property – 'The British Constitution was an instrument for men who were agreed about the way of life the English State should impose' (Laski 1938: 68).

Once this agreement was challenged, as it would be by a Labour Party committed to socialism and with a parliamentary majority, then there was a great danger that those who stood to lose by continuing to play the parliamentary game by the rules would break the rules and overturn the board. Indeed parliamentary government was threatened from both sides, for if it was employed to radical ends it risked a counter-revolution, whereas if it only maintained itself in being by doing nothing to alter the existing distribution of property, it would lose the support of the mass of the people: 'Parliamentary government, to retain its hold, must give the promise of great results. If it fails to do so, the electorate will look elsewhere for them' (Laski 1938: 35).

The anticipation of conflict could lead, as it led Laski in the 1930s, to a determined expectation, though not precipitation, of political struggle. It could also lead, as it later led Laski, to a new degree of caution and restraint. The events of the years between 1920 and 1950, both at home and abroad, gave a new impetus to a retreat from overt general argument. Paradoxically, the very violence of the ideological and the physical, military clash and grind between fascism and communism, and the oppression which increasingly appeared to characterize regimes based on them, led to a reaction in Britain – and elsewhere – against ambitious political schemes and argument, and a renewed stress on cautious and conservative methods in politics. This strengthened an already existing desire for harmony and reconciliation in policy, and eager competition amongst those of different political persuasions to appear more constitutional in their methods and arguments than their opponents.

The experience of the First World War led some into pacifism, and was responsible for many more feeling an aversion to military solutions to international disputes. The policy of appeasement, which subsequently attracted general odium, led easily and reasonably out of the determination to avoid any revisitation of the disasters and horrors of 1914 to 1918. The spirit of appeasement informed domestic as well as international politics. Industrial conflict after 1918, culminating in the General Strike of 1926, caused many, particularly amongst conservatives, to seek an accommodation between what were coming to be known as the two sides of industry. Order was to be re-established by rationalization and integration, whilst involvement and participation were to be widened by social and more specifically by economic partnership. One of the more important contributions of the Conservative leader Stanley Baldwin to political discussion in the inter-war years was his employment of this notion of industrial partnership and his appeal for 'peace in our time' in the relationship between workers and employers: 'I am whole-heartedly with those men who talk about disarmament on the Continent, peace on the Continent, and the removal of suspicion on the Continent, but far more do I plead for disarmament at home' (Baldwin 1937: 41).

European totalitarianism encouraged a search for more liberal solutions to public policy problems. Thus Harold Macmillan's middle way was both a middle way between socialism and pure capitalism, and a middle way between totalitarianism on the one hand, and economic and social disorder on the other: in one case a blending compromise, in the other an avoidance of both Scylla and Charybdis. Karl Popper's *Poverty of Historicism*, though not published until

1944, was completed in outline in 1935 in the early years of 'the historicist superstitions of the Third Reich' (Popper 1961b: iv). It proposed an end to grand schemes of reform, and argued that 'instead of trying to find the laws of social development' there should be an attempt to 'look for the various laws which impose limitations upon the construction of social institutions' (ibid.: 46). The appropriate method of government was thus the cautious and ad hoc tactic of 'piecemeal social engineering' (Popper 1961a). Hayek's *The Road to Serfdom* was written in 1944 with specific reference to the example of totalitarianism, while the philosopher R.G. Collingwood detected in the Nazi regime an example of mass irrationalism which required an urgent attention to political education in free societies (Collingwood 1942).

The debut of the Labour Party as a significant parliamentary presence and the arguments following the ending of the second Labour government in 1931 were accompanied by the elaboration of a traditionalist theory of parliamentary democracy. An attempt was made both to describe and defend a British alternative to the dictatorships which were emerging on the continent, and to assimilate organized labour and any challenge which through the pursuit of socialism it might make to the existing order. R.G. Bassett, in *The Essentials of Parliamentary Democracy*, extracted lessons from an account of British politics which he employed to place constitutional restrictions on the radicalism with which any government might behave. Ruling parties ought to limit themselves to what would not outrage or antagonize opposition parties, and Parliament ought to exercise the same restraint towards the tolerance of the electorate. To act otherwise would involve the destruction of parliamentary democracy: 'any attempt to carry out an abruptly drastic transformation of our economic and social structure involves the abandonment of our political institutions and methods, and the risk, amounting almost to a certainty, of a revolutionary situation' (Bassett [1935] 1964: 157). For the Labour Party and for parliamentary socialism Basset believed and argued that there were particular consequences of this view:

> The party must face the facts that, under democratic conditions, there can be no abrupt revolutionary changes, and that, therefore, it must be prepared to do things which are not in strict conformity either with abstract Socialist principle or Five-Year Socialist Plans, or even with the kind of election programmes which it has hitherto

presented. There must be continuity of policy, even in 'fundamentals', even with 'capitalism'.

(Bassett [1935] 1964: 185–6)

But the notion of the constitution as a device for regulating politics,
and within which all parties and groups should operate, was not found
only among conservatives, and was accepted with equal enthusiasm by
those, such as Laski, whom Bassett attacked. Laski who was in one
respect a radical critic of the constitution in the 1930s was willing and
eager, provided that the entire system of parliamentary government
was neither overthrown nor subverted, to work within and to develop
what he conceived to be its conventions. His account of the threats to
parliamentary government were just that, and the institution which he
felt to be threatened was valued despite its apparent dependence on the
progress of history. A growing recognition of the intolerance,
oppression and simple violence which would ensue if politics were
conducted without any conventions about tactics led to a new
emphasis being placed upon matters which earlier would have been
regarded as purely procedural. Constitutionalism gained a new appeal
in Britain after it had seemed discredited by the events of 1931. The
authors of *The Next Five Years* believed in 1935 'that the democratic
system is on its trial' not only because of its violent supersession on the
continent by 'dictatorial violence' but, more disturbingly, because it
had to 'prove capable of achieving new tasks more complex than those
for which it was built up' (Abercrombie et al. 1935: 4). But whilst the
viability of democracy might be in jeopardy, the constitutional
arrangements whereby it was carried on in Britain were less
contentious than they had been before 1918 when disputes involving
antagonistic beliefs about the proper distribution of power both within
Parliament and within the population had threatened constitutional
stability in a way in which the arguments of the inter-war years never
did. The conception of the constitution became less a series of different
political alternatives, and more an attempt to place political arguments
within the context of a system whose general structure and function
were not seriously contested. Even those who felt no great enthusiasm
for the constitution as they perceived it accepted it after consideration.
E.M. Forster in 1935 described himself as 'a bourgeois who adheres to
the British constitution, adheres to it rather than supports it' (Forster
[1936] 1967: 77).

Those who were initially enamoured of grand Manichean politics
had in many cases become disillusioned by the end of the second
quarter-century. Either the exposure of Stalinism, whether it came late

or early, or the Nazi–Soviet pact, or what appeared to be the consequence of armed principle between 1939 and 1945, or the final and full revelations of both German and Soviet atrocities induced a desire for caution and quietness. John Strachey, after the Nazi–Soviet pact, shifted from the revolutionary politics of *The Coming Struggle of Power* to an interim reformism which was to sustain both democracy and progress pending the final supersession of capitalism. It remained 'the indispensable task of humanity to build a socialist system of production for use', and such a system 'will alone enable us to live' (Strachey 1940: 5). But in the meantime some kind of extension of state power was inevitable, and socialists must seize the opportunity to do what they could with the existing situation:

> If we fail to realise this possibility, and therefore inevitability, and dissipate our energies in struggling for objectives which cannot in the nature of things be realised in the next phase of development, all that we shall do is leave the reactionaries free play to carry through the job in their own way.
>
> (ibid.: 166)

Hence public enterprise would be extended, credit facilities and publicly controlled banking introduced, social services improved, and income redistributed through taxation.

So with the climax of the violent politics of the second quarter of the century which came with the Second World War, a synthesis was attempted by several writers between the politics of democratic moderation and the politics of radical enthusiasm. The most violent assault on orderly, predictable, peaceful politics did not produce a total retreat into caution and conservatism but rather, at least amongst some, an assertion of the values both of political conduct and of substantive policy. Strachey proposed democratic progress, Orwell wrote *The Lion and the Unicorn* and Laski developed the argument, implicit in *Parliamentary Government in England*, that both democracy and radical reform had to be cultivated. Like Orwell, Laski argued that in order to retain faith in democracy, democracy must be shown to work and to be capable of promoting social reform: 'every evil which defaces our national life, every injustice which can be exploited in our system, every problem we fail to tackle, is a weapon in the hands of Hitlerism' (Laski 1943: 158). And not only had democratic government to achieve reform in order to justify the claims made for it and the expectations laid on it, but if it did not, people would employ other, revolutionary means, to pursue reform. And though the ends of revolutionary politics might be desirable, a revolution would follow the pattern it had followed both in France in 1789 and in Russia in 1917; revolution 'ushers in an iron age' (ibid.: 161). Unless by the beginning of the peace

> the foundations of a world have been laid in which men can discover the right to hope they will think too differently to settle their disagreements in terms of peace. The margin between their assumptions will be too wide to be bridged by discussion, by the give and take of rational compromise. If that becomes the position, it is obvious that the preservation of democracy will no longer be possible.
>
> (ibid.: 168)

The war was the climax of two decades of political conflict and violence which had aroused enthusiasms both for radical policies and for the value of democratic and open politics. Laski's wartime arguments illustrated a balance between the value of free politics and a hostility to despotism on the one hand, and a commitment to radical reform on the other. It had been Laski's argument and Orwell's that the relation between the two was not accidental, but that each complemented the other. Nonetheless there was always the possibility that a concern for substantive policies could tumble over into a pursuit of those policies with little regard for what would normally be thought of as politics, while the adherence to calm and tolerant politics could equally tumble into a flight from radical policies lest they prove contentious. The years immediately after the war were to demonstrate the second of these possibilities.

7 Arrivals and departures

Political ideas in the third quarter of the twentieth century

CAUTION AND CONSENSUS

Before the Second World War political enthusiasms had become attached to extra-British events. But at the same time the very destructiveness of those events and the continued intensity and violence of the Cold War in Europe and the hot war in Asia further strengthened the flight from political discord. The post-war generation, as E.P. Thompson put it, 'grew to consciousness amidst the stench of the dead, the stench of the politics of power' (Thompson et al. 1960: 188). Consensual, authoritative and traditionally ordered ways were given increased respect not necessarily because they seemed right but because they seemed safe. Laski in 1951 argued that 'the real alternative to the House of Commons is the concentration camp' (Laski 1951: 9). Even allowing for the fact that Laski's enthusiasm for the established political institutions was increased by the presence of a Labour government, the emphasis of his argument had shifted not only from the critical constitutionalism of the 1930s but from the revolutionary democracy of the early 1940s. One political scientist observed in 1955 that the generations before the mid-1940s 'dreamed of realizing Utopia; this generation hopes to escape disaster, whether in the form of economic collapse or atomic destruction' (Peardon 1955: 488). It was the age of the lifebelt, and people, giving up dangerous ideas of grand voyages, clung on to anything which looked as if it would float, never mind where to, provided it was not far away. Even those who like Michael Oakeshott, Laski's successor at the London School of Economics, aspired to grander craft nevertheless eschewed all thought of anticipated arrivals. There was 'neither starting-place nor appointed destination. The enterprise is to keep afloat on an even keel' (Oakeshott 1967: 127). And because the familiar was accepted because it was familiar, because it seemed safe rather than because it seemed right, certainties and simple principles were replaced by relativism and qualified judgements. There was a belief in the pragmatic politics of economic efficiency and advancing overall living standards as opposed to any contest between high socialism and pure libertarianism or any general debate about the direction of public policy in terms of transforming or even reforming goals. The suggestion was that British politics in the 1950s were characterized by consensus about the general manner of government and politics and about the one general aim of not having any general aims other than that of managing the existing system. This had the conservative function of putting on one side radical disagreement about political and social structure, and of presenting politics as a matter of housekeeping, of distributing the available goods and benefits and of husbanding resources. In its stress on a middle way between ambitions and enthusiasms of all kinds and between socialism and unbridled capitalism, the argument was a reiteration and a development of what had been said in the 1930s. It was also a restatement of the move from politics to administration of the kind variously envisaged by the Webbs, Wells and later Laski and by the whole broad oligarchic tradition in its technocratic form.

Akin to the notion of consensus politics was a renewed belief in the efficacy of reforms of the machinery of government. The movement for reform drew its vitality from a confidence in the absence of any major divisions of political opinion. Its arguments were characterized by appeals not so much to principles or preferences which were asserted or championed, as by a reliance, often implicit, on a common sense which all citizens were presumed to share. But the reform movement was also a response to a disappointment, even a despair, with the country's economic performance, or apparent lack of it, epitomized for Brian Chapman by the 'haughty exclusion' of Britain when she attempted to join the Common Market (Chapman 1963: 7). There had of course always been a concern with such matters as the proper functioning of Parliament. But by the early 1960s this concern had both grown and become less clearly associated with the articulation of broad political preferences. The Hansard Society for Parliamentary Government in its 1961 review of parliamentary reform felt able to exclude from consideration those proposals of the previous thirty years which had been 'put forward from an extremely partisan point of view and which would appear to be little more than propaganda for some particular body or interest' (Hansard Society 1961: 8). The principal contribution to the debate was made by Bernard Crick, first in a Fabian pamphlet of 1959, and then in a book four years later. Crick based his advocacy of particular reforms – an extension of the Commons committee system and the provision of assistance to MPs – on the argument that Parliament had two important functions: to render government more efficient by making opposition more vigorous, and to illuminate, excite and educate the public as part of a continuous election campaign (Crick 1964). But Crick's method was not typical, and he was even accused of 'ogee argumentation' by one writer who exemplified those who were content to work within the kraal of common sense (A. Barker 1965: 267). The prolific writing on parliamentary reform in the 1960s had little to say on what it was all for. Yet at the same time it relied on the underpinning of its rhetoric by terms such as 'democratic'.

This implied belief that political principles were most aptly expressed tacitly in institutional arrangements was further illustrated by the new status of loyal opposition. There was little discussion of the role of opposition in British politics, and what there was was conducted by political scientists concerned to describe government and politics, rather than by writers whose intention was to persuade. Nonetheless, changes in the status of opposition were occurring in the 1960s which reflected the shift from the politics of principle to the politics of technique. The place of opposition in parliamentary politics had been recognized for over a hundred years: J.C. Hobhouse had introduced the expression 'His Majesty's Opposition' in 1830. But for most of that time it had been thought of as, like Parliament and like party, a means of refining government policy and arriving at a truer perception of supposedly common, national needs. Criticism was not considered to be the proposition of alternatives, but the dialectical pursuit of a single national interest. As Sir Ernest Barker put it in 1942, the more political opposition 'fulfils its ultimate constructive duty, the more it hastens the pace of considered and effective action, weighted with the volume of general consent, and moving with the momentum which only that volume can give' (E. Barker 1967: 203). It was thus an indication of an important change in perceptions of opposition when before the 1964 general election it was argued that a Labour victory was desirable not because its policies were better than those of the Conservatives or its leaders more capable, but in order to maintain a healthy alternation in governing parties. The acceptance of opposition in this sense, as proposing alternatives out of office and providing for regular alternation of rulers and measures, was the outcome of the eschewal of grand causes. If the pursuit of political ends with zeal and dedication led to disaster, then it was wise to give no final allegiance to any single principle, but to place one's faith instead in a set of constitutional institutions which sustained variety in policy, prevented hegemony, and which implied a relativism towards what were normally thought of as political values and principles. Further, not only did the support of opposition as alternative and alternation suggest that final and total allegiance should be given to no single set of political goals other than those expressed in the rules of the game, but it implied that such differences of value and opinion as did exist were not of fundamental importance. Had they been so, then their restraint by constitutional institutions would have been unjustified.

It was not only Parliament that was caught up in the trawl of reform. Local government and the civil service were similarly discussed, and the discussion frequently relied on a use of words such as 'democracy' or 'efficiency' whose contribution to the discussion consisted of the clouds of glory which they trailed from their use in other contexts, rather than of any sustained or critical use to which they were put in their new setting. Academic political scientists were much involved in these movements. One branch of political science, public administration, had from its inception been directed to institutional efficiency within the existing structure and its existing justifying assumptions, a characteristic illustrated by F.F. Ridley when he claimed that 'the study of government should have a reformist intent' (Ridley 1975: 7).

One response to this situation was to assert that political argument in the manner in which it had previously been conducted was dead, that there was an 'end of ideology'. The notion of an 'end of ideology' was an invention of political writers in the United States, and it was an indication of the changed ambience of politics and political argument that views from that source, rather than from continental Europe, should have become an important part of political discussion in Britain. Reporting on a conference promoted by the Congress for Cultural Freedom and attended by several British academics, the American sociologist Edward Shils wrote of the

> obscuring of the once clear distinction between 'left' and 'right', the discovery that over the past thirty years the extremes of 'right' and 'left' had disclosed identities which were much more impressive than their differences, the disasters of governing societies by passionate adherence to formulae, the crimes committed in the names of sacred principles of policy in Nazi Germany and the Soviet Union.
>
> (Shils 1955: 53)

Shils described 'a very widespread feeling that there was no longer any need to justify ourselves *vis-à-vis* the Communist critique of our society' (ibid.: 54). The doctrine of 'an end of ideology' was not as complacent as this might suggest. It was a stick with which to beat state communism, and became a great universal shibboleth wherewith to divide the godly from the ungodly. But the consequences of this preference for caution and compromise in the methods of politics, and conservatism in the substance of policy, were odd and far from impartial. E.P. Thompson commented on the way in which healthy stock had become scattered in the division of sheep and goats in the post-war years: 'It seemed that on one side there was progress, historical necessity, humanism, totalitarianism, Zhdanov, concentration camps, 1984; on the other there was integrity, the Christian tradition, empiricism, personal relations and piecemeal social reform' (Thompson et al. 1960: 188).

But by the end of the 1950s the notions of consensus and of an 'end of ideology' were being increasingly challenged. The very assertion that British political argument was characterized by piecemeal discussion over technical detail was a factor in this ceasing to be the case. The assertion that old controversies were dead was itself controversial. There was a renewed assertion that the politics of the centre, far from representing consensus, ignored important divergences of opinion, and by 1968 the German notion of extra-parliamentary opposition had begun to seem both pertinent and attractive. It had begun to be pointed out that the enthusiasms of the observers and champions of consensus were partisan, and that the doctrine of 'an end of ideology' was itself 'ideological'.

THE BEGINNING OF IDEOLOGY: SOCIALISM – JOHN STRACHEY, C.A.R. CROSLAND, RICHARD TITMUSS, E.P. THOMPSON, RAYMOND WILLIAMS

Those in Britain who elaborated the consensual case frequently did so by attempting to put a gloss upon it and to develop it either in the direction of competitive market economics or in that of egalitarian socialism. On the one hand, socialists such as C.A.R. Crosland argued for a use of public power that was managerial and directive, rather than concerned with nationalization, and which emphasized equality and the quality of life. On the other, market conservatives such as Macleod and Powell argued for a limitation of public economic and social services to a safety net and the encouragement within the margins thus set of libertarian enterprise.

In the case of the socialists, the belief in the pragmatism of the electorate and in the importance and possibility of uncontentious and distributive politics was modified by the stress on the quality of life which included notions of participation and control. The experience of Britain during the ten years 1940–50 had provided a practical application of the common sense of state collectivism, and the starting point for renewed reflection at a more general level. During these years, both in response to the exigencies of war and under the Labour government of Clement Attlee, the state advanced farther and faster than ever before. By 1950 the practical implications had been worked out of the broad policies whose foundations had been laid in the first quarter of the century. The years after 1950 saw reflection on these practical outcomes. This reflection took place both within the practical discussion of politics and more broadly. Its vigour increased more after the experience of peacetime Labour government than in the years of wartime coalition, perhaps because a sense of crisis and national unity restrained criticism before the end of hostilities, but also because whilst wartime measures might seem temporary responses to emergency, peacetime measures were clearly intended to be permanent, and were indicators of a settled direction of policy. There was no longer the possibility that encouraging or appalling changes – according to one's tastes – were simply temporary. The translation of wartime improvization to peacetime permanence, symbolized by the Nissen hut, required an intellectual response of equal likely longevity.

The force of consensual, technical argument had been weakened by the reaction against it, by its own increasingly evident partiality and by the limited effects of the reforms it proposed. At the same time discussion continued both within the broad context of state collectivism, and in terms of hostility towards the operations of the modern state. In 1952, sixty-three years after the first *Fabian Essays in Socialism*, a collection of *New Fabian Essays* were published under the editorship of R.H.S. Crossman. The general tone of the collection was what subsequently became known as 'revisionist'. This set of arguments was well expressed in the writings of the contributor of the essay on 'Tasks and Achievements of British Labour', John Strachey. Strachey explained the change from his communist Marxism of the 1930s by the influence of Keynes, and of Douglas Jay's *The Socialist Case*, and he tactfully located his change of heart 'about 1938' – a year before the Nazi–Soviet pact which had rocked his assumptions before Keynes ever shook them. He now argued that it was possible to subordinate the behaviour of capitalism to the political decisions of a democratic state. Given the combination of democratic institutions, sufficient technical skill and capacity (which Keynes had provided), and 'the existence of a politically mature electorate and of effective and united popular political parties, capable of sustaining governments of the left', it was possible, he believed, 'to drive contemporary capitalism out of its normal channels of development, to devote its vast productive energies to raising the standard of life of its own population instead of taking the fatal course of stagnation at home qualified by imperialist expansion abroad' (Strachey [1952] 1970: 189). This supremacy, or potential supremacy, of politics over economics involved the general and varied exercise of governmental power, and thus did not necessarily involve a simple reliance on extensions of public ownership. What it did necessarily involve was what Strachey termed 'the shift of political power and influence between social groups' (ibid.: 187). The admiration for Keynesian techniques and the limited, by implication, adherence to public ownership did indeed constitute a 'revision' of the mainstream British socialism which had flowed through and around the Labour Party. On the other hand the insistence upon the importance of power and its distribution between social groups both drew on a central element in the Marxist tradition and provided an intimation of a new emphasis which was to emerge in political discussion in post-war Britain, particularly from the later 1960s.

The location of power within the argument for socialism was given further and greater weight in Strachey's *Contemporary Capitalism* published four years later in 1956. Hugh Thomas has suggested that Strachey 'reverted to Marx ... in opposition' whilst forgetting him when in power and when writing for *New Fabian Essays* (Thomas 1973: 277). But both in office and out of it and in *New Fabian Essays* and in *Contemporary Capitalism*, Strachey had a view of the power of private capital which derived from Marx, and a view of the power of politics which expressed the democratic socialism of the Labour Party. The chief difference between the arguments of 1952 and those of 1956 was that the latter were a trifle less optimistic, but the conflict which they envisaged was the same. The tendency of capitalism, Strachey argued, was to accumulate and to concentrate; that of democracy, to disperse. The dispersal of power was essential and socialism could not be achieved without it, or rather a socialism which was achieved by other means could not, at a later stage, discard those means: 'if we have learnt anything in our epoch, it is that the means and methods profoundly condition the goal. A socialism achieved by democratic means will inevitably be a basically different thing from a socialism achieved by dictatorial coercion' (Strachey 1956: 276). But the victory of democracy over capitalism would not be easy. First, because although the power of democracy was increasing, so were the centralization and enhancing of the power of capital: 'now economic power is reaching a critical degree of concentration which threatens to become incompatible with the still growing diffusion of political power. Economic power threatens to submerge political power unless political power can at the critical moment obtain control of economic power' (ibid.: 180). The second difficulty arose because the power of economic privilege lay not only in the economic sphere, but in the political sphere as well. Strachey argued both that the state was, or had been, a class state, and that it could be democratically controlled for other ends. But the obstacles were both practical and ideological. For the upper classes, he pointed out, for 'several generations the State had been their State.... Nevertheless, over recent decades, and in particular, of course, during the six years of the third Labour Government, they encountered the profoundly disturbing possibility that the state apparatus might become responsive to the wishes of the wage earners' (ibid.: 261). Hence without any insincerity there was a resurgence of libertarian and anti-state doctrines. Strachey cited the views of, amongst others, Talmon, Oakeshott, Berlin, Beloff and Utley and commented on 'the fact that these fatal characteristics of democracy have been discovered just at the moment when majority rule, working, as we have seen, almost as powerfully upon the party of the right as on the party of the left, is pushing the economy along paths profoundly unwelcome to "the 10%"' (ibid.: 271). This was of course no new discovery, as Strachey suggested. But it was a revival of arguments which had received little currency since the First World War. Inter-war politics had given little substance to fears of a predatory democracy; the Attlee government appeared to do so.

Strachey's analysis employed the notion of power and implied the possibility of conflict. Other contributors to the 1952 essays preferred a more traditionally Fabian scenario of encroaching rationalism. For the editor of the volume, R.H.S. Crossman, though there were privileges attaching to private ownership, the conflict was between materialism and moral progress rather than between classes. In so far as greater control was exercised by the state, it was a control expressive of national agreement rather than of the limitation of the power of one group by another:

> The true aim of the Labour Movement has always been not the dramatic capture of power by the working class, but the conversion of the nation to the socialist pattern of rights and values.... Sceptical of the Marxist doctrine of inherent conflict, the Labour Party has tenaciously assumed that British People can be persuaded

by an act of collective conscience to subject economic power to public authority and to civilise the conflict inherent in social change.

(Crossman [1952] 1970: 26)

A concern with the nature of class divisions and the appropriate public response towards them lay at the centre of the writing of the most influential of the 1952 essayists, C.A.R. Crosland. In his 1952 essay on 'The Transition from Capitalism' and in his *The Future of Socialism* published four years later in 1956, Crosland distinguished between the achievement of the supremacy of the political world over the economic world, which he termed statism, and socialism. By the end of the 1945–51 Labour government, 'statism' had emerged, and 'Britain had, in all the essentials, ceased to be a capitalist country' (Crosland 1970: 42). In making this judgement Crosland was disassociating himself from the ideas of many British socialists and in particular from what he himself saw as the considerable influence of the ideas of Marx on the British left since the 1930s: 'in my view Marx has little or nothing to offer the contemporary socialist, either in respect of practical policy, or of the correct analysis of our society, or even of the right conceptual tools or framework' (Crosland 1956: 20–1). The expectation of a capitalist collapse was rejected, first because the economic system had in fact produced a rising standard of living, and second because it had been so transformed as to be no longer adequately described as capitalist. The increased economic powers of the state, the greater power of trade unions in their dealing with employers, the separation of ownership from control, the changing ethics of businessmen – 'aggressive individualism is giving way to a suave and sophisticated sociability' (ibid.: 37) – all these meant that capitalism had been left behind. The new powers of the state, moreover, were being used, partly in response to socialist policies and partly in response to the electoral power of the working class, to secure more equitable treatment for the working population. One consequence of all this was that 'the rich are distinctly less rich, and the poor are much less poor' (ibid.: 53). But though the new powers of the state could be and should be used to pursue socialism, the mere possession of those powers did not constitute socialism. It was necessary, Crosland argued, to consider what socialism now meant and to do so, not by returning to any of a number of rival fundamentals, but to examine general socialist aspirations in the light of changed historical conditions. He quoted Tawney writing in *Socialist Commentary* on the need 'to treat sanctified formulae with judicious irreverence and to start by deciding what precisely is the end in view' (ibid.: 97). It was an appropriate reference since Crosland's view of socialism was close to Tawney's. He identified five aspirations which had characterized socialist argument: the protest at the material poverty which accompanied capitalism; the call for social welfare; the call for equality and a classless society; the call for co-operation and fraternity; and the indictment of the inefficiency of capitalism. Of these, Crosland selected equality and classlessness, as Tawney had done. What was necessary was 'to eradicate this sense of class, and to create in its place a sense of common interest and equal status' (Crosland [1952] 1970: 62).

Crosland argued that the major economic problems had been solved. The state had sufficient powers over the economy, and Britain stood 'on the threshold of mass abundance' (Crosland 1956: 515). But inequality and class antagonism still disfigured Britain, and there were severe material restrictions on the exercise of individual liberties. So on the one hand the aim of public policy should be to take particular care of the most vulnerable and needy groups and categories, and on the other to move towards equality by ending segregation and social hierarchy in education, to reduce, by capital gains and inheritance taxes, substantial inequalities of wealth, and to erode class distinctions by levelling up the provision of public services. It was an optimistic argument which, because it assumed that there were no present major problems or future major conflicts of power, could anticipate a difficult but feasible programme of continuing reform. But Crosland was far from arguing that little needed doing. Nearly twenty years later he was more dissatisfied than he had been in 1956, writing that 'British society – slow-moving, rigid, class-ridden – has proved much harder to change than we supposed. Looking back with hindsight, the early revisionist writings were too complacent in tone; they proposed the right reforms, but under-rated the difficulty of achieving them' (Crosland 1975: 44). In 1956, too, Crosland was warning of the dangers to a programme of socialist reform, but not so much from the power of capital as from the power of the state. An increasing sense of communal unity was to be combined with freedom and variety in private and group affairs, and with restraints on further exercise of public regulation: 'socialists should recall (though they often do not) that they have anarchist blood in their veins, and that it is no part of their creed always to back the State against the individual' (Crosland 1956: 165).

But the investigation of precisely what was involved in achieving these aims caused socialists to become less optimistic about the relative easiness of progress. If the old problems had been solved, and the old aims were no longer relevant, it did not follow that the new problems were any less mighty. Nor was it so certain that all the old aims could be set aside. Crosland had looked to the traditions of socialism to find the moral basis for his critique of orthodox Labour Party socialism and his proposition of democratic and participatory reform. Others did the same, and did so in a combative manner. Writing in 1958 in a collection of essays entitled *Conviction*, the journalist Norman MacKenzie argued 'it is now quite clear that the programme on which the Attlee Government worked so hard was designed in its essentials to liquidate arrears, to create the social and economic pattern which was the alternative to Baldwin's England'. MacKenzie quoted William Morris on the dangers of achieving no more than, and being satisfied with, social reform capitalism, and spoke of the need to break out of 'the bridgehead' that the Labour Party by 1951 had 'wedged into the acquisitive society' (MacKenzie 1958: 18, 21). The phrase was taken from Tawney, and it was that part of the socialist tradition which was concerned with the nature of work, the quality of life and the power which people exercised over their own life on which another contributor to the essays concentrated. Iris Murdoch urged the need to move on from welfare socialism to deal with those problems of the nature of labour raised by Morris, Marx and the Guild Socialists (Murdoch 1958).

Not only was the socialism achieved by a social service state considered an inadequate expression of the socialist vision, but the actual material benefits provided were called into question. It was pointed out that the middle class gained more from the welfare state than did the working class, a paradox which led the social scientist Brian Abel-Smith to entitle a discussion of this fact 'Whose Welfare State?' But like other socialists in the late 1950s, Abel-Smith was concerned not only with the material level of benefits provided, but with the relations of power and status which were involved. The agents of the social service state still treated the people as if they were the recipients of charity, rather than as clients: 'Why is the customer always right and the citizen usually wrong?' (Abel-Smith 1958: 67). The practical examination of the operation of the welfare state provided a context for a moral rather than a material assessment of public policy, and for a rejection of the idea that politics could now be reduced to a series of material adjustments and technical solutions. As R.M. Titmuss, a pioneer of social administration, the academic study of social policy and its impact, put it in an essay of 1959, the doctrine of consensus 'constitutes a threat to the democratic process. If it is thought that less divides us, there is less to argue about' (Titmuss 1963: 220). Titmuss insisted that important differences of power and of advantage remained, and that they were sustained by a dangerous growth of private and hence irresponsible power. In the case of groups, the public, open, and responsible was subordinated to the private, sectional, closed, and hence, because not undertaken in the light of public goals, irresponsible. In the case of the attitudes and priorities of citizens, this growing withdrawal into the private sphere was equally damaging: 'All the impulses and ideals of the 1940s to recreate, rebuild and replan have collapsed.... This is retreat from Government; a retreat into irresponsibility' (Titmuss 1963: 241).

Responsibility thus involved relating particular activities to general principles, and principles which were public in that they represented the considered judgement of society. Thus in a specific area of academic enquiry – social administration – which was developing a degree of autonomy, there was at the same time a relation of argument to a context beyond the particular discipline. Titmuss's language was suffused with the cadences of social justice, and he could write, with a more than merely technical eloquence, of the principles of equality and of 'the welfare of the politically obscure minorities; the powerless groups; the dependent poor, the disabled, the deprived and the rejected' (Titmuss 1963: 217). This relation of the details of social policy and of the detailed operation of discrete parts of the state and the economy to general purposes had implications not only for what was done by the state but for what was done elsewhere. In his 1959 essay on 'The Irresponsible Society' Titmuss argued that a consequence of the great power of the private insurance companies was that 'Social policies will be imposed without democratic discussion; without consideration of the moral consequences which may result from them. In this sense they will be irresponsible decisions' (Titmuss 1963: 216). It followed that much that was presented as merely technical debate about public policy was nothing of the kind. Particular social policies had constantly to be considered in the light of 'general social objectives'. The differences between partisan ideologies were far more than glosses on essential agreements: 'Socialist social policies are, in my view, totally different in their purposes, philosophy and attitudes to people from Conservative social policies. They are (or should be) pre-eminently about equality, freedom and social integration' (Titmuss 1968: 116).

Both Titmuss's egalitarian radicalism and his conservative preference for central, public measures rather than for particular, group initiative and assertion were neatly expressed in an essay of 1967. Writing of the failure of the United States poverty programme and of the beliefs which caused that failure he argued: 'it has not been seen as a universalist problem of inequality, social injustice, exclusion. The faults were not political and structural; technical know-how, project innovation, self-help and consumer aggression could eradicate the "poverty disease".' He went on to identify the problem of 'how to include poor people, and especially poor coloured people, in our societies' (Titmuss 1968: 114). The notion was closely similar to MacDonald's conception of socialism. It was radical in that it wanted an extension of citizenship to the whole adult population; it was conservative in that it involved giving the right to participate. When Titmuss detected group autonomy he saw it as being exercised against the public interest by powerful and secretive minorities, spoke of "'The Pressure Group State'", and deplored 'professional syndicalism' (Titmuss 1963: 231). He quoted Hogg on the secondary importance of politics for conservatives as an example of the bad and growing predominance of private pleasures and purposes over public respon-sibility (ibid.: 223–4). Both in Titmuss's moralism and in his stress on fraternity and co-operation, there was thus a strong affinity with the socialism of Tawney. In his last book, *The Gift Relationship*, Titmuss argued not only for the moral obligations which social life imposed, but for the creation of opportunities for moral activity:

> It is the responsibility of the state, acting sometimes through the processes we have called 'social policy', to reduce or eliminate or control the forces of market coercion which place men in situations in which they have less freedom or little freedom to make moral choices or to behave altruistically if they so will.
>
> (Titmuss 1970: 273)

If there was a strong vein of Tawney, there was also a trace of Green. Crosland, in his 1956 *The Future of Socialism*, had commented on and complained about what he termed 'a curiously strong tendency within the Labour Party towards a suspicious, militant, class-conscious Leftism' (Crosland 1956: 195). He was registering the existence, a worrying existence for a believer in rational and uncontentious progress, of socialist arguments based on perceptions of conflicts of power and interest. He was thinking in particular of Aneurin Bevan, whose *In Place of Fear* Strachey had quoted with approval, to the effect that either 'poverty will use democracy to win the struggle against property, or property in fear of poverty will destroy democracy' (Bevan 1952: 3, quoted in Strachey 1956: 180). The tradition of socialism represented by Bevan shared many elements with the egalitarian consensual reformism of Crosland. In *In Place of Fear* Bevan attacked the irrationality of unbridled capitalism, argued the need for planning, invoked a sense of community as a social good which needed to be included in calculations of the costs of economic decisions. But Bevan was also, as Kenneth Morgan has put it, 'the prophet of working-class power' (K. O. Morgan 1976: 1615). His journalism and speeches were often a better indication of his arguments than the unusual event of a book, and in *Tribune* he insisted on the central importance of 'the struggle for power in the State' (*Tribune*, 13 June 1952, quoted in Foot 1973: 371).

Crosland, in 1956, had declared that capitalism had been left behind, and that the way forward consisted not of any radical or revolutionary reconstruction of society or redistribution of power, but in the careful but deliberate cultivation of a more varied and egalitarian society, through the use of state power informed by a revised socialism. But though Crosland had declared radical socialism irrelevant, it was by no means dead. The New Left which emerged from the end of the 1950s was a broad and varied movement of oppositional political thought, formed of radical socialists and of former communists who had left the party after Hungary in 1956, of anarchists, communitarians, feminists, and libertarians. It was a movement of the left, and a movement closely allied with socialism. All its ramified sections presented alternatives to the view put forward by Crosland, both in terms of what needed to be achieved, and in terms of the analysis of the present condition. The New Left encompassed a wide range of arguments, from revived collectivism to almost pure anarchism, and such unity as it possessed lay in its aversions and its aspirations, rather than in its arguments and its alliances. There was a common hostility to the Cold War, to the attack on 'ideology' and the assertion, by right or left, that politics was characterized by 'consensus'. Thirteen years of Conservative government between 1951 and 1964, and the American involvement in the Vietnam war, combined with a growing awareness or acknowledgement of the nature of Soviet government, fuelled a broad hostility to the degree to which politics, both in east and west, was seen to be organized from above. This was complemented by a subsidiary opposition to materialism or, as the fashionable term had it, consumerism. When this was combined with a belief that parliamentary socialism had failed to deliver any substantial benefits, whilst party Marxism in Eastern Europe had produced despotism and secrecy, there was a broad base of aversion and aspiration to fuel a movement far wider than any single organization, argument, or journal. There was a re-assertion of direct politics, including workers control, a discovery of a 'liberated' Marx who could be used to discuss alienation and ideology, and a revived attention to the nature and quality of work drawing on William Morris and on Marx, to anarchism, and to cultural, as against a simply or rigidly class, approaches to both analysis and prescription.

The qualified collectivist wing of the New Left was most clearly expressed in the writings of those who were, sometimes, briefly, associated with the *New Left Review*. E.P. Thompson, writing in the collection of essays *Out of Apathy*, in 1960 argued for the radical possibilities of politics, and the desirability of revolutionary transformation. Thompson started with the case which had been made against grand causes in reaction against both fascism and communism, a case which had sustained the revisionism of men such as Crosland, and the general 'end of ideology' and 'consensus' arguments. He turned this case upside down, citing the orthodoxy and quiescence which characterized both Stalinism and doctrines of consensus politics, thus suggesting that principled and ambitious politics were the way ahead out of old disasters:

> The Western disenchanted delivered themselves over, by their own hand and in confessional mood, to McCarthyism, just as an earlier generation of Communist intellectuals had, by their capitulation before the 'infallible' party, delivered themselves over to Zhdanov and to Beria. In Natopolitan culture today, no swear-word is more devastating than 'romantic', just as the 'Utopian' or 'idealist' is the butt of Stalinist abuse. It was left to Mr. Amis to make the ultimate definition of political romanticism: 'an irrational capacity to become inflamed by interests and causes that are not one's own, that are outside oneself'.
>
> (Thompson 1960 et al.: 168)

The idea of 'practicality', argued Thompson, imposed a partisan character on political life just as surely as did supposedly 'ideological' approaches. Making the comparison once again with Stalinism, he wrote that if 'in the one, evil may be justified in the name of "historical necessity", then in the other it is accepted as a necessary part of the "human condition"' (ibid.: 155). Political events would occur whether people exerted themselves to direct them or not. The only difference between activism and quiescence was that 'if *we* do not change circumstances, circumstances will change nonetheless; and they are likely to change for the worse' (ibid.: 181).

On the one hand, therefore, Thompson insisted on a radical alternative to the existing order. Socialists could never 'pull themselves up by the bootlaces of capitalism' (ibid.: 14). But on the other he saw the sources of this radical challenge within the political traditions of Britain. The socialism which he asserted though it involved a specific preference for the public and political over the private, was a socialist humanism in reaction against the centralized rigidities of both institutional communism and established capitalism. And this humanism he found within the British labour movement, and the kinds of argument expounded by Morris:

> The wholesome dislike of the reasons of state, the values of intellectual and artistic integrity, a sense of the real strengths within British traditions – all these, once learnt, need not be cast aside.... Perhaps, without our knowledge, the key to change has been tossed into British hands, and the world waits impatiently upon us to turn the lock? The materials for a definition of socialist humanism lie on every hand. Our own intellectual traditions rise to meet our needs.
> (Thompson et al. 1960: 192–3)

The demand for a radical approach in politics marked Thompson off very clearly from revisionists such as Crosland. Yet both shared an insistence on the need for progress to be made from below, Crosland in his call for more gaiety and variety, Thompson in his opinion that a 'socialist state can do little more than provide "circumstances" which encourage societal and discourage acquisitive man; which help people to build their own, organic community, in their own way' (ibid.: 194). Norman Birnbaum, in his foreword to *Out of Apathy* found, or thought his readers might find, the incorporation of culture within politics which this implied, odd. But if it was an oddity, it was one which extended beyond the New Left.

It was also, as the work of another contributor to these discussions showed, an oddity which extended far back into political writing in modern Britain. Birnbaum had mentioned the contribution of Raymond Williams, an adult education teacher of English literature. Williams's *Culture and Society* had been published in 1958, and had discussed the political and social, as well as the conventionally 'literary', character of such writers as Orwell, Tawney, Mallock, Eliot and Lawrence. His book *The Long Revolution* published in 1961 contained an examination of what this concern with the political quality of life implied. Williams rejected the notion of material consumption as an adequate account of people's needs, and insisted on the importance of 'social use as one criterion of our economic activity'. The market, since it could not register or express the value of social use, was hence an inadequate means of reaching decisions, and in fact discriminated against social value: 'we think of our individual patterns of use in the favourable terms of spending and satisfaction, but of our social patterns of use in the unfavourable terms of deprivation and taxation' (Williams 1961b: 324). Against the methods of competition Williams advanced the fraternal traditions of the labour movement as providing examples, or at least hopes, 'of ways of living that could be extended to the whole society, which could quite reasonably be organised on a basis of collective democratic institutions and the substitution of co-operative equality for competition as the principle of social and economic policy' (ibid.: 328).

Such 'co-operative equality' required the cultivation of more direct forms of democratic self-government. It was not sufficient to increase the electoral leverage of citizens over the existing centralized political institutions, a system which Williams likened to a court which ruled as it saw fit whilst occasionally taking notice of demands made upon it:

> The pressure has been to define democracy as 'the right to vote', 'the right to free speech', and so on, in a pattern of feeling which is really that of the 'liberty of the subject' within an established authority. The pressure now, in a wide area of our social life, should be towards a participatory democracy, in which the ways and means of involving people much more closely in the process of self-government can be learned and extended.
>
> (ibid.: 342–3)

Williams's work, more clearly than that of any other socialist writing at the time, emphasized the case for democracy at both ends. On the one hand, public ownership should be extended in order to ensure that the larger economic decisions were taken in response to overall public needs whilst, on the other, power should be distributed downwards. There was a need to end the impudence of the official in the public services by creating more directly democratic forms of control so that, for instance, public housing estates might have management committees elected from amongst their tenants. In industry, boards of directors elected from amongst the workers in the industry or service would promote self-government. Williams's invocation of existing patterns of working-class co-operation as providing suggestions for a wider dissemination of democracy had affinities in different ways with both Hobhouse and Orwell. Moreover, his arguments represented an attempt to reassert the rights and functions of smaller units within the central collectivist state in a way which modified the operation of the state without, as had happened earlier in the century, absorbing the case made on behalf of the citizen organized on a smaller pattern into a scheme of enlarged central competence.

The concern with the quality of life in a broader political discussion was reciprocated by a political dimension in literature. The plays of

Arnold Wesker dealt with the way in which people lived with public
and political, as well as private and domestic, aspirations and
limitations. *Chips with Everything*, about class and hierarchy in the
armed forces, dealt with precisely that distribution of power which had
concerned Williams.

THE BEGINNING OF IDEOLOGY: LIBERTARIANISM, CONSERVATISM AND ANARCHISM – ENOCH POWELL, MICHAEL OAKESHOTT, F.A. HAYEK, COLIN WARD

The advocacy of the use of public power and of the pursuit of public
solutions to socially perceived problems had been conducted at its
most articulate level in the third quarter of the century largely by
socialists. But within the body of socialist argument there was variety
and disagreement, and an increasing insistence not only on public
power but also on group power. Within the arguments of those who
resisted collectivism there was equal variety and equal radicalism, and
a concern as great for the power of groups outside the institutions of
the state. There were three elements in continuing anti-state arguments:
first, libertarianism; second, a preference for hierarchies, conventions
and authority other than those represented by the state; and third,
communistic anarchism. The first and second were distinguished from
each other more by emphasis than by any firm division of political
tastes or recommendations, and there was much overlap and shared
prescription. Nor were purely libertarian arguments ever expressed, so
that the matter becomes one of determining the degree and kind of
state activity accepted, and of establishing the character of the
unmolested or relatively unmolested set of social arrangements which
were presented as desirable. Some of the attacks on the modern state
were forthright and unqualified. John Jewkes, writing two years after
the formation of the Attlee government, identified that government as
the turning point – and indeed the measures and policies of 1945–51
were, as Strachey had pointed out, the occasion for a revival of various
kinds of libertarian arguments. Arguments between the advocates of
economic planning and their opponents, wrote Jewkes, might seem to
be simply about quantities. But they were in fact about liberty,
tolerance and variety: 'the depths of human wretchedness and a
centrally planned economy have invariably gone together' (Jewkes
1968: 49). Centralized economic planning, he argued, destroyed
initiative, created irresponsible central power, corruption and privilege.
It reduced individuality, and

ultimately turns every individual into a cipher and every economic decision into a blind fumbling, destroys the incentives through which economic progress arises, renders the economic system as unstable as the whims of the few who ultimately control it and creates a system of wirepulling and privileges in which economic justice ceases to have any meaning.

(ibid.: 53)

Against this gloomy condition Jewkes opposed the price mechanism and the free market, which were scientific just as planning was arbitrary. They were also democratic, for a true economic democracy consisted of unconstrained consumer power to make economic choices. The libertarian economics expounded by Jewkes were not novel: he referred to Hayek's 1944 *The Road To Serfdom*, and the tradition was much longer than that. Jewkes's significance lay not in what he said, but in when he said it.

Jewkes said little about the political arrangements which he preferred or was prepared to accept. But when libertarian critics of the state did do so, they revealed a variety of limitations and qualifications on what might be termed 'pure' libertarianism. The Conservative politician Enoch Powell, whilst he vigorously attacked state economic collectivism, indicated also in his writings the points at which behaviour in society might be restrained or ordered other than by the sanctions of the market. The state must of course, argued Powell, do some things. But it had two general modes of operation: 'government by specific prescription' and 'government by the maintenance of a spontaneous or automatic system of decision' (Douglas and Powell 1968: 48). In some areas such as defence or the maintenance of law, government acted with specific intention. But specific decisions of this kind were incommensurable – they were taken for their own sake and could not be expressed in terms of measurable, monetary benefits or costs. Such decisions when taken in economic matters involved making incommensurable what normally would be commensurable through the market mechanism and the comparative standard of monetary value. They thus involve the assumption either that government could determine with superior skill which of a series of alternatives was to be adopted, or that it could predict the result of a perfect operation of market forces. The proper course was clear:

The market decentralizes power right down to every individual consumer, so that a grand, continuous general election is in progress the whole time, a vote being cast whenever a share or a security or an article or a service is bought and sold. This is an economic democracy in which there are no privileges – everybody's dollar is as good as everybody else's dollar – and where the mightiest of corporations and capitalists have had to bow to the collective wishes of the humblest citizens.

(ibid.: 68)

Such a system was valuable both because it ensured freedom, and because it worked. It was 'the subtlest and most efficient system mankind has yet devised for setting effort and resources to their best economic use' (Powell 1965: 15). The 'capitalist free economy' was

much more than a mechanism for ensuring that the nation gets the best material return from its energies and resources: we uphold it as a way of life, as the counterpart of the free society, which guarantees, as no other can, that men shall be free to make their own choices, right or wrong, wise or foolish, to obey their own consciences, to follow their own initiatives.

(ibid.: 6)

The free market was not in other words simply an economic device: it was a means of distributing power as widely as possible. This distribution, Powell argued, was the alternative to socialism, and the only alternative for those who opposed the centralization of power in the hands of government: 'if the country's future is limited by the vision and knowledge of a small group of people, it will be poor and stunted' (ibid.: xi).

But Powell's libertarianism was tempered by two features. First was a belief that there were certain functions the state should perform beyond the maintenance of order and the defence of the realm. Through the social services for instance it had the task 'of providing for the members of the community, or for a section of it' those conditions which community action, and only community action, can provide' (Powell 1965: 28). Second, the historical, national tradition provided both restraints and a context within which any policy must be pursued. This was in part an immediate condition of politics: 'any government has to reckon with the facts as it finds them, including the results of its predecessors' policies' (ibid.: 1). Further, it had, in so far as it was limited by those policies, to pursue them effectively. As T.E. Utley put it, Powell believed it necessary 'to see to it, in fact, that the neo-socialist society into which we were moving was as efficiently administered as was compatible with its nature' (Utley 1968: 84). But there was also a much wider setting for government action:

I am only politically self-conscious in a particular society, in this particular society, namely, that of Britain. So far as I have ideals, which is an inappropriate word – I prefer to say political objects – they are much more concerned with the removal of blemishes or the avoidance of dangers than with the assimilation of the British Constitution to a platonic idea of a democracy which pre-exists in the mind.

(Douglas and Powell 1968: 146–7)

Thus libertarianism was blended with a conservatism which expressed a sense of national tradition. It was this sense of a national, English tradition and character – 'the unbroken life of the English nation over a thousand years' and institutions which 'appear in England almost as works of nature' – on which Powell drew in his attacks on immigration from the black Commonwealth, which introduced those whom he depicted as 'strangers' (Powell 1969: 340, 304).

The mixing of conservatism and libertarianism which Enoch Powell expressed in party and parliamentary politics was executed at one remove from the platform by the political scientist Michael Oakeshott. Oakeshott's arguments were both libertarian and conservative. As a libertarian, he argued for limited government as the complement of freedom. And this freedom was construed not as the application of some general principle, but as a term which described certain actual conditions which had developed: 'we consider ourselves to be free because no one in our society is allowed unlimited power – no leader, faction, party or "class", no majority, no government, church, corporation, trade or professional association or trade union' (Oakeshott 1967: 41). Freedom was thus characterized by 'the absence from our society of overwhelming concentrations of power' (ibid.: 40). Power was to be diffused not only within a society but over time – people should not do too much, lest they bind their successors, and a free society 'will find its guide in a principle of *continuity* (which is a diffusion of power between past, present and future) and in a principle of *consensus* (which is a diffusion of power between the different legitimate interests of the present)' (ibid.: 48).

In such a society, government would have two characteristics: it would not itself constitute an overwhelming concentration of power, and it would operate in order to regulate in a law-governed and predictable way, relations within the state. Oakeshott expressed this ideal by the term 'the rule of law', and his use of the phrase was similar to Dicey's: governments operated under fixed and general laws which bound both them and their subjects, and their actions were concerned with the upholding of these general laws, rather than with the achievement of specific objects. The notion might be better expressed – though some of its persuasive force would be lost – by the term, 'the rule of general, formal law'. Such a notion was incompatible with what Oakeshott viewed as the collectivist drift of the times:

> Collectivism depends for its working upon a lavish use of discretionary authority. The organization it imposes upon society ... must be kept going by promiscuous, day-to-day interventions – controls of prices, licences to pursue activities, permissions to make and to cultivate, to buy and to sell, the perpetual readjustment of rations, and the distribution of privileges and exemptions – by the exercise, in short, of the kind of power most subject to misuse and corruption. The diffusion of power inherent in the rule of law leaves government with insufficient power to operate a collectivist society.
>
> (ibid.: 512)

Thus the public sphere of activity was opposed to the private, and the activities of states distinguished in terms of *societas* and *universitas*, the first a relationship in terms of rules of conduct, the second in terms of common public enterprise (Oakeshott 1975). The former was the condition of the rule of law, of government 'by means of the enforcement by prescribed methods of settled rules binding alike on governors and governed' (Oakeshott 1967: 4–3).

In the condition of things which Oakeshott presented as preferable, three broad kinds of rights would be observable: rights of speech, of association and of property. Oakeshott argued that labour was a form of property, and from this that a wage system with a multiplicity of employers was necessary to preserve this form of property right:

> That a man is not free unless he enjoys a proprietary right over his personal capacities and his labour is believed by everyone who uses freedom in the English sense. And yet no such right exists unless there are many potential employers of his labour. The freedom which separates a man from slavery is nothing but a freedom to choose and to move among autonomous independent organizations, firms, purchasers of labour, and this implies private property in resources other than personal capacity.
>
> (ibid.: 46)

Unlike Powell, Oakeshott did not enthusiastically assert the virtues of capitalism; but it was clear what he meant.

Oakeshott's rejection of abstract principle was complemented by his conservatism: by a preference for the familiar, and a discussion of, for

instance, freedom not in terms of human rights in general but in terms
of the freedoms enjoyed in England. Politics ought not to involve the
construction or application of blueprints or grand plans, but the
'pursuit of intimations', the development and application of existing
customs and conventions. It was a conservative version of the
distinction which Geddes had drawn between utopia and eutopia. It
has been suggested that there was a contrast between this aspect of
Oakeshott's writings and his equal enthusiasm for variety and
individuality (Barber 1976: 456–7). But this is to misunderstand the
way in which the preference for freedom and the taste for conservatism
complemented and qualified each other in Oakeshott's work. The
freedoms preferred were not any that might be enjoyed by any body of
people, but those enjoyed at a particular time. To put the argument in
terms which Oakeshott did not employ, but which his argument
implied, it was a preference for an existing distribution of powers,
preserved against any redistribution which might be attempted by the
state. Hence it was also a conservative disposition, a disposition as
Oakeshott put it, 'appropriate to a man who is actually aware of having
something to lose which he has learned to care for' (Oakeshott 1967:
169). So the conception of conservatism and the conception of freedom
were merged. To be simply conservative in the 1950s would have been
to have accepted the legislative work of the Attlee government, which
Oakeshott clearly did not. To this extent the conservatism was
selective. It was

> the observation of our current manner of living combined with the
> belief (which from our point of view need be regarded as no more
> than an hypothesis) that governing is a specific and limited activity,
> namely the provision and custody of general rules of conduct, which
> are understood, not as plans for imposing substantive activities, but
> as instruments enabling people to pursue the activities of their own
> choice with the minimum of frustration, and therefore something
> which it is appropriate to be conservative about.
>
> (ibid.: 184)

The persuasive force of this argument depended on freedom, and the
account of the proper task of government, being defended on grounds
of conservatism, and presented as the given, historically evolved
condition of things in Britain. Society, which was conservative,
pluralist and cautious, was under threat from government which was
ambitious, dynamic and radical. But historically, Oakeshott's arguments were just as radical as the policies he attacked. They involved
championing one element in the political tradition, which was felt to be

under threat, against another which was felt to be in the ascendant. The juxtaposition of a centralizing state with a widely dispersed body of power in society implied that the kind of pluralism which was desired already existed, or could be produced with a few small adjustments, and that it was challenged by the actions of the state. Substantial satisfaction within society at the relative distribution of power within it was a necessary condition for a conservative libertarianism such as Oakeshott advanced. The assumption of consensus sustained the advocacy of ad hoc adjustments. So on the one hand, if the state aroused substantial opposition from the existing holders of power, it was ipso facto condemned, whilst if either state or groups or individuals attempted to alter the distribution – other than in the negative way of breaking up undue concentrations of power – they too could be accused of tampering with the free, in the sense of unconstrained by the state, exercise of existing freedoms, freedoms which were after all justified not by any abstract principle of freedom, but by the historical and conservative principle of being actually exercised by existing corporations. In dealing with the first point, Oakeshott argued that 'overwhelming power would be required only by a government which has against it a combination so extensive of the powers vested in such a variety of different individuals and interests as to convict the government of a self-interest so gross as to disqualify it for the exercise of its proper function' (ibid.: 42).

In dealing with the second point, Oakeshott designated syndicalism as joining with collectivism to form the 'two great, mutually exclusive contemporary opponents of libertarian society as we know it' (ibid.: 50). But his attack on syndicalism almost inevitably reads like an attack on a parody of his own views: 'Syndicalism is a contrivance by means of which society is disposed for a perpetual civil war in which the parties are the organized self-interest of functional minorities and a weak central government.' The attack was related to his other statements on the concentration and dispersal of power by the suggestion that all 'monopolies are prejudicial to freedom, but there is good reason for supposing that labour monopolies are more dangerous than any others'. But its coherence with the rest of his writing was weakened by the invocation of a 'community as a whole' whose interest was adversely affected by the 'monopoly prices and disorder' which result from trade union power (ibid.: 50, 53).

Conservative arguments such as those both of Oakeshott and of those advocates of greater trade union or employer power whom he termed syndicalist, represented an application of the assertion of group rights. The conservative argument was a defence of the powers and rights of existing associations, and of the existing powers and rights of those associations, rather than an assertion of the value of group powers and functions as such. The naturalness of such associations was thus frequently stressed. T.E. Utley in his *Essays in Conservatism* in 1949 wrote that 'The family, the tribe, the nation, are all forms of natural association which result from the interdependence of men. All of them are prior to the state, and the family and the nation have rights which do not derive from the *fiat* of the State' (Utley 1949: 4). Since the existing distribution of power and advantage was in general preferred, politics and state activity were valued as a means of preserving and when necessary adjusting that distribution, and hence they had a secondary importance. Utley distinguished between 'those who regard politics as supremely important and those who conceive it to be the hand-maid of religion, art, science and society. The Left are in the first category, Conservatives are in the second' (ibid.: 1). An extension of politics or state competence in new ways would involve a diminution in the powers of existing associations and it was perhaps more in defence of the advantages which he himself valued and spoke for, rather than in fear of the frustration of the hopes of socialists, that Utley argued that the Left 'failing to appreciate that politics is power, are perpetually inclined to extend the range of political action. Regarding political action as essentially beneficent, they legislate without realizing that they are extending the range of those human relationships which are conducted on the basis of command and obedience' (ibid.: 2).

The assertion of the market against the possibility of any central state direction of the economy and allocation and distribution of goods and services to groups and individuals had been made by Hayek in the 1930s and 1940s. The consolidation of the inter-party and wartime commitment to state welfare responsibility and the development of that commitment by the Attlee government was the occasion for a restatement of his position. The argument was set out in its fullest form in *The Constitution of Liberty*, first published in 1960 after nine years of Conservative government which, whatever glosses it had put on newly acquired public responsibilities and powers, had left them largely intact. This book raises a difficulty about the limits of an essay on political argument in Britain. Hayek taught at the London School of Economics from 1931 to 1950, but before that he worked in Vienna, and after that in Chicago, Freiburg and Salzburg. When *The Constitution of Liberty* was published he had been out of the United Kingdom for nearly ten years.

To what extent may his work be considered a part of a British

debate? In one sense there is no problem: the work was read and
quoted, as Marx or Maurras were read and quoted. But Marx, for
example, would not be considered to be more directly a part of a
British debate by virtue of his having spent the last years of his life in
Britain. Hayek's English-language work is more clearly part of an
Atlantic and European debate than of a specifically British one. The
problem is created by the existence of the United States of America
and by the especial accessibility of work written in that country to
English audiences. With Hayek's work in German there is no such
difficulty. Hayek seems to have been aware of this problem himself, and
in the preface to the book commented that perhaps

> the reader should also know that, though I am writing in the United
> States and have been a resident of this country for nearly ten years, I
> cannot claim to write as an American. My mind has been shaped by
> a youth spent in my native Austria and by two decades of middle life
> in Great Britain, of which country I have become and remain a
> citizen. To know this fact about myself may be of some help to the
> reader, for the book is to a great extent the product of this
> background.

(Hayek 1960: 8)

So the discussion of Hayek's work after 1950 involves some problems.
If one were dealing with his form of liberalism it would be appropriate
to do so in a context which went far beyond the politics of the United
Kingdom. There is thus a double abridgment of reality in including
him here, both because he is abstracted from what is his more
appropriate context, and because his claim for inclusion is not as clear
as that, for instance, of Kropotkin.

Hayek repeated his charges of incompetence, bureaucracy, extravagance and oppression, and called for a rule-maintaining rather than
a housekeeping state. Unlike opponents of the modern state such as
Oakeshott who had based a part of their arguments on conservatism
and a rejection of rationalist politics or policies deduced from general
principles, Hayek insisted on the necessity for precisely this. The
objection to conservatism was both that it committed one to going
with the drift of things, and that it provided only a limited and
expedient case against growing state responsibility: 'In general, it can
probably be said that the conservative does not object to coercion or
arbitrary power so long as it is used for what he regards as the right
purposes' (ibid.: 401). In distinction from conservatism Hayek
advanced a case for what he termed freedom or liberty, 'the condition
of men in which coercion of some by others is reduced as much as is

possible in society' (ibid.: 11). This definition was refined by introducing the notion of arbitrariness, freedom being that condition 'in which a man is not subject to coercion by the arbitrary will of another or others' (ibid.: 11). The consequence of this qualification was to imply a distinction between the constraints which men regularly place on others and which are thus part of the condition of things, and unpredictable constraints. Liberty thus 'leaves us to decide what use we shall make of the circumstances in which we find ourselves' (ibid.: 19). There was a small qualification of this view in the admission that coercion could involve the situation in which 'somebody else has power so to manipulate the conditions as to make him act according to this person's will rather than his own' (ibid.: 13). But the crucial word there was 'manipulate', which suggests unusual or particular intervention. For all his attack on conservatism, Hayek was bound to defend existing institutions and structures by his doctrine of freedom.

This is clear when the character of what Hayek terms the free society is examined. Despite his insistence that he was defending individual freedom, what in fact he was defending was the freedom of individuals within particular societies and subject to its restraints, conventions and hierarchies, from coercion by governments other than such coercion as was necessary to maintain an orderly structure for the conduct of human relations. The choice was not between individual freedom on the one hand, and uniformity on the other. Rather it was between an enforced and rigid uniformity maintained by the coercive power of the state on the one hand, and an informal and flexible uniformity maintained by social convention and hierarchy on the other. Elites would and should continue to exist, but they would not be sustained by law, and would have 'to prove themselves by their capacity to maintain their position under the same rules that apply to all others' (ibid.: 403). This argument made Hayek, in his own alternative terminology, a Whig rather than a liberal or a libertarian. The 'value of freedom', as he put it, 'consists mainly in the opportunity it provides for the growth of the undesigned, and the beneficial functioning of a free society rests largely on the existence of such freely grown institutions. . . . Paradoxical as it may appear, it is probably true that a successful free society will always in a large measure be a tradition-bound society' (ibid.: 61). The consequences of these arguments were that liberalism was employed to justify conservatism, for the kind of freedom which Hayek advocated had, as he put it, 'never worked without deeply ingrained moral beliefs . . . coercion can be reduced to a minimum only where individuals can be expected as a rule to conform voluntarily to certain principles' (ibid.: 62). It was the society which was to be free of the state, rather than the individuals who were to be free of the society.

This doctrine of liberty employed in the defence and promotion of hierarchy and orthodoxy presaged the tone of much political argument against the collectivist state. At its roughest this tradition of argument could be redolent of the social Darwinism of the years before 1914. A.M. Ludovici in a defence of property, hierarchy and aristocracy complained not only of the 'fraud, self-indulgence and sloth' created by social reform legislation but also of 'its twofold effect in character deteriorisation and in penalising the more industrious, thrifty, responsible and self-reliant members of the population for the sake of the indolent, profligate, unscrupulous and least disciplined' (Ludovici 1967: 170). But this was not the prevalent tone. More common, among conservatives who realized that whilst consensus might mean no extension of socialism, it also meant no contraction of it either, and amongst supporters of existing, threatened hierarchies, was a series of particular critiques of areas of public policy in the light of libertarian, conservative, market and hierarchic principles. The Institute of Economic Affairs provided through its publications a medium for those who from market preferences attacked the economic and social service activities of the state. A retreat from universal, monopoly services was recommended, either by means of the introduction of private enterprise alternatives, or by a system of public provision in cash or vouchers which would give consumer freedom to citizens. In education, the contributors to a series of *Black Papers* from 1968 onwards attacked the egalitarianism which underlay much public educational policy and advocated a market in education together with a differentiation of pupils by measurable ability. There was a defence of social convention which juxtaposed the conservative with the libertarian face of the protest. The libertarianism of the young in culture and morals was not regarded with enthusiasm.

In the writing of Hayek there had been a considered and measured adherence to democracy. For a few opponents of state collectivism, particularly in the 1970s, this adhesion was placed under severe strain. There was a long tradition of associating democracy with despotism. Dicey had articulated it before 1914, and it had been revived by the critics of the expanding responsibilities of the post-Second World War state. International events after 1970 exacerbated this suspicion of, and hostility to, democratic government and increased the fears and beliefs of those who believed that liberty was based on a diffusion of private property and were fearful of popular political power. The journalist

Robert Moss in *The Collapse of Democracy* took this tension between a belief in private property and a qualified adhesion to parliamentary democracy beyond the limits where both could be supported. For Moss a free society rested on a dissemination of property and hence of economic power. The power of parliamentary democracy to impede or alter this had to be curbed by a device such as a bill of rights. Moss's book represented a mixture of libertarianism and the defence of privilege, and like many of those who after the war years mingled conservatism, pluralism and libertarianism, he was discriminating in the group and social rights which he championed. It was vain to suppose, he argued, that trade unions could be made responsible by giving them more power. You could not turn 'poachers into gamekeepers' (Moss 1975: 116) – the peasants, in fact, had to be kept off the estate.

Not all those who recommended the virtues of the market against those of state collectivism, however, were committed to existing hierarchies or orthodoxies in morals and culture. For Samuel Brittan the values of what had by then come to be called 'the permissive society' were sustained by a free and competitive market: 'to the extent that it prevails, competitive capitalism is the biggest single force acting on the side of what [it] is fashionable to call "permissiveness", but what was once known as personal liberty' (Brittan 1973: 1). Brittan's argument was unusual for, as he pointed out, many defenders of private enterprise gave only qualified support to freedom and competition in all areas of life. Hence he was able to argue that there were affinities between a socialist humanism and genuine capitalism: 'the time is ripe for a realignment in which the more thoughtful members of the New Left and the more radical advocates of competitive free enterprise realise that they have a common interest in opposing the corporate industrial state' (ibid.: 36). But it was not simply a matter of economics. The general principles of libertarianism and competition which underlay capitalism 'have a great deal in common with contemporary attitudes, and in particular with contemporary radical attitudes. Above all they share a similar stress on allowing people to do, to the maximum feasible extent, what they feel inclined to do rather than conform to the wishes of authority, custom or convention' (Brittan 1973: 1). This was a thoroughgoing libertarianism that was not characteristic of most attacks on the post-war state.

Brittan's invitation to the New Left and the New Right to join hands illustrated once again the affinities which lay beneath the apparent alliances of political attitude and aspiration. The right to be left alone was, when stated without further qualification, a libertarianism which could be invoked in support of a range of activity, and if an Englishman's home was his castle, so was an Englishwoman's commune hers. From the reformist wing of the post-war Conservative Party Quintin Hogg had asserted another version of the primacy of the private, unpolitical activities of life.

The public sphere was of secondary importance to Conservatives he wrote, 'the simplest among them prefer foxhunting – the wisest religion' (Hogg 1947: 10). The defence of privacy – meaning, not secrecy, but the right to conduct one's own affairs as one wished – and the right to free expression were not defended solely by left or by right. When the editors of the magazine *Oz* were convicted in 1971 of publishing an obscene article, the right-wing *Spectator* was the only journal to criticize not only the sentence but the conviction, arguing that the 'right of any man to express himself as he wishes should not be constrained unless he interferes with his neighbour's right not to listen or look' (quoted in Palmer 1971: 268). In the matter of rights, the principles involved were always various and often confused. Discussions of a bill of rights after 1970 involved on the one hand the demand that constitutional restraints should be placed upon what Parliament might do, and on the other that the state guarantee the right to fair and equal treatment of disadvantaged groups such as women. The first had affinities with anti-state arguments, and was most frequently heard from politicians of the right. The second had affinities with state collectivism. But there was no simple division, and by the late 1960s the National Council for Civil Liberties was arguing both for the removal of obstructions to free behaviour and for public intervention to create conditions of equality.

The links which cultural and moral anarchism on the left had with libertarianism of the right were matched by affinities between market politics and the older anarchist tradition. Anarchism provided just that 'blood' for the New Left which Crosland had urged socialists always to be mindful, and proud, of. It was both a combative doctrine against the power of capitalism and the state, and a doctrine of living now as if the revolution had already occurred. The first element was articulated by Stuart Christie and Albert Meltzer, who concentrated their attention on the oppressive role of the state. Particular reforms, such as those pioneered in education by A.S. Neill, were 'not enough. Allied to education must be the movement to alter society' (Christie and Meltzer 1972: 37). The revolution, to be successful, had to be total. But the other aspect of the anarchist tradition stressed the immediate possibility and practicality of co-operation, self-help, and the control by people of their own immediate environments. Colin Ward, who edited at various times both the monthly *Anarchy* and the weekly *Freedom*, put forward a case for an anarchism that, 'far from being a speculative vision of a future society ... is a description of a mode of human organisation, rooted in the experience of everyday life, which operates side by side with, and in spite of, the dominant authoritarian trends in our society' (Ward 1973: 11). This application of the anarchist tradition involved not only the advocacy of a total alternative to existing social, political and economic relations, but the immediate pursuit in particular situations of co-operative and uncoerced form of education, the treatment of children, domestic life, sexual relations and work.

In its necessarily practical application this form of anarchism contained many arguments which were similar to sentiments in the work of advocates of private property and the market. Ward quoted with approval the Italian anarchist Giancarlo de Carlo to the effect that 'The home is man's affirmation in space' (Ward 1976: 169), and pointed out the benefits which followed from, if not the ownership of private property, then certainly the control of domestic property: 'how is it that on one side of town, substandard private housing is cherished and continuously improved by its occupants, while on the other Parker Morris expensively built council housing begins its cycle of deterioration the moment it is occupied?' (ibid.: 97). Modern planning, argued Ward, took no account of the variety of people's needs, nor of the active contribution which dwellers themselves could and should make to the improvement and hence the creation of their dwellings:

> The traditional unplanned city had a fine grain: there was always at some level or another, a space for everyone. But the doss-houses, common lodging houses, Rowton Houses and other forms of cheap lodging are rapidly being upgraded or planned out of existence. The planned, re-developed, improved city is coarse-grained: it admits only a restricted range of citizens.
>
> (ibid.: 159)

Ward came very close at times to advocating unregulated private enterprise for personal use in housing, and attacked the restrictions which planners and planning regulations placed on citizens building their own homes how and where they wished: 'our responsible authorities, themselves incapable (as they are bound to be within our economic structure) of solving the housing problem, take punitive action against people with enough initiative and independence to solve it for themselves' (ibid.: 66). But whereas right-wing libertarianism was radical towards government but conservative towards society, anarchism had always sought a revolution in the distribution not only of political but of social and economic power.

Anarchism had not been, however, a doctrine of simple revolution with a concomitant belief that until the revolution, nothing could be accomplished. Working in the tradition of Kropotkin and Geddes, both of whose work he cited, Ward argued for both the long-term solution and the particular, immediate and small-scale application of anarchist principles within an unreformed society. As he put it in 1976, 'one of the tasks of the anarchist propagandist is to propagate solutions to contemporary issues which, however dependent they are on the existing social and economic structure, are anarchist solutions' (ibid.: 10). Geoffrey Ostergaard made the same point in the monthly journal *Anarchy*: 'The task of the anarchist is not ... to dream about the future society; rather it is to act as anarchistically as he can within the present society' (in *Anarchy*, October 1962, quoted in Stafford 1971: 9). These practical but anarchist solutions in housing and planning involved 'dweller-control', tenants' cooperatives, squatting, all intended to acknowledge and develop the role of those who lived in houses as actively involved in using and developing their houses and not simply receiving benefits from public bodies. Established public policy on housing only made sense, Ward argued, 'if we assume that the only factors in the provision of housing are the technocrats and the bureaucrats and the capitalist building industry. The missing factor, left out of all the calculations, is popular involvement' (Ward 1976: 98). What could be done in housing and the creation and growth of towns could be done also in education, in the workplace, in the organization of social services.

NEW PLURALISMS

There was of course an element of piecemeal reform about this kind of anarchism, even though it also implied a theory of permanent revolution rather than of a transforming cataclysm. Not all those who participated in the revival of anarchist argument from the early 1960s shared this approach, working rather in the tradition of Bakunin and the revolutionary overthrow of the existing order. And in addition to those who despaired of the existing order of things and worked for, and waited until, their complete overflow, there were those who from a similar immediate despair moved not towards total confrontation, but towards withdrawal. The year which provided visions and memories for radicals and the left in western Europe, 1968, saw the publication of *Communes*, the journal of the commune movement. The significance of the self-conscious commune movement was both ambiguous and various. Abrams and McCulloch caught some of this ambiguity when in their study of communes they commented that

> in an oblique but unmistakable sense, communes had something to say about the politics of revolution. Appearing in the context and the aftermath of some spectacular failures of direct political action, and against the background of many sobering demonstrations of the power and unresponsiveness of institutionalised politics, communes suggested the possibility of a political detour.
>
> (Abrams and McCulloch 1976: 6)

But what kind of a detour? There was no break in the long continuum from being a cultural and ideological fallout shelter for the fugitives from an infected society, to being a small light in a naughty world, burning not for the sake of the candle but to illuminate the darkness for those who still inhabited it. There was no discernible break in the line which ran from a withdrawn and alternative culture, through the culture which either fructified the whole or made it richer by variety, to a counter-culture which was a basis for opposing and a sketch for replacing or succeeding the existing, dominant order. Thus do political beliefs which have apparently been happily sufficient in the withdrawn seclusion of the wilderness begin to emerge with the dust of the desert about them and denounce the sovereign order at the foot of its very throne. Arks have a persistent tendency to turn first into gunboats and then into heavy cruisers.

The outward spiral of state activity and state responsibility was accompanied and followed not only by the continued and renewed assertion of libertarian and collectivist arguments, but by the assertion of the claims of particular groups and classes. This involved claims for the autonomous activity of groups. But the claim was only in part a form of libertarian pluralism, since it involved or implied consequences for collective, public, state policy. The pluralism of the first quarter of the twentieth century had eventually become an aspect of the broadening focus of politics, a means of incorporating activities into the ambit of the collectivist state rather than of asserting their independence from it. The pluralist political arguments of the latter 1960s accompanied a continuing expansion of state responsibility – but they also involved a reaction against the centralization of power which that involved, and had not by the mid-1970s become themselves assimilated into a yet broader centralized collectivism. They made radical demands on the state, but also asserted autonomy from it. Although British socialism had always been, amongst other things, about power, the main emphasis had been on power exercised in a single way and through a single channel. The people were to enjoy power through democratic politics and the influence which that gave them upon the operations of the state. So power was to be exercised centrally over all the various and particular aspects of life by the state, which was in its turn to be subject to the will of democracy. In industry and work, the spread of democracy thus meant the spread of national control, not the introduction of self-government as advocated by the guild socialists. Workers were, in this sense, to control the publicly owned industries in which they worked in exactly the same way, but only in that way, in which they controlled industries in which they did not work: through the ballot box.

By the end of the Attlee government the actual experience of widespread nationalization had led to a dissatisfaction with this scenario which was to feed a further strand of the New Left. The very success of achieving public ownership through nationalization led to second thoughts, which drew upon the traditions of functional control and worker's self-government. The nationalization of major industries did not lead to substantial changes in the position of the workers in those industries, whilst such participation or consultation as there was seemed in part to justify the Webbs' warnings about the capturing of the trade union opposition if it compromised its critical, independent, bargaining role by becoming involved with management. Management itself gave some unwitting support for these suspicions by its enthusiasm which, in so far as it adopted the forms of participation rather than of control, made such schemes appear an instrument of the management rather than of the workers. Profit-sharing as a form of industrial partnership had been encouraged by the individualist opponents of trade unionism before the First World War, and G.D.H. Cole has spent much effort in threading a distinction between acceptable encroaching control and unacceptable absorption by the capitalist system. When Crosland wrote in *Encounter* in 1959 that a 'great deal can be done ... by enlightened personnel management' he was expressing precisely that aspect of participation which aroused the suspicion and hostility of advocates of greater working-class power in industry (Crosland 1962: 226). Crosland, together with Crossman and Strachey, his fellow-contributors to the *New Fabian Essays* in 1952, were opposed to workers' control, preferring instead the application of existing centralized democracy to the economy. Strachey wrote of the importance of 'a large industry which is ultimately responsible to elected representatives of the whole population, instead of to a motley, ever changing, but relatively narrow, group of shareholders' (Strachey 1956: 278).

But at the same time Crosland, Crossman and Strachey all spoke of the need for a diffusion of power and for greater participation, Crossman calling for a general increase in 'the citizen's right to participate in the control not only of government and industry, but of the party for which he votes, and of the trade union whose card he carries' (Crossman [1952] 1970: 29). Crosland spoke of a diminution of differences of status between employers and employees, proposed a theory of society and of socialism in terms of status and power, and attempted to give an account of the citizen which made him or her more than a claimant or a resource and an occasional elector. The improvement in the quality of life and in the workers' influence over their environment which Crosland detected was not presented as arising from or likely to be sustained by workers' control, but rather by workers' bargaining power exercised through trade unions. Nonetheless the stress laid on the qualitative aspect of socialism shifted argument away from the kinds of consideration that had characterized earlier, managerial conceptions of public ownership.

In the writings of the New Left control over people's immediate environment, including the workplace, held an important place. The very first number of *New Left Review* in the spring of 1960 complained that the 'present form of nationalization is not a socialist form: it does not give ordinary men and women direct control over their own lives' (quoted in Stafford 1971: 8). The new accessibility, for English readers, of Marx's *1844 Manuscripts* and the subsequent discussion of alienation, and the reviving interest in the work of socialists such as William Morris, were part of a condition of thought in which Raymond Williams, in 1958, could describe Guild Socialism, which had been increasingly neglected since the 1950s, as a 'creative and indispensable' element in British culture (Williams 1961a: 191). Three years later in *The Long Revolution* he wrote that it was 'difficult to feel that we are really governing ourselves if in so central a part of our living as our work most of us have no share in decisions that immediately affect us' (Williams 1961b: 332). The nationalized industries were particularly criticized by Williams because they ought to have been characterized by a break with pre-socialist relationships and forms of organization, whereas in fact they had 'reproduced, sometimes with appalling accuracy, the human patterns, in management and working relationships, of industries based on quite different social principles' (Williams 1961b: 330). So in their different ways both the revisionists and the New Left argued for the importance of the quality of life and the free action of citizens. In one case this facilitated arguments for workers' control, in the other, it was an essential part of such arguments. The tradition of argument represented by Cole and by Tawney was thus revived. The political scientist H.R.G. Greaves, in a lecture in 1964, spoke in terms reminiscent of those employed by Tawney in 1920 when, recommending workers' participation, he said that it depended on

> the mutual acceptance by all concerned of what can best be called a status of membership, entailing at least certain elements of freedom, responsibility and equality. Joint consultation is an attempt to express them. They articulate the principle of partnership in a common concern. They contrast the idea of men as partners in production, with the idea of men as the human instruments of production set on a par with the other machinery of production, and similarly directed and controlled.
>
> (Greaves 1964: 5)

So a re-examination of the arguments for workers' control was made possible. The particular occasion for this re-examination was the unlikely combination of the election of a Labour government in 1964 and 1966, and the events of May 1968. The first reintroduced nationalization as a question of practical left-wing politics, the second aroused new enthusiasms for popular action. Within particular trade unions such as the AEU and the NUR there had for some years been agitation for some form of workers' control, and in 1966 a series of conferences were begun which led in 1968 to the formation of the Institute for Workers' Control as a centre for discussion, education and propaganda. The arguments of prominent members and associates of the IWC, such as Ken Coates, Tony Topham and Michael Barratt Brown, contained many traditional and familiar elements. Workers' control was, as it was for the syndicalist, a use of the power most readily available to the worker for the supplanting of capitalism. But William Morris's assertion that no man is good enough to be another's master was frequently quoted, and status was involved as well as power. Coates and Topham, for instance, advocated in 1972 an approach to industrial organization which would ask

> What a man's life is for. It will hold out human horizons beyond the sums of production statistics. It will challenge the power of one man over another, in order to develop the social capacity of all men within nature ... it will also wage implacable war against

subordination, manipulation, and all authority that is not freely and spontaneously required by those over whom it is exercised.

(Coates and Topham 1972: 38)

Workers' control was also advocated as a mixture of short-term and long-term policy: the first to improve the condition of the workers, the second to move towards a socialist society. As Ernie Roberts put it in 1973, it was 'concerned both with the first level of achievement that we have in industries and unions at the moment, and with the achievement ultimately of workers' power: the power to control our lives, our industries, and the country in which we live' (Roberts 1973: 9). From this point of view workers' direct action was part of a wider political strategy. Unlike syndicalism it did not rely entirely on industrial strength, but recommended a mixture of political and industrial tactics, as had Miliband in his 1961 study of the Labour Party, *Parliamentary Socialism*. But the advocates of workers' control shared with the syndicalist the notion of action changing consciousness. As Roberts put it,

> it is primarily through their own practical everyday experiences that the workers will learn about the nature of the capitalist state, and how to consolidate and extend their control over various aspects of their working lives. As a result of their experiences, they will evolve a theory and practice which will lead to the complete overthrow of the existing order and its substitution by a worker-controlled state.
>
> (ibid.: 59)

One of the problems facing the proponents of workers' control had always been the counter-demand for profitability. If, for instance, the workers rather than the management were to control appointments, promotions and dismissals, might not employment policies be pursued which would damage or even eliminate profitability? In an attempt to place the argument on quite different grounds, the notion of social costs or social audit was introduced, whereby the consequences of policies were viewed in a context wider than that of the individual factory or industry. In one sense there was nothing new in this. Aneurin Bevan had insisted on the need to take into account not only immediate industrial costs but social costs as well. But in its new form the argument served a double purpose. For it met a second objection to any form of workers' control, and one frequently put by the Webbs, that production ought to be subject to the national interest as represented by the totality of citizen consumers. To give power over a particular industry or factory to its workers was to establish a sectional and potentially monopolistic fly in the communal ointment. The notion of social audit answered this objection by widening the context of the discussion to take in the interests of communities other than the controlling workers and, potentially, the whole national community. Thus Michael Barratt Brown proposed linking various social audit groups by means of research and exchange centres and by the creation of national social audit groups, a solution reminiscent of the federal superstructure of guild socialism. The management's economic perspectives were thus transcended, and the charge of self-interest rebutted.

As well as trade union leaders such as Jack Jones, politicians such as Tony Benn were associated with the IWC. Benn contributed to the 1973 pamphlet, *Workers' Control: How Far Can the Structure Meet Our Demands?*, and a year later was to be in a position to give governmental encouragement to his socialist colleagues. But though in doing so he was acting within a well-established tradition of British politics, that tradition had by then broadened beyond the boundaries of the factory. The early 1970s were characterized not only by the resurgent interest in workers' control but also by an engagement in participatory politics and direct, functional groups. The formation of tenants' groups and claimants' unions drew on two beliefs which underlay the arguments for workers' control: that people's interests were best-served when they took direct responsibility for promoting them; and that it was in itself desirable that individuals and groups should manage their own affairs, for by so doing they augmented their social humanity.

The debate over workers' control involved a re-examination of the character of citizenship and of the various forms of political participation, activity and representation. The idea of functional representation rather than representation in geographical constituencies was revived (Roberts 1973: 263), and the potential and limitation of reliance on parliamentary representation discussed (Miliband 1961). The nature of citizenship was also raised again in the arguments over sex and nationality as categories of political activity and political oppression. From the end of the 1960s, there was a revival of feminist argument in Britain. One approach to the disappointing consequences of the enfranchisement of women had been to argue that legislative reform was not yet completed and that for instance support for equal pay for equal work was required. But the political arguments of feminism from the late 1960s went far beyond such reforms, to constitute the most substantial and radical component of the New Left.

The argument involved the identification of inequalities and oppression in areas which had previously not readily been thought of as political, particularly relations between men and women in the family, but also the characterization of women in the culture and ideology of society, and the consequences of concepts of sexual divisions and differentiations. In a conventional sense much of the feminist writing from the late 1960s was not about 'politics' but about something far wider (e.g. Mitchell 1971, Rowbotham 1973). The extension involved not only the argument that matters were properly subject for public concern which had previously not been thought to be so. It also involved arguing that they were already political in that political and governmental institutions were deeply involved in maintaining certain patterns of advantage and disadvantage. It was pointed out, for instance, that 'the state upholds the family in its present form and, thereby, forces women into a position of dependence on men'. (Women's Liberation Campaign for Legal and Financial Independence 1975:1) This allegation that the activity of the state was wider and more partial than was generally supposed or publicly accepted was one which divided feminists from most of those who had argued either in favour of or against the collectivist state, and who had seen the state as in general distinct from society, and acting upon it in a way which could be increased, reduced or altered. Marxists and anarchists, on the other hand, had seen a relation between state and society whereby the state in its character, structure and operation sustained, administered and enforced a particular kind of society in the interests of particular groups and particular values. This conception of the partiality of the state also emerged from feminism. Hence radical demands were made upon the state both for it to cease upholding the existing subordination of women, and for it actively to work for their liberation. The feminist arguments constituted a critique of the adequacy of existing notions of citizenship – somehow women got left out. But at the same time the formal promises implied in the notion of citizenship led to demands that the state fulfil its obligations. What were claimed on behalf of the state and of citizenship in theory stimulated and supported demands for transformation of what was available in reality.

THE MOVE TO THE ACADEMY, BRITAIN IN THE WORLD, THE CONTINUATION OF POLITICAL ARGUMENT

The nationalist arguments of the 1960s and 1970s, unlike the revived and expanded feminist case, added little to what had been said earlier in the century. The statement of Gwynfor Evans and Ioan Rhys that 'Those of us who wish to see more frontiers in the world, whether we be Welsh or Scots or Catalan or Basques or Breton, also wish to see all frontiers made lower' would have received sympathetic recognition from Chesterton (Edwards et al. 1968: 24). But though there were differences, there were also similarities. A feature of both feminist and nationalist argument and of political argument in general which marked off the middle of the twentieth century from the years before the First World War was the change in its location. Not only was intellectual life becoming, as Collini put it, less concentric (Collini 1991: 21), but political argument was conducted increasingly in the environs either of the political parties or of the universities. Crosland and Robson, Powell and Crick, replaced Morris and Spencer, Chesterton and Shaw, as the man of letters whilst not disappearing, became rarer and rarer.

The contribution of political scientists and of academics in general to political argument has been subjected to scorn and criticism. Ernest Benn wrote in 1932 of the establishment by the professors of 'a new class called experts, to act as a buffer between the politician and his folly' (Benn 1932: 153). Hayek rebuked economists in 1944 for having been 'absorbed by the war machine, and silenced by their official positions' (Hayek 1944: v). What Hayek was doing was no more than a particular application of the general view arising within the Marxist tradition, that intellectuals were the ideological agents of the power of the state and of capitalism. Alasdair MacIntyre wrote in 1960 of the university teacher that as 'the supporter of the dominant ideas in our culture he is gradually transformed into a trustworthy guardian of our society's ideology' (Thompson et al. 1960: 209). But if academics in general and political scientists in particular had become lions under the throne, both this event and the exceptions to it need explanation. For both Hayek and MacIntyre, when they made their observations, were themselves university teachers and had thus taken the king's shilling. Moreover revolutionary socialism, feminism, anarchism and workers' control, the radical arguments of the 1960s and 1970s, whilst drawing their initial vigour from outside the universities, had also been developed, sustained and transmitted within them.

It is not as surprising as many found it at the time that active dissent occurred so frequently within the universities in the 1960s and early 1970s, for this was the obverse of the academicization of political argument. Even a movement such as the Campaign for Nuclear Disarmament, although not a university movement, was more of a students' movement than any previous mass lobby. The move to the academy was associated with an openness to ideas from other countries through the university connection. This resulted in an increase in the variety and vitality of political argument, though it had other characteristics. Many of the issues discussed were international or even universal as well as specifically British, concerned with capitalism, or communism, or imperialism. When Britain commanded an empire which covered the world, to discuss any of these topics was to discuss British politics. Indeed the politics of these wider issues could almost seem a subordinate theme within an essentially British argument. But whereas the rivers of argument formerly flowed outwards from Britain, the tide had now been reversed, and British politics easily became an instance in matters which had continental or universal significance.

Political argument in Britain in the second quarter of the century had been characterized by an increasing importance of political events occurring, and political ideas being stated, outside the United Kingdom. The world provided both a point of reference and a subject of attention. This was even more the case from the 1950s, as foreign events and causes appeared more and more relevant to internal political discussion. Earlier in the century, enthusiasms had been directed towards the examples of regimes, in Russia, in Germany, in Italy. By the third quarter of the century, although there were regimes which aroused enthusiasm, in Cuba, in China or in Yugoslavia, there were fewer people who detected the future working in any existing system. Rather it was the struggles of dissident groups, revolutionaries, nationalists, in Vietnam, Chile, Russia or Southern Africa, or the internal political contests in France, or Portugal, which lured and roused political hopes.

One consequence of this was that a great deal of political argument which was immediately and initially about Britain was also about politics in general or the world as a whole. The arguments which took place over the purpose and methods of workers' control in the 1970s were not so much about the politics of Britain, as about the politics of socialism and capitalism (e.g. Hyman 1974; Brown et al. 1975). Racism, or capitalism, or bureaucracy, or socialism in Britain became instances in wider events, or tests of universal doctrines. It was not only the increase of international political and intellectual communication which facilitated this. Such economic autonomy as Britain had ever enjoyed was increasingly diminished. Decisions were made in other countries which determined the price and availability of raw materials, whilst as commercial organizations became international, it became implausible to argue that their activities were subordinated to public policy or state regulation or initiative.

Yet political ideas were still set out in a recognizably national context. The New Left which grew out of the betrayals and revelations of 1956 was characterized by placing itself in a British popular tradition. The political values for which it argued were picked neither from the air nor from abroad, but from what were presented as indigenous, submerged and resistant political traditions. Thus when E.P. Thompson gave an account of his own location in a Marxist tradition, it was a British location, not one without historical context – one, rather, which was both distinctively Marxist and distinctively British. The setting for opposition was thus a democratic one and a national one, and Thompson wrote with some degree of assertive pride of 'an ancient Protestant island' and associated himself with 'English empiricism, romanticism, traditionalism' – 'our best moralism has been contextual' (Thompson 1974: 14, 12, 14). British political circumstances and traditions became the medium within which arguments of wider significance were pursued.

The example of the New Left emphasized what had always been the case, that political argument in Britain has not been undertaken by people whose eyes were shielded by glasses which tinted automatically at the appearance of a thought from abroad. The growth of an international academic community would by itself have ensured this, just as would the international revolutionary and socialist movement in the nineteenth century. At the same time writers in Britain have occupied and have insisted upon an intellectual tradition which is particular without being insular. So by this insistence, and by the growth and exploitation of a national tradition to which specific reference can be made and from which directions and inspiration can be gained, a body of argument has continued which is recognizably British.

This body of argument has been made up of many and various strands and no one element within it can be presented as the traditional or natural or properly British manner of arguing about politics. There is no one essential set of aims and values. But this is not to reduce the variety to a bazaar in which the richness of the display transcends and synthesizes the variety of the items. Although none can either be excluded or claim a monopoly, neither do the elements form a consistent whole lacking in antagonisms. The fact that the arguments both for a technocratic planning elite and for producer control have been put within the context of a single political culture does not make them compatible. Workers' control and welfare paternalism are mutually antagonistic; if Tawney on equality is accepted, Mallock on oligarchy must be rejected; if Morris's assertions as to how people might live are allowed, Wells's samurai must go out of the window. Were this not the case, no one would have bothered to put the arguments in the first place.

So the years after 1950 saw a continued and revived vigour and variety in political argument. Those who had suggested that the old arguments were dead had nonetheless drawn particular and contentious conclusions from this, and had developed, rather than been quiescent in the face of, the notion of a new consensus. Political philosophers were soon to detect tremors of life in their own supposedly moribund discipline (Greaves 1960; Laslett and Runciman 1962). The scope of political discussion was widened so that political argument in Britain became increasingly a part of argument in, and about, Europe, America and the world. At the same time the scope of the political was enlarged, and the number of issues and areas where, in particular, questions of power were detected was widened. There was renewed discussion of the diffusion of power, of functional control and of the distribution amongst citizens and groups of what state collectivism had centralized as part of a representative social and economic democracy. Attempts were made to shorten the logistical chain between representatives and those they represented, by a functional and geographical devolution and dissemination of power. Ernie Roberts, writing of workers' control in a socialist society, insisted that the 'fight for democracy does not stop at the crisis point of "taking power" – in fact, it should never stop' (Roberts 1973: 30). Just so political argument continued, for the achievement of one aim, or the obsolescence of one idea, simply prepared the way for another. As one common sense is established, new challenges are made to it. It is in this manner that political argument continues, and in this manner that it revises, subverts and circumvents established conceptions and perceptions, and creates new ones which in their turn are the starting point and the subject matter of further argument. In such a debate, whether each truth is believed to encapsulate its predecessor, or there is thought to be a continuous process of both gain and loss of insight and comprehensiveness, there can be no conclusion.

So I rhetorically ended in 1978. But this should not be taken to mean that an account of political argument in the twentieth century would simply be a matter of one damn thing after another. To talk of arrivals and departures is one metaphor. Another would be to talk of the conceptual worlds or languages which were available in the last part of the twentieth century or, as it has been put, after the end of the short twentieth century, and the ways in which they both drew on elements from earlier languages, and invented new ones. This entails an account of the recessive elements in the short twentieth century which were to emerge as major or dominant elements thereafter. The next ten years were to see two events: the governmental and intellectual rise of the New Right, and the collapse of managerial communism in Eastern Europe and the Soviet Union, which were to transform political thinking. It is to the consequences and circumstances of this that the three final chapters are devoted.

8 The death of conservatism and the dispersal of liberalism

THE DEATH OF CONSERVATISM

Some time in the last quarter of the chronological twentieth century, over a period of years rather than at one single date, but indubitably and irrevocably by the end of the 1980s, conservatism vanished as a significant presence in British political thinking. It did not disappear utterly and without trace. There were still hints and shreds of it to be found in pamphlets, speeches, and even the occasional academic textbook. But it was no longer a major part of political debate. It was killed, so it seemed, by its successor the New Right which like many patricides went to some lengths to try to convince people that nothing had changed, that the old order was still in place, and the old values still followed. This impression was given initial credibility by the circumstances of the transition. The ascendancy of the New Right was not only an intellectual ascendancy, but an ascendancy of parties and governments which had previously been the vehicles of traditional conservatisms: not only in Britain under Margaret Thatcher but in the United States under Ronald Reagan; in France under Maurice Chirac; and in what was still then West Germany under Helmut Kohl. Institutional continuity helped sustain the illusion of ideological continuity.

But the demise of conservatism was not a simple consequence of the rise of the New Right, and both were part of a series of changes whose circumstances were not simply domestic. Conservatism had developed in response to two revolutions on the mainland of Europe, and their repercussions – or feared and supposed repercussions – at home. The French Revolution of 1789 and the Russian Revolution of 1917 raised up the two great challenges against which conservatism, as a defensive account of government and society, gave itself shape. The revolutions of 1989, in bringing to an end the division of Europe and of the world which Europeans inhabited into two military, ideological and economic camps, deprived conservatism of its second historical rationale at a time when the New Right was usurping its domestic intellectual function. There is a paradox here. Conservatives, despite the elegance with which many of them wrote, had habitually presented themselves as people of instinct and convention, rather than of rational planning. Grand theories and the politics which were ostensibly derived from them were for others: liberals, socialists, and continental Europeans of a certain kind. Yet the New Right employed precisely such arguments from principle. Only the revolutions of 1989 eventually spared it, but not for several years, the possibility of being classed with the politics of ideology, alongside conservatism's principal example of that particular error, the Soviet Union and its Eastern European satellites.

In Britain the demise of conservatism began in circumstances which seemed at the time to be not a death but a renewal and a resurgence. In 1979 a Conservative government under the premiership of Margaret Thatcher took office, and remained in power under her leadership for the next eleven years, and under that of her successor John Major for a further seven years. The combination of policy, action, and rhetoric which characterizes any party or government soon came to be described, in the case of the Conservative Party and government, as 'Thatcherism', a phenomenon about which a great deal came to be written, and whose precise place in the broader category 'New Right' was and continues to be the subject of a great deal of discussion.

Any characterization of a style or form of political conduct – action and thinking qualifying each other – stands at one remove from a characterization of political thinking, which is broader than the ethos of any institution whether that institution is a party or a government. But the various accounts of 'Thatcherism', in their disagreement as to whether it was a continuation of traditional Conservative Party politics or a radical departure from them, paralleled the differing accounts which were given of the morphology and mortality of conservatism as a network of political thinking. The principal discussion was precisely over continuity and identity. Was 'Thatcherism' a break with conservatism, a fulfilment of it, or a subtle continuation of old aims with new rhetoric? The answers to these questions form a substantial discussion and an abundant literature. They are a topic in themselves, and I have not considered them here. Nonetheless some of the answers given, and some of the uncertainties and problems identified, indicate that the conclusion of old patterns and the emergence of uncertain new ones was a feature not only of political thinking, but of political life as a whole.

The speeches and actions of politicians and rulers stand at one remove from the arguments of political thinkers, and even from their own arguments in print or on the platform. Nonetheless the Thatcher government turned the 1980s into a decade distinguished by the New Right's ascendency both intellectually and in office. The successes of government gave encouragement and prestige to the body of ideas from which those governments, at the same time but in their own terms, drew justifications for what they wished to do, and goals to which they might aspire.

But the continued success of a party whose title described it as conservative concealed the fact that it was that very success that was the institutional base for the jettisoning of conservatism. This illustrated the symbiotic relationship between the activity of political thought and the campaigning, administrating, policy making activities of a party. Each draws strength from the other, without simply expressing or being determined by it. It is a form of mutual dependence that can be described as the 'Constantine relationship' (R. Barker 1996a) and in the case of conservatism and the New Right it concealed the fact that the political thinking which sustained, and was sustained by, party conservatism was by the end of the 1980s quite different from that which had been associated with the party in the past. Were it not for this relationship, were political thought a form of politics carried on without any connection or reciprocal influence with the activities of institutions such as parties, then there would have been less reason for the growth of the New Right to have been the occasion for the death of conservatism.

There were a number of cautious obituaries and farewells. Neville Johnson wrote in 1992 that 'there may no longer be any substantial social or moral foundation for a body of practice and thought that can realistically be designated "conservative"' ('What will you conserve?', Times Literary Supplement 972, October 1992, 10, quoted in Miliband 1994: 4). John Gray, even though he thought there was still life in conservatism, considered it to have been deposed and driven into exile by 'Maoism of the Right' (Gray 1993a, 1995b: 87), whilst Roger Scruton, in the midst of a vigorous explication of conservative 'dogma', euphemistically conceded that 'the Conservative Party has often acted in a way with which a conservative may feel little sympathy' (Scruton [1980] 1984: 15). Even those who claim to have caught sight of conservatism, by their very descriptions identify a phenomenon which existed in the earlier part of the century, but had vanished by its closing years. If, like Charles Covell, they identify the representatives of contemporary conservatism as writing 'in the context of the reversal of the postwar consensus which culminated in the Conservative victory of 1979' (Covell 1986: 202), they have at the very least to reconcile traditional accounts of conservatism with the idea of sharp historical and intellectual breaks. Covell himself, whilst arguing that there is still something appropriately called conservatism in the late 1980s, is aware too of how easily it might be accounted for as no more than a 'dissenting intellectual strategy', 'romantic disdain', or 'reactionary or nostalgic' (ibid.: 209). If, as Philip Norton claims (1994: 40), the two principal characteristics of conservatism are scepticism and natural conservatism, there have been no notable conservatives in the latter twentieth century. Attempts such as those of Lincoln Allison to set out even at a level of moderate abstraction an account of conservatism are faced with the difficulty that the passionate advocacy of markets simply does not fit with the caution and pragmatism which conservatism had been able to enjoy. There were 'important beliefs which are, in England, recognisably conservative, which are in logical opposition to the main tenets of marketism' (Allison 1984: 15). Scepticism has been replaced by fierce dogma, and a conservative disposition by crusading partisanship. Though supporters of the change might present it in a different colour, the substance of their judgement was the same. In an admiring comment on the contribution of F.A. Hayek to contemporary debate, John Gray observed that 'a contemporary conservative who values private property and individual liberty cannot avoid being an intellectual and moral radical' (Gray 1984: 134). Paternalism, the defining feature of the Tory strand within conservatism, vanished equally completely. The Tory tradition which with Maine saw elites as the cultivators of progress, tolerance, and cultural advance, or with Mallock as the guardians of the material well-being of the people, or with Baldwin as the responsible trustees of their fellow citizens, or with Macmillan as moderate and moderating patricians – all of that was pushed aside as 'nannying', as elite presumption, or as liberal arrogance (Scruton 1984).

The themes which occupied the place which conservatism had previously filled had been termed as early as the 1960s, when they were in their relative infancy, as the 'New Right' (Collard 1968). But if that title implied that there had been an old right, it was misleading. What emerged at the close of the short twentieth century was something in spirit more akin to continental European right-wing thinking of the nineteenth and early twentieth century, and for some the extra-parliamentary right of France and Germany were cited not only as examples of what to avoid, but as valuable 'restatements of things that have been fundamental to our own Conservative tradition, and should not be lost from sight' (Griffiths 1978: 134). The New Right was not an alternative to either conservatism or economic liberalism, but a progression from both of them in circumstances which made each inappropriate or implausible as means of pursuing the ends, and maintaining the values and institutions, with which they had traditionally been associated. When the political scientist John Gray, who had been an enthusiastic commentator on the work of F.A. Hayek, parted company with the New Right, his sojourn with traditional conservatism, though imaginative, was brief, since there was nowhere left to sojourn (Gray 1993a). Conservatism had depended upon a homogeneous culture regulated and cultivated by a secure hierarchy. The values and practices it supported could then be defended without recourse to broad principle, without radicalism or dogma. But once that society was replaced, or, which is what matters, once the common perceptions were not of such a society, but of a society with a plurality of values and practices, the advocacy of any particular culture could only be partisan in character and doctrinaire in advocacy.

The disappearance of conservatism was not simply a matter of some of the aspirations and aversions which conservatives had shared being taken up in a different form by the New Right. As Bernard Shaw had earlier pointed out, 'tories' were to be found in all parties, and the paternalist element within conservatism, whilst it suffered a massive rebuff at the end of the century, could still be found, in exile, on the left, in the arguments for society's responsibility towards its most vulnerable members, and in advocacy of government's responsibility actively to intervene where the well-being of the commonwealth, that interest which all had in common, was threatened.

THE DISPERSAL OF LIBERALISM

If conservatism passed away, that was at least a discernible event, a move from presence to absence. The history of liberalism was less straightforward. For much of the twentieth century, whether chronological or 'short', there was little or no liberal equivalent to the conservatism of Mallock, or Cecil, or Baldwin, or Oakeshott, or to the socialism of Cole, or Tawney, or Laski, or Orwell or Crosland. Yet though there was no body of liberal political writing, liberal ideas were everywhere. Classical liberal economics in various levels of dilution formed one pole of the debates of economists and non-economists alike; appeals to democracy, individual rights and freedom, constitutional government or the rule of law presupposed, though less frequently invoked, liberal principles and assumptions. The absence of sustained arguments for liberalism was complemented by the presence of liberal assumptions at almost every point in the discussion of public affairs. Liberalism was present in another arena as well. If the everyday dialect of political language had a liberal inflexion, the contribution of liberalism to academic political philosophy was large, grew larger, and continued to expand. Yet this liberalism, both in the political and the academic worlds, was composed of two elements which, since the time of Hobhouse and New Liberalism, had kept each other company less and less: political liberalism and economic liberalism. The first saw politics either as the most powerful instrument for the preservation of individual rights and the promotion of individual interests, or as a form of human activity whereby individual autonomy and individual flourishing were enhanced. The second saw government as a necessary coercive institution for making possible the exercise of utilitarian individual choices in an economic market, and viewed politics with suspicion as a threat to such unconstrained, rational and materialist human activity (R. Barker 1996a).

So both at an academic level and at the level of ordinary discussion, fragmented liberal themes flourished. It was only in the middle ground that so little seemed to be happening. And it was in the middle ground that the New Right created a set of political arguments which finally registered the dismemberment of liberalism into political and economic segments, and which catalysed economic liberalism into its own distinctive fusion which drew on, yet moved far beyond, the liberal intellectual parentage.

THE NEW RIGHT

The most novel feature of the New Right is indicated in its title: not the word 'new', for as has often been pointed out, none of the particular ideas were in themselves new, or if they were, they were derived from familiar conservative and liberal ancestors (Gamble 1983; King 1987: 2; Hoover and Plant 1989), but the word 'right'. Before the emergence of the New Right, though left and right continued in popular identification of political and partisan allegiances, the use of the terms had been criticized either for exaggerating the extent of disagreements, or for identifying the wrong ones (Brittan 1968). The division of political thought into 'left' and 'right', despite its subsequent usages, had after all its origins in the political divisions of the French

Revolution, before any polarization between socialism and capitalism, or any tripartite division between socialism, conservatism and liberalism had occurred. The use of left and right descriptions or categories depicted both sides as partisan, both as arguing for causes and principles, both, equally, as enthused by visions of desired and alternative social orders. The 'right' in New Right was an appropriate word to describe a vehemence in argument which had previously been the almost exclusive preserve, during the class politics and government of the middle part of the century, of critics, whether liberal or socialist, of existing social and economic arrangements. With the eclipse of conservatism by the New Right, a new player joined that particular activity.

The first question to be answered however is not 'is there really a New Right?' or 'what is the real character of the New Right?' nor 'how did it achieve the success that it has achieved', but 'what are the predominant forms of political thought after the end of the short twentieth century, and what term or terms best briefly indicate their general character?' In attempting to answer this question it is not necessary to show that every argument which is described as 'right' rather than 'left' springs logically from one common principle, nor that what is termed 'right' is always and everywhere the same, nor that there is an absence of explicit disagreement or implicit contradiction. What is required is to point to a historically existing cluster of arguments, rather than a logically feasible or coherent set of positions. I have not followed the implication therefore of some writing on the New Right which in talking of 'fusion' or 'new ideological synthesis' (Levitas 1986: 5–6) suggests a greater degree of integration or coherence, either internally or functionally, than can in fact be observed.

The point is not whether some pure New Right exists, but whether there is an identifiable association of aspirations and aversions, or a similarity of goals and enemies, such that it is appropriate to group together a number of arguments, or writers, and identity them with a single title. It is important not to imagine that there is some teeming historical entity called 'the New Right' of which all manner of political actions, from books to casual remarks, from developed arguments to brief and dogmatic assertion, can be seen as symptoms or expressions. Such a view, which with the narrow meshed, broad mouthed fishing net of the term 'Thatcherism' has at times helped to trawl in a great mass of varying politics, makes it easy to condemn, but does not give much help in understanding. But though the idea of single sources or principles of the variety of New Right thinking deserves being treated with scepticism, the variety does not. The new right, whatever its original components, involved a clear cluster of aversions and aspirations which gave it a character which did not depend on, and was not qualified by, the variety of arguments used to support them. It is in this comprehensive if diverse social vision, rather than in any single principle, that the most obvious coherence of the New Right lies. Certainly when its features are simply listed, they have the appearance more of a buffet of political aspirations and aversions, than of an ordered political argument, and the dissonance is often as obvious as the affinities. But aspirations, and often even more aversions, are a sure way of identifying the character of a body of thought. A brief listing would include: hostility to socialism and Keynsian economics; active support of capitalism; antagonism towards contemporary and 'progressive' education (Cowling 1989); military pugnacity allied, to begin with, with anti-Soviet and anti-communist rhetoric; hostility to universal social services and a fear of a 'dependency culture' amongst the ordinary working population; championing of the market, of property, and of the positive functions of economic inequality; moralism and patriarchy, a puritan suspicion of 'permissiveness', of feminism, and of unorthodox households; a combination of nationalism with religious and racial defensiveness or intolerance; individualism both normative and methodological, sustaining an advocacy of individual responsibility in opposition to collective provision; a 'no-nonsense' anti-intellectual populism; an aversion to paternalism in both government and the arts, but not in business, education, or morality.

Such a listing gives no more than an impression of a phenomenon, and it should not be taken as an anatomization of a single coherent doctrine or set of principles. At the loosest level, the unity of the New Right lies in no more than the historical contiguity of various beliefs, aspirations, aversions and arguments which more often than not seem to be found in each other's company, or in each other's vicinity, whilst sharing an antagonism to other liberal or left clusters of belief, or being linked in a chain or circle of overlapping aspirations and aversions. But whereas conservatism had been able to defend what could be seen as an established and homogeneous social and political structure, whose divisions were horizontal ones of rank, power and advantage, the New Right responded to a quite different situation. Civil society appeared to be divided vertically by different religions and ethnic groups, by different conceptions of individual life and household character. In these circumstances the defence of strong preferences could not be limited to the cultivation of established values, but had to involve either or both of a partisan championing of some values against others, and a rational or principled defence of the preferred social pattern.

This championing of preferences differed from conservatism, though not from liberalism, in one important aspect. There was within the New Right a use of international, universalist principles to sustain arguments. Conservatism in its nature could not, did not appeal to general principles or conceptions of universal human, social, or economic nature. British conservatism had always expressed suspicion or downright hostility towards general theories, particularly if they came from beyond the shores of the United Kingdom, and had frequently insisted that its own thinking was not the development of a set of principles, but the distillation of an existing body of practice, convention, and institutions. But a radical argument is frequently in need of precisely the kinds of support which conservatives eschewed, and in its use of such support the New Right marked itself off yet more clearly from the past. Even though aspirations could therefore be found amongst the New Right which were shared with earlier conservatives or economic liberals, radical advocacy had a different tone from conservative defence, and involved a quite different attitude towards existing arrangements and towards the principles which were to be applied for the transformation of those arrangements.

INTERPRETING THE NEW RIGHT

Partly because of the way in which it appeared to have transformed the agenda of political discussion, partly because it seemed such a break with the more consensual styles of the earlier years of the twentieth century, the New Right rapidly attracted a substantial body of analysis and explanation. There have been widely different accounts, as there have been widely different questions asked, and widely different conceptions of what it was that required explanation. Richard Cocket sees at least some of the success of the New Right as the result of years of dedicated persuasion and propaganda by organizations such as the Institute of Economic Affairs (Cockett 1994), whilst Desai has added the further cause of the links between New Right thinkers and 'prominent financial journalists' (Desai 1994: 23). Friends of the New Right see its rise as no more than the appropriate result for an analysis and a prescription which matched changing historical realities, whilst another explanation would say no more than that ideas grow until they compose the major set of intellectual tools which are available for people to think and argue with.

Analyses of the character, as opposed to the causes, of the New Right have been equally varied. A common starting point has been the New Right's mixture of political cohesion and intellectual variety. It was 'not a single, coherent system of ideas but rather an eclectic mixture of themes and policies brought together, in Britain and elsewhere, more by the contingencies of circumstance than by logic' (Gray 1993a: v ; cf. Brittan 1983: 49). Some have been led, in an attempt to identify coherence, to concentrate on some one particular aspect of the New Right. Political scientists, for instance, have concentrated on the New Right approach to political analysis (e.g. Dunleavy 1991), writers whose principal interest is in economic theorizing set on one side moral and cultural doctrines which seem more conservative than liberal in origin (Bosanquet 1983), whilst advocates and sympathetic analysts have presented the New Right as more simply coherent than it was by concentrating on its liberal economic aspect (Green 1987). Much discussion of the New Right presents it wholly as a carbuncle of liberalism.

But attempts to explain the apparent incoherencies in New Right thinking as existing merely at the level of the various theories and methods employed to achieve ends which were shared, suggests further dimensions. Amongst the various shared goals, such as an electoral alliance whereby the unegalitarian outcomes of a liberal market are justified by 'social and moral conservative principles' (King 1987: 8) attention has been drawn to the central role of the family (David 1986; King 1987). The New Right 'embraced the twin goals of restoring class forces in favour of capital and of restoring gender relations in favour of men' (Tusscher 1986: 76). If each acre in the hands of the peasantry was another musket for the defence of property, it seemed as if each Telecom share passed down through the middle class might be another vote for the defence of the New Right, and each extra jot of power in the hands of the patriarchal head of the family an extra shot in the locker against feminism, permissiveness, and the excessive independence of the young. A new alignment, of patriarchy without paternalism, and markets without political liberalism brought the zealous promotion of conservative ends by un-conservative means and the promotion of liberal economies in un-liberal societies together in an alliance which was to demonstrate both pragmatic and theoretical cohesion.

The property owning family which was at the same time the conduit for property accumulation and the nursery of virtues both civic and domestic, even though it did not play a prominent part in New Right thinking, was one of the fusion points for the various aspirations and, in their wake, the various theories, of the New Right. A conception of the family provided a meeting point for disparate elements in New Right thinking. There has been an insistence on the privacy of the family, in the sense of immunity from public and political gaze or state regulation, combined with a clear moral vision of what such family life should be like. Georgina Waylen (Waylen 1986: 94) has drawn attention to the argument in Hayek's *The Constitution of Liberty* on the necessity of keeping relations within the family or the household beyond the reach of the state. The full quotation, (Hayek 1960: 138) is even richer than the abbreviated version which Waylen gives. She comments on the passage that marriage, being a voluntary contract, should be kept free from state interference. She does not comment on, though she quotes, Hayek's use of the term 'personal domestic service' to describe the work of members of the family. But by the use of the phrase, hierarchies of employment and patriarchy are neatly merged.

The economic role of the family could be justified by allowing at least one collective actor in the liberal market, its cultural and moral role by reference to the post-conservative social vision. In an account of the family presented by contributors to an Institute of Economic Affairs collection on *Liberating Women... From Modern Feminism* (Quest 1994), tasks and responsibilities are divided by gender, and while the male pursues a career, the female is dependent but caring. These divisions are based on the different biologically rooted capacities and aptitudes of men and women. At the same time, the beneficial consequences of such an ideal are compared with the social costs of feminism. Without state subsidy for childcare, a woman 'will not be able to afford to work full-time. If she does not work full-time, then she is unlikely to be able to compete with men, and the most efficient use of her time will, therefore, be looking after her own children' (ibid.: 4). The state should use the tax system in order to re-introduce some of the features of the 'family wage', the practice of paying men more than women because they are deemed to be the principal earners in a family (Morgan 1994: 24). Writing on the family, gender, and feminism drew on both the social vision and the argumentative arsenal of the New Right in a way which demonstrated how an isolated and intensified economic liberalism and a cultural rightism could sustain each other.

'CONSERVATISM' AND THE NEW RIGHT

One school of interpreters would deny there is any break with conservatism in the political thinking of the New Right, since conservatism is merely an opportunist juggling with whatever values and conceptions happen, from time to time, to be most useful for maintaining an elite in power. This is, specifically, the argument of Ted Honderich (Honderich 1990). Others have argued that the New Right is to be seen as at one and the same time a development of conservatism and a departure from its essential principles. The New Right, argued John Gray, 'brought into conservative discourse a sectarian spirit that belongs properly not with conservatism, which is sceptical of all ideology, but with the rationalist doctrines of the Enlightenment' (Gray 1993a: viii). But there was also within the New Right an intensification of the commitment to cultural orthodoxy which had been one element of Toryism, a particularist, anti-enlightenment assertion of the claims of tradition. This was indeed a 'sectarian spirit', but one which intensified what had previously been muted, and gave prominence to what had been merely recessive. So long as the fabric of institutions, culture, religious affiliation, governmental responsibilities and political practices which conservatives admired or hoped for was recognizable in either the practices of the present or at least in their implications or possible growths or adjustments, conservatism could be tolerant, flexible, conservationist. But by the end of the 1970s, conservatives could no longer be confident that this was so. Keith Joseph and Jonathan Sumption saw a belief in equality as 'deeply embedded in the language and unspoken assumptions of political thinking' and so much part of 'the pale of intellectual premises within which alone civilised debate is possible' that someone such as Hayek was only 'a formidable but solitary figure' (Joseph and Sumption 1979: 2). Once the distance between what was seen and what was desired became deep and visible, however, there was a choice either of accepting a society that in terms of the inherent preferences associated with conservatism was profoundly uncongenial, or of advocating, in a thoroughly unconservative manner, the creation or reconstruction of a social, economic, and political order which fulfilled those aspirations which present circumstances denied or frustrated. Whether this was to be achieved by a 'return to Victorian values' or by the creation of an enterprise society made no difference in terms of the radicalism of what was proposed and the distance from existing social arrangements. In these circumstances conservatism was replaced by an assertive, campaigning style, an attempt to introduce or as the argument would have it, restore, valued practices, conventions, or institutional methods, a partisan claim like any other rather than a defence of a dominant position.

This element within the New Right, the apparently conservative writers who have abandoned conservatism, is best represented by the work of Roger Scruton. Scruton faces the charge that conservatism is 'no longer "available"' (Scruton 1984: 11), with the reply that, when circumstances require it conservatism can be presented as a set of beliefs that are 'systematic and reasonable' (ibid.), and as a belief which will assist a search for 'something greater' than the world people presently inhabit (ibid.: 12). The world which the conservative values may be in 'ruins', but that does not mean that the old ways as they are seen and valued by conservatives cannot be re-established: 'a conservative is also a restorationist' (ibid.: 21). But the refusal to search, to have goals and visions, was precisely what had distinguished conservative from radical doctrines. Correspondingly, the commitment to ideological long marches marked off the 'conservatism' of the 1980s from everything that had gone before. So Scruton, writing of 'what was once called "the alien wedge"' lists this as one of the areas where 'conservatives must fight' (ibid.: 68 and 69). In such a transformation, a right-wing argument develops which, utterly unlike the conservatism of the short twentieth century, no longer defends preferences which can be presented as dominant, but advocates some values and stigmatizes others in a society whose pluralism it both notes and refuses to accept. It thus provides a programme for an entire culture and polity, and does so in terms of an orthodoxy which it seeks the service of the state to cultivate and, if necessary, impose. Similar views were expressed by Maurice Cowling who, in a collection of *Conservative Essays* published in 1978, wrote that the 'immigration of alien communities in the last twenty-five years' has damaged a common national identity. But any departure from the aspiration for a single national identity is firmly rejected: 'the sense of national identity that existed in Britain until at least twenty years ago, with its mixture of common memories, images and expectations, may in places already have been eroded; intelligence and skill will be needed if it is to be restored and, more important, extended to those who have never felt it' (Cowling 1978a: 16). It was a form of right-wing argument not previously very familiar in Britain.

In constructing such an argument, Scruton employs a form of reasoning which has always, necessarily, been part of the conservative case, but which becomes employed in a far more vigorous way in the circumstances of the New Right-wing politics. On the one hand, the conservative seeks to put aside assessment of the worth or reasonableness of social arrangements. This is done by saying that there are no criteria external to the society within which those arrangements exist, and which they help constitute, whereby they can be assessed, and that our character as members of that society is shaped by reference to them. This is an argument which proceeds from fact to value, as in the subordination of contract to the prior existence of society and government, or the statement that family and civil society are a universal and essentially unchanging natural response to 'natural necessity' (Scruton 1984: 31). Nature and natural necessity can be quite generously invoked in this kind of argument, and Scruton justifies aspects of the existing constitutional arrangements of Britain by citing a natural allegiance to monarchical government, an argument which, like Filmer's three hundred years previously, moves analogously from the family to the state. This form of argument presents tradition as something that is always received, never made. The individual 'must see himself as the inheritor, not the creator, of the order in which he participates' (ibid.: 66). But of course he is both, and if traditions were not created, they could not be inherited.

On the other hand, Scruton's conservative does not wish to endorse all arrangements simply because they exist and have existed for some time. He or she therefore requires, on occasion, to seek just those external criteria which were previously dismissed as mere wraiths of liberalism. So Scruton argues:

> I considered the possibility that there might be *general* principles of justice, which carry an authority greater than the authority of a particular constitution. I claimed that there are such principles, that they are in deep and inevitable conflict with the ethic of 'social justice', and that they cannot be viewed as the instrument of power. Their generality stems from the general condition of the social order. Hence, even the conservative view of law, which gives special weight to existing social arrangements, can generate a criterion of validity that applies beyond the *status quo*. In virtue of that, it is possible for a conservative to deny that each and every arrangement deserves to be conserved. But when an arrangement deserves that favour, it demands along with it the institution of a rule of law.
>
> (ibid.: 93)

In a similar manner Scruton's eloquent account of the purpose of private property entails the elaboration of general principles of human life, rather than the particular embedded experiences of an historical society. Man, he writes, has 'an absolute and ineradicable need of private property' (ibid.: 99). The ensuing argument about taxation, public ownership, markets and capitalism is conducted in a way quite different from the initial exposition of the conservative position. It pursues, rather, what is implied in beliefs about the desirable purpose of property and government, and the subordination of economic judgments to ones of social value.

Scruton's arguments in this direction have been politely rebuked from a more traditional conservative position by John Gray, arguing that a 'legitimate concern for the moral foundations of civil society cannot justify policies of social engineering aiming to revive a lost (and doubtless partly imaginary) moral solidarity' (Gray 1993a: 51). Certainly they share with other forms of social engineering the belief that what people want and what they think they want are not the same. 'The dogma of conservatism will therefore prove startling and even offensive to many whose feelings it none the less quite accurately describes' (Scruton 1984: 25). They share too the belief that, despite the denials of having any truck with universal principles, there is a universal human nature whose understanding should be the basis of public life and of government (ibid.: 31, 35).

Conservatism as depicted by Scruton is a desire for a particular kind of order. It is no accident that Scruton begins by quoting Peel in the Tamworth Manifesto on the need for 'the maintenance of order and the cause of good government' (ibid.: 15). But the social and political order to which this 'restorational' conservatism aspires is one in which any form of social contract as the basis of government, and any form of democracy as the sanction of policy, is dispensed with. Democracy can be dismissed as a contagion, and the public discussion by its citizens, 'popular opinion', as something which it may be one of the few beneficial functions of Parliament to have protected the 'social organism' against (ibid.: 58). There may well be circumstances, from this standpoint, when truth is best kept from the majority, in order to advance one's own 'true' policies: 'It is a philosophical question whether relativism is *true*. Politically speaking, however, it is better that few men believe it. Like Plato, a conservative may have to advocate the "Noble Lie"' (ibid.: 139). Constraints on speech are justified in the maintenance of the traditional values of society, and it is their removal, not their imposition, that needs justifying. Yet the opinions of the mass of the population can, on other issues, be presented as the social bedrock against which the foundations of legislators must rest, while liberalism is dismissed because it lacks this popular rootedness, and is merely 'the creed of an elite, and an impossible substitute for the pieties of ordinary existence' (ibid.: 81).

Such 'restorational' conservatism is defined both by what it aspires to and by how it describes and perceives its enemies. In Scruton's version, conservatism is a doctrine of government, and thus inherently opposed to liberal individualism:

In politics, the conservative attitude seeks above all for government, and regards no citizen as possessed of a natural right that transcends his obligation to be ruled. Even democracy – which corresponds neither to the natural nor to the supernatural yearnings of the normal citizen – can be discarded without detriment to the civil well-being as the conservative conceives it.

(ibid.: 16)

It is necessary from such a position to argue on the one hand that there is an organic society, rooted in tradition, membership of which, rather than any individual rights, gives meaning to the life of men and women, and on the other hand that the nature of this social life is not properly understood by many people, and threatened by some who are its enemies. Society is thus on the one hand justified because it is, and then defended because it isn't. Such a society as embattled or resurgent orthodoxy then becomes the goal of conservative politics: 'a society really does have enemies ... those enemies seek to undermine it, and ... it is the duty of the government, as it is the expectation of the citizens, that they should be prevented by every means to hand' (ibid.: 18). And such a society really exists, it has a character and personality and will – though not purpose (ibid.: 23). The problem, of course, is identifying them, just as there is a problem in characterizing society, though the two activities arise from each other.

The emergence of a form of right-wing argument which, whilst related to conservatism, is a different historical being is a part of the realignment of political thought after the end of the short twentieth century. The argument is marked off from conservatism by its militancy and by its appeal to general principles. It has been pointed out how an appeal both to tradition and to reason and principle causes internal strains in a conservative argument (Wendelken 1996). But it does more than that, for it carried the argument beyond conservatism. The contribution to the New Right from this direction was principally in the form of the vigorous assertion of aspirations and aversions. For the fuller development of the general advocacy, it was necessary to look to a development of one of the fragmented strands of liberalism.

LIBERALISM AND THE NEW RIGHT: THE CONTRIBUTION OF HAYEK

The strand within the New Right which both drew on and replaced conservatism needed to call in aid principles derived in a similar manner from liberalism, since its aspirations for social and economic change needed far more justification than conservatism could ever provide. As Cowling put it, describing what he was still calling conservatism, but which was a relatively early exposition of the cluster of views which characterized the New Right, talk of freedom 'is a way of not saying what they want, a way of attracting sympathy and support for, and attributing principle to, a social structure which they wish to conserve or restore' (Cowling 1978a: 9). The growth out of economic liberalism does not in itself provide a sufficient key to the character of the New Right, but it is in arguments which have economic liberal roots rather than in those which have conservative ones that the most effective contribution to the coherence of the New Right is found. But the end result is not a liberal one, anymore than it is a conservative one.

There is a conjunction, both strategic and intellectual, between the 'authoritarian conservatism' or 'radical conservatism' which forms a prominent part of post-twentieth century political thought, and arguments developed from economic liberalism. There is no better illustration of this than in the development of the thinking of F.A. Hayek. Hayek's particular development of economic liberalism into a political argument had been available well before the publication of *The Road to Serfdom* in 1944. But even after that date, it had been a recessive theme in political thinking, and lay largely fallow for over a quarter of a century, despite continuing and prolific publication by its author. The Hayek who was known principally as the author of *The Road to Serfdom* was treated, and marginalized, as an extreme advocate of laissez faire. The Hayek who provided the intellectual underpinnings of the New Right contributed a far more subtle interweaving of strong government, orthodox social structures and economic markets. The Hayek of the 1940s, 1950s and 1960s is in that sense a different intellectual presence from the Hayek of the 1980s, just as is the Morris of the 1920s from the Morris of the 1970s. In this change there is a two-way relationship, as Andrew Gamble has pointed out. On the one hand Hayek's reputation 'was closely linked with the revival of the fortunes of economic liberalism', whilst on the other his work 'became one of the main inspirations for many of the currents of thought which made up the New Right' (Gamble 1996: 3).

Hayek is frequently presented as no more than an extreme kind of liberal (King 1987: 16; Levitas 1986: 1). Even John Gray, who in one of the best accounts of Hayek's political thought described it as a liberalism grounded in the kind of socially located, pragmatic 'conservative view of reason' found in Hume (Gray 1984: 130), in his own later writings presented Hayek in terms of his liberal economism, to the detriment of his social and institutional conservatism (Gray 1993a: 52).

Hayek's principal importance is neither as an exemplar of the New Right nor as an exponent of liberalism, but as a writer who provides a theoretical tie between the economically liberal rooted strand and the conservatively rooted strand in the New Right. Even so, this tie is not, in Hayek's writing, between two fixed elements in this thinking, but a relationship between components whose relative weight changes with the historical circumstances in which they are expressed. Hayek's writing is central, in both rounding off and making sharper and more militant old themes, and in presaging new ones.

Amongst those who have paid attention to Hayek's social doctrines, and have detected the presence of two apparently incompatible, or at least mutually uncongenial, strands, there have been two principal responses: to deny that there is an inconsistency because the overall position expresses a coherent liberalism, or to dismiss the overall intellectual position as simply incoherent. The first account is given by John Gray, who has argued that whilst the use of tradition draws heavily on conservatism, it does so to create a 'more humble, sceptical and modest form of liberalism' which has freed itself from rationalism but which yet remains in the liberal tradition (Gray 1984: 130). But the attempt to establish ancestral credentials, quite apart from the lopsidedness of a liberal lineage derived principally from David Hume (ibid.), detracts from what is historically novel and specific about what Hayek was attempting to do. Gray goes on to argue that Hayek is in fact morally radical, in that he believes that major changes will be necessary in order to develop an ethical framework in which markets will be safe (Gray 1984: 130–4). The account may set up defences for Hayek against the charge of inconsistency, but at the same time it shows very clearly how his doctrine stands beyond both liberalism and conservatism. The second account is given by Samuel Brittan who sees in Hayek an unworkable 'blend of radical evolutionary fervour and conservative insistence on rule observance' (Brittan 1983: 52). Hayek, argues Brittan, is 'attracted to two different political philosophies: classical liberalism (based on limited government, free markets, and the rule of law) and a conservative philosophy which stresses tradition and the hidden wisdom of existing institutions'. There might have been times in the real or imagined past when the two systems could 'seem in harmony' but in either authoritarian or collectivist situations, there was a 'tension between the two ideals' (Brittan 1983: 54).

Brittan's suggestion that it may be as much historical location as internal logic which determines whether doctrines will be in tension with one another provides a clue for the understanding of Hayek's place in the New Right. It was because both classical liberalism and conservatism had come to an end that the character of his arguments is best understood with reference to neither, but as an evolving element in new political circumstances.

The connections which link Hayek to earlier economic liberalism should not obscure his movement beyond the perimeters of that liberalism, nor the fact that this movement was a matter of shifting emphasis from more orthodox beginnings. When Hayek's writing first made an impact on political thinking, with the publication in 1944 of *The Road to Serfdom*, he appeared as a liberal, albeit a particularly uncompromising one. And indeed the arguments of 1944 were principally economic and political, and caused no problems to those who wanted to place Hayek firmly within the liberal tradition. As his argument was expanded over the following half century, it became clear that economic liberalism was only one component of his thinking. The other was an increasingly uncompromising social and cultural conservatism, but a conservatism so assertive as to move beyond the permitters within which that title could appropriately be applied. Gray's remark that Hayek's society is 'held together solely by the impersonal nexus of market exchange' (Gray 1993a: 52) does insufficient justice to this dimension of his argument. The direction in which the emphasis was shifting was clear in the 1960 *The Constitution of Liberty* as it makes clear the possibilities which Hayek's argument present for a transition from old economic liberalism and old conservatism to something different from either. The appendix on 'Why I am Not a Conservative' is something of a smoke screen, for the socially repressive principles appear far more clearly in this book than they had done sixteen years earlier in *The Road to Serfdom*. One vehicle for the transition is the appeal to tradition.

INDIVIDUALS AND INSTITUTIONS: THE FREEZING OF TRADITION AND THE RATIONALIZATION OF CUSTOM

Hayek's use of tradition increasingly displays the radical character of right-wing thought, and the way in which an argument which in conservative hands had been defensive and paternalist, in the circumstances at the end of the twentieth century becomes aggressive and partisan. Oddly, for a cluster of aspirations and aversions which seem to depend so heavily on principled radicalism, the New Right case drew heavily on the mixture of cultural partisanship and rule governed neutrality which characterized the presentation of tradition.

It was the point where the disparate strains which fed the New Right came closest together, the loyalty to particular cultural forms being sustained by the argument that they had been tested by evolutionary quality assurance, the attraction to abstract rules of government sustained by the demonstration that they would lead to particular desirable outcomes. The argument of an Oakeshott for indigenous practices selected through the grid of libertarian principles comes at this point closest to that of a Hayek who argues for market principles and demonstrates their support for orthodox social outcomes.

As used earlier in the century both by Hayek and by conservatives such as Oakeshott, the argument from tradition contained fundamental inconsistencies. Had Hayek simply continued to employ that argument, he would have been open to the simple criticism of contradiction, which has at times been directed at him. Ellen Frankel Paul, for instance, has argued that there is an incompatibility between Hayek's liberal economic values, and his relativist, positivist, evolutionary theory:

> it is not clear whether Hayek intends this concept of spontaneous orders to be normative or descriptive. With such statements as this one – that it is never rational to combine spontaneous order with organization in governing a society – the concept seems to be prescriptive. But this interpretation runs counter to the whole tenor of Hayek's thought, which is to make social theory scientific by observing the known regularities of the social order and viewing these regularities as the result of evolutionary, unintended growth.
>
> (Paul 1988: 257)

Paul points out that in the absence of a moral stance on liberal principles, Hayek is open to having to accept any regime which survives. It would be a basic and devastating criticism, since it is precisely on his refusal to take any normative stand on such things as the market as a distribution mechanism that Hayek rests his case, were Hayek's writings not increasingly characterized by a clear recommendation of values, conduct and institutions, though not ones of a particularly liberal kind.

The conservatism, or rather the assertive right-wing culturalism, serves to solve, or explain, the contradiction in Hayek's use of tradition. It also replaces the problem by replacing the argument, and making it one markedly different from that used both by Hayek and by conservatives earlier in the century. Without that replacement, Hayek's argument would be dependent solely on his idea of spontaneous order as creating a society formed out of the various intentional acts of individuals and groups, but reflecting none of those intentions. The problem then arises not in simultaneously seeking liberal or any other outcome, but in giving an account of individual choice. The dilemma which Paul identifies at a theoretical level then becomes a concrete problem of how individual actions are to be understood, and what proposals are being put forward, on the one hand for analysing them, on the other for seeking to regulate or guide them.

By allowing Hayek to claim less than he does, his case could be made more coherent. Since he terms himself a Whig rather than either a liberal or a conservative, he should be taken to be aware of and attempting to reconcile the potential conflict between a conservative account of history and a liberal recommendation as to conduct. He does not argue that all societies are necessarily governed by tradition, but that those that are are both more free and more efficient. That is not where the problem lies. The problem lies in his account of how people should act if they are convinced of the correctness of his argument.

It is not clear what, for Hayek, is the nature of the constraint which the traditionally evolved social order places on individual action. He speaks of civilization being made possible by 'subjugating the innate animal instincts to the non-rational customs which made possible the formation of larger orderly groups' (Hayek 1979: 155), and of 'the obedience to learnt rules' as a necessary alternative to 'the direct pursuit of felt needs or perceived objects' (ibid.: 160). But it is unclear whether he envisages an objective constraint, which would fit with the interpretation of the argument as an explanatory one, or a self imposed restraint arising from a person's rational perception of the likely function of rules which she cannot understand, which would fit with an interpretation of Hayek's argument as a prescriptive one. If it is neither of these, but simply another way of saying that this person or these people just happen to behave in one way rather than another, and just happen to have one set of institutions rather than another, then words like restraint and discipline are no more appropriate than talking of ants observing the discipline of the ant hill or wolves the discipline of the hunt. Hayek himself does not generally give examples, but the possible implications of his argument may be clarified if one is used. A shopkeeper setting up business in a community where there is a strong moral convention against the consumption of alcohol would clearly be constrained if he devoted a large part of his stock to wines and spirits. The constraint would arise from the reluctance of customers to buy, and if that reluctance persisted, he would either go out of business or modify his wares. In this case he would clearly have been constrained by the traditional beliefs of his potential customers, and despite his intentions, would have failed to do any business in selling alcohol. It would of course also be possible that as a result of his attempts, a taste for alcohol would develop which would modify the traditions of the community in which he set up shop. If that is all Hayek means, then he is simply saying that we all have to take our chance in the market, and some of the things we try will work, some won't, and many of them will lead to results different from those which we intended.

But at times he seems to mean something quite different, and to argue that people should modify their conduct in advance, not as the result of the play of circumstance, but in (rational?) deference to a tradition which they may neither accept nor comprehend. In that case the shopkeeper, in deference to the traditions of the community – and out of deference alone, and not in an attempt to curry favour with customers who might buy his other goods – would exclude alcohol from his wares.

When Hayek does pursue the question of what people are doing when they act within the conventions of institutions, he sometimes gives a double layered explanation. Some people or groups 'break' existing rules or behave in ways which ignore or move beyond them. When this behaviour is seen to make them prosper, others imitate them (Hayek 1979: 161). But in neither case is the 'rule keeping' of the kind that Hayek recommends. The innovators, whether by accident, temperament, or design, are acting in a way which he seems to condemn, whilst the imitators are acting on a rational calculation of material advantage. Neither of these gives the results Hayek appears to want.

So Hayek employs both description and prescription. A Hayekian traditionalist, the moment she (though it is more likely to be he) identifies and attempts to abide by a tradition or convention, seems guilty of precisely that attempt to give society a conscious purpose which Hayek so condemns in others.

Hayek describes the social order that he simultaneously describes and prescribes as 'spontaneous'. But his use of the word 'spontaneous' is probably misleading. The order is not spontaneous at all, but the naturally selected consequence of innumerable individual decisions. The implication of the word spontaneous is that the cause of the order comes from within society, as opposed to from the minds of men, and society is thus reified. It sits ill with the notion of natural selection, which would see order not as a system generated by society, but as the way things happen to be constituted in social arrangements which survive.

Since any social order is the result of individual decisions, it is at any time the consequence of a permanent process. Indeed, were individual decisions to cease, the source of social order would also cease to operate. Thus it is not consistent with the original descriptive understanding of social order to recommend that a necessary dynamic process be treated as complete, and as henceforward placing rational, moral constraints on hitherto interest maximizing individuals. Hayek's idea of spontaneous order is of society as formed out of the various intentional acts of individuals and groups, but as reflecting none of those intentions. But when he tries to subordinate the actions of individuals to the resulting body of traditions and conventions, he is attempting to deny the very process which led to the establishment and growth of his spontaneous order in the first place. It is like trying to subordinate the insects to the coral which their remains form, and to prevent their pre-reef activities.

There are two ways in which traditions might order and constrain human societies. They may do so by presenting each individual with a series of external obstacles or conditions which qualify her intentions and actions. Traditions in this sense form the raw material or starting conditions for individual action. This is a view not unlike Marx's that 'men make their own history, but they do so in circumstances not of their own choosing'. Such constraints or order are external, a matter of the beliefs and actions of others. But there may also be internal constraint, a belief that whatever I might wish to do, I ought to be governed by traditional values. These two forms of constraint are not of course mutually exclusive. Nor do they, in their artificial simplicity, give an adequate account of actual historical conduct or circumstances. External constraints may be internalized not only as a conscious willed restraint on my ambitions, but as an unconscious supposition about what the world is like, and an unconscious moulding of wants and aversions. In other words the conditioning of tradition is not simply a series of constraints on wants once they have been identified. It is present far earlier in the very formation of those wants.

But it is not this form of externalized objective influence that Hayek can be recommending. Precisely because it is unconscious and part of the raw material we have before we begin to think, it is not something we can do anything about. The same is true of external constraints. They are there, and whilst all kinds of stratagems may be employed to accept, circumvent, or exploit them, they cannot just be cancelled out. The only case where it makes any sense to recommend action to individuals is in their conscious and deliberate response to norms, values, institutions in the societies which they inhabit when those norms, values, or institutions imply different courses of action to those which the individual would otherwise follow. And here Hayek is quite explicit. Individuals should subordinate their plans to these values even when they can see no good reason to do so.

The use made by Hayek of the idea of tradition contained elements which pulled in different directions. But its importance did not lie in that. A similar division had existed in conservative political thinking. But there it had been employed as a means of the selective defence of existing practices, and the selective stigmatizing of others. What Hayek's usage permitted, and increasingly in his own writings moved towards, was an active propagation of new institutions, values and customs in order to sustain an imagined or hoped for social and economic order. A device of conservatism became a weapon of the right.

This more aggressive use of the ambiguities of the argument for tradition was found in the speeches and writing of politicians, as for instance in the calls by Norman Tebbitt in the mid-1980s for moral regeneration: there was a need to 'return to traditional values of decency and order' because 'the defence of freedom involves a defence of the values which make freedom possible' (Norman Tebbitt, *Britain's future – A Conservative Vision*, London: Conservative Political Centre: 15–16, quoted Durham 1991: 134). It was not a bad paraphrase of Hayek.

The increasing importance of the socially didactic, culturally right-wing aspect within Hayek's writing appeared in the three volumes collected together under the title *Law, Legislation, and Liberty*. Two features of the argument about culture and morality mark these volumes off from Hayek's earlier writing. The first is a much greater emphasis on the ways in which individuals ought to be subordinate to social institutions: 'there can be no excuse or pardon for a systematic disregard of accepted moral rules because they have no understood justification' (Hayek 1979: 171). The second, paradoxically, is an insistence on the need for radical changes in those institutions in order to make the world safe for markets. So on the one hand Hayek can talk approvingly of the power of social ostracism in enforcing conduct, and on the other of the undesirable resistance placed by group solidarity in the onward course of universal principles of association in a market society (Hayek 1973, 1976, 1979).

The style of these books of the 1970s is invocational, and reliant on the authority of 'acknowledge leaders' in whatever field Hayek happens to be drawing on – the 'head-man' approach, which constitutes his shorthand for most pre-industrial society. But as Hayek develops it, it is a doctrine, antipathetic to anything but the most unthinking conservatism in every branch of life. Yet if society is to progress in the way that Hayek clearly believes that it does, will, and should, then since at any time any person must be faced with a choice of habits, some critical and active thought is necessary in order to explain why we are still not going to mass every day and riding horses on uncobbled streets. Hayek's cultural evolution makes mind, far more so than does even vulgar Marxism, the servant, and the lobotomized servant, of the material development of society.

THE ESTABLISHMENT AND EROSION OF THE NEW RIGHT

Like the bee which dies in stinging, the New Right was, if not destroyed, then certainly enfeebled by its success. By the end of the short twentieth century the New Right had, relatively briefly, established itself as a new paradigm, and both lost its predominance at the level of theory whilst many of the aversions and aspirations which it expressed had become a part of the coinage of political thinking. This paradoxical result has arisen because on the one hand New Right arguments about markets, about the relative efficiencies of public and private bureaucracies, about innovation, flexibility and change, had become a part of contemporary common sense. Many of the values championed by the New Right, individual choice, individual wants rather than collectively determined needs, privacy, the private possession and accumulation of property, ceased to be monopolies of the right, and became, or became more obviously, in ways which drew on their earlier left-wing ancestry, components both of a newer left and of feminism.

But such values and assumptions were only a part of 'common sense' assumptions, and at the same time some of the disadvantages of the version of New Right policies pursued in the United Kingdom have become increasingly apparent: low investment, inadequate education and training, private monopolies in place of public ones, and the erosion of public goods, whilst abroad the application of market remedies has failed to produce the expected transformation of the economies of Eastern Europe and the former Soviet Union. It may not be sufficient to say, as Desmond King predicted in 1987, that the New Right was 'a passing intellectual fashion' (King 1987: 2), but its high point has nonetheless clearly passed, or passed into something else.

The New Right, like any other body of political thinking, was both defined by and dependent on its daemonology. New age travellers, single mothers, feminists, trade unionists, Marxists, and elitist intellectuals at home were supplemented by communism and collectivist economic planning abroad. Thus the retirement or abdication of Lucifer with the revolutions of 1989, and the associated fading of the intellectual influence of Marxism, was an event of profound significance in right-wing cosmology. If right-wing thinking flourished during the Cold War and the cold economic and political contest which accompanied it, it suffered correspondingly from the revolutions of 1989 and their aftermath. Deprived of its principal and most effective example of the alternative to markets by the dissolution of the Soviet Union and the pell-mell flight of the countries of Eastern Europe away from economic state collectivism, the New Right lost both a principal justification for its radicalism and principal weapon in its rhetorical arsenal. Paradoxically the destruction of one-party managerial communism, for which the right had so vigorously called, was to prove deeply destabilizing and debilitating. For if Satan and sin abdicate their powers, what need is there to listen to promises of salvation?

HOW FAR DOES THE EMERGENCE OF THE NEW RIGHT MAKE APPROPRIATE A RE-READING OF THE PAST?

The aversions, aspirations and arguments which constituted the New Right were partly old ideas which were re-asserted in new forms and with a new intensity, and partly a new phenomenon. This gave them a dual relationship with earlier themes: as revenants and as descendants. But in both of those relations to the past, the New Right has drawn on recessive themes within economic liberalism and conservatism. In the case of economic liberalism, the recessive element is clear enough. Hayek's prominence was a feature of the end of the chronological century, from the 1970s onwards. But what remains his best known work, *The Road to Serfdom*, had been published in 1944, and his attacks on collectivist economic planning went back to the 1930s. Yet it was not unfair for Nicholas Bosanquet to refer to *The Constitution of Liberty* as something which, though placed in an intellectual reservation at the time of its publication by being termed a 'magnificent dinosaur', had become by 1986 'a dinosaur that is revived and is trumpeting around the world' (Cohen et al. 1986: 18). This changing presence of arguments over time is evident in the very writing of my own book. In the first edition, although attention was paid to Hayek, he was not treated as a figure of major importance. The final volume of what was to become the trilogy, *Law, Legislation, and Liberty*, was not published until after the first edition of this book had appeared. But it is not that alone which explains the greater attention paid to Hayek in the new chapters of the revised edition. Hayek's argument has developed and its emphasis has changed since 1944. But there is more involved than recording the subsequent history of political thinking. As Alan Ryan has pointed out, a book or an article has several identities, one of which is what the author intended or meant, but another of which is shaped by the interaction of the book, having left the author's hands, with the minds of readers (Ryan 1984: 3–4). In the first sense Hayek's arguments have changed over time; but in the second sense there is a double change, since the earlier works are now read in the light of the impact of the later ones.

When an account is given of both the New Right and the recessive themes on which it has drawn, it is not only the latter phenomenon, but the earlier themes, which may be interpreted in terms of the new relationship. Does the writing of Michael Oakeshott look at all different from the view point of the 1990s? Are there elements of transition in his political thinking? Alan Ryan, writing after the development of the New Right, finds Oakeshott liberal by comparison with neo- or post-conservatives, and liberal to a degree which would not have been so evident in the 1950s or 1960s. Writing in 1986, Charles Covell was already portraying Oakeshott's *Rationalism in Politics* not so much as conservative text, as one which marked a breach with the existing consensus.

The role that the arguments, aspirations and aversions that made up the New Right have at the end of the twentieth century is both in spite of and because of the disruption of their cohesion, and the fact that the pure doctrine, in the form set out by Hayek, has passed its high point of public presence. The economic rationalization of the market has proved unsuited to holding societies together, whilst the fierce advocacy of cultural specificities has proved dangerously effective in prising them apart. But whilst the very intellectual neatness of the arguments made them vulnerable, the aspirations to which they gave expression and support have survived into the fluid debates of the century's end. Several of the aspirations and aversions which gave substance to the New Right were shared, with varying degrees of difference, with other traditions of political thinking. The championing of the nuclear heterosexual family, the stress on individual autonomy, the suspicion of government and of politics, which were never a monopoly of the right, have become part, in a variety of forms, of a broader debate. The market as a device for making actual demand rather than hypothetical need the principle on which goods and services are distributed has been taken up with almost as much enthusiasm on the left as on the right. The constituent, though fragmented, elements of the New Right, some in forms that their original champions would scarcely recognize, continue to be fragments, and important fragments, in political thinking. What is wholly unclear and uncertain is the overall pattern, the general direction.

9 The death of socialism and the rise of the left

SOCIALISM, RADICALISM, AND THE LEFT

Towards the end of 1994 a volume of essays appeared on the future of the left (D. Miliband 1994). That in itself was not remarkable. Several such volumes appeared each year, with various titles and authors, discussing the underlying principles and purposes of radical politics, assessing recent successes and failures in achieving, pursuing or catching sight of goals, and considering the sorts of policies most likely to achieve them in the future. The right may not have been the stupid party, but compared with the left it had always been the reticent one. And especially in the years after the emergence of the New Left, the left had been the party of publication. Journals and publishing houses multiplied, there were years books, anthologies, series and collections. *The Socialist Register*, published annually, institutionalized the process, but it was by no means the only contributor to the debate. The left, as reformists, were more inclined regularly to look to the future – their own and the country's – than were the right. They were after all seeking to improve the condition of the country and of its institutions in the light of either principles or example. The right, at least up until the demise of conservatism, were only trying to keep things more or less as they were. The appearance of volumes of articles and essays, by one, two or a collection of authors, was part of the annual round of political discussion. To that extent, there was nothing unusual about *Reinventing the Left*. What distinguished the volume edited in 1994 by David Miliband was the almost complete absence from its pages of the word 'socialism'.

The contributors to *Reinventing the Left* covered the principal topics which socialists would have covered, but did so from the perspective of values and rhetoric which presented a case both wider than the old socialist one, and more eclectic in its frame of ethical reference. The terms in which the argument was carried out were now autonomy, individual, community, equality, and power, which both reflected and departed from the older reference points of welfare, society, class, equality and wellbeing. And whilst the designers of a newer left moved on from the past by seeming to be almost wholly unaware of any such word or set of proposals as socialism, their perspective on the condition of political thinking was confirmed by those disgruntled supporters of the old arguments who complained that there was, in the present debates, nothing of the old to be seen. Socialism, it had been insisted by some of its defenders (Cohen 1995: 1), was inseparable from common ownership, because its aims of equality could not be achieved without equal access to 'what's valuable in life for everyone', an equality which was not compatible with a division into capital and labour, nor with private ownership of the means of production. But the conclusion drawn from that definition was identical to that implied, but not stated, in the crafters of a newer left: the old arguments were no longer to be found, the old proposals had vanished, and in that case, socialism was either dead or suffering distant exile. Socialism, like conservatism, had faded from the language of politics, and the new competition between left and right was being conducted in ways which both departed from and transcended past themes.

Political ideas are the medium in which politics is conducted. The transformation of the old landscape of conservatism and socialism was not confined to books, and was to be seen too in the ways in which the political parties presented themselves to their members, their supporters, their opponents and the public in general. During 1995 the Labour Party revised the policy sections of Clause IV of its constitution. The formula devised in part by Sidney Webb in 1917 had been intended to encompass the aspirations of those who wanted workers' control, those who wanted municipal ownership, and those who wanted nationalization, without committing the party to any particular solution. But it had come to be seen as mobilizing the party around nationalization, and defining socialism as public ownership under the control of the central state. The replacement of this clause by an advocacy of citizen fulfilment was only the rhetorical symptom of a far more substantial change. Shifting the emphasis away from the state as the guardian or expression of popular power, towards a tactically but also logically less precise advocacy of various unpredictable forms of citizen autonomy, was the partisan and propagandist expression of a transformation in the structures of political thought.

THREE HISTORICAL SHIFTS: NEW RIGHT, CLASS, AND COMMUNISM

Ideas situate themselves around institutions and events at the same time as they give them form. In defining socialism and in order to understand the course of its decline, it is necessary to identify not an essential principle or principles, but a cluster of historically located aspirations and aversions. The context of socialism, as of conservatism or liberalism or feminism, is in this sense historical, rather than logical or intellectual in any abstract sense. Socialism had passed away not as a result of any abstract intellectual re-assessment by either friends or enemies, but in response to and as part of quite specific historical circumstances. The move from socialism to post-socialism, from old polarities to a postmodern left, was accomplished in a series of responses to three major historical shifts.

THE INFLUENCE OF THE NEW RIGHT

The initial response of the left to the New Right was to attempt to defend existing positions. An advocacy of markets, and a stress on culture as hierarchical, seemed to add little save by degree to the arguments of opponents, and to require little more than simple rebuttal, bringing well-tried arguments to bear on well-known enemies. The historical detail might be new, and the detailed empirical evidence would have to be extracted, but the broad case on each side contained little or nothing unfamiliar. Occasional critical attacks from the left on what was already being called the 'New Right' had after all appeared in the 1960s (Collard 1968), and the views of writers such as Hayek had been available for very much longer than that. *The Road to Serfdom* had been reviewed by Orwell (Orwell 1968b: 142–3). But ideas cluster around parties and governments, and it was the election victory of Margaret Thatcher in 1979 which turned what many had dismissed as eccentric and idealistic theories into perceived challenges. The election victory of 1979 marked the move from the study and the publishing house to Whitehall and Westminster, and the level of intellectual activity increased correspondingly. Nonetheless the initial response was to see the arguments of the right as challenges which required no more than that they be repulsed, rather than as arguments which might shift the very structures within which debate would take place. It was not only the first responses which were wholly defensive or dismissive, and one strand of critical writing about the New Right, though a diminishing one, has limited itself to dismissing all its

arguments as fallacious, empirically unsound, or ethically unacceptable. But the successes, electoral, governmental and intellectual, of the
New Right presented the left with challenges at the level of both tactics
and theory. The New Right had presented an account of liberty and of
anti-elitism in which individual choice was wholly unaccountable save
to the law, and in which popular power could be advanced, not
through the state, but as an alternative to it. It had been an assumption
of democratic socialism, and an argument of social democrats, that
whether as the working class or as the people, the power of ordinary
men and women was most effectively advanced through the agency of
representative governmental institutions. The argument that popular
power was not necessarily or even probably state power hijacked both
the democratic and the libertarian carriage of the left, and questioned
the whole majoritarian theory of democracy.

The ascendancy of the New Right drew attention to, or revived, a
resentment of paternalism which had always been a recessive theme of
the left. Socialism for ordinary people, George Orwell had written in
The Road to Wigan Pier, meant amongst other things 'nobody bossing
you about' (Orwell [1937] 1962: 154), whilst a theme of the New Left of
the 1960s and 1970s had been a suspicion of orthodoxy and a revolt
against gerontocracy. Paternalism could take very specific forms, and
the resentment of it could shape itself around the prosaic and the
mundane. One of the lasting contributions of the New Right was to
root into political thinking the view that personal consumption,
whimsical choice, idiosyncratic or even vulgar wants were not inferior
to collective decision making, and that politics, as a collective process,
has no universal or inherent superiority to smaller units of choice. Why
should council tenants not be able to paint their front doors in colours
of their own choosing? But the left was slow to rediscover this aspect of
its tradition, though it was assisted in so doing by the inconsistencies
within the New Right's anti-elitism. Bureaucrats, experts, and the
'nanny' state might come under attack, but leaders and managers were
the emissaries of the future. To begin with, therefore, the left simply
reversed the daemonology.

THE REVOLUTIONS OF 1989

The impact of the New Right had been a slow process suddenly
accelerated and confirmed after 1979. Of equal significance was the
evaporation of the existing scale of polar opposites which had been
sustained by the existence of the Soviet Union as the custodian of
managerial state socialism and the representative, for both democrats

and capitalists, of the antithesis of the institutions and values which they themselves prized. On one side despotic one party state control, on the other liberal democracy. For thinkers across a wide range of political sympathies, the existence of the Soviet Union and Eastern Europe made possible a Manichean world view, whether Soviet party communism provided a 'pole of attraction', an 'alternative "world view"' (R. Miliband 1994: 150), or a pole of repulsion. But such perspectives can be restricting in their very simplicity. Over thirty years previously, the events of 1956 with their massive discrediting of party communism had seemed to involve a great intellectual liberation, freeing Marx from the canons of both orthodoxy and anathema. But quite how much the structures of political argument remained set by the communist/managerial-despotic and capitalist/liberal democratic polarity was not clear until 1989 blew the whole structure away. After 1989, neither communists nor anti-communists could claim that socialism was, whatever the attraction of its values and aspirations, most substantially represented by the regimes of Eastern Europe and the Soviet Union. The revolutions of 1989 in Eastern Europe un-demonized socialism, and made possible a less restrained, because less defensive, examination of its possibilities.

What did not disappear was the polarity between left and right. The collapse of managerial communism made possible a presentation of left and right which was not exclusively or even predominantly about economic resources, their control or distribution. It was not just, as Perry Anderson put it, that the revolutions of 1989 'struck away mental fixtures of Left and Right' (Anderson 1992: 301), but that they introduced a new demonology, and made possible a new pantheism. If 1917 was one crucial date for twentieth century socialism, then by the same token 1989 was the other.

The overthrow and abdication of managerial communism in Eastern Europe and the Soviet Union not only deprived the right of its demonology. It abolished an international polarity of capitalist versus communist and democratic versus despotic within which political argument had been constricted, and to which the terms 'right' and 'left' had been tethered. The adjective 'right' could even be used, much to the distaste of Conservatives such as Norman Tebbitt, to describe old communists in Russia. Whilst the breadth of application of the terms left and right lacked precision, and could not survive any precise assessment of the accuracy of the words as means of categorizing beliefs, a new and more flexible discussion was nonetheless underway which, if it lacked precise ground markings, showed continuing imagination, innovation and variety.

The abdication of East European autocracies made even more irrelevant a juxtaposition of socialist planning with capitalist markets. All modern states use both, and the question has become one of the role of the state in facilitating the free choices of citizens, whilst the experience of the new post-communist systems illustrated the unhelpfulness of assuming rigid or automatic relationships between liberal democracy, limited government and flourishing market economies. The lessons of both domestic and Eastern European experience were complex. The popular demands of the people of Eastern Europe, so long canonized by the right, were seen to be more complex and more varied, and to include not simply a desire for the fruits of capitalism, but a desire for the collective services and structure of socialism, and the political liberties of liberalism.

A CHANGE OF CAST

Socialism had always accorded itself a special relationship with the working class. They were the group who had most to gain from a transformation of capitalist society, the ones who more than any others suffered from its injustice and inequalities, and whose sense both of fairness and of self-interest would provide the electoral fuel for socialism's democratic advance. The oppression of the working class was the necessary and unavoidable corollary of capitalism, and the advance of the workers and the abolition of capitalism were, equally, component parts of a single historical process. By the last decade of the chronological twentieth century, most of the assumptions on which this special relationship had been based were either destroyed or under challenge.

Two things seemed clear from the Eastern European revolutions of 1989. One was that the working class, whilst it had always been allotted a principal role as the engine, or at least the infantry, of socialism, could act just as decisively, or even more so, to promote capitalism, markets, party despotism or nationalism. The working class was not necessarily a revolutionary or even a radical force in relation to property, consumption or the values of the individualist capital-acquiring or capital-desiring household and family. The other was that whilst the term 'people' or 'citizens' had a non-specific inclusiveness suitable for encompassing the very great variety of workers, students, intellectuals, Catholics and Protestants, small farmers, liberals, writers, parents and patriots who mobilized against the old regimes, 'working class' was a term and a concept which was of limited and diminishing explanatory or categorizing usefulness.

But the special place of the working class in socialist thinking was being undermined earlier than the East European revolutions, and closer to home, in the United Kingdom. Even before 1989, socialists were pointing to a decline in class voting, as the link between manual occupations and left-wing aspirations seemed less and less self-evident to manual workers themselves. 'The evidence we have suggests that people like having cash in their hands and buying their goods and services competitively: they feel secure and self-confident in a way that they often do not when dealing with public agencies' (Miller 1989a: 49). The Labour leader Neil Kinnock was making a similar point when he asked whether it made sense to promise to free a car owning, Spanish holiday taking worker from his chains (Kinnock 1992: 130). Not only was the propensity of the working class to replace the existing order increasingly called into question, but a decline in its relative size made it less and less likely that anyone could look to it to do so even had it wanted to. At the same time there was an awareness of the rise of other dimensions of allegiance. While the working class was losing its role as a principal actor in either politics or the theories devised to explain it, other actors – students, women, members of religions and ethnic cultures – were emerging as increasingly important participants. Identity through religion and gender began to assume a larger and larger place in political argument, as class was upstaged by fideism and feminism. The recognition of this increasingly emerged even in more traditional socialist writing, and in 1992 Perry Anderson was juxtaposing an observation that 'labour forces have been feminized' with the comment that 'working-class identification has declined' (Anderson 1992: 324).

Anderson's comment points in the direction of one more reason why class had become seen by some on the left as not the best motor of progress. Feminists had argued that the fraternity which was presented as one of the cultural values and political weapons of class was just that: a closing of ranks by the brothers. The conceptualization of class politics in heroic terms, on a social landscape which excluded the household where women worked and produced without wages, and much of the waged work which they did as well, was one more cause of the increasing search for other social relationships on which to base political action.

The traditional motors of socialism had been either a democratic working class, or an enlightened collectivist elite. Both of these disappeared as plausible identities, leaving a socialist future, even if it were to be desired, without any credible progenitors. At the same time as the progenitors of any plausible socialism were removed, so were its active, and passive, components were it to be established, its rulers and its subjects. The dissipation of the idea of a single science of government which could be mastered, and of a disinterested class or community that could apply it, was balanced by the disappearance of any single identity, working class or anything else, whereby the citizen or subject could be described and hence the purposes of government defined. Once the character and hence the wants or needs of citizens could no longer be assumed to be uniform or readily predictable, the nature and purposes of government lost the direction, certainty and coherence which had underlain the expectations of socialism.

But if simple class analysis was eclipsed, it was eclipsed by a postmodernism which pointed in no single direction. There were both populist and elitist implications of this. On the one hand, why should the people not have what they want? But on the other, might not some forms of public (elite) provision be the only ways of making culture available and enabling it to flourish?

THE DEFENCE OF SOCIALISM

The government which came to power in 1979 echoed many of the themes of the new right in its general principles and rhetoric, was anti-collectivist and radical rather than conservative in economic policy and social provision. The Conservative electoral victory of 1979, followed by success in 1983 and 1987, faced the left with something more than a cyclical dip in its fortunes. As such it called forth a response different from that with which socialists had in the past met their opponents. But the governmental and party phenomenon swiftly labelled 'Thatcherism' was easier to respond to than the intellectual phenomenon of the New Right. There was disagreement over how 'Thatcherism' was to be characterized and explained, but a broad agreement that it was in some sense original. 'Thatcherism' could be accounted for as a strategy or a tactic, and its undeniable political success attributed to its skill in mobilizing media, commercial and electoral support. To acknowledge this aspect of the advance of the right however defined did not involve any suggestion that coherent, illuminating or valuable elements were to be found in its thinking. It was less easy to accept either the originality or the merit of the New Right as an interpretation of politics or as a prescription for government. The success of the New Right as a body of political thinking was difficult for its opponents to come to terms with. Rejection and refutation, on grounds of coherence, ethics or empirical evidence was one response. Far more was at stake in admitting that an opponent's ideas had some merit, than in acknowledging the skill of her tactics.

The initial response to the flourishing of New Right thinking was a re-assertion and development of existing socialist themes. Because of the very novelty of the views being expressed by the New Right, its intellectual ascent called forth to begin with a defensive restatement of old socialism. Martin Loney's attack of 1986 proclaimed its position in its title, *The Politics of Greed*, condemning and dismissing the New Right on ethical grounds. Claims that the New Right's success could be at all explained by any support amongst the electorate for shifting resources from public to private services were not taken seriously (Loney 1986: 1). A collection published the same year under the editorship of Ruth Levitas was broader in the grounds of its criticism, but no more inclined to treat the New Right's thinking as any less mistaken or inconsistent, or any more popular in touching on genuine electoral resentments or aspirations. Whilst New Right thinking was treated as having an intellectual presence, which was indeed the subject of the volume, the ideas were taken to be internally flawed. Though the New Right was treated as an ideology, it was thought to have escaped from the tethering cords of class or sectional interest, and gained an independent intellectual life. Hence the necessity to combat it on the plane of political thinking (Levitas 1986: 10). What was not in doubt was that on this level total defeat was possible. The suggestion that the New Right 'addresses people's real needs and experiences in a way which the Left fails to do', that the left should acknowledge popular resentment at bureaucracy, paternalism and condescension, and popular liking for some forms of market provision, was dismissed on two counts. First that it represented 'colluding' with the right, and second that people's 'experiences and needs are constructed' within ideological contexts (ibid.: 13–16) and so 'the New Right's connection with need and experiences is illusory' (ibid.: 16). This initial response, though increasingly muted and infrequent, continued into the 1990s. When in 1990 a collection of *Reactions to the Right* was published, the editor Barry Hindess warned of the pursuit of an 'illusory individual freedom' (Hindess 1990: 31) and warned that the view that socialism was about liberty could obscure 'important political issues concerning the power and significance of corporate actors in the modern world' (ibid.: 2). The response of Jim Tomlinson, another of the contributors, to the advocacy of market socialism was that it was little more than 'a socialist gloss' on the theories of Schumpeter and Hayek (ibid.: 45). Hindess's answer to the dissatisfactions of citizens laid stress on more effective or more democratic methods of political control of public agencies, not in any direct citizen power (ibid.: 29–20). Ralph Miliband, in his last book, identified capitalism, defined as the extraction of profit from formally independent wage-earners, as the root of our present system and the source of its evils: not just ordinary inequality, but racism, sexism, nationalism and cruelty of all kinds. And if the workers seemed better off, their conditions of work were still undemocratic and their incomes insecure. The socialist alternative was co-operation, fraternity and public ownership in a democratic community where power had been abolished. To create such a society would involve a difficult and arduous transformation of both the structures and values of existing society (R. Miliband 1994). The years since 1979 had not changed that task, however more difficult they might have made it.

For some even more optimistic writers the history of the left, and the significance of the New Right, was to be seen principally as a flowering of the socialist tradition which the New Right succeeded only in stimulating or provoking. Perry Anderson argued that

> a regime of the radical Right part confronted, part created an overall cultural drift to the left. Prompted by social resentment and doctrinal animus, its attempt at a *Gleichschaltung* of the academy tended to raise up the very adversaries it sought to stamp out, even as its drive to impose the values of the counting-house and constabulary on society swept forward elsewhere.
>
> (Anderson 1992: 200)

In the analyses of writers such as Anderson or Rustin, the old structures of class and capitalism continued to shape both the description and the prescription. On such a reading, the spread of New Right arguments was a vaccine provoking a response which, however imaginative, was essentially defensive.

But as it became obvious that some of the recessive themes of socialism were being employed with great success as dominant themes in the New Right, a more radical reassessment began, which led not so much to the transformation or revision of socialism, as to its final metamorphosis into something else, just as conservatism had given way to the radicalism of the New Right.

URBAN LEFTISM

In this process, a transitional role was performed by what was frequently referred to at the time as the 'new urban left'. A major element in the 'new urban left' of the 1980s was determined by the policies of the New Right, or by a government to which a large amount of New Right influence was attributed. Opposition to cuts in services, or of levels of council employment, and to increases in rates, constituted an important plank in the programme, which was in that respect a defensive politics of the status quo. The Greater London Enterprise Board, set up by the 'new urban left' GLC stressed the defence of existing jobs, and old opportunities for men, rather than new opportunities for women. But there was in those defences an echo of earlier recessive themes, and a development of the potential for radical rethinking. The New Left of the 1960s and 1970s had been associated with a belief in the value of the small, the communal and the direct in politics. The 'new urban left' of the 1980s represented a transition between this and the newer left of the 1990s. It was also a move away from the merely defensive response to the advance of the New Right, beginning from the recognition that the terms of the debate were changing, and that some of the suppositions on which socialists had previously based their arguments had to be questioned or abandoned. Writing in 1984 in a collection of essays on *The Future of the Left*, Doreen Massey, Lynne Segal, and Hilary Wainwright argued that

> Changing the terms of the debate is essential, since Thatcher's attack has been successful precisely because there WAS so much to criticize. Nationalized industries are unresponsive to both worker and consumer. On a day-to-day level many people do experience the welfare state as undemocratic, impenetrable, even hostile – not that Thatcher's state is any less so, of course. We don't want the old, social democratic state back either. If the public sector is to be defended, whether it be the National Health Service or local authorities, we have to rethink from the beginning what it is about the public nature of provision which should be attractive and beneficial – a publicly available resource to be drawn upon rather than the heavy hand of the state.
>
> (Massey et al. 1984: 215)

A link between the New Left of the 1960s and 1970s and the new urban left of the 1980 was provided by the arguments set forward in 1979 by Sheila Rowbotham, Lynne Segal and Hilary Wainwright in *Beyond the Fragments*. The starting point of the discussion was feminism, but a feminism which made connections between the various, fragmented parts of a broad and variegated left-wing constituency. The most evident drawing back was from the vanguard politics of Leninism, but the simplifications of representative parliamentary politics and, at least in its most common form, a political analysis based on class came in for equal retirement after criticism.

Whereas the older left had looked to national representative democracy, and a central social democratic state, to pursue the interests of either the people or the working class as a whole, the 'new urban left' placed far more emphasis on local and municipal politics and government. Its institutional alliances were not so much with politics at Westminster, as with local councils and political organizations, particularly with the Greater London Council under the leadership of Ken Livingstone between 1981 and 1985. It was pluralist, but still socialist, and local but still collectivist. Its pluralism was bounded within the concept of a single, however loosely connected, movement, which faced a single, if many faceted, enemy which was, before all else, capitalist. The phrase 'rainbow coalition' was used to describe an alliance drawn from the hitherto neglected segments of the electorate categorized by ethnicity, sexuality or gender, just as auxiliary help had been sought in the Great War from the empire and the colonies, to supplement the contribution from the domestic shires. But whilst the interests of women, ethnic minorities or gays might have distinct elements to them, they could not be pursued in isolation since the causes of their exploitation were interconnected. The groups were assumed to have an overall unity, just as the enemy was, even if many headed, still one beast. When the feminist authors of *Beyond the Fragments* recommended in 1979 a strategy which laid some of the theoretical foundations for the new urban left, they argued for a recognition both of distinct interests and of interconnectedness: 'it is precisely the connections between these sources of oppression, both through the state and through the organization of production and culture, which makes such a piecemeal solution impossible' (Rowbotham et al. 1979: 4). Class remained the comprehensive category, and the various new, or newly recognized, political groups and movements were still 'fragmented working-class activities' (ibid.: 10). The idea of a 'rainbow coalition' was frequently a refinement of the older notion of a working-class movement, variegating the idea of class, rather than complementing it with alternative and additional categories. 'The different interests within the working class, of gender, race, region and work, asserted themselves with confidence, aspiring to redefine the common interests of class – a human pluralism against the monolithic tendencies of capital' as Wainwright put it in a reflection on the new urban left's successes and failures (Wainwright 1987a: 14).

Such a socialist pluralism was group politics rather than identity politics. The components were still seen as distinct categories, rather than as the collective facets of a part of several individuals lives. The various segments of the rainbow, too, were in the first place public and political, and neither private nor economic. Groups would play their part in the overall enterprise through their inputs into the political process, not through politically unco-ordinated market choices of the kind that market socialists were subsequently to favour. And though the link between the personal and the political was asserted, it was not because people's sexual predilections or household arrangements were their business and nobody else's, but because politics was assumed to permeate sexuality and household arrangements. Where George Herbert had written that 'Who sweeps a room as for thy laws, Makes that and th'action fine', the secular version was that even sweeping a room had to be seen in the context of the overall liberation struggle.

Once it was clear that the intellectual opposition was not destroyed by such attacks, a second response was to examine more closely and more sympathetically whether there might not be some strengths in the New Right position which explained its vigour. The revolutions of 1989, by providing a potentially clean agenda for the whole of Eastern Europe, stimulated such enquiries, and facilitated a response to the arguments of economic liberals such as Hayek which conceded the value of some of the New Right aspirations, whilst grafting them on to traditional socialist aspirations. At the same time, the attraction for many in the newly democratic nations of Eastern Europe of the vision of markets and liberty provided by writers such as Hayek provoked a further effort on the left to examine in a manner both more critical and less hostile the arguments of the New Right (Wainwright 1994: viii–xi). Hilary Wainwright's 1994 *Arguments for a New Left* contained an ingenious attempt to accept Hayek's account of markets as effective means of transmitting economic information, but to collectivize or at least to pluralize many of the sources of that information, replacing or supplementing the individual consumer with groups whose functions were at least in part political. Taking the New Right seriously involved recognizing, among other things, that far from being simply a hostile intellectual force, New Right ideas and left-wing ideas shared, if not remarkably similar concerns on some issues, then some unduly obscured common parentage. As Wainwright commented, in its Thatcherite form the New Right had managed to 'appropriate the libertarianism of 1968, extracting its entrepreneurial spirit from its values of social solidarity' (ibid.: xvi). Hilary Wainwright's response to Hayek countered the economic liberal description of a market choice with a version of economic information provision which straddled both the promise of liberalism and the collectivism of old socialism. It was a posthumous agenda for the new urban left, and thus an agenda for a revived old left, rather than for a new or newer left. As workers organizing their own work, and collaborating with each other in 'inter-enterprise systems of direct co-ordination' and as members of 'community based' associations of one kind and another, people could provide 'social relations that are neither market nor plan, neither the haphazard outcome of individual activity nor the design of an all-knowing central authority' (ibid.: 148).

The new urban left, despite the novelty indicated by its title, drew on the recessive themes of socialism and on the tradition, running back to anarchism and the communism of William Morris in the nineteenth century, which saw local communities as the forum for a freer, more imaginative and direct form of politics, with citizens directly and collaboratively arranging their own affairs without the intermediary activity of professional politicians or representatives. Whilst at the level of municipal politics it failed in its radical defensive strategy, intellectually it provided a crucial bridge to the future.

MARKET SOCIALISM

The new urban left had incorporated in its working assumptions the criticisms made by the New Right of collectivist state provision. But they had remained committed to collective, political methods, albeit on a far smaller and more local scale, for allocating the resources which the New Right wanted distributed through market choices. The first post-socialist response to the New Right, in that it absorbed the argument in favour of market rather than collective, political allocations, was market socialism. Though the arguments of the market socialists were assisted by the revolutions of 1989, they were developed before the collapse of East European state socialism. The term 'market socialism' disguised how far the argument had moved from left-wing collectivism. It differed from the pluralist socialism of the new urban left in two principal respects: the relative emphasis placed on class, and the relative balance within civil society of political and private activity. In 1989 a collection of essays edited by Julian LeGrand and Saul Estrin under the title *Market Socialism*, and a fuller exposition by one of the contributors, David Miller, *Market, State and Community*, set out the essentials of what to some of the authors was a rethinking of the consequences of the essential principles of socialism, but which to others both on the left and the right could be presented as the first step, or perhaps the third or fourth step, in the radical rethinking or even abandonment of socialism altogether. LeGrand and Estrin spoke of a confusion between socialist ends and socialist means, much as Crosland had done over forty years earlier in *The Future of Socialism*, and implied that the objection to markets was simply the result of such a confusion (LeGrand and Estrin 1989: 2). Miller on the other hand wrote of 'a radical redefinition of the meaning of socialism' (Miller 1989b: 1) and of market socialism as an 'alternative' to 'older forms of socialism' which are 'outdated' (Miller 1989b: 5).

The New Left of the 1960s and 1970s had been about liberty, variety and autonomy, and this gave an unexpected continuity with the left response to the New Right use of the idea of markets. The attachment of socialism and markets to one another was not new, and had been discussed as a means of achieving desirable ends of production by Alec Nove in 1983 (Nove 1983). There are two very different arguments to be found amongst socialist advocates of markets. One is that markets, like socialism, are a means of maximizing choice and freedom. The other is that markets, like socialism, are a means of promoting economic efficiency. The first draws on the traditions of liberal individualism, the second on those of collective efficiency. But both are responses not only to reason but to both domestic and international circumstance. Whether or not central planning and collective decision worked, there appeared to be considerable electoral support for the promise of markets, whilst the failures of the managerial communist systems of Eastern Europe, in the shape of economic inefficiency and, after 1989, political collapse and abdication, subverted the structure of political discussion which had pure centralized collectivism and anarchic capitalism as its polar opposites.

But the clear attractions of some aspects of markets for consumers and citizens, and the success of the New Right in using this attraction to promote a far wider agenda, led to a reassessment on the left of the old preferences for collective action, and of the old suspicions of individual choice rather than public deliberation and collective allocation. It was now argued that

> Since we are all citizens and consumers, since most of us are (or have been, or will be) workers, and since the majority own, or would like to own, capital in some form (a house, savings accounts, pension rights, insurance policies, stocks and shares), it is not surprising that none of these traditional 'models' of how the economy should be organized finds favour.
>
> (LeGrand and Estrin 1989: 23)

So whilst for those whose concern was overall economic efficiency, markets might be a means of promoting efficient production, for those whose arguments began with citizens, workers or voters markets not only promised to take the waiting out of wanting, or at least the politics out of wanting, but provided a form of autonomy for those who, for whatever reason, shared Oscar Wilde's antipathy to political consultation and decision by meetings because socialism did cut into one's evenings so dreadfully. There was also a feeling that collective solutions were not, anyway, either ones that truly did involve ordinary citizens, or lead to effective results: 'Mistrust of the intentions of bureaucrats and the effectiveness of public intervention leads market socialists to seek to err on the side of *laissez-faire*' (ibid.: 1). If the end of socialist policies was to promote the interests of citizens, then structuring markets in such a way that they successfully met individual interests might be better than trying to determine what was in the interests of people collectively, and pursuing it through central policy. This meant altering 'the environment in which markets operate to ensure that such outcomes are in the private interests of individuals, rather than use the state to impose the public interest from above' (ibid.).

Purists of left and right have insisted that markets and socialism are incompatible. One reply to that view is that they are mistaken in imagining that the real world can be accommodated to abstract simplicities. Another is that even in their own terms the opposite of socialism is not markets but atomized individualism, the opposite of markets, not socialism, but centralized planning. Even so, the initial advocates of market socialism were over-sanguine in their insistence that socialism was about ends not means, and that the means which they sought were the same as had always informed socialist argument. The distinction between ends and means can be misleading, in that the means employed will themselves express some way of social organization and social relating. Moreover, once the market is introduced, so is the possibility of a variety of often unpredictable individual purposes, and the likely impossibility of any socialist goal which involves collective ends save of the broadest, enabling kind of allowing everyone as much autonomy as possible.

A further obstacle faced by the advocates of market socialism was a deeply seated moral or cultural suspicion of 'random' individual choices, and a sense that collective decisions were morally preferable to each person simply going their own way. There was a long puritan tradition within English socialism, which Tawney exemplified when he defined how much happiness was 'good for any of the children of Adam' (Tawney 1920: 83). In dismissing such collective paternalism as simply 'indefensible', market socialists such as David Miller (1989a: 31) have paid more attention to the logical strength than to the historical depth of their opponent's views. At its most radical, this socialist puritanism dismisses the pursuit of individual objectives as mere selfishness, to which altruism and the pursuit of either the common good or the good of others ought always to be preferred. To this the market socialist has no answer, save to say either that most people are in fact motivated by a desire for their own good, or that to insist on a particular form of altruism is only to insist on one conception of what the good life entails for an individual, and that in the presence of a great variety of such conceptions, and the absence of any agreed or agreeable conception of the good life, what should be aimed for are circumstances where individuals can as far as possible pursue their own ideals.

PRODUCERS' POWER

The New Right promised to give ordinary people the power of choice. But this individual power was to be exercised in the marketplace rather than in the workplace where, indeed, the right of managers to manage was the preferred slogan. In setting out the case for market socialism, there was therefore both a limitation in the extent of the individual powers offered by the opposition, and a potentially profitable ambivalence within the socialist tradition. Marx was not the only socialist to have argued that the worker was deprived of powers and benefits which were rightly his or hers, and that under capitalism the owner or the employer exploited the worker by expropriating what was the result of the worker's own productive labour. One response to this was to argue that since these expropriated benefits were, like so many other advantages of social life, the product of society as a whole, they should be managed by the state on behalf of and for the benefit of all. Another response, however, was to say that the worker had property right in his or her own labour and in its products, and that these should be expressed in some form of worker's control.

So whilst the New Right promised to give people power, or choice, as consumers, market socialism promised it to them as producers as well. Miller's account of market socialism involved a recommendation of workers' co-operatives. As such, market socialism was open to the old criticism of Beatrice and Sidney Webb, that producer power was undemocratic, whereas consumer power extended democracy. As producers, people were in two senses a faction or group: they were only a part of the whole community, and they produced only one thing, whereas the consumer was by contrast a universal figure.

MARKETS AND EQUALITY

When Crosland had based his account of socialism on the most basic principles that could be identified in the socialist tradition, he chose equality. To do so invoked a lineage even older, going back to 1789. The arguments of market socialists such as Miller assumed equality rather than argued it, but assumed it not as a fundamental principle, but rather as a working rule. Nonetheless by taking seriously some of the arguments of the New Right, Raymond Plant was able to place on new foundations the case for equality which earlier socialists had placed on an ethical base. Plant uses the economic liberal argument that there is no criteria by which goods can be distributed to argue the egalitarian case that therefore 'no individual merits more or less in the distribution of those basic resources which are necessary to enter the market on a fair basis and thus those resources should be distributed as equally as possible' (Plant 1989: 67). This rational presumption in favour of equality was employed by Miller to advocate the use of markets to promote older socialist aspiration. Thus if welfare were desirable, then one policy was 'to redistribute resources so that markets bring about a more equal distribution of welfare' (Miller 1989a: 29). The point here is not that the argument starts from a principle of equality, and then proceeds to ask what the implications of that commitment are in areas of income, education, career, etc., but rather it identifies certain goods and then takes as a working rule that, other things being equal, everyone's desires for those goods should be placed on an equal footing. Mainstream socialist theories of equality had stressed equality of condition, of enjoyment of goods, services and opportunities. Such a form of equality, if it did not necessarily entail a paternalist state, albeit a democratic one, was quite compatible with it. But if equality began at the other end, not as an equal division of social goods, but as an equal possession of individual rights, the paternalist conclusion was not only not implied, it was precluded. Markets could be employed to achieve this. But markets were not natural things, existing instead in chosen and contrived conditions. A socialist market therefore presupposed a range of equalities even more radical than those assumed by traditional collectivists socialists.

The principal contribution of market socialist arguments such as those of Miller and Plant was, despite the care and detail with which they were set out, not so much to add new aspirations to the agenda of the left, as to exorcize old bogey men. One of the first steps in the market socialist argument was to detach markets from capitalism, and socialism from collectivist planning, to assert, as David Miller put it, that it was 'quite possible to be for markets and against capitalism' (Miller 1989a: 25). Many of the arguments in favour of the usefulness of markets were similar in major respects to those put forward by less cautious and more radical advocates on the right such as Hayek. It was not therefore the novelty of the arguments so much as the context in which they were placed that shifted the location of left-wing arguments, making both suspicion of collective activity and provision, and active support for individual autonomy, respectable elements in the debate. Market socialism was a radical development within socialism with equality on one face and rights on the other. Its advocates nonetheless retained the assumption that there were socialist goals, however plural, which markets could be cultivated in order to produce, and that there were some wants which should be replaced by needs, since the customer was not always right, particularly 'in the case of goods like medical care and education, where the recipients are unlikely to be well placed to make an informed judgment about the quality of the service they are given' (Miller 1989b: 317). So both in being rather more suspicious of consumers than of producers, and in envisaging a major re-organizing and organizing role for the state, market socialism retained strong continuities with what had gone before. On the other hand, the inhabitants of a socialist market would, rather like those of the Fabian state, be citizens and producers above all else, though the way in which they would perform those roles would be very different from that envisaged by the Fabians.

COMMUNITY, COMMUNITIES, AND PUBLIC LIFE IN A CLASSLESS SOCIETY

When the Labour leader Tony Blair began to speak of community in 1995, some commentators traced the concept across the Atlantic to the American sociologist Amatai Etzionni. But it was an unnecessary and unhelpful diversion. Community was a word and a concept that already had a long and vigorous domestic history both in political philosophy and in political thinking and writing. Not only had Raymond Plant, one of the advocates of market socialism, been writing about community over twenty years previously (Plant 1974), but the idea that there were non-material benefits to be gained from a collaborative and fraternal relationship with one's fellow human beings, and that this was expressed and sustained by some shared values and responsibilities encompassed by the term 'community', was one which ran back through the New Left via Tawney to William Morris. And it was characteristic of a notion with such varied ancestry that it could take many forms, from a desire to discover a foundation for national life in a working-class or popular culture, to a belief that politics had to start by listening to the mundane desires of ordinary people. The idea of community has been a persistent one in socialist thinking. Or more precisely, ideas of community have been persistent, for the images to which the term referred varied widely. For Morris, community had been classless because class society had been left far behind, though it had been united by a shared involvement in creative work. For others, though in differing ways, community had been at root a matter of class, whether the decent English working class into which Orwell wished everyone to merge, or the working-class culture of fraternity, solidarity and revolutionary potential described by the writers and historians of the New Left. As such, community can be a Trojan Horse for the pluralism of a Paul Hirst, the cultural socialism of a Raymond Williams, or the market socialism of a David Miller and Raymond Plant.

But the principal reason for the revival of community in the last decade of the chronological twentieth century was the abandoning of fraternity based on class, and the distrust of solidarity based on nationalism. Community offered a way forward which stressed the practical and moral value of seeing individual action as taking place in relation to other members of society.

In the writings of market socialists, community, in the form of the nation, took a further shape, and was advanced as the necessary condition of a socialist market society (Miller 1989b: 245), with what Raymond Plant described as 'the individual consumer as a bearer of common identity within an otherwise plural society' (Plant and Barry 1990: 4). The market socialist case pointed in the direction of the kinds of social structures and relationships which would be the condition and context of socialist markets, in a way which either excluded or transcended differences of culture. Nor did such a citizenship community incorporate or express more than a part of the life of its members. On the contrary, such a limited community was a necessary alternative to those comprehensive communities which led so readily to hostility towards non-members, and in which xenophobia and intolerance flourished. Citizenship, argued Miller, 'represents the only viable form of society-wide community under modern conditions' (ibid.: 16–17).

Community was both wider and less encompassing than collectivity.

Wider because it was varied and even discordant, and because it involved more people, not just representatives and manager/bureaucrats; less encompassing because the claims it made on people were less comprehensive. Although socialists like Tawney had envisaged community being founded on a common culture, it was precisely this which the communitarians of the 1990s rejected. The criticisms of writers such as Hayek, together with the evident multi-culturalism of British society, made the assumptions of earlier socialist such as Tawney of the possibility of finding common purposes or a common culture untenable. Common purposes and fraternity were replaced by citizenship and tolerance, and an extended importance given to the private sphere, within which at least a part of economic activity was now assumed to fall. In its strong version, set out in the nineteenth century by writers such as Morris, community had involved altruism and duty and, as Cohen argued against the socialist use of markets, service and a belief that each should contribute according to his abilities, and receive according to his needs (Cohen 1994). But once both needs and abilities were seen as varied and unpredictable, even a premise of altruism and duty came to be seen as best implemented through the flexibilities of markets.

But if community was not an ideal, but a response to 'actually existing humanity', whilst it might provide opportunities for radical argument, it clearly placed restraints on it as well. If the existing values, customs, and aspirations of citizens were to form the content of community as a positive and guiding set of values, then policies some radicals would find uncongenial seemed to follow. In the arguments of market socialists community and market were devoid of content, though they needed to be structured in a way that safeguarded rights. Matters which other users of the notion of community tried to build into their account, whether to acknowledge them or transcend them, such as gender, were specifically excluded. On the one hand 'community' provided the context for market socialism and the liberal pluralism of the newer left. But on the other there was a recurring insistence on the dissimilarities between people or, which was the obverse of the same point, the absence of any identity save as individuals making choices in a market. Markets did not treat people as workers, or men or women, and so, the argument ran, the old broad categories were inadequate, and inadequate moreover because individuals were likely to occupy different categories on different occasions, and to be adequately summed up by no single one of them. Socialist markets seemed to offer a system which at the least was consistent with varieties of identities, and probably supported them.

RIGHTS, ENTITLEMENTS AND CITIZENSHIP

The left of the 1990s developed a complex relationship with the thinking of the New Right, on the one hand taking up its idea, which was also an old liberal idea, of consumer rights, whilst developing against the New Right state the rights of citizens. Socialism had traditionally assumed the beneficence or capturability of the apparatus of government. The success of Conservative governments after 1979 in increasing centralized power and reducing public services was the occasion for serious rethinking for two reasons. If the beneficence of the state could not be taken for granted, then even socialist citizens might need rights against it. And if the state, even if it could be electorally captured for socialist policies, might for substantial periods of time be in the hands of the right, then citizens needed protection during times of right-wing ascendancy. So the left turned its attention to citizenship and to rights (Andrews 1991; Coote 1992; D. Miliband 1994). If market socialism expressed the departure from collective activity and collective provision and decision making in economic terms, rights and citizenship expressed it in civil and political terms. Citizenship in a nation which was to form the context for a community within which market socialism operates 'must be a social role which is partly, but not wholly, defined in terms of rights' (Miller 1989b: 245). The term 'citizenship' was not a familiar one in British political discussion, and though there were precedents in the arguments of radicals such as Paine, it had played little part in more recent thinking on the left (Wright 1993). A stress on citizenship arose from a commitment to politics which was alien to the culture of the short twentieth century, and a form of social life facilitating, if not composed of, varieties of allegiance and membership. The attention to citizenship marked a shift from old rights to new. Old rights were to specific objective needs, collectively defined, sanctioned and provided. New rights were rights to the unpredictable exercise of individual choice, and were exercised by citizens as entitlements, analogous to the rights of the customer rather than the claim of the subject on the paternalism of the community.

The argument had two principal components. First the belief, a largely unfamiliar one on the left, that there were reasons and ideologies of government which were independent of the purposes of politicians or the wishes of electors. A subordinate part of this belief was that governments, whatever programme they were elected on, could not be trusted to devote themselves to that and to nothing else. This view that government was not necessarily to be trusted, was complemented by the second belief, that the surest guarantee of the interests of citizens was if they held sufficient power in their own hands not to be dependent on others for the promotion or safeguarding of those interests. The arguments which had underlain the distribution of power down to each consumer via the market was seen to have other dimensions which markets alone or unstructured could not deal with. If the citizen needed individual and direct power in the market, so did she in other spheres.

Equally, the broad distribution of power which the market promised needed to be matched in government and politics. There had always been arguments, expressed alike amongst socialists, liberals and conservatives, for a broad distribution of governmental power as a check against oppressive government. To that argument was added the view that, since in any society, there will be a variety of values pursued, in order to express this, and give both weight and protection to these, there must be institutional pluralism (Miller 1989b: 4–5). There were precedents for much of this in the recessive themes of the left, from the Webbs's doubts about excessive state power, to anarchism and to Laski's plural sovereignty (R. Barker 1989).

CONSTITUTIONAL RADICALISM

The New Left of the 1960s had found its heroes in revolutionaries and artists. In the 1990s the past was redescribed around political radicals, and 1995 saw a 'political life' of Tom Paine which set out in part to discuss Paine not as an historical, but as a contemporary figure (Keane 1995). By the 1990s, there was the almost forgotten event of a stirring of public debate over the monarchy. Charter 88 had from the end of the 1980s provided an umbrella for all those who wanted more open government, the placing of royal prerogatives under the authority of parliament and statute, electoral reform and freedom of information.

The argument for constitutional reform, more than any other aspect of political argument at the close of the short twentieth century, illustrated both the breadth and the novelty of the new character of the left. A stimulus to constitutional radicalism had been created both by the 1979 Conservative government's heavy use of power, and by its demolition of constitutional safeguards against over-centralized power, in particular its growing subordination of local government, some of which, such as the GLC, it abolished completely. Arguments for constitutional reform covered a broader span of the old political spectrum than any other issue, encompassing those who might in other contexts have been classified as liberals, socialists, feminists or even in one or two instances conservatives. The demand for constitutional reform, far more than the debate over citizenship, was popular as well as academic, and not restricted to academic journals. There were widespread proposals for untangling, spreading out and making more public the exercise of government (Barnett et al. 1993; Brazier 1991; Institute for Public Policy Research 1993; Marr 1995; Jenkins 1995; Hutton 1996).

The demand for constitutional reform more than anything else marked the post-socialist left off from its socialist predecessors. Old socialists, like old conservatives, had not been disposed to see the political sphere as something markedly independent of social and economic patterns and objectives. The demand for constitutional reform expressed a liberal view of the distinctiveness, and desirable neutrality, of the political sphere. The proposals of organizations such as Charter 88 were met with either suspicion or disdain by the more traditional kinds of socialist. Perry Anderson damned the whole project with faint praise:

> Too radical for Labour leadership, it was modest compared with Conservative designs. For the comprehensive programme of social engineering that gave the Thatcher regime its dynamism, the swathe of measures calculated to reshape the British social landscape and entrench the power of the Tory Party over it, elicited no alternative of similar scope.
>
> (Anderson 1992: 301)

It is a judgement which places the old socialist and the new right on one side of the line that divides a liberal conception of politics from all those views which do not admit of a distinct political sphere, but both accept and intend to work with an enmeshment of political institutions and practices with social and economic institutions and powers. When, two years later, Anderson came to look more favourably on the movement for constitutional reform, it was still principally because he was able to associate with it one of the champions of an older socialism, Tony Benn (ibid.: 347) who had argued from the early 1970s that the constitutional arrangements of the United Kingdom needed radical reform in order to make socialist democracy possible (Benn and Hood 1993). But Benn's argument, like that of others from Laski on who saw political reform as the instrument of substantive social and economic change (Laski 1938; Elliott 1993) was for political and constitutional reform as a necessary part of socialism, rather than as a freestanding, or at least semi-detached, ambition for the left. In many ways too, though radical at a time when constitutional reform was not on the agenda at all, Benn's proposals for the abolition of the monarchy and the House of Lords, coupled with a robust defence of the Commons and a dismissal of proportional representation (Benn and Hood 1993) had come to look a little cautious by the 1990s.

If democracy meant not rule by the majority, which the working class were presumed to be even if, electorally, they frequently failed to act as such, but rule by the people, then to recommend democracy involved a commitment to variety and unpredictability, since the people were not a single thing nor possessed of a single or unchanging voice. The demand for constitutional reform involved a new or rediscovered conception of the political community and hence a different conception of nationalism(s) or at least one different from that which had prevailed in the short twentieth century.

CONTINUITIES AND DISCONTINUITIES: THE RECESSIVE THEMES OF THE LEFT

Had there been a simple, sudden and comprehensive break, old socialists would have found few affinities with the newer left. That was not the case, and a part of the reason why it was not was that new arguments were composed in considerable part of the recessive themes of the past. So was the short twentieth century a long diversion, with few lasting consequences? If citizenship and constitutional reform are back on the agenda, is political debate simply taking up where it left off before the arrival of socialism? The similarities are illuminating, but they do not by themselves provide an adequate account, and are not themselves even properly understood if considered alone. One important difference between the beginning and the end of the 'short twentieth century' is that the opponent of constitutional reform and citizenship is a New Right which is quite different from the nineteenth century opposition to liberal politics. In the circumstances of the 1990s, too, constitutional and political reform almost unavoidably involves Europe – it is no longer something contained within the geographical borders of Britain until the moment comes to export its lessons for the rest of the world. But left-wing thinking at the end of the century drew on, and developed, in innumerable and often surprising ways, on earlier themes.

When in 1960 E.P. Thompson wrote that the 'materials for a definition of socialist humanism lie on every hand. Our own intellectual traditions rise to meet our needs' (Thompson et al. 1960: 192–3), he was assuming a single, developing tradition of which the then contemporary thinking of the New Left was no more than a late

276 Death of socialism, rise of the left

flowering. But the New Left of the 1960s and 1970s, and even more so the radical left of the century's end, whilst it drew on recessive themes from the past, did not necessarily do so within a single tradition. Both Orwell and Thompson had detected the working materials for a socialist future in a working-class present. That comparison ought in itself to warn that there may be no one, homogeneous tradition on which present or future may draw. Such an assumption divided the short twentieth century from what followed. Both Thompson and those with whom he had argued over the exact nature of the English, or British, problem, had written in terms of a single or dominant culture, and of a subordinated or disadvantaged or controlled or hegemonized class which was equally homogeneous in its essential character and its essential needs. Traditions might be both dominant and suppressed, but there remained an essential coherence on each side of the dividing line between those who employed hegemony and those who were subordinated by it. The radical left of the 1990s drew on a broader store of 'traditions', some of which would have been regarded with little enthusiasm, though for different reasons, by Orwell or Thompson or Williams.

The New Left of the 1960s and 1970s had worked within, and to that extent been constrained by, a world view which was socialist in its assumptions about class and about collective activity and provision. This set a limit to the extent to which arguments based around gender, or locality, or nation, could achieve a major place. For some arguments, most notably for feminism, this meant that increasingly the discussion was carried on outside or beyond socialism. The events of 1989 were thus a final trauma which shattered the containing shell of socialism – and conservatism – and finally gave unfettered play to other themes.

As the left, in the uncertain closing years of the millennium, drew on its recessive themes, it rediscovered a belief in the dissemination of political power, and a suspicion of governmental authority. As the Labour MPs Anthony Wright and Gordon Brown put it, writing optimistically between general elections, 'For a hundred years the socialist message has inevitably had to be that the State should assume power on behalf of the people. Now it is time that the people take power from the state.' 'In short, while as a government we take power, we do so not to entrench it but to give it away' (Brown and Wright 1995: 26). In an argument which owed more to anarchism or to the New Liberalism of Hobhouse than to either Marxism or social democracy, Wright and Brown argued that power 'can concentrate at the expense of individuals within the State as well as within private capital and that the State can, like private capital, be a vested interest' (ibid.: 17).

Discussing forms of political organization which gave proper attention to the particular experience of grass roots political movements, Sheila Rowbotham had in 1979 taken the discussion back to the syndicalist *Miners' Next Step* of 1912 (Rowbotham et al. 1979: 79). In much the same way republicanism and tolerance emerged as recessive traditions of the left. Workers' control, guild socialism, syndicalism, feminism, intellectual pluralism, domestic utopianism with the household rather than the collective community as the starting point provided rediscovered and newly developed raw material. Pluralist and anarchist traditions could adapt to the re-alignment of political thought in a way that traditional social democracy could not. In an argument that was socialist in its understanding of human life, but liberal and pluralist in its proposals for political and public organization, Paul Hirst argued for 'associational' democracy, drawing on Figgis, Cole and Laski on the one hand, and Proudhon on the other (Hirst 1989, 1994). For whilst the left may have gone to market, more important, but implied by that journey, was going to the forum. The left, by the beginning of the twenty-first century, was principally about politics, whereas during the short twentieth century it has been principally about government and about economics. And politics, unlike government, is necessarily about diversity.

One account of this proliferation of identities has described it as postmodernism, a replacement of one single theory or explanation by a variety of specific and limited ones. Certainly socialism has not been succeeded on the left by any new intellectual empire, but rather by fragmentation and fluidity. There is no shortage of optimistic claims, such as those of Geoff Mulgan that whereas old politics followed the patterns of industrial organization, was hierarchical in form and economic in substance and policy, postmodern politics is free of this, and the older, ethical concerns can now re-emerge (Mulgan 1994). Such a postmodernism might look very like old pluralism entering into its inheritance. But whether the post-twentieth century left is described as pluralist or as postmodern, one aspect which marks its novelty is the elements from other dispersed traditions that play an important part in constituting the new position. It is frequently observed that the New Right was composed of both liberal and conservative strands. It would be truer to say that it eclipsed both conservatism and the economic component of liberalism. Yet liberalism, which had fragmented far earlier in the century, was eclipsed only in part by the New Right, since its political and cultural aspects followed quite different historical courses. Any suggestion that the New Right can be treated principally as an inheritor of liberalism would thus miss the rather different course that the large part of the liberal political tradition took. From the unravelled threads of liberalism, autonomy, self direction, the pursuit of wants within a framework of law and equal respect for the liberty of others were garnered by a post-twentieth century left to replace the paternal provision for needs.

The affinity between market socialism and New Liberalism has been pointed out before, by both admirers and critics (Desai 1994: 188). A number of threads dropped or pushed to one side sometime around or before the First World War were taken up and re-woven. The stress on equal liberty, and on public action to enable individuals effectively to pursue their own varied purposes come straight out of Hobhouse, who is invoked in support by Brown and Wright (1995: 22). In a similar vein Miller talks of investment agencies assisting co-operatives, and socially-owned but worker-used capital, in a manner redolent of both Hobson and Tawney (Miller 1989b: 10). But the insistence by some contributors on process rather than goals shows why even a post-liberal like Hayek can have a fascination for the left. Wainwright tries to save Hayek from himself by deploying Mill, in whose writing she finds 'belief in workers' self-management and in an egalitarian pluralism' (Wainwright 1994: 147).

But the salvagings were not restricted to political liberalism, and even more striking than the use made of a liberal inheritance, is the use made of a conservative one. The idea of community had distinctly conservative affinities at a time when the death of conservatism meant that its legacy was available for distribution. From the wreckage of conservatism, continuity, trusteeship, historical identity were salvaged, and there were even calls from one friendly observer for the left to draw upon a '"philosophic conservatism" – a philosophy of protection, conservation and solidarity' (Giddens 1994b: 27). By 1996 the journalist Will Hutton was calling for stakeholding which, if not specifically invoking Burke, was redolent of his arguments (Hutton 1996). Stephen Tindale, on the other hand, made free with the intellectual diaspora of conservatism, citing Burke and applying the concept of a trusteeship towards the world we inherit as guardians between former and future generations to the stewardship of the physical environment (Tindale 1994: 194–6). Gordon Brown became strangely Oakeshottian when he called for 'safeguards against entrenched interests, including the state' (Brown 1994: 113).

THE IMPORTANCE OF ENEMIES

It may well be true that you can tell a lady by the company she keeps. But the enemies someone makes, or imagines, can be just as revealing about what sort of person they have become or are trying to become. The identity of any set of political beliefs will frequently be defined as much by who are regarded as enemies as by who are thought of as friends and allies. The enemies of socialism had been a clear if sometimes heterogeneous collection: class, private capital, consumerism, self-interest, property, inequality, injustice and non-collectivism. Just as there are recessive themes, so there are recessive enemies. For a left which sees at least a part of its task as political or constitutional reform, the enemies will be those against whom radical attacks were made before 1917, before 1914, even before the emergence of modern socialism in the 1880s. So the enemies of the short twentieth century were replaced at its close by orthodoxy, regulation, poverty and power. At first glance the enemies of the post-twentieth century left look remarkably like those of the New Left of the 1960s and 1970s. But there was a crucial difference. The old enemies had been presented as if not a single group, then a cluster of groups. They had a social identity, and one which was not far removed from capitalism, or the military industrial complex. But the new enemies were not people or groups in this sense, but attitudes, values, forms of behaviour, which could be exhibited by many people and groups without wholly characterizing them, and which could give them a theoretical unity which co-existed with an absence of any necessary historical coherence or single social identity.

10 Definitions and doormats
The rise of feminism

THE CONTEXTS OF FEMINISM

Feminism was both the most lasting and the most radical of the strands of political thinking which made up the New Left of the 1960s and 1970s. From the vantage point of the time, feminist political thinking could be presented as an extension or auxiliary of the rainbow alliance of causes and aspirations which constituted the New Left. From the vantage point of the 1990s, a different account is possible. The socialism of the New Left, developing out of well-established traditions, and doubly checked at the end of the short twentieth century by the revolutions of 1989 and the ascendancy of the New Right, can be contrasted with the growth and diversity of the feminism of the New Left.

In a rough chronology of the development of feminist thinking in the last four decades of the chronological century, the 1960s, 1970s and 1980s can be seen as producing arguments which, though they had not disappeared by the 1990s, were becoming much less prominent, whilst the body of more conventional feminist scholarship continued to increase. Whether one sees the late 1960s as the start of a 'second wave' of feminism, as Shulamith Firestone has termed it (Firestone 1971), or as a particular moment in a permanently flowing tide (Spender 1983), feminist argument formed a major component of the New Left, as both its major internal critic and its major legacy. And whether one talks of waves or tides, the chronology and context of feminism was different from that of other forms of political thinking. Though feminism flourished at the same time as the socialist, Marxist and anarchist components of the New Left, the contexts in which it did so were in important respects different. Though it was far from lacking roots, it had a tradition and a development which stood in important respects at one remove from those of socialism, and which was not affected in the same manner by the events of the 1980s. The changes which brought to an end the last wave of socialism and conservatism did not have the same effect on feminism, which continued to flourish and proliferate as socialism and conservatism declined.

In one respect feminism shared with other forms of political thinking a characteristic which had become increasingly marked by the end of the short twentieth century: the internationalization of political argument. The writer who gave currency to the title 'second wave' was an American, a fact which usefully draws attention to a further characteristic of much political thinking in the last decades of the twentieth century, and of feminism in particular. There is a sense in which talking of British feminism is artificial. All political thinking in Britain in the last quarter of the chronological century was conducted in an international forum. Not only paper publication, radio and television, but fax and e-mail provided a wider invisible college, or invisible library and debating hall, than had existed before. Even the British unreadiness to read languages other than their own was to some extent weakened, and French writing in particular became a distinct presence. Some of the major influences on British feminist thinking were continental European or North American: de Beauvoir, Freidan, Millett, Delphy, Firestone or Daly. Feminism, presenting women as the most alienated section of society, could claim most in common with women and with feminists across the world, and had least expectation of gaining sustenance from the dominant traditions of their own society. Even the recessive traditions were frequently difficult to detect to begin with, a difficulty that has sometimes been described as a further barrier, in part deliberately constructed, to the autonomy of women (Spender 1983) whose achievements, and thoughts, had been 'hidden from history' (Rowbotham 1973a). Feminism was in consequence more aware of the function of recessive themes, once they had been identified, than were other political traditions, being itself a kind of massive recessive theme, and one which, more than any other, was aware of the need for 'an enormous interrogation of the past' (Rowbotham et al. 1979: 58).

In its internationalism, feminism, just as it had made the major innovative contribution to the New Left in the 1970s and late 1960s, was the most postmodern of the political doctrines of the 1990s, for it had no particular national homeland, but as many variants as there were nations or regions. Yet at the same time there has been a particular British confluence of and development of arguments. The openness of British feminism to thinking from North America made it, not a mere geographical location of an international debate but, in its equal openness to socialism and to European thinking, a particular consequence of eclecticism (Lovenduski 1988).

A distinction is widely made between liberal, socialist (or Marxist) and radical feminism, though like all categorization, this has an initial usefulness which can constrict understanding if it limits further discussion. For some, the very freezing of movement and change involved in such naming signals a 'sclerosis' (Delmar 1986: 9). The tripartite distinction can be useful for identifying the major strands of feminist thinking in the 1960s and 1970s, and is worth briefly spelling out. Thereafter it is less and less used, and increasingly gives a misleading picture of a body of thought which has developed rapidly beyond its earlier assumptions and arguments. Each of the three categories is thus useful for giving an account of the 1960s and 1970s, but by the 1980s different or further descriptions are necessary.

LIBERAL FEMINISM

One of the continuing traditions of feminist thinking in Britain which connected the Edwardians to the women of the last quarter of the century was liberal in its assumption that rational argument could remove the injustices suffered by women, and transform a society characterized by sexual inequality into one where men and women were on an equal footing. There was within this tradition an assumption that women had been overlooked by those who had imperfectly applied the familiar principles of liberalism. Equality in the public worlds of employment and politics was still flawed by barriers placed in the way of women, but these could be removed once rational enquiry had identified them, and rational discussion drawn attention to them.

Yet it was a mark of the shadowed existence of this tradition that when similar ideas were articulated with renewed vigour in the 1960s and 1970s, the immediate sources of the resumed discussion were North American and French, not British. Simone de Beauvoir's *The Second Sex* had been published in English translation in 1953, but its influence was much delayed. Betty Freidan's *The Feminine Mystique* was published in Britain in 1963, and the two books between them provided for several years the historical context for British thinking, and for the identification of the immediate domestic discontent.

Not only was liberal feminism in its 1960s and early 1970s form initially American and French in its articulation. It formed a background of assumptions, rather than a foreground of argument. The articulation was to come later, perhaps at the end of its influence, in defence of liberal feminism against more radical and, it was argued, dangerous and ineffective forms. It was not until 1980 that Janet Radcliffe Richards set out the case for a feminism of reason, advancing its case against opponents who were as likely to be mistaken as to be defending any vested interest. But the argument was as much a defence of a position as positive attack using that position as a starting point, devoting considerable attention to the tactics and conduct of radical and socialist feminists (Richards 1980). Feminism was an application to a particular form of oppression or injustice, of general principles which could be elaborated in the first instance without reference to women: 'The other unexpected result of defining feminism as a movement opposed to the systematic social injustices suffered by women because of their sex is that feminism turns out to be not only not a movement *of* women, but not a movement FOR women either' (ibid.: 4–5). Feminism is not concerned 'with *a group of people it wants to benefit, but with a type of injustice it wants to eliminate*' (ibid.: 5). Thus the intellectual ground on which the argument was to be conducted was, to that extent, familiar, and feminists should take care not to speak too often in ways which, to other occupants of that ground, were incomprehensible. 'It is essential that *in addition to* their concern for individuals and their experiences feminists must learn the logic and science which have been the traditional preserve of men' (ibid.: 31). For Richards the implications of this were both that feminists must set out their case by reference to principles which, though employed in feminist argument were not themselves feminist, since they were the basis of opposing injustice as such, and that the argument had to be conducted in a way which was not only logical, but persuasive, as much by not frightening away people whose expectations were conventional as by attracting them with new ways of thinking.

> The feminist who can see the oppression of women in the trivia of everyday life, in much the same way as the religious believer can see the hand of God in what is to the atheist the unremarkable course of nature, may also incline to the common religious view that since the truth is manifest the fallen state of the heathen can be imputed only to Sin, or, in this case, vested interests and conditioning.
>
> However, the feminist way of looking at things is not at all manifest, and feminists must do their opponents the justice of recognising this.
>
> (ibid.: 268–9)

The assumption was not only that the essential injustice could be solved by reason, but that it required changes not in the structure or formation of social life, but only in the distribution of goods and advantages: 'The principal complaint of feminists, reduced to its barest essence, is that men have contrived by various means to get for themselves an inordinately high share of the good things of life, leaving women with a corresponding disproportion of the bad' (ibid.: 63).

Such liberal feminism avoided in consequence, if not in intention, one of the difficulties faced by radical feminists. If there were insights into inequality, or the relations between men and women, or the distribution of power by gender, which could best be understood by women, or if there were virtues which characterized women, then in a perverse way the divisions of social life along lines of gender seemed partially justified. For Richards the problem was swept to one side with the arguments which led to it. So whilst on the one hand she commented that the 'feminist sees what is generally invisible, finds significance in what is unremarkable, and questions what is pre-supposed by other enquiries.... Without a feminist view of things even the best-founded of feminist pronouncements may appear nonsensical' (ibid.: 267), this is countered by the observation that the 'fact is that if women accept that they have been deprived of the opportunity for full development and are therefore less than they should be, they cannot at the same time be full of confidence about the accuracy of their own intuitions' (ibid.: 31).

SOCIALIST FEMINISM

It is a mark of the vital role which enemies play in the formulation of political arguments that just as liberal feminism, whatever its apparent historical priority, was articulated most clearly in response to socialist and radical feminism, so socialist feminism was to begin with a reaction against the quiet and not so quiet patriarchy of much existing socialism. One of the criticisms made of liberal feminism was its apparent inability to conceive that there might be powerful interests hostile to the advancement of women (Bryson 1993: 201). Socialist feminism had a different problem, which was to determine which of two contenders, capitalism and patriarchy, was the principal enemy.

In the 1960s feminism, though a clearly powerful strand in the cluster of New Left political thinking, had frequently been treated as something of an outsider in need of incorporation within the intellectual universe. This approach was particularly found amongst socialists, and even those who have tried to be kind to the male intellectuals of the *New Left Review* have described them as taking 'a rather orthodox defensive position' against feminism (Chun 1993: 168).

Yet feminism had been the most vigorous and innovative of all the component parts of the New Left, the one recessive theme that had, all along, been not so much recessive as alternative or parallel. So feminism had a complex relationship with the rest of the New Left: on the one hand, the most subversive and innovative strand in the tangled skein of the New Left, on the other developing in reaction to the patriarchal attitudes which more traditional forms of New Left thinking constantly betrayed.

So one part of socialist feminism was a reaction against and from the New Left: to that extent there was a specific historical issue and occasion. 'The emergence of radical feminism was also in part a reaction to Marxist attitudes to women .... The Marxist left tended to dismiss feminist issues as bourgeois deviations from the real struggle' (Weedon 1987: 8). This theoretical dismissal was compounded by the conduct of men in left-wing and protest movements and the way in which those movements were structured (ibid.: 9). Whereas on the one hand feminism was open to an international agenda of argument, on the other its development was not so much assisted as provoked by the domestic practices of established socialism. Its inspirations were in this sense global, its irritations provincial.

The problems, and the evolution, of socialist feminism are illustrated in the work of Juliet Mitchell. An essay originally published in 1966 drew attention to the absence of women from the cast of so much ostensibly revolutionary analysis and prescription: 'today, in the West, the problem has become a subsidiary, if not an invisible element in the preoccupations of socialists' (Mitchell 1984a: 19). The title of the essay, 'Women: the longest revolution', carries echoes of Raymond Williams's *The Long Revolution*, published five years earlier. An argument grounded in Marxism but not limited to or dependent on it, Mitchell's essay extended the analysis of subordination beyond class to the condition of women. There were, she argued, four components of subordination: production, reproduction, sexuality, and child rearing. Women were responsible for production in the household, which was where a major part of any society's production was both carried on and, in conventional accounts, concealed. At the same time they were responsible for the most menial areas of public, waged production. Woman's 'social weakness' has made her the 'major slave' in production (Mitchell 1984a: 29). Mitchell thus argued that change needed to take place in all four areas before the subordination of women could be ended. Although the argument was inspired by a substantial body of socialist writing on sexual inequality, and to that extent departed from the assumptions of liberal feminism, women's subordination was none-theless subordination without a subordinator.

This gap was remedied in Mitchell's 1971 *Woman's Estate*. The discussion in that book made clear the climate in which Mitchell's feminist argument had developed: various liberation movements of the 1960s raised principles which involved applying general principles of freedom or equality to particular groups, but in each case excluding the largest group of all: women. The 1971 book, though it incorporated the 1966 essay, introduced terms such as 'patriarchy' and 'male chauvinism' which indicated a wider stance than that taken in 1966. It also discussed though by no means invented the notion of 'conscious-ness raising'.

Mitchell's work illustrated the potential strains within socialist feminism. Unlike liberal feminism, which assumed that change could occur through rational persuasion, socialist feminist identified the oppression of women as arising from more than a simple mistake or misunderstanding. There was therefore a problem when it came to identifying the beneficiaries of women's condition. If the oppression arose solely from capitalism, an argument from which Mitchell had clearly stood aside in identifying four distinct strands of oppression, then the position of men remained that which was implied in liberal theory: accessories, but innocent or, less flatteringly, ignorant accessories. If on the other hand capitalism was only one the beneficiaries, if, as Sheila Rowbotham argued, the 'oppression of women differs too from class and race because it has not come out of capitalism and imperialism' (Rowbotham 1973b: 117), then male socialists stood, for some purposes at least, in the enemy camp, or in one of them.

One attempt to resolve this tension within socialist feminism was made by Michèle Barrett in 1980 in *Women's Oppression Today*. Barrett argued that the origins of gender division were to be found in the pre-capitalist 'family-household complex'. However capitalism, being an exploitative and opportunistic phenomenon, made use of whatever was to hand, and thus had incorporated gender inequality not out of any necessary logic of its own, but simply because it was one of the social raw materials to hand (Barrett 1980).

Another response to the dilemma posed by the mutual presence of a socialist and a feminist analysis was made in 1979 by Sheila Rowbotham, Lynne Segal and Hilary Wainwright. In a collection of articles appropriately entitled *Beyond the Fragments: Women and the Making of Socialism*, they turned the problem on its head. Whereas in the 1960s there had been numerous attempts to find feminism a place within socialism, and to slot the oppression of women in as a sub-category of the oppression of workers, Rowbotham, Segal and Wainwright argued that it was feminism, both as an analysis and as a pattern of political practices, which provided the vantage point from which to co-ordinate the increasingly disparate elements of the left. Feminism, it was argued, had consequences for the whole range of political issues, whether immediately and apparently associated with gender or not. 'If the left is to achieve the change in consciousness and the growth in self-organisation which is a condition for resolving the problem of power, then there is much that socialists can learn from the women's movement's values and ways of organising' (Rowbotham et al. 1979: 2). This was reminiscent of the argument of Woolf's *Three Guineas* – the social situation of women, and conversely of men, underlay far more than sexual inequality alone. It was at one and the same time a recognition of diversity which prefigures postmodernism; a presentation of feminism as a comprehensive theory within which the claims of other groups, and even other classes, can be set, understood and applied; and a radical alternative to orthodox politics on both the left and the right. It drew, too, on recessive themes both feminist and non-feminist within political thinking in a manner which illustrated once again how far the feminism of the 'second wave' and of subsequent waves, however innovative it might be, nonetheless had behind it a long radical tradition.

RADICAL FEMINISM

Whereas liberal feminism treated any injustice suffered by women as a matter for rational redress, and socialist feminism related it, albeit in a variety of ways, to capitalism, radical feminism presented women's oppression as a distinct form of oppression, termed patriarchy, meaning domination by men. Radical feminism has often been attributed in considerable degree to transatlantic sources: 'Most of the important and influential radical-feminist texts are American in origin' (Weedon 1987: 6). Certainly Shulamith Firestone was a major influence, as was Kate Millett (Firestone 1971; Millett 1971). But there is a French influence too, whilst if more popular books, such as Greer's *The Female Eunuch* (1970) are included, the overseas dependence is less marked. The broad sweep of radical feminism, insisting on the priority of sexual divisions, but demolishing the conventional boundaries both between 'feminist' and 'non-feminist' issues, and between the public sphere work and politics and the 'private' sphere of household, family and sexuality, has precedents in feminist writing in both the immediate and turn of the century past. A discussion of radical feminism soon indicates how artificial or at least fragile distinctions such as that between liberal, socialist and radical feminist can be. Although Juliet Mitchell dismissed Greer's work as that of an 'anarchist individualist' (Mitchell 1971: 68 n.1), the two writers shared an identification of women as suffering from a distinctive form of oppression which could not be understood simply as a sub-division or particular application of capitalism. Radical feminism was distinctive in the emphasis it placed on patriarchy as the most fundamental form of inequality and oppression, on its pervasiveness, and on the need for a transformation of patriarchy as the chief task for radicals. A book such as Greer's contained a call to change everything, which was necessarily invocational rather than specific, and which specifically rejected reform or compromise. Those conservatives who saw the entry of women 'to politics and the profession' as 'the undermining of our civilization and the end of the state and marriage were right after all' as Greer put it, taking the bull by rather more than the horns (Greer 1970: 329).

Once the pervasiveness of patriarchy had been asserted, an analysis of every aspect of social life in terms of gender divisions became appropriate. Whilst for the right property was a bastion of the patriarchal family, theories of property had implications for gender politics as well, and for the insistence on the control by women of their own persons and their own space. Once every theory was questioned, it became just as possible as to use one's opponents' weapons oneself, or to turn them into ploughshares, as to spike them. Language, which for a liberal feminist might be an at least potentially neutral medium of communication and discussion, could be seen as structured and formed in a manner which sustained patriarchy. Male power, argued Dale Spender, was based on the myth of male superiority. Men had made a language which polarized any account given of reality into male and female, or rather into male and minus-male. Since the language was both the medium of communication and the constructor of reason, arguments against its structure, or arguments which did not accept its terms, could be dismissed as unreasonable. Within a human community in which patriarchy systematically subordinated women, those women who rejected the entire system were necessarily against men, but with the abolition of patriarchy, that antipathy, which patriarchy has created, would disappear (Spender 1980).

THE DEVELOPMENT OF FEMINISM PURE, BUT NOT SIMPLE

Long before the demise of the New Left, feminist argument had developed to a point where the liberal, socialist, radical distinction was increasingly limited and unhelpful, and where if distinctions were to be made, they needed making more and more in terms which were specific to feminist argument itself. By the 1980s a body of feminist argument had developed which, whilst in no way being homogeneous, had drawn upon and transcended the separate insights of liberal, socialist and radical feminism, to articulate a feminism which was particular, and not in need of qualification by any adjective drawn from other political traditions even though affinities with and dialogues between them were clear. At the same time, whilst continuing to take its ethical starting point from the condition of women, feminism increasingly became an analytical viewpoint from which gender division could be employed as a method of comprehensive social analysis. Just as Marxism described both labour and capital, so feminism described both males and females, the entire set of social relations constructed on gender. The distinctions between radical and socialist feminists became less firm, and less important, whilst a engagement with public life or a consideration of ways in which it might be changed or transformed, which had previously been largely the preserve of liberal feminism, became more widespread (Lovenduski and Randall 1993: 7). Such a feminism was radical by default, in that it began with the assumption that the situation of women was special, did not simply derive from larger inequalities, and gave a particular character to society as a whole. Gender suffused everything or, as Anne Phillips put it: 'gender challenges all our political perspectives' (Phillips 1991: 2). The change which this represented, from studying women to studying gender, transformed the leverage of feminism, and at the same time made it increasingly difficult to identify a single feminist position. A broad and eclectic feminism developed which was radical by default in relation to other political arguments, but not necessarily radical within feminism. 'Women's liberationists took a sideways step closer to radical feminists and became "feminists"' (Mitchell and Oakley 1986: 2).

The distinction between challenging an existing order by developing alternatives, and challenging it by pursuing those alternatives within existing structures can be sometimes merely semantic, but is usually troublesome. In the case of feminism it involved a discussion of the relative merits of sisterhood and collective non-hierarchical political action on the one hand, and a more opportunistic approach, less radical, but not necessarily less imaginative in the methods used, on the other. This implied amongst other things a re-assertion of the liberal individualism which had previously seemed so insufficient, against the disadvantages of collective identity and action (Mitchell and Oakley 1976: 11–13) and the liberal insistence of both rational discussion and individual choice were brought into play when a stress on collective action appeared to bring the possibility of new oppressions and new orthodoxies (ibid.: 10–14).

As the development of feminism occluded the distinctions between liberals, socialists and radicals, terms and concepts which had been divisive developed new functions. The phrase 'the personal is political' had marked off the liberals from the radicals, and caused some inconvenience to socialists. But once it was possible to use liberal reason to show how liberalism had failed even in its own terms, to point to the comprehensiveness of gender distinctions and the structured nature of 'private' and 'personal' actions and relationships, a position was reached which could claim to transcend the weaknesses, and incorporate the strengths, of the previously distinct strands of feminism.

INDEPENDENT FEMINISM AND POLITICS

Diana Coole remarks interestingly when she discusses feminism 'as a theory of politics' that she will be concentrating 'predominantly on radical feminist innovations' (Coole 1988: 251). To be able to write this in 1988 indicated what a transformation had taken place. Edwardian feminism had seen the vote, and the life of the citizen, as goods which were withheld from women by statutory restriction. Once the law was changed, the constitution both as a formal legal framework and as a set of practices which constituted politics would permit women full participation. But by the 1960s the whole gamut of conventional politics had come to be regarded, and dismissed, with suspicion by radical feminists (Delmar 1986). A part of this suspicion of politics amongst radical feminists in the 1960s and 1970s rose from a confirmed suspicion that formal rights were only a part of political power, and that the social and domestic structures upon which those rights rested were a necessary part of any effective citizenship. The conclusion drawn by many was that politics in any conventional sense was therefore a useless and indeed distracting activity in patriarchal society. But this suspicion of existing forms of government, then 'a deep mistrust of the public political sphere' (Lovenduski and Randall 1993: 6), was one side only of a double approach, particularly in the

1960s and 1970s, whereby there was also a broadening and plural understanding of government and politics. Leadership, hierarchy and the histrionics of male charismatic rhetoric and campaigning could be dismissed, but the alternative could equally be the proposition of alternative ways of conducting things, not just with a women's movement, but in a reformed public political sphere. This had been in part precisely what the authors of *Beyond the Fragments* had been arguing for (Rowbotham et al. 1979).

A different use of insights into the connection between formal constitutions and working political systems was developed as feminist argument moved into its 'particular' phase. In the work of writers such as Carol Pateman (1983, 1988, 1989) or Anne Phillips (1991, 1993, 1995), the sceptical understanding of formal liberal politics became, not a rejection of politics, but a demand for its radical restructuring. If liberal claims could not be sustained within the existing arrangements, then they, and the conditions in which they might operate, need rethinking.

> It has been left to feminists to explore how far the relentless privileging, not just of real living men, but of the very category male itself, has formed and deformed political theory and practice. And at one level it seems almost too obvious for argument that inserting women into the previously 'gender neutral' (for which read male-defined) pre-occupations of political theory will prove a qualitative as well as a quantitative change.
>
> (Phillips 1991: 2)

Methods of organization and the ordering of policy priorities became matters for specific feminist discussion, and the examination of democracy became not so much a matter of how democracy could be extended in order to include women, as a question of what kind of democratic theory was needed in order to employ the insights and meet the demands of a feminist position. Speaking of the debate between supporters of participatory democracy and the advocates of representative democracy, Anne Phillips commented that the 'importance of feminism is not that it will add its weight to one or other of two sides, but that its concerns might change the shape of the discussion' (Phillips 1991: 13). At the same time though as shifting the ground of the discussion, the existing discussion is, it was claimed, thrown into clearer relief: 'It is when we add in gender that the picture becomes clearer' (Phillips 1991: 18). Nor did an occupation, or a re-occupation, of the public sphere of democratic politics involve leaving behind a concern with the 'private' world of the household. The argument, on the contrary, hinged on the insistence that the privacy and social invisibility of the household was a key instrument in the oppression of women and their continual demotion within conventional liberal theory. Participatory democracy, which had been discussed initially in the context of the factory, now became a means of ending the ghettoization of the household and the subordination of women within it (Pateman 1983a and b).

POSTMODERNISM?

If there is such a thing as postmodernism, the replacement of grand theories by smaller, particular workable ones, and the replacement of universal human nature and universal identities by varied, multi-faceted and historically particular identities, then feminism in its end of century form might seem well tuned to it. 'The current feminist preoccupation with heterogeneity and difference combines easily with this, for arguments that highlight the "man" in humanity lead on to more general scepticism over any universalizing claims' (Phillips 1991: 6). Feminism in its current phase was already well in place before the demolition of class and it replacement by varied and more shifting forms of identity, and there is both a postmodernist feminism and, since there is in postmodernism a disposition against any overall theory, a feminist element within postmodernism.

The feminist debate over postmodernism, and the debate between feminists and other postmodernists (Frazer and Lacey 1993; Hoffman 1995; Lovibond 1989, 1992; Mouffe 1993; Nicholson 1990; Squires 1993), illustrates a special character of feminism, which is that more than any other body of political thinking or academic enquiry, it works across and to an extent ignores or transcends the boundary between the academic, enquiring argument and the political, instrumental one (Fraser 1995). The discussion of postmodernism, especially but not exclusively on the part of those feminists who are critical of it, deals not only with the explanatory potential of postmodernism, but with its likely political consequences (Zalewski 1991).

The reception of postmodernist arguments amongst feminists was far from universally welcoming however. Those who suspected postmodernism of being conservatism disguised as relativism had their suspicions strengthened by what has been termed 'family feminism', of which Germaine Greer's 1984 *Sex and Destiny* was taken to be a leading example. On one reading, the development of either post-feminism, neo-conservative feminism, or family feminism, is an inevitable feature of the colonization of social and political thought by feminism. The sympathetic or positive feminist account of the family and maternity then becomes evidence of permeation by feminist perspectives, when even 'conservative' political argument draws on feminist accounts. On another reading such thinking constitutes a backlash (Stacey 1986). Whatever view is taken, the difference has arisen in part over an attempt to deal with an issue which it was possible, in the 1960s and 1970s, to obscure or defer in favour of the task of setting out the broad feminist case. But once that was done, an awkward gap was left between a simple rejection of the family as an unacceptable and exploitative form of domestic life on the one hand, and a liberal optimism that men could be argued into taking up domestic responsibilities on the other. A growing body of feminist writing was neither radically revolutionist, nor merely liberal, and there thus existed a space within which an argument over the family developed. One strand within this argument is what Stacey has termed conservative pro-family feminism (ibid.: 220): 'The pain and difficulties experienced by a generation of feminists who self-consciously attempted to construct alternatives to the family are a major social psychological source of the emergence of pro-family feminism, and one, as I will elaborate later, that may fuel the pro-family retreat from sexual politics' (ibid.: 231). But the principal British contribution to what Stacey presents as a backlash is slightly more difficult to classify than this. It constitutes not a defence of the 'traditional' nuclear family, but of what Greer calls Family, with a capital 'F' – a matriarchal, extended sorority in which women's particular skills are recognized, nurtured and applied (Greer 1984). It is a mark of the breadth and ambition of feminist thinking at and after the end of the short twentieth century that it can incorporate such a wide scale of different positions on issues spanning virtually the entire range of human social life.

DEFINITIONS AND DOORMATS

Writing at a time when feminist argument still occupied a marginal if radical position, Rebecca West had been able to allege some difficulty in defining feminism: she didn't know what feminism was, but men always accused her of it when she refused to behave as a doormat. Three-quarters of a century later there was still a problem, no longer because feminism remained difficult to pin down, but because its profusion made any one account inadequate. Rosalind Delmar could identify the problem of definition as arising, not from the paucity of established accounts, but from their variety, quantity and permeation of every area of intellectual life. It made 'more sense to speak of a plurality of feminisms than of one' (Delmar 1986: 9). When feminism could be represented, as it could at the beginning of the twentieth century, as both radical and peripheral, simply to stand together with other writers whose arguments tended in much the same direction was a sufficient basis for intellectual identity, and a sufficient answer to the question 'what is feminism?' But the successes, even though they were limited, of feminism in the later twentieth century meant that whereas in 1910 there had been one unifying objective, the vote and political citizenship, eighty years later the goals were as varied as were the arguments advanced in support of them. Not only were there many forms of feminist argument, but those arguments addressed the state and politics, domestic work and the household, the nature of the public sphere, life in organizations and institutions, sexuality, the relations of domestic power, pornography, violence, art, literature, work and religion. At the same time feminist dimensions were to be found in philosophy, political science, economics and virtually the whole range of academic disciplines. So on the one hand feminism was adding to the areas of human life which were analysed and described, and on the other it was transforming the manner in which all areas of life were understood.

What was described by some as the 'second wave' of feminism (Firestone 1971) from the late 1960s onwards had placed a greatly enhanced body of feminist thinking on the agenda, and had done so in two ways. First more was being written from the end of the 1960s. Second this work in its turn rapidly led to a revised vision of feminist thinking which revealed, or recalled, how much work had continued to be done within the feminist tradition at times when it had seemed in abeyance but had in fact simply been 'hidden' (Rowbotham 1973a). By throwing new light on its own past, and insisting that there had 'always been a women's movement this century' (Spender 1983), the feminism of the 1960s and 1970s came to appear, not as an innovation or even as a revival, but as a continuation. The very variety and complexity of feminist writing encouraged analytical reflection as well as optimistic campaigning, and as Mitchell and Oakley put it, 'has drawn us into reflecting on our past and present where once we more gaily planned our future' (Mitchell and Oakley 1986: 7). The growing attention of feminist scholars to history was, far from being a diversion from the elaboration of contemporary feminist theory, a contribution to and condition of it.

The presentation of its own past underlined the claim that feminism was not a mere development out of socialism or liberalism, but rather 'a profound challenge to other political ideologies' (Bryson 1993: 21) which at the same time dealt with questions 'increasingly difficult to place anywhere along the traditional political spectrum from left to right' (Eisenstein 1984: 127, quoted Coole 1988: 258). Yet feminism did have some elements in common with both liberalism and socialism. It was possible to claim that feminism was pursuing doctrines of equality to their logical conclusion in a way that the predominant political theories had shied away from doing. Sometimes this meant that the development of feminist argument was given added impetus, not so much by the promises of liberalism or socialism, as by the inadequacies of 'actually existing' liberalism and socialism, and the traditionalism of actually existing liberals and socialists. With conservatism or the right, on the other hand, feminism appeared to share little or nothing. Yet it was evidence of the extent to which feminism had, like a river delta, spread across the intellectual landscape, that there was there, too, writing which even whilst criticizing much feminist argument, at the same time claimed to be setting out a case which was both practically in the interests of women and theoretically feminist in a radical manner (Taylor 1994).

THE PECULIARITY OF FEMINISM. IS IT A POLITICAL THEORY AT ALL?

It has occasionally been objected that a discussion of feminism is out of place in an account of political thinking (Minogue 1991: 649). The charge makes a vice out of what would otherwise be presented as virtuous innovation. Feminism does not fit the categories that are adequate and appropriate to describe the previously dominant themes of political thought. Not only does it challenge the status of existing theories and accounts, but it employs different conceptions of politics, both as a world of public concern, and as a method of criticizing and affecting policy. If feminism is to be included within accounts of political thinking, new definitions of politics need to be elaborated.

A slightly different response to feminism has been not to deny its place within political thinking, but to locate it outside the limits of 'central' or 'fundamental' or 'primary' political concerns: the nature of government, the character of politics, and the making and application of public policy. Gender then becomes simply a subordinate category in such investigations, like geographical location, age or occupation. Even to do this, however, is to establish feminism on the intellectual map, so that accounts which leave gender on one side, implicitly or explicitly, nonetheless take a stance in response to feminist claims. If on the other hand the presence of feminist political argument is accepted, the lack of 'fit' with previously conventional ideas of what political thinking is principally about becomes an occasion not for marginalizing feminist writing but for reconsidering the breadth and adequacy of previous intellectual conventions.

In one further and final respect feminism differs from the other principal political traditions. It is at one and the same time a range of political doctrines, and a theoretical approach to the understanding of the entire range of human social life. There are historians whose general approach is clearly integrated with or affected by their doctrinal predilections, just as there are political theorists who are left or right, radical or conservative, liberal or socialist. There is a feminist political science – and history, sociology, law, anthropology – to a far greater degree than there is a liberal, conservative or socialist academic sphere. Feminism differs, too, from liberalism, in that the liberal academic presence outside political science and economics is negligible, whereas feminist scholarship is both widely active in the social sciences and the humanities and, at a fairly preliminary stage, in subjecting work in all of those disciplines to critical examination and rethinking. Feminism spans a comprehensive academic range as well as a doctrinal one, in a way which makes it, in the twentieth century or its aftermath, unique.

If that is accepted, several possible ways of writing an account of political thinking then require examination. In order to take account of feminism, a different framework will be necessary from that which served to describe socialism, liberalism and conservatism, pluralism, collectivism, and individualism. A peculiar difficulty is created too by the fact that feminist political thinking has represented a combination of both recessive and parallel themes. Feminist thinking has been so firmly excluded from the mainstream, in other words, that rather than being a recessive theme, it has been a parallel one. A framework which takes adequate account of feminist thinking could be used either once feminism was a clear presence requiring explanation, or retrospectively to give a revised account of the entire short twentieth century and of preceding periods. If the latter, this may reduce the descriptive force of accounts of non-feminist thinking. On the other hand it may involve placing them in a fuller or illuminatingly different perspective, since feminism has contributed a valuable re-description of previous history. If the former, problems will be raised by a change of descriptive context for non-feminist thinking not necessarily because it has changed, but because it no longer occupies such a dominant or monopolistic position. Clearly its relation with feminism will be a novel factor, but does this mean that its own character has changed also? One might argue that it has, in that non-feminist political writing begins to take account of, to address, and to respond to feminist argument, even if only to allege that it lies outside its own delineation of important issues or political problems.

Feminism is distinct in two further ways. First, feminism has not developed around a party, organization or institutionalized interest. This distinguishes it from socialism and conservatism. It has none-theless had a constituency. This distinguishes it from liberalism. Second, it has involved, not uniquely but to a degree greater than of any other body of political thinking, the use of drama, spectacle and theatrical direct action. Feminism has developed the theatre and cabaret of politics, drawing to a degree on its own recessive themes in the tactics of the Edwardian suffrage campaigners. In the politics of abortion, or in the anti-nuclear weapons protests at Greenham Common, comedy and satire have been employed as subversive instruments of public discussion. Such 'theatre of politics' has been used because much feminist argument not only challenges the coherence or evidence base of existing political thinking, but the perception on which it is founded or upon which it depends. It challenges existing thinking, in other words, from the outside, and in terms which are sometimes incomprehensible to those whom it criticizes. The use of forms of expression or communication which dramatize or demonstrate a different perspective has thus been particularly appropriate. Such dramatized political communication has been the public face of consciousness raising, an aspect of feminist practice which at the same time reflected an assumption about how gender divisions were to be understood, the limitations of existing theories and perceptions, and the manner in which more adequate understanding could be attained. Consciousness raising meant stepping outside the perceptual limitations of the dominant order. It has been carried into the forum, to become a means of public expression, and a method of challenging and altering the presumptions upon which public discussion is conducted and politics carried on.

PLURALISM AND UNIVERSALISM: THE PARADOX OF FEMINISM

Feminism has become an established part of a pluralist, postmodern debate in which the variety and multiplicity of identities, and the specificity of individual and group character, is an important assumption. Yet at the same time feminist thinking has developed and employed the concepts of gender to analyse and describe the entire range of human social life, abolishing the distinction between the public and the private, the political and the personal, individual choice and collective structure. So on the one hand feminism has contributed to a new pluralism, on the other it appears to claim a new universalism. This has affinities with the simultaneous presence of classical and romantic forms of argument within feminism, the one stressing universal human values, the other particular female virtues (Vogel 1986). It has frequently been pointed out that a tension exists between identifying women as a particular group with particular virtues, and calling for an end to gender differentiation (Mitchell and Oakley 1986).

Perhaps more than any other of the available doctrines at the close of the short twentieth century, feminism presents the possibility of a series of linked but not monolithic descriptions of the range of human social life, not only subsuming the distinction between private and public, but that between descriptive and prescriptive. But at the same time feminist political thinking, in confronting the problems raised by multiple identities, faces the wider problem generated by postmodernism as such. For an identity – as a feminist, a nationalist, a market socialist, or anything else – to work with other identities, it must be informed by a recognition of its limitation, both temporal, spatial and social. Yet for it to work for the person whose social life it expresses, it must be more than simply one picture amongst many. It must have a special quality which raises at least the possibility of its wider, even its universal, application.

In describing the character of feminism at and after the end of the short twentieth century, and in giving account of its relation to other forms of thinking – which is part of describing the character of feminism – terms such as post-feminism have been employed. But it would be as true to describe the general world of political thinking as feminist, as to identify a particular strand of it as post-feminist. For in expanding, diversifying and spreading delta-like across the landscape, feminism has become not so much a particular coherent doctrine, but an aspect of the whole. No argument can, or does, now ignore the dimension of gender or the various feminist claims and accounts. Not only has gender, and the account of gender given from a variety of feminist writings, become a prominent dimension of political thinking, but the response to gender and the account given of gender has now become one of the central characteristics which, in giving an account of a thinker or doctrine, it is considered necessary to describe. This is the reverse of the process described by Delmar whereby coherence can facilitate marginalization (Delmar 1986: 10). So in writing about the spectrum of left and right-wing political thinking at the close of the twentieth century, both what is said and what is not said about gender and about the arguments of feminists becomes an integral part of the description.

By contrast with feminism the mainstream traditions of political argument – socialism, liberalism and conservatism – were complete and exhausted by the end of the third quarter of the present century. They had dominated the 'short twentieth century' (Hobsbawm 1994; R. Barker 1995) but by the 1990s were well advanced in a lengthy process of fragmentation and realignment which was to create quite different clusters and alliances in political thinking. Liberalism had long ago divided into economic and political strands, socialism and conservatism had ceased to exist in any recognizable form.

Feminism by contrast, though it had always been characterized by variety, was neither dismembered nor absorbed. It was still evolving, and was to become 'complete' as the other traditions began to mutate and disintegrate. More so even than liberalism, it was placed to flourish in the open and flexible environment of postmodernism. It would be possible to respond that feminism and liberalism are not simply different political ideas, but different kinds of ideas. Feminism is an analysis about one dimension of political and social life, and a series of recommendations about the responses to it. Liberalism, in contrast, though resting on assumptions about how social life is arranged and carried on, does not present analyses in the same way, while offering a comprehensive, as contrasted with a one-dimensional, set of recommendations about how social and political life should be carried on. But this would require the analytical and descriptive contributions of feminism always to be considered in conjunction with the political theory, whilst at the same time leaving on one side such history, sociology or anthropology as might be informed by a liberal view of the world. It would also involve accepting that feminism was about women, whereas increasingly feminist thinking has dealt with gender as an organizing division within society and politics.

An alternative description would be to say that feminism had always been complete, but with a chronological context different from that of the old dominant doctrines, and hence with a life cycle which differed also. The chronology of feminism, and its historical context, had always been different from that of the more dominant traditions of political thinking. They had developed within a domestic setting of class politics and competition for governmental power, and an international setting of revolution and Cold War. Neither of these contexts had the same importance for feminism, though the dissipation of both the old domestic and the old international context by the last decade of the chronological century meant not so much that feminism had a vacuum to occupy, as that its attention to other problems and other conflicts ceased to be eclipsed by the old orthodoxies.

11   Conclusion

At the end of the historical century and the approach of the chronological millennium, there is plenty of temptation to predict the new age, as Fukuyama and many other have done (R. Barker 1996a). But about the only certainty to emerge is the clear evidence of wild and vigorous disagreement. I have tried to follow the less spectacular but possibly safer course of indicating possibilities and uncertainties, but steering clear of confident prediction. The fading away of conservatism and socialism, and the arrival of lefts and rights which are both radical and variegated, has loosened or severed the link between ideas and institutions, and left political thinking unusually unsustained and untethered by organized interests. As political parties with comprehensive programmes have seemed less and less the vehicles, even for those who do no more than hitch a ride, for plausible or coherent political thinking, voluntary associations, single cause or issue groups, 'new social movements' have taken the initiative both in placing issues on the agenda of politics and in relating political thinking to public policy.

Many of these movement have contributed to the beginnings of political thinking which not only does not sit within the old divisions of collectivist and libertarian, or socialist, liberal and conservative, but has no obvious relationship either with the fluid categories of left and right, pluralist or feminist. A concern with the environment, and a desire to 'tread lightly on the earth' is associated with a post-industrial mood, and may be informed both by collective conscience and by a deep worry about the quality of human life. It is clearly political, but when attempts have been made to throw bridges across to either old or new bodies of political thinking (Gray 1993a; Red-Green 1995), the structures have been too rickety to take any serious traffic.

The dangers of being over-confident about the future are matched by the equal dangers of being over-confident about the past. The view that traditional socialism and traditional conservatism no longer play any significant part in political discourse has stimulated a revision of their histories. The disappearance of any unique connection between class and reform, or between politics based on the working class and progressive policies, had led to questioning whether their importance in the past had been overrated. It seems at times as if socialism and conservatism are being nibbled away at both ends in the contemporary accounts of the short twentieth century and its precursor.

A cautious pluralism in anticipating the future direction of political thinking, and a desire to be able to accommodate variety, suggests that arguments which seem undogmatic in their choice of outcomes should be looked on favourably. The New Right, or at least the contribution made to it by F.A. Hayek, might seem to have provided one possible path to a plural society. Hayek's arguments involved the predictability of uncertainty, and his *Constitution of Liberty* was dedicated to 'the unknown civilisation that is growing in America' (Hayek 1960). But Hayek's apparently open society turns out to be deeply hostile both to cultural variety and innovation, and to constitutional experimentation.

Postmodernism similarly fails to fulfill its promise to provide a basis for plural and undogmatic political life. As a descriptive vantage point it can take in the variety of identities. But each identity draws sustenance from the perception that it is not contingent, but universal. Worse by far for the optimistic postmodernist, it involves the identification of enemies amongst precisely those people with whom the postmodernist assumes a kind of liberal co-existence or even co-operation will be possible.

The first edition of this book had a good deal to say about liberalism. There is on the face of it little about liberal ideas in the new chapters. Yet liberalism has not disappeared so much as shifted ground: its various components have mingled with the new doctrines of left and right, and its higher theory has become a theology which shadows the politics of the end of the twentieth century (R. Barker 1996a). The 'long twenty first century' may turn out to be a liberal or at least a liberal pluralist one. If the latter, then the pluralism will be more important than the liberalism, and politics and public life will be conducted on the basis neither of class nor of individual, but of identity groups whose claims and constitution will offend the rationalist aspirations and claims of both. In a sense, *all* discussion at the close and after the close of the twentieth century is liberal, in two important senses. First, the left, the right and feminism are all manoeuvring with fragments of the liberal inheritance. Second, the assumptions about liberty and choice to which everyone feels the need to defer, if only rhetorically but normally substantially as well, provide a liberal environment within which all discussion is conducted.

The fact that Britain remains a virtually monoglot state, so that writings from the United States are still more accessible than anything written in the rest of Europe should not obscure the fact that political thinking in this country is nonetheless, and possibly despite itself, re-entering the world. Perry Anderson has claimed that Britain is uniquely placed to become a crossroads of ideas:

> Only recently the most self-contained of the larger NATO cultures, it was now to become in some ways the least closed to the surrounding world. The terms of this change were basically set by its peculiar crossroads position: geographically part of Europe and linguistically tied to America. By the late 1980s, there was probably no other country where influences from both sides of the Atlantic intermingled so freely.
>
> (Anderson 1992: 201)

If the move from being an imperial power at the start of the short twentieth century, to being a nation in greatly reduced circumstances at the start of the unpredictable twenty-first has meant, paradoxically, that Britain is more open than ever to intellectual influences, whilst retaining a distinctive manner of responding to them, then whatever the impossibility of prediction, it is reasonable to suppose we may still live in interesting times.

Bibliography

Abel-Smith, B. (1958) 'Whose Welfare State?', in N. MacKenzie (ed.) *Conviction*, London: McGibbon & Kee.

Abercrombie, L. et al. (1935) *The Next Five Years: An Essay in Political Agreement*, London: Macmillan.

Abrams, P. and McCulloch, A. (1976) *Communes, Sociology and Society*, Cambridge: Cambridge University Press.

Ackers, Peter (1993) 'The "Protestant Ethic" and the English Labour Movement: The Case of the Churches of Christ', *Labour History Review*, 58(3), Winter.

Addison, P. (1975) *The Road to 1945, British Politics and the Second World War*, London: Jonathan Cape.

Adonis, Andrew and Hames, Tim (1994) *A Conservative Revolution? The Thatcher–Reagan Decade in Perspective*, Manchester: Manchester University Press.

Alcock, Peter, Gamble, Andrew and Gough, Ian (1989) *The Social Economy and the Democratic State*, London: Lawrence & Wishart.

Alexander, Sally (1988) *Women's Fabian Tracts*, London: Routledge.

Allett, John (1981) *New Liberalism: The Political Economy of J.A. Hobson*, Toronto: University of Toronto Press.

Allett, John (1990) 'The Conservative Aspect of Hobson's New Liberalism', in Michael Freeden (ed.) *Reappraising J.A. Hobson: Humanism and Welfare*, London: Unwin Hyman.

Allison, Lincoln (1984) *Right Principles: A Conservative Philosophy of Politics*, Oxford: Blackwell.

Amenta, E. (1986–7) 'Compromising Possessions: Orwell's Political, Analytical, and Literary Purposes in *Nineteen Eighty-Four*', *Politics and Society*, 15(2): 157–88.

Anderson, Perry (1992) *English Questions*, London: Verso.

Andreski, Stanislav (1971) *Herbert Spencer: Structure, Function and Evolution*, London: Nelson.

Andrews, Geoff (ed.) (1991) *Citizenship*, London: Lawrence & Wishart.

Annan, N. (1960) 'Kipling's Place in the History of Ideas', *Victorian Studies*, 3(4), June.

Apter, D.E. and Joll, J. (eds) (1971) *Anarchism Today*, London: Macmillan.

Arblaster, Anthony (1977) 'Anthony Crosland: Labour's Last "Revisionist"?', *Political Quarterly*, 48(4).

Arblaster, Anthony (1989) 'Tawney in Retrospect', *Bulletin of the Society for the Study of Labour History*, 54(1).

Arblaster, A. and Lukes, S. (eds) (1971) *The Good Society*, London: Methuen.

Armytage, W.H.G. (1961) *Heavens Below: Utopian Experiments in England 1560–1960*, London: Routledge & Kegan Paul.

Asher, Kenneth (1995) *T.S. Eliot and Ideology*, Cambridge: Cambridge University Press.

Ashford, Nigel and Davies, Stephen (eds) (1991) *A Dictionary of Conservative and Libertarian Thought*, London: Routledge.

Ashton, Frankie (1987) *Feminist Theories and Practical Policies*, Bristol: School for Advanced Urban Studies.

Aughey, Arthur, Jones, Greta and Riches, William (1992) *The Conservative Political Tradition in Britain and The US*, London: Pinter.

Baker, Kenneth (ed.) (1993) *The Faber Book of Conservatism*, London: Faber.

Baldwin, Stanley (1937) [1926] *On England*, London: Penguin.

Balfour, A.J. (1928) *Introduction to Walter Bagehot, The English Constitution*, London: Oxford University Press.

Banks, O. (1986) *Faces of Feminism: A Study of Feminism as a Social Movement*, Oxford: Blackwell.

Banks, Olive (1993) *The Politics of British Feminism, 1918–1970*, Aldershot: Edward Elgar.

Barber, B. (1976) 'Conserving Politics: Michael Oakeshott and Political Theory', *Government and Opposition*, 2(4), Autumn.

Barker, A. (1965) Review in *Political Studies*, 8(2), June.

Barker, D. (1973) *G.K. Chesterton*, London: Constable.

Barker, D.L. and Allen, S. (1976) *Dependence and Exploitation in Work and Marriage*, London: Longmans.

Barker, E. (1915a) 'The Discredited State', *Political Quarterly*, February.

Barker, E. (1915b) *Political Thought in England from Herbert Spencer to the Present Day*, London: Williams & Norgate.

Barker, E. (1967) [1942] *Reflections on Government*, London: Oxford University Press.

Barker, Rodney (1971) *Studies in Opposition*, London: Macmillan.

Barker, Rodney (1974) 'Socialism and Progressivism in the Political Thought of Ramsay MacDonald', in A.J.A. Morris (ed.) *Edwardian Radicalism 1900–1914*, London: Routledge.

Barker, Rodney (1975) 'Guild Socialism Revisited?', *Political Quarterly*, 46(3), July–August.

Barker, Rodney (1976) 'Political Myth: Ramsay MacDonald and the Labour Party', *History*, 61(201), February.

Barker, Rodney (1984) 'The Fabian State', in Ben Pimlott (ed.) *Fabian Essays in Socialist Thought*, London: Heinemann.

Barker, Rodney (1989) 'Harold Laski', in W. Euchner (ed.) *Klassiker des Sozialismus*, Munich: C.H. Beck.

Barker, Rodney (1992) 'Dworkin on Disobedience: the Case of Greenham Common', *Political Studies*, 40(2), June.

Barker, Rodney (1994) *Politics, Peoples and Government: Themes in British Political Thought Since the Nineteenth Century*, Basingstoke: Macmillan.

Barker, Rodney (1995) 'Why Are There No More Socialists or Conservatives?', *Contemporary Politics*, 1(2), Summer: 129–33.

Barker, Rodney (1996a) 'A Future for Liberalism or a Liberal Future?', in James Meadowcroft (ed.) *The Liberal Political Tradition: Contemporary Reappraisals*, Aldershot: Edward Elgar.

Barker, Rodney (1996b) 'Political Ideas Since 1945, or How Long Was the Twentieth Century?', *Contemporary British History*, 10(1), Spring: 2–19.

Barker, Rodney and Howard-Johnston, X. (1975) 'The Politics and Political Ideas of Moisei Ostrogorski', *Political Studies*, 23(4), December.

Barnett, Anthony, Ellis, Caroline and Hirst, Paul (eds) (1993) *Debating the Constitution: New Perspectives on Constitutional Reform*, Cambridge: Polity.

Barrett, Michele (1980) *Women's Oppression Today: Problems in Marxist Feminist Analysis*, Verso: London.

Barrow, L. (1969) 'The Origins of Robert Blatchford's Social Imperialism', *Bulletin of the Society for the Study of Labour History*, 19, Autumn.

Barrow, Logie and Bullock, Ian (1996) *Democratic Ideas and the British Labour Movement*, Cambridge: Cambridge University Press.

Barry, E.E. (1965) *Nationalisation in British Politics*, London: Cape.

Bassett, R.G. (1964) [1935] *The Essentials of Parliamentary Democracy*, London: Frank Cass.

Bax, E.B. (1885) *The Religion of Socialism*, London: Swan Sonnenschein.

Bax, E.B. (1887) *The Ethics of Socialism*, London: Swan Sonnenschein.

Bax, E.B. (1913) *The Fraud of Feminism*, London: Grant Richards.

Bax, E.B. and Levy, J.H. (1904) *Socialism and Individualism*, London: P.S. King & Son.

Beddoe, Deirdre (1984) 'Hindrances and Help-Meets: Women in the Writings of George Orwell', in Christopher Norris (ed.) *Inside the Myth: Orwell and the Left*, London: Lawrence & Wishart.

Beer, S.H. (1965, 1969) *Modern British Politics*, London: Faber.

Beevers, R. (1987) *The Garden City Utopia: A Critical Biography of Ebenezer Howard*, London: Macmillan.

Beilharz, Peter (1992) *Labour's Utopias: Bolshevism, Fabianism and Social Democracy*, London: Routledge.

Belchem, John (1996) *Popular Radicalism in Nineteenth-Century Britain*, Basingstoke: Macmillan.

Bellamy, E. (1887) *Looking Backwards*, Chicago and New York: M.A. Donohue & Co.

Bellamy, Richard (ed.) (1990) *Victorian Liberalism: Nineteenth Century Political Thought and Practice*, London: Routledge.

Bellamy, Richard (1994) '"Dethroning Politics": Liberalism, Constitutionalism and Democracy in the Thought of F.A. Hayek', *British Journal of Political Science*, 24(4).

Belloc, H. (1927) [1912] *The Servile State*, London: Constable.

Belloc, H. and Chesterton, C.E. (1911) *The Party System*, London: Stephen Swift.

Benewick, R. (1972) *The Fascist Movement in Britain*, London: Allen Lane.

Benn, E.J.P. (1925) *The Confessions of a Capitalist*, London: Hutchinson & Co.

Benn, E.J.P. (1930) *Account Rendered 1900–1930*, London: Ernest Benn.

Benn, E.J.P. (1932) *Honest Doubt: Being a Collection of Papers on the Price of Modern Politics*, London: Ernest Benn.

Benn, E.J.P. (1946) *Benn's Protest: Being an Argument for the Restoration of our Liberties*, London: John Gifford.

Benn, T. (1974) *Speeches by Tony Benn*, Nottingham: Spokesman Books.

Benn, T. and Hood, A. (1993) *Common Sense – A New Constitution for Britain*, Hutchinson: London.

Benn, T. et al. (1973) *Workers' Control: How Far Can the Structure Meet Our Demands?*, Nottingham: Spokesman Books.

Bennett, A.J. (1977) 'The Conservative Tradition of Thought: A Right Wing Phenomenon', in N. Nugent and R. King (eds) *The British Right: Conservative and Right Wing Politics in Britain*, Farnborough: Saxon House.

Bentley, Michael (ed.) (1993) *Public and Private Doctrine: Essays in British History Presented to Maurice Cowling*, Cambridge: Cambridge University.

Bergonzi, B. (1972) 'Myth Man at Heart', *New Society*, 27 January.

Berki, R.N. (1975) *Socialism*, London: Dent.

Berlin, I. (1950) 'Political Ideas in the Twentieth Century', *Foreign Affairs*, 28(3), April.

Bernstein, Eduard (1993) [1899] *The Preconditions of Socialism*, ed. Henry Tudor, Cambridge: Cambridge University Press.

Besant, A. (1889) 'Industry under Socialism', in G.B. Shaw (ed.), *Fabian Essays*, London: Allen & Unwin.

Bestor, A.E. Jr. (1948) 'The Evolution of the Socialist Vocabulary', *Journal of the History of Ideas*, 9.

Bevan, A. (1952) *In Place of Fear*, London: Heinemann.

Beveridge, W.H. (1907) 'The Problem of the Unemployed', *Sociological Society Sociological Papers*, 3.

Beveridge, W.H. (1944) *Full Employment in a Free Society*, London: Allen & Unwin.

Biagini, Eugenio F. (1992) *Liberty, Retrenchment and Reform: Popular Liberalism in the Age of Gladstone, 1860–1880*, Cambridge: Cambridge University Press.

Biagini, E.F. and Reid, A.J. (1991) *Currents of Radicalism: Popular Radicalism, Organized Labour and Party Politics in Britain 1850–1914*, Cambridge: Cambridge University Press.

Birch, A.H. (1964) *Representative and Responsible Government*, London: George Allen & Unwin.

Blackburn, H. (1902) *Record of Women's Suffrage*, London: Williams & Norgate.

Blackwood, Caroline (1984) *On the Perimeter*, London: Heinemann.

Blatchford, R. (1894) *Merrie England*, London: The Clarion Press.

Blatchford, R. (1902) *Britain for the British*, London: The Clarion Press.

Blease, W. L. (1913) *Votes for Women. Against Prejudice. A Reply to Professor Dicey*, London: Women's Freedom League.

Blinkhorn, Martin (ed.) (1990) *Fascists and Conservatives: the Radical Right and the Establishment in Twentieth-Century Europe*, London: Unwin Hyman.

Boardman, P. (1944) *Patrick Geddes: Maker of the Future*, Chapel Hill, N.C.: University of North Carolina Press.

Bosanquet, B. (ed.) (1895) *Aspects of the Social Problem*, London: Macmillan.

Bosanquet, B. (1923) [1899] *The Philosophical Theory of the State*, London: Macmillan.

Bosanquet, Nick (1983) *After the New Right*, London: Heinemann.

Bottomore, Tom (1990) *The Socialist Economy: Theory and Practice*, Hemel Hempstead: Harvester Wheatsheaf.

Boucher, David (1989a) *The Social and Political Thought of R.G. Collingwood*, Cambridge: Cambridge University Press.

Boucher, David (ed.) (1989b) *Essays in Political Philosophy by R.G. Collingwood*, Oxford: Oxford University Press.

Boucher, David (1993) *A Radical Hegelian: The Political and Social Philosophy of Henry Jones*, Cardiff: University of Wales Press.

Boucher, David (ed.) (1994) *Collingwood Studies: vol. 1 1994: The Life and Thought of R.G. Collingwood*, Swansea: R.G. Collingwood Society.

Bouchier, D. (1983) *The Feminist Challenge*, London: Macmillan.

Bowman, S.E. (1962) *Edward Bellamy Abroad*, New York: Twayne Publishers.

Boyd, I. (1972) 'Chesterton and Distribution', *New Blackfriars*, August:

Bradshaw, David (ed.) (1994) *The Hidden Huxley: Contempt and Compassion for the Masses*, London: Faber.

Bramwell, Anna (1989) *Ecology in the 20th Century: A History*, New Haven: Yale University Press.

Brazier, Rodney (1991) *Constitutional Reform: Re-Shaping the British Political System*, Oxford: Clarendon.

Brecht, A. (1959) *Political Theory*, Princeton: Princeton University Press.

Bridson, D.G. (1972) *The Filibuster: a Study of the Political Ideas of Wyndham Lewis*, London: Cassell.

Briggs, A. (ed.) (1962) *William Morris: Selected Writings and Designs*, Harmondsworth: Penguin.

Briggs, A. and Saville, J. (eds) (1971) *Essays in Labour History 1886–1923*, London: Macmillan.

Brinton, C. (1933) *English Political Thought in the Nineteenth Century*, London: Ernest Benn.

Bristow, E. J. (1970) 'The Defence of Liberty and Property in Britain 1880–1914', unpublished PhD thesis, Yale University.

Bristow, E. (1975) 'The Liberty and Property Defence League and Individualism', *The Historical Journal*, 18(4), December.

Britain, Ian (1982) *Fabianism and Culture: a Study of British Socialism and the Arts, 1884–1914*, Cambridge: Cambridge University Press.

Brittan, Samuel (1968) *Left or Right: the Bogus Dilemma*, London: Secker & Warburg.

Brittan, Samuel (1973) *Capitalism and the Permissive Society*, London: Macmillan.

Brittan, Samuel (1983) 'Hayek, Freedom and Interest Groups', in *The Role and Limits of Government: Essays in Political Economy*, London: Temple Smith.

Brown, Gordon (1994) 'The Politics of Potential: A New Agenda for Labour' in David Miliband (ed.) *Reinventing the Left*, Cambridge: Polity.

Brown, Gordon and Tony Wright (eds) (1995) *Values, Visions and Voices: An Anthology of Socialism*, Edinburgh: Mainstream Publishing.

Brown, I. (1920) *The Meaning of Democracy*, London: Richard Cobden-Sanderson.

Brown, K. D. (ed.) (1974) *Essays in Anti-Labour History: Responses to the Rise of Labour in Britain*, London: Macmillan.

Brown, M.B., Coates, K. and Topham, T. (1975) 'Workers' Control versus

"Revolutionary" Theory', in R. Miliband and J. Saville (eds) *The Socialist Register*, London: Merlin Books.

Brown, Tony (ed.) (1991) 'Edward Carpenter and Late Victorian Radicalism', *Prose Studies*, special issue, London: Frank Cass.

Bryce, J. (1921) *Modern Democracies*, 2 vols, London: Macmillan.

Bryson, Valerie (1992) *Feminist Political Theory: An Introduction*, London: Macmillan.

Bryson, Valerie (1993) 'Feminism', in Roger Eatwell and Anthony Wright (eds) *Contemporary Political Ideology*, London: Pinter.

Buchanan, Tom (1991) *The Spanish Civil War and the British Labour Movement*, Cambridge: Cambridge University Press.

Buck, P. (ed.) (1975) *How Conservatives Think*, Harmondsworth: Penguin.

Bullock, A. and Shock, M. (eds) (1956) *The Liberal Tradition from Fox to Keynes*, Oxford: Clarendon Press.

Burrow, J. W. (1970) *Evolution and Society*, 2nd edn, Cambridge: Cambridge University Press.

Butler, Eamon (1983) *Hayek: His Contribution to the Political and Economic Thought of our Times*, London: Temple Smith.

Cachin, Marie-Francoise (1990) '"Non-governmental society": Edward Carpenter's Position in the British Socialist Movement', in Tony Brown (ed.) *Edward Carpenter and Late Victorian Radicalism*, special issue of *Prose Studies*, 13(1), May.

Cahm, Caroline (1990) *Kropotkin and the Rise of Revolutionary Anarchism, 1872–1886*, Cambridge: Cambridge University Press.

Caine, Barbara (1992) *Victorian Feminists*, Oxford: Oxford University Press.

Callaghan, J. (1987) *The Far Left in British Politics*, Oxford: Blackwell.

Callaghan, John (1990) *Socialism in Britain since 1884*, Oxford: Blackwell.

Callaghan, John (1993) *Rajani Palme Dutt: A Study in British Stalinism*, London: Lawrence & Wishart.

Campbell, Beatrix (1985) 'Orwell – Paterfamilias or Big Brother?', in Christopher Norris (ed.) *Inside the Myth: Orwell and the Left*, London: Lawrence & Wishart.

Campbell, Beatrix (1987) *The Iron Ladies*, London: Virago.

Candidus (1910) *The Reform of the Electorate Based upon the Professions and Trades in Place of Local Constituencies*, London: Frank Palmer.

Canovan, Margaret (1977) *G.K. Chesterton, Radical Populist*, New York and London: Harcourt Brace Jovanovich.

Canovan, Margaret (1981) *Populism*, London: Junction Books.

Canovan, Margaret (1982) 'Two Strategies for the Study of Populism', *Political Studies*, 30(4).

Carey, John (1992) *The Intellectuals and the Masses: Pride and Prejudice among the Literary Intelligentsia, 1880–1939*, London: Faber.

Carpenter, E. (1889) *Civilization: Its Cause and Cure*, London: George Allen.

Carpenter, E. (1896) *Love's Coming of Age*, London: George Allen & Unwin.

Carpenter, E. (1897) 'Transitions to Freedom' in *Forecasts of the Coming Century by a Decade of Writers*, Manchester: Labour Press.

Carpenter, E. (1905) [1883] *Towards Democracy*, London: George Allen & Unwin.

Carpenter, E. (1906) [1887] *England's Ideal*, London: Swan Sonnenschein.

Carpenter, L.P. (1973) *G.D.H. Cole: An Intellectual Portrait*, Cambridge: Cambridge University Press.

Carpenter, L.P. (1976) 'Corporatism in Britain 1930–45', *Journal of Contemporary History*, 2(1), January.

Carr, G. (1975) *The Angry Brigade*, London: Victor Gollancz.

Carrington, C. (1955) *Rudyard Kipling*, London: Macmillan.

Carter, April (1988) *The Politics of Women's Rights*, London: Longman.

Carter, Ian (1989) 'Human Nature and the Utopianism of the New Right', *Politics*, 9(2).

Carvel, J. (1987) *Citizen Ken*, London: Hogarth Press.

Catlin, G. (1950) [1939] *A History of the Political Philosophers*, London: George Allen & Unwin.

Catlin, G. (1952) 'Contemporary British Political Thought', *American Political Science Review*, 46(3), September.

Cecil, Lord H. (1912) *Conservatism*, London: Williams & Norgate.

Chace, W. M. (1973) *The Political Identities of Ezra Pound and T.S. Eliot*, Stanford, Calif.: Stanford University Press.

Chamberlain, J. (1971) [1885] *The Radical Programme*, (rep. Brighton 1971, together with T.H.S. Escott, *The Future of the Liberal Party*, ed. and intro. D.A. Hamer), Brighton: Harvester.

Chapman, B. (1963) *British Government Observed: Some European Reflections*, London: Allen & Unwin.

Chappelow, A. (1969) *Shaw: The Chucker Out*, London: Allen & Unwin.

Chesterton, C.E. (1910) *Party and People*, London: Alston Rivers.

Chesterton, G.K. (1904) *The Napoleon of Notting Hill*, London: John Lane/The Bodley Head.

Chesterton, G.K. (1905) *Heretics*, London: John Lane/The Bodley Head.

Chesterton, G.K. (1909) *George Bernard Shaw*, London: The Bodley Head.

Chesterton, G.K. (1912) [1910] *What's Wrong with the World*, London: Cassell.

Chesterton, G.K. (1914) *The Flying Inn*, London: Methuen.

Chesterton, G.K. (1926) *The Outline of Sanity*, London: Methuen.

Chesterton, G.K. (1936) *The Autobiography of G.K. Chesterton*, New York: Sheed & Ward.

Christie, S. and Meltzer, A. (1972) [1970] *The Floodgates of Anarchy*, London: Sphere Books.

Chun, Lin (1993) *The British New Left*, Edinburgh: Edinburgh University Press.

Churchill, W.S. (1909) *Liberalism and the Social Problem*, London: Hodder & Stoughton.

Clark, J.C.D. (ed.) (1990) *Ideas and Politics in Modern Britain*, London: Macmillan.

Clarke, J., Cochrane, A. and Smart, C. (eds) (1987) *Ideologies of Welfare*, London: Hutchinson.

Clarke, P.F. (1971) *Lancashire and the New Liberalism*, Cambridge: Cambridge University Press.

Clarke, P.F. (1972) Introduction to *L.T. Hobhouse, Democracy and Reaction*, ed. P.F. Clarke, Brighton: Harvester.

Clarke, P.F. (1974) 'The Progressive Movement in England', *Transactions of the Royal Historical Society*, 5th series, 24.

Clarke, Peter (1978) *Liberals and Social Democrats*, Cambridge: Cambridge University Press.

Clutton-Brock, A. (1914) *William Morris: his Work and Influence*, London: Thornton Butterworth.

Coates, K. (1976) 'How Not to Reappraise the New Left', in R. Miliband and J. Saville (eds) *The Socialist Register 1976*, London: The Merlin Press.

Coates, K. and Topham, T. (1972) *The New Unionism: the Case for Workers' Control*, Harmondsworth: Penguin.

Coates, K. (ed.) (1968) *Can the Workers Run Industry?*, Nottingham: Spokesman Books.

Cockett, Richard (1994) *Thinking the Unthinkable*, London: HarperCollins.

Cohen, G.A. (1994) 'Back to Socialist Basics', *New Left Review*, 207, September/October.

Cohen, G.A. (1995) *Is Socialism Inseparable from Common Ownership?*, Socialist Renewal, European Labour Forum, Pamphlet no. 1, Nottingham: Spokesman.

Cohen, G., Bosanquet, N., Ryan, A., Parekh, B., Keegan, W. and Gress, F. (1986) *The New Right: Image and Reality*, London: The Runnymede Trust.

Coker, F.W. (1934) *Recent Political Thought*, New York: D. Appleton-Century.

Cole, G.D.H. (1929) *The Next Ten Years in British Social and Economic Policy*, London: Macmillan.

Cole, G.D.H. (1953–8) *A History of Socialist Thought*, London: Macmillan.

Cole, G.D.H. (1972) [1917] *Self-Government in Industry*, London: Hutchinson.

Cole, G.D.H. (1973) [1913] *The World of Labour*, London: G. Bell.

Cole, G.D.H. and Mellor, W. (eds) (1933) *Workers' Control and Self-Government in Industry: A Memorandum Prepared by a Group of Trade Unionists and Socialists as a Basis for Consideration by the Working-Class Movement*, London: New Fabian Research Bureau.

Cole, M.I. (ed.) (1949) *The Webbs and their Work*, London: Muller.

Cole, M.I. (1971) *The Life of G.D.H. Cole*, London: Macmillan.

Cole, M.I. (1973) [1955] 'Beatrice and Sidney Webb', in M. Katanka (ed.) *Radicals, Reformers and Socialists – from the Fabian Biographical Series*, London: Charles Knight.

Coleman, Janet (1990) *Against the State: Studies in Sedition and Rebellion*, London: BBC Books.

Collard, David (1968) *The New Right: A Critique*, London: The Fabian Society.

Collingwood, R.G. (1939) *An Autobiography*, Oxford: Oxford University Press.

Collingwood, R.G. (1942) *The New Leviathan, or Man, Society, Civilization and Barbarism*, Oxford: Clarendon Press.

Collini, S. (1974) 'Laissez-Faire and State Intervention in Nineteenth Century Britain', *History*, 59(195), February.

Collini, S. (1975) 'Idealism and "Cambridge Idealism"', *The Historical Journal*, 18(1).

Collini, S. (1976) 'Hobhouse, Bosanquet and the State: Philosophical Idealism and Political Argument in England 1880–1918', *Past and Present*, 72, August.

Collini, S. (1977) 'Liberalism and the Legacy of Mill', *The Historical Journal*, 20(1).

Collini, Stefan (1979) *Liberalism and Sociology: L.T. Hobhouse and Political Argument in England 1880–1914*, Cambridge: Cambridge University Press.

Collini, Stefan (1991) *Public Moralists: Political Thought and Intellectual Life in Britain 1850–1930*, Oxford: Clarendon.

Collins, H. (1971) 'The Marxism of the Social Democratic Federation', in A. Briggs and J. Saville (eds) *Essays in Labour History 1886–1923*, London: Macmillan.

Colls, R. and Dodd, P. (eds) (1986) *Englishness: Politics and Culture 1880–1920*, London: Croom Helm.

Conway, David (1992) 'Do Women Benefit from Equal Opportunities Legislation?', in Caroline Quest (ed.) *Equal Opportunities: A Feminist Fallacy*, London: IEA.

Conway, K. St John and Glasier, J.B. (1890) *The Religion of Socialism*, Manchester and Glasgow: The Labour Press Society.

Cook, Alice and Gwyn Kirk (1983) *Greenham Women Everywhere*, London: Pluto.

Coole, Diana (1988) *Women in Political Theory*, Brighton: Harvester.

Coote, Anna and Campbell, Beatrix (1987) *Sweet Freedom*, 2nd edn, London: Picador.

Coote, Anna and Pattullo, Polly (1990) *Power and Prejudice: Women and Politics*, London: Weidenfeld & Nicolson.

Coote, Anna (ed.) (1992) *The Welfare of Citizens – Developing New Social Rights*, London: Rivers Oram.

Coren, Michael (1989) *Gilbert: The Man who was G.K. Chesterton*, London: Jonathan Cape.

Coren, Michael (1993) *The Invisible Man: The Life and Liberties of H.G. Wells*, London: Bloomsbury.

Corrin, Jay P. (1981) *G.K. Chesterton and Hilaire Belloc: The Battle Against Modernity*, Athens/London: Ohio University Press.

Cort, John C. (1988) *Christian Socialism*, London: Orbis Books.

Cott, Nancy F. (1986) 'Feminist Theory and Feminist Movements: The Past Before Us', in Juliet Mitchell and Ann Oakley (eds) *What is Feminism?*, Oxford: Blackwell.

Covell, Charles (1986) *The Redefinition of Conservatism: Politics and Doctrine*, London: Macmillan.

Cowley, John (1992) *The Victorian Encounter with Marx: A Study of Ernest Belfort Bax*, London: British Academic Press.

Cowling, Maurice (1978a) *Conservative Essays*, London: Cassell.

Cowling, Maurice (1978b) 'The Present Position' in Maurice Cowling (ed.) *Conservative Essays*, London: Cassell.

Cowling, Maurice (1985–6) *Religion and Public Doctrine in Modern England*, 2 vols, Cambridge: Cambridge University Press.

Cowling, Maurice (1989) 'The Sources of the New Right: Irony, Geniality, and Malice', *Encounter*, November.

Cox, C.B. and Dyson, A.E. (eds) (1968) *Fight for Education: A Black Paper*, London: The Critical Quarterly Society.

Cox, C.B. and Dyson, A.E. (eds) (1969) *Black Paper 2*, London: The Critical Quarterly Society.

Cox, C.B. and Dyson, A.E. (eds) (1970) *Black Paper 3*, London: The Critical Quarterly Society.

Cox, H. (1907) *Socialism in the House of Commons*, London: Longmans, Green & Co.

Craig, Cairns (1982) *Yeats, Eliot, Pound and the Politics of Poetry*, London: Croom Helm.

Cramb, J.A. (1900) *Reflections on the Origins and Destiny of Imperial Britain*, London: Macmillan.

de Crespigny, A. and Minogue, K. (eds) (1976) *Contemporary Political Philosophers*, London: Methuen.

Crick, B. (1964) *The Reform of Parliament*, London: Weidenfeld & Nicolson.

Crick, B. (1980) *George Orwell: A Life*, London: Secker & Warburg.

Crick, B. (1987) *Socialism*, Milton Keynes: Open University Press.

Crofts, W.C. (1885) *Municipal Socialism*, London: Liberty & Property Defence League.

Crofts, W.C. (1892) *Municipal Socialism*, London: Liberty & Property Defence League.

Croham, Lord (1981) 'The IEA as seen from the Civil Service' in Arthur Seldon (ed.) *The Emerging Consensus: Essays on the Interplay Between Ideas, Interests, and Circumstances in the First 25 Years of the IEA*, London: Institute of Economic Affairs.

Crook, D.P. (1984) *Benjamin Kidd: Portrait of a Social Darwinist*, Cambridge: Cambridge University Press.

Crosland, C.A.R. (1956) *The Future of Socialism*, London: Jonathan Cape.

Crosland, C.A.R. (1962) *The Conservative Enemy*, London: Jonathan Cape.

Crosland, C.A.R. (1970) [1952] 'The Transition from Capitalism', in R.H.S. Crossman (ed.) *New Fabian Essays*, London: Dent.

Crosland, C.A.R. (1975) *Socialism Now*, ed. Dick Leonard, 2nd edition, London: Jonathan Cape.

Crossman, R.H.S. (ed.) (1970) [1952] *New Fabian Essays*, London: Dent.

Crowder, George (1991) *Classical Anarchism: The Political Thought of Godwin, Bakunin, and Kropotkin*, Oxford: Clarendon.

Crowley, Brian Lee (1987) *The Self, the Individual and the Community: Liberalism in the Political Thought of F.A. Hayek and Sidney and Beatrice Webb*,

Crozier, B. and Seldon, A. (1984) *Socialism Explained*, London: The Sherwood Press.

Curran, James (1984) *The Future of the Left*, Cambridge: Polity and New Socialist.

Dahl, R. (1947) 'Workers' Control of Industry and the British Labour Party', *American Political Science Review*, 41(5).

Dahlerup, D. (ed.) (1986) *The New Women's Movement: Feminism and Political Power in Europe and the USA*, London: Sage.

Dale, Alzina Stone (1982) *The Outline of Sanity: A Life of G.K. Chesterton*, Grand Rapids, Michigan: William B. Eerdmans Publishing Co.

Dale, Jenny (1980) *Feminists and State Welfare*, London: Routledge.

David, Miriam (1983) 'The New Right in the USA and Britain: A New Anti-Feminist Moral Economy', *Critical Social Policy*, 2(3): 21–45.

David, Miriam (1986) 'Moral and Maternal: The Family in the Right', in Ruth Levitas (ed.) *The Ideology of the New Right*, Cambridge: Polity.

Davies, A.J. (1995) *We, The Nation: The Conservative Party and the Pursuit of Power*, London: Little, Brown, & Co.

Davies, Charlotte Aull (1989) *Welsh Nationalism in the Twentieth Century*, London: Praeger.

Deane, H.A. (1955) *The Political Ideas of Harold J. Laski*, New York: Columbia University Press.

Delavenay, E. (1971) *D.H. Lawrence and Edward Carpenter*, London: Heinemann.

Delbez, L. (1964) 'Quelques reflexions sur la pensee politique anglaise', *Revue politique des idees et institutions*, 53(3–4), February.

Delmar, Rosalind (1986) 'What is Feminism?', in Juliet Mitchell and Ann Oakley (eds) *What is Feminism?*, Oxford: Blackwell.

Denham, Andrew (1997) *Think Tanks and British Politics*, London: UCL.

Dennis, N. and Halsey, A.H. (1988) *English Ethical Socialism: From Thomas More to R.H. Tawney*, Oxford: Clarendon Press.

Derfler, L. (1973) *Socialism Since Marx*, London: Macmillan.

Desai, Radhika (1994) 'Second Hand Dealers in Ideas: Think Tanks and Thatcherite Hegemony', *New Left Review*, 203 January/February.

Devigne, Robert (1994) *Recasting Conservatism: Oakeshott, Strauss, and the Response to Post-modernism*, London: Yale University Press.

Dewey, C.J. (1974) '"Cambridge Idealism": Utilitarian Revisionists in Late Nineteenth Century Cambridge', *The Historical Journal*, 17(1).

Dicey, A.V. (1959) [1885] *An Introduction to the Study of the Law of the Constitution*, London: Macmillan.

Dicey, A.V. (1962) [1905] *Lectures on the Relation between Law and Public Opinion in England during the Nineteenth Century*, London: Macmillan.

Dicey, A.V. (1909) *Letters to a Friend on Votes for Women*, London: John Murray.

Dicey, A.V. (1913) *A Fool's Paradise: Being a Constitutionalist's Criticism of the Home Rule Bill 1912*, London: John Murray.

Dickson, Lovat (1972) [1969] *H.G. Wells: His Turbulent Life and Times*, London: Macmillan, Pelican.

Dobson, Andrew (1990) *Green Political Theory: An Introduction*, London: Unwin Hyman/Routledge.

Dodd, Kathryn (ed.) (1993) *A Sylvia Pankurst Reader*, Manchester: Manchester University Press.

Donisthorpe, W. (1886) *Empire and Liberty, a Lecture on the Principles of Local Government*, London: Liberty & Property Defence League.

Donisthorpe, W. (1889) *Individualism, a System of Politics*, London: Macmillan.

Donisthorpe, W. (1893) *Love and Law: An Essay on Marriage*, London: W. Reeves.

Donnachie, Ian, Harvie, Christopher and Wood, Ian S. (eds) (1989) *Forward! Labour Politics in Scotland 1888–1988*, Edinburgh: Edinburgh University Press.

Douglas, P. and Powell, J.E. (1968) *How Big Should Government Be?*, Washington D.C.: American Enterprise Institute for Public Policy Research.

Douglas, R. (1976) *Land, People, and Politics*, London: Allison & Busby.

Dunleavy, P. (1991) *Democracy, Bureaucracy and Public Choice: Economic Explanations in Political Science*, Hemel Hempstead: Harvester Wheatsheaf.

Dunn, J.H. (1977) 'The Language and Myths of the New Right', *New Society*, 40(761), 5 May.

Durbin, Evan F.M. (1940) *The Politics of Democratic Socialism*, London: Routledge.

Durbin, E. (1949) *Problems of Economic Planning*, London: Routledge & Kegan Paul.

Durbin, E. (1985) *New Jerusalems: The Labour Party and the Economics of Democratic Socialism*, London: Routledge & Kegan Paul.

Durham, Martin (1991) *Sex and Politics: The Family and Morality in the Thatcher Years*, London: Macmillan.

Dyhouse, Carol (1976) 'Social Darwinistic Ideas and the Development of Women's Education in England, 1880–1920', *History of Education*, 5(1).

Dyhouse, Carol (1989) *Feminism and the Family in England 1880–1939*, Oxford: Blackwell.

Eagleton, Terry (1976) 'Criticism and Politics: The Work of Raymond Williams', *New Left Review*, 95.

Eagleton, Terry (1989) *Raymond Williams: Critical Perspectives*, Cambridge: Polity.

Eatwell, Roger and Wright, Anthony (eds) (1993) *Modern Political Ideologies*, London: Pinter.

Eccleshall, Robert (1977) 'English Conservatism as Ideology', *Political Studies*, 35.

Eccleshall, Robert (ed.) (1986) *British Liberalism: Liberal thought from the 1640s to the 1980s*, London: Longmans.

Eccleshall, Robert (ed.) (1990) *English Conservatism since the Restoration: An Introduction and Anthology*, London: Unwin Hyman.

Eco, Umberto (1994) *Apocalypse Postponed*, London: British Film Institute.

Edgar, David (1983) 'Bitter Harvest', *New Socialist*, 19–24, September/October.

Edwards, D. (1974) 'The New Liberalism of C.F.G. Masterman', in K.D. Brown (ed.) *Essays in Anti-Labour History: Responses to the Rise of Labour in Britain*, London: Macmillan.

Edwards, Owen Dudley, Evans, G., Rhys, I. and McDiarmid, Hugh (1968) *Celtic Nationalism*, London: Routledge & Kegan Paul.

Edwards, Owen Dudley (ed.) (1989) *A Claim of Right for Scotland*, Edinburgh: Edinburgh University Press.

Eisenstein, H. (1984) *Contemporary Feminist Thought*, London: Unwin.

Eliot, T.S. (1928) *For Lancelot Andrewes, Essays on Style and Order*, London: Faber & Faber.

Eliot, T.S. (1934) *After Strange Gods*, London: Faber & Faber.

Eliot, T.S. (1939) *The Idea of a Christian Society*, London: Faber.

Eliot, T.S. (1948) *Notes Towards the Definition of Culture*, London: Faber.

Elliot, B. and McCrone, D. (1987) 'Class, Culture and Morality: A Sociological Analysis of the New Conservatism', *The Sociological Review*, 35(3).

Elliott, Gregory (1993) *Labourism and the English Genius: The Strange Death of Labour England?*, London: Verso.

Ellis, R.W. (ed.) (1930) *Bernard Shaw and Karl Marx: A Symposium*, New York: Random House.

Ellison, Nick (1994) *Egalitarian Thought and Labour Politics: Retreating Visions*, London: Routledge.

Emy, H.V. (1973) *Liberals, Radicals and Social Politics*, Cambridge: Cambridge University Press.

Englander, David and O'Day, Rosemary (1995) *Retrieved Riches: Social Investigation in Britain 1830–1914*, Aldershot: Scolar Press.

Evans, Mark (1995) *Charter 88: A Successful Challenge to the British Political Tradition?*, Aldershot: Dartmouth.

Evans, Judith et al. (1986) *Feminism and Political Theory*, London: Sage.

Fairlie, H. (1960) 'Aneurin Bevan and the Art of Politics', *History Today*, 10(10), October.

Favil Press (1927) *Bernard Shaw and Fascism*, London: Favil Press.

Fawcett, M. (1912) 'Introduction' in *J.S. Mill, Three Essays*, ed. Millicent Fawcett, London: The World's Classics.

Fforde, Matthew (1990) *Conservatism and Collectivism 1886–1914*, Edinburgh: Edinburgh University Press.

Fielding, Steven and Thompson, Peter and Tiratsoo, Nick (1995) *England Arise! The Labour Party and Popular Politics in the 1940s*, Manchester: Manchester University Press.

Figgis, J.N. (1913) *Churches in the Modern State*, London: Longmans.

Fildes, S. (1987) *Contemporary Feminist Theory*, Brighton: Harvester.

Finlay, J.L. (1972) *Social Credit, the English Origins*, Montreal and London: Mcgill-Queen's University Press.

Firestone, Shulamith (1971) *The Dialectic of Sex: The Case for Feminist Revolution*, London: Jonathan Cape.

Fisher, H.A.L. (1927) *James Bryce*, 2 vols, London: Macmillan.

Fishman, W.J. (1975) *East End Jewish Radicals*, London: Duckworth.

Fleming, Marie (1979) *The Anarchist Way to Socialism: Elisee Réclus and Nineteenth Century European Anarchism*, London: Croom Helm.

Foot, M. (1962, 1973) *Aneurin Bevan: A Biography*, 2 vols, London: McKibbon Kee, Davis-Poynter.

Foot, Michael (1995) *The History of Mr. Wells*, London: Doubleday.

Foot, P. (1965) *Immigration and Race in British Politics*, Harmondsworth: Penguin.

Forbes, I. (1986) *Market Socialism: Whose Choice?*, London: Fabian Society.

Ford, D.J. (1974) 'W.H. Mallock and Socialism in England' in Kenneth D. Brown (ed.) *Essays in Anti-Labour History*, London: Macmillan.

Forster, E.M. (1965) [1951] *Two Cheers for Democracy*, Harmondsworth: Penguin.

Forster, E.M. (1967) [1936] *Abinger Harvest*, Harmondsworth: Penguin.

Forsyth, Murray (1988) 'Hayek's Bizarre Liberalism: A Critique', *Political Studies*, 36(2), June: 235–250.

Fowler, W.S. (1967) 'The Influence of Idealism upon State Provision of Education', *Victorian Studies*, 4(4), June.

Francis, Mark and Morrow, John (1994) *A History of English Political Thought in the Nineteenth Century*, London: Duckworth.

Franco, Paul (1990) *The Political Philosophy of Michael Oakeshott*, London: Yale University Press.

Fraser, Nancy (1995) 'From Redistribution to Recognition? Dilemmas of Justice in a "Post-Socialist" Age', *New Left Review*, 212, July/August.

Frazer, Elizabeth and Lacey, Nicola (1993) *The Politics of Community: A Feminist Critique of the Liberal Communitarian Debate*, Hemel Hempstead: Harvester Wheatsheaf.

Freeden, Michael (1978) *The New Liberalism*, Oxford: Clarendon.

Freeden, Michael (1986) *Liberalism Divided: A study in British Political Thought 1914–1939*, Oxford: Clarendon.

Freeden, M. (ed.) (1988) *J.A. Hobson: A Reader*, London: Unwin Hyman.

Freeden, Michael (1990a) 'The New Liberalism and its Aftermath', in Richard Bellamy (ed.) *Victorian Liberalism: Nineteenth Century Political Thought and Practice*, London: Routledge.

Freeden, Michael (1990b) 'The Stranger at the Feast: Ideology and Public Policy in Twentieth-Century Britain', *Twentieth Century British History*, 1(1).

Freeden, Michael (ed.) (1990c) *Reappraising J.A. Hobson: Humanism and Welfare*, London: Unwin Hyman.

Fulford, R. (1957) *Votes for Women*, London: Faber.

Fuller, Timothy (ed.) (1990) *The Voice of Liberal Learning: Michael Oakeshott on Education*, London: Yale University Press.

Fuller, Timothy (ed.) (1993) *Michael Oakeshott: Religion, Politics and the Moral Life*, London and New Haven: Yale University Press.

Gainer, B. (1972) *The Alien Invasion*, New York: Crane Russack & Co.

Gamble, Andrew (1983) 'Thatcherism and Conservative Politics', in Stuart Hall and Martin Jacques (eds) *The Politics of Thatcherism*, London: Lawrence & Wishart.

Gamble, Andrew (1993) 'The Entrails of Thatcherism', *New Left Review*, 198, March/April.

Gamble, Andrew (1995) 'The Crisis of Conservatism', *New Left Review*, 214, November/December.

Gamble, Andrew (1996) *Hayek: The Iron Cage of Liberty*, Cambridge: Polity.

Garner, Les (1984) *Stepping Stones to Women's Liberty: Feminist Ideas in the Women's Suffrage Movement 1900–1918*, London: Heinemann.

Geddes, P. (1915) *Cities in Evolution: An Introduction to the Town Planning Movement and to the Study of Civics*, London: Williams & Norgate.

Gelb, J. (1986) 'Feminism in Britain: Politics without Power?', in D. Dahlerup (ed.) *The New Women's Movement: Feminism and Political Power in Europe and the USA*, London: Sage.

George, H. (1911) [1880] *Progress and Poverty*, London: J.M. Dent.

George, V. and Wilding, P. (1985) *Ideology and Social Welfare*, London: Routledge & Kegan Paul.

Germino, D. (1967) *Beyond Ideology: The Revival of Political Theory*, New York: Harper & Row.

Giddens, Anthony (1994a) *Beyond Left and Right*, Cambridge: Polity.

Giddens, Anthony (1994b) 'Brave New World: The New Context of Politics', in David Miliband (ed.) *Reinventing the Left*, Cambridge: Polity.

Gilbert, B.B. (1970) *British Social Policy 1914–1939*, London: Batsford.

Gilhespy, D., Jones, K., Mainwaring, T., Neuburger, H. and Sharples, A. (1986) *Socialist Enterprise: Reclaiming the Economy*, Nottingham: New Socialist/Spokesman.

Gilmour, Ian (1977) *Inside Right*, London: Hutchinson.

Glass, S.T. (1966) *The Responsible Society: The Ideas of the Guild Socialists*, London: Longmans.

Glickman, H. (1961) 'The Toryness of English Conservatism', *Journal of British Studies*, 1.

Goode, J. (1971) 'William Morris and the Dream of Revolution', in J. Lucas (ed.) *Literature and Politics in the Nineteenth Century*, London: Methuen.

Goodrich, Carter L. (1975) [1920] *The Frontier of Control*, London: Pluto.

Goodway, David (ed.) (1989) *For Anarchism*, London: Routledge.

Gordon, Peter and White, John (1979) *Philosophers as Educational Reformers: The Influence of Idealism on British Educational Thought and Practice*, London: Routledge & Kegan Paul.

Gorham, D. (1975) 'English Militancy and the Canadian Suffrage Movement', *Atlantis: A Woman's Studies Journal*, 1(1), Autumn.

Gorham, Deborah (1990) '"Have We Really Rounded Seraglio Point?": Vera Brittan and Inter-war feminism', in Harold L. Smith (ed.) *British Feminism in the Twentieth Century*, Aldershot: Edward Elgar.

Gorham, Deborah (1996) *Vera Brittain: A Feminist Life*, Oxford: Blackwell.

Gorman, Clem (1975) *People Together: A Guide to Communal Living*, Frogmore: Paladin.

Grainger, J.H. (1986) *Patriotisms: Britain 1900–1939*, London: Routledge & Kegan Paul.

Gray, John (1984) *Hayek on Liberty*, Oxford: Blackwell.

Gray, John (1986) *Liberalism*, Milton Keynes: Open University.

Gray, John (1989) *Liberalisms: Essays in Political Philosophy*, London: Routledge.

Gray, John (1993a) *Beyond the New Right*, London: Routledge.

Gray, John (1993b) *Post-Liberalism: Studies in Political Thought*, London: Routledge.

Gray, John (1995a) 'Harnessing the Market', *New Left Review*, 210, March/April.

Gray, John (1995b) *Enlightenment's Wake: Politics and Culture at the Close of the Modern Age*, London: Routledge.

Gray, John (1995c) *Isaiah Berlin*, London: HarperCollins.

Gray, John with Kukathas, Chandran, Minford, Patrick and Plant, Raymond (1992) *The Moral Foundations of Market Institutions*, London: IEA.

Gray, Tim (1990) 'Herbert Spencer's Liberalism: From Social Statics to Social Dynamics', in Richard Bellamy (ed.) *Victorian Liberalism: Nineteenth Century Political Thought and Practice*, London: Routledge.

Greaves, H.R.G. (1960) 'Political Theory Today', *Political Science Quarterly*, 75(1), March.

Greaves, H.R.G. (1964) *Democratic Participation and Public Enterprise*, L.T. Hobhouse Memorial Trust Lecture No. 34, London: The Athlone Press.

Green, D.G. (1987) *The New Right: The Counter-Revolution in Political, Economic and Social Thought*, Brighton: Harvester.

Green, T.H. (1886) 'Lectures on the Principles of Political Obligation', *The Works of Thomas Hill Green*, ed. R.L. Nettleship, vol. 2., London: Longman.

Green, T.H. (1888) 'Liberal Legislation and Freedom of Contract', *The Works of Thomas Hill Green*, ed. R.L. Nettleship, vol. 3. London: Longman & Co.

Greengarten, I.M. (1981) *Thomas Hill Green and the Development of Liberal-Democratic Thought*, Toronto: University of Toronto Press.

Greenleaf, W.H. (1966) *Oakeshott's Philosophical Politics*, London: Longmans.

Greenleaf, W.H. (1973) 'The Character of Modern British Conservatism', in R.

Benewick, R.N. Berki and B. Parekh (eds) *Knowledge and Belief in Politics*, London: George Allen & Unwin.

Greenleaf, W.H. (1975a) 'Toulmin Smith and the British Political Tradition', *Public Administration*, Spring.

Greenleaf, W.H. (1975b) 'The Character of Modern British Politics', *Parliamentary Affairs*, 28(4), Autumn.

Greenleaf, W.H. (1981) 'Laski and British Socialism', *History of Political Thought*, 2(3).

Greenleaf, W.H. (1983a) *The British Political Tradition, vol. 1: The Rise of Collectivism*, London: Methuen.

Greenleaf, W.H. (1983b) *The British Political Tradition, vol. 2: The Ideological Heritage*, London: Methuen.

Greenleaf, W.H. (1987) *The British Political Tradition, vol. 3: A Much Governed Nation*, 2 Parts, London: Methuen.

Greer, Germaine (1970) *The Female Eunuch*, London: McGibbon & Kee.

Greer, Germaine (1984) *Sex and Destiny: The Politics of Human Fertility*, London: Secker & Warburg.

Griffith, Gareth (1993) *Socialism and Superior Brains: The Political Thought of Bernard Shaw*, London: Routledge.

Griffith, John (1983) *Socialism in a Cold Climate*, London: Unwin.

Griffiths, Richard (1978) 'British Conservatism and the Lessons of the Continental Right', in Maurice Cowling (ed.) *Conservative Essays*, London: Cassell.

Griggs, Edwin (1991) 'Hayek on Freedom and the Welfare State', *Politics*, 11(1): 37–42.

Gummer, John Selwyn (1971) *The Permissive Society*, London: Cassell.

Guy, Josephine (1991) *The British Avant-Garde: The Theory and Politics of Tradition*, Hemel Hempstead: Harvester.

Haas, Richard and Knox, Oliver (eds) (1992) *Policies of Thatcherism: Thoughts from a London Thinktank*, London: CPSU Press of America.

Hain, P. (ed.) (1976) *Community Politics*, London: John Calder.

Haldane, R.B. (1902) *Education and Empire*, London: John Murray.

Hall, J. and Higgins, J. (1976) 'What Influences Today's Labour M.P.s?', 'What Influences Today's Tory M.P.s?', *New Society*, 2 and 9 December.

Hall, Stuart and Jacques, Martin (1983) *The Politics of Thatcherism*, London: Lawrence & Wishart.

Hamilton, A. (1971) *The Appeal of Fascism*, London: Anthony Blond.

Hamilton, Cicely (1981) [1909] *Marriage as a Trade*, London: The Women's Press.

Hamilton, M.A. (1934) *Sidney and Beatrice Webb*, London: Sampson Low.

Hansard Society (1961) *Parliamentary Reform 1933–60; A Survey of Suggested Reforms*, London: Hansard Society.

Hardie, J.K. (1906) *The Citizenship of Women: A Plea for Women's Suffrage*, London: Independent Labour Party.

Hardie, J.K. (1907) *From Serfdom to Socialism*, London: George Allen.

Harris, D. (1987) *Justifying State Welfare: The New Right versus the Old Left*, Oxford: Blackwell.

Harris, J. (1972) *Unemployment and Politics: A Study in English Social Policy, 1886–1914*, Oxford: Clarendon Press.

Harris, Jose (1993) *Private Lives, Public Spirit: A Social History of Britain 1870–1914*, Oxford: Oxford University Press.

Harris, Jose (1995) 'Between Civic Virtue and Social Darwinism: The Concept of the Residuum', in David Englander and Rosemary O'Day (eds) *Retrieved Riches: Social Investigation in Britain 1830–1914*, Aldershot: Scolar Press.

Harris, Jose (1996) 'Political Thought and the State', in S.J.D. Green and R.C. Whiting (eds) *The Boundaries of the State In Modern Britain*, Cambridge: Cambridge University Press.

Harris, S.H. (1943) *Auberon Herbert: Crusader for Liberty*, London: Williams & Norgate.

Harrison, F. (1918) [1893] 'Family Life', in *On Society*, London: Macmillan.

Harrison, J.R. (1966) *The Reactionaries*, London: Victor Gollancz.

Harrison, Royden (1987) 'Sidney and Beatrice Webb', in Carl Levy (ed.) *Socialism and the Intelligentsia, 1880–1914*, London: Routledge.

Harvey, Charles and Press, Jon (1991) *William Morris: Design and Enterprise in Victorian Britain*, Manchester: Manchester University Press.

Harvie, Christopher (1976) *The Lights of Liberalism*, London: Allen Lane.

Harvie, Christopher (1991) *The Centre of Things: Political Fiction from Disraeli to the Present*, London: Unwin Hyman.

Haseler, Stephen (1996) *The English Tribe: Identity, Nation and Europe*, Basingstoke: Macmillan.

Haworth, Alan (1995) *Anti-Libertarianism: Markets, Philosophy and Myth*, London: Routledge.

Hayek, F.A. (1935) *Collectivist Economic Planning*, London: Routledge.

Hayek, F.A. (1944) *The Road to Serfdom*, London: Routledge.

Hayek, F.A. (1949) *Individualism and Economic Order*, London: Routledge.

Hayek, F.A. (1960) *The Constitution of Liberty*, London: Routledge & Kegan Paul.

Hayek, F.A. (1973) 'Rules and Order', in *Law, Legislation and Liberty*, London: Routledge & Kegan Paul.

Hayek, F.A. (1976) 'The Mirage of Social Justice' in *Law, Legislation and Liberty*, London: Routledge & Kegan Paul.

Hayek, F.A. (1979) 'The Political Order of a Free People', in *Law, Legislation and Liberty*, London: Routledge & Kegan Paul.

Hayek, F.A. (1982) *Law, Legislation and Liberty*, London: Routledge & Kegan Paul.

Hayek, F.A. (1988) *The Fatal Conceit: The Errors of Socialism*, London: Routledge.

Hearnshaw, F.J.C. (1933) *Conservatism in England, an Analytical, Historical, and Political Survey*, London: Macmillan.

Henderson, A. (1911) *George Bernard Shaw: His Life and Works*, London: Hurst & Blackett.

Henderson, A. (1932) *Bernard Shaw: Playboy and Prophet*, London: D. Appleton & Co.

Henderson, A. (1956) *George Bernard Shaw: Man of the Century*, New York: Appleton-Century-Crofts.

Henderson, P. (ed.) (1950) *The Letters of William Morris to his Family and Friends*, London: Longmans, Green & Co.

Henderson, P. (1967) *William Morris: His Life, Work, and Friends*, London: Thames & Hudson.

Herbert, A. (1880) *The Choice between Personal Freedom and State Protection.*

Herbert, A. (1884) *A Politician in Trouble about his Soul*, London: Chapman & Hall.

Herbert, A. (1885) *The Free Mind in the Free Body: Anti-Force Papers no. 1*, London: Women's Press Society.

Herbert, A. (1898) 'Salvation by Force', *The Humanitarian*, October.

Herbert, A. (1908) *The Voluntarist Creed*, London: W.J. Simpson.

Herbert, A. and Levy, J.H. (1912) *Taxation and Anarchism*, London: Personal Rights Association.

Hewart, Lord (1929) *The New Despotism*, London: Ernest Benn.

Higginbottom, Melvyn David (1992) *Intellectuals and British Fascism: A Study of Henry Williamson*, London: Janus.

Hill, Christopher and Beshoff, Pamela (eds) (1995) *Two Worlds of International Relations: Academics, Practitioners and the Trade in Ideas*, London: LSE/ Routledge.

Hill, D.M. (1974) *Democratic Theory and Local Government*, London: George Allen & Unwin.

Himmelfarb, G. (1974) *On Liberty and Liberalism: The Case of John Stuart Mill*, New York: Alfred A. Knopf.

Hindess, B. (1987) *Freedom, Equality, and the Market: Arguments on Social Policy*, London: Tavistock.

Hindess, Barry (ed.) (1990) *Reactions to the Right*, London: Routledge.

Hinton, J. (1973) *The First Shop Stewards' Movement*, London: George Allen & Unwin.

Hinton, James (1989) *Protests and Visions: Peace Politics in 20th Century Britain*, London: Hutchinson Radius.

Hirst, Paul (ed.) (1989) *The Pluralist Theory of the State: Selected Writings of G.D.H. Cole, J.N. Figgis, and H.J. Laski*, London: Routledge.

Hirst, Paul Q. (1990) *Representative Democracy and its Limits*, Cambridge: Polity.

Hirst, Paul (1994) *Associative Democracy: New Forms of Economic and Social Governance*, Cambridge: Polity.

Hobhouse, L.T. (1893) *The Labour Movement*, London: T. Fisher Unwin.

Hobhouse, L.T. (1918) *The Metaphysical Theory of the State, a Criticism*, London: George Allen & Unwin.

Hobhouse, L.T. (1964) [1911] *Liberalism*, New York: Oxford University Press.

Hobhouse, L.T. (1972) [1905] *Democracy and Reaction*, Brighton: Harvester.

Hobsbawm, E.J. (1972) [1964] *Labouring Men: Studies in the History of Labour*, London: Weidenfeld & Nicolson.

Hobsbawm, Eric (1990) *Nations and Nationalism since 1780: Programme, Myth, Reality*, Cambridge: Cambridge University Press.

Hobsbawn, Eric (1994) *Age of Extremes: The Short Twentieth Century 1914–1991*, London: Michael Joseph.

Hobson, J.A. (1898) 'Rich Man's Anarchism', *The Humanitarian*, June:

Hobson, J.A. (1904) *John Ruskin Social Reformer*, London: James Nisbet.

Hobson, J.A. (1909) *The Crisis of Liberalism: New Issues of Democracy*, London: P.S. King.

Hobson, J.A. (1921) *Problems of a New World*, London: Allen & Unwin.

Hobson, J.A. and Ginsberg, M. (1931) *L.T. Hobhouse: His Life and Work*, London: Allen & Unwin.

Hobson, S.G. (1917) [1914] *National Guilds: an Enquiry into the Wage System and the Way Out*, ed. A.R. Orage, 2nd edn, London: G. Bell.

Hoffman, John (1995) *Beyond the State*, Cambridge: Polity.

Hogg, Q. (1947) *The Case for Conservatism*, West Drayton: Penguin.

Hollis, C. (1970) *The Mind of Chesterton*, London: Hollis & Carter.

Holloway, H.A. (1963) 'A.D. Lindsay and the Problems of Mass Democracy', *Western Political Quarterly*, 16(4), December.

Holton, B. (1976) *British Syndicalism 1900–1914: Myths and Realities*, London: Pluto.

Holton, R. (1972) 'The Daily Herald and the Labour Unrest', *Bulletin of the Society for the Study of Labour History*, 25, Autumn.

Holton, Sandra Stanley (1987) *Feminism and Democracy: Women's Suffrage and Reform Politics in Britain, 1900–1918*, Cambridge: Cambridge University Press.

Holton, Sandra Stanley (1990) 'In Sorrowful Wrath: Suffrage Militancy and the Romantic Feminism of Emmeline Pankhurst', in Harold L. Smith (ed.) *British Feminism in the Twentieth Century*, Aldershot: Edward Elgar.

Honderich, Ted (1990) *Conservatism*, London: Hamish Hamilton.

Hoover, Kenneth R. (1987) 'The Rise of Conservative Capitalism: Ideological Tensions Within the Reagan and Thatcher Governments', *Comparative Studies in Society and History*, 29: 245–68.

Hoover, Kenneth and Plant, Raymond (1989) *Conservative Capitalism in Britain and the United States: A Critical Appraisal*, London: Routledge.

Horton, John (1990) 'Weight or Lightness? Political Philosophy and its Prospects', in Adrian Leftwich (ed.) *New Developments in Political Science*, Aldershot: Edward Elgar.

Howard, E. (1898) *To-morrow: A Peaceful Path to Social Reform*, London: Swan Sonnenschein.

Howe, Stephen (1993) *Anticolonialism in British Politics: The Left and the End of Empire, 1918–1964*, Oxford: Clarendon.

Howell, D. (1986) *A Lost Left: Three Studies in Socialism and Nationalism*, Manchester: Manchester University Press.

Howell, G. (1891) 'Liberty for Labour', in Thomas Mackay (ed.) *A Plea for Liberty*, London: John Murray.

Hughes, H.S. (1959) *Consciousness and Society: The Reorientation of European Social Thought 1890–1930*, London: McGibbon & Kee.

Hughes, H. Stuart (1988) *Sophisticated Rebels: The Political Culture of European Dissent, 1968–1987*, London: Harvard University Press.

Hulse, J.W. (1970) *Revolutionists in London: A Study of Five Unorthodox Socialists*, Oxford: Clarendon Press.

Humm, Maggie (1992) *Feminisms: A Reader*, Hemel Hempstead: Harvester/Wheatsheaf.

Hunt, Karen (1996) *Equivocal Feminists: The Social Democratic Federation and the Woman Question 1884–1911*, Cambridge: Cambridge University Press.

Hutton, Will (1996) *The State We're In*, 2nd edn, London: Jonathan Cape.

Huxley, A. (1946) [1932] *Brave New World*, Harmondsworth: Penguin.

Huxley, A. (1962) *Island*, London: Chatto & Windus.

Huxley, T.H. (1898) [1894] *Evolution and Ethics and other Essays*, London: Macmillan.

Hyman, R. (1974) 'Workers' Control and Revolutionary Theory', in R.

Miliband and J. Saville (eds) *The Socialist Register 1974*, London: The Merlin Press.

Hyndman, H.M. (1881) *The Text Book of Democracy: England for All*, London: E.W. Allen.

Hyndman, H.M. (1884a) *The Coming Revolution in England*, London: W. Reeves.

Hyndman, H.M. (1884b) *The Social Reconstruction of England*, London: W. Reeves.

Hynes, Samuel (ed.) (1971) *Twentieth Century Interpretations of 1984*, Englewood Cliffs, N.J.: Prentice-Hall.

Hynes, S. (1972) *Edwardian Occasions, Essays in English Writing in the Early Twentieth Century*, London: Oxford University Press.

Hynes, S. (1976) *The Auden Generation*, London: The Bodley Head.

Ingle, Stephen (1993) *George Orwell*, Manchester: Manchester University Press.

Inglis, Fred (1995) *Raymond Williams*, London: Routledge.

Institute of Public Policy Research (1993) *A Written Constitution for the United Kingdom*, Poole: Cassell.

Ironside, Philip (1996) *The Social and Political Thought of Bertrand Russell: The Development of Aristocratic Liberalism*, Cambridge: Cambridge University Press.

Jardine, Lisa and Swindells, Julia (1989) 'Homage to George Orwell: The Dream of a Common Culture and Other Minefields', in Terry Eagleton (ed.) *Raymond Williams: Critical Perspectives*, London: Polity.

Jay, D. (1947) [1938] *The Socialist Case*, London: Faber.

Jeffreys, Sheila (1986) *The Spinster and her Enemies: Feminism and Sexuality 1880–1930*, London: Routledge & Kegan Paul.

Jenkins, Simon (1995) *Accountable to None: The Tory Nationalisation of Britain*, London: Hamish Hamilton.

Jevons, W.S. (1910) [1882] *The State in Relation to Labour*, 4th edn, London: Macmillan.

Jewkes, J. (1968) *The New Ordeal by Planning: The Experience of the 40s and 60s*, London: Macmillan.

Johnson, Paul (1994) *Wake Up Britain! A Latter Day Pamphlet*, London: Weidenfeld & Nicolson.

Jones, A.R. and Thomas, G. (eds) (1973) *Presenting Saunders Lewis*, Cardiff: University of Wales Press.

Jones, G. (1986) *Social Hygiene in Twentieth Century Britain*, London: Croom Helm.

Jones, J.R. (1965) 'England', in H. Rogger and E. Weber (eds) *The European Right*, Berkeley: University of California Press.

Jones, Sir H. (1910) *The Working Faith of the Social Reformer*, London: Macmillan.

Jones, Sir H. (1919) *The Principles of Citizenship*, London: Macmillan.

Jones, Stuart (1995) *Political Thought in 19th Century Britain*, London: Macmillan.

Jordan, Grant (1993) *Public Policy and the New Right*, London: Pinter.

Joseph, Keith and Sumption, Jonathan (1979) *Equality*, London: John Murray.

Joyce, Patrick (1994) *Democratic Subjects: The Self and the Social in Nineteenth Century England*, Cambridge: Cambridge University Press.

Julius, Anthony (1995) *T.S. Eliot, Anti-Semitism and Literary Form*, Cambridge: Cambridge University Press.

Kaye, Harvey J. and McClelland, Keith (1990) *E.P. Thompson: Critical Perspectives*, Cambridge: Polity.

Keane, John (1995) *Tom Paine: A Political Life*, London: Bloomsbury.

Kedourie, E. (1970) 'Conservatism and the Conservative Party', *Solon*, 1(4), October.

Kedourie, E. (1972) 'Salisbury as a Conservative Intellectual', *Encounter*, June.

Kendall, W. (1969) *The Revolutionary Movement in Britain, 1900–1921*, London: Weidenfeld & Nicolson.

Kenny, Michael (1991) 'Facing Up To The Future: Community in the Work of Raymond Williams in the Fifties and Sixties', *Politics*, 11(2), October: 14–19.

Kenny, Michael (1995) *The First New Left: British Intellectuals After Stalin*, London: Lawrence & Wishart.

Kent, John (1992) *William Temple: Church, State and Society in Britain, 1880–1950*, Cambridge: Cambridge University Press.

Kidd, B. (1895) [1894] *Social Evolution*, London: Macmillan.

King, D.S. (1987) *The New Right: Politics, Markets and Citizenship*, London: Macmillan.

King, Desmond S. (1988) 'New Right Ideology, Welfare State Form, and Citizenship: A Comment on Conservative Capitalism', *Comparative Studies in Society*, 30(4).

King, Desmond (1994) 'The New Right and Public Policy', *Political Studies*, 42(3), September.

King, Desmond and Stoker, Gary (1996) *Rethinking Local Democracy*, Basingstoke: Macmillan.

King, Desmond and Waldron, Jeremy (1988) 'Citizenship, Social Citizenship and the Defence of Welfare Provision', *British Journal of Political Science*, 18: 415–43.

Kinnock, Neil (1992) *Thorns and Roses: Speeches 1983–1991*, London: Hutchinson.

Kirk, R. (1954) *The Conservative Mind*, London: Faber.

Kitchen, P. (1975) *A Most Unsettling Person: An Introduction to the Ideas and Life of Patrick Geddes*, London: Gollancz.

Kley, Roland (1994) *Hayek's Social and Political Thought*, Oxford: Oxford University Press.

Koebner, R. and Schmidt, H. (1964) *Imperialism: the Story and Significance of a Political Word, 1840–1960*, Cambridge: Cambridge University Press.

Kojecky, R. (1971) *T.S. Eliot's Social Criticism*, London: Faber.

Kramnick, Isaac and Sheerman, Barry (1993) *Harold Laski: A Life on the Left*, London: Hamish Hamilton.

Kropotkin, P. (1899) *Fields, Factories and Workshops*, London: Hutchinson.

Kropotkin, P. (1902) *Mutual Aid*, London: William Heinemann.

Kukathas, Chandram (1989) *Hayek and Modern Liberalism*, Oxford: Clarendon Press.

Kumar, K. (1987) *Utopia and Anti-Utopia in Modern Times*, Oxford: Blackwell.

Kumar, Krishan (1995) 'Introduction', *William Morris, News from Nowhere, or an epoch of rest: being some chapters from a Utopian Romance*, Cambridge: Cambridge Texts.

Kymlicka, W. (1989) *Liberalism, Community and Culture*, Oxford: Clarendon.

Kymlicka, Will (1991) *Contemporary Political Philosophy: An Introduction*, Oxford: Clarendon.

Lane, J. (1978) [1887] *Anti-Statist, Communist Manifesto*, Sanday, Orkney: Cienfuegos Press.

Laski, H.J. (1925) *A Grammar of Politics*, London: George Allen & Unwin.

Laski, H.J. (1938) *Parliamentary Government in England: A Commentary*, London: George Allen & Unwin.

Laski, H.J. (1943) *Reflections on the Revolution of our Time*, London: George Allen & Unwin.

Laski, H.J. (1951) *Reflections on the Constitution: The House of Commons, the Cabinet, the Civil Service*, Manchester: Manchester University Press.

Laski, H.J. (1968) [1917] *Studies in the Problem of Sovereignty*, London: George Allen & Unwin.

Laslett, P. and Runciman, W.G. (eds) (1962) *Philosophy, Politics and Society*, Oxford: Blackwell.

Lawrence, D.H. (1930) 'Introduction to F.M. Dostoievsky, The Grand Inquisitor', in E.D. McDonald (ed.) *Phoenix: The Posthumous Papers of D.H. Lawrence*, London: Heinemann.

Leach, Robert F. (1983) 'Thatcherism, Liberalism and Tory Collectivism', *Politics*, 3(1).

Leach, Robert (1991) *British Political Ideologies*, Hemel Hempstead: Philip Allan.

Lecky, W.E.H. (1896) *Democracy and Liberty*, 2 vols, London: Longman.

Lee, Francis (1988) *Fabianism and Colonialism: The Life and Political Thought of Lord Sydney Olivier*, London: Defiant Books.

LeGrand, J. (1982) *The Strategy of Equality*, London: Allen & Unwin.

LeGrand, Julian and Estrin, Saul (eds) (1989) *Market Socialism*, Oxford: Clarendon.

Leruez, J. (1975) *Economic Planning and Politics in Britain*, London: Martin Robertson.

Letwin, S.R. (1965) *The Pursuit of Certainty*, Cambridge: Cambridge University Press.

Letwin, Shirley Robin (1978) 'On Conservative Individualism', in Maurice Cowling (ed.) *Conservative Essays*, London: Cassell.

Letwin, Shirley Robin (1992) *The Anatomy of Thatcherism*, London: HarperCollins.

Levin, Michael (1992) *The Spectre of Democracy: The Rise of Modern Democracy as Seen by its Critics*, London: Macmillan.

Levine, Philippa (1987) *Victorian Feminism 1850–1900*, London: Hutchinson.

Levitas, Ruth (1985) 'New Right Utopias', *Radical Philosophy*, 39: 3–9.

Levitas, Ruth (ed.) (1986) *The Ideology of the New Right*, Cambridge: Polity.

Levitas, R. (1990) *The Concept of Utopia*, Oxford: Philip Allan.

Levy, Carl (ed.) (1987) *Socialism and the Intelligentsia, 1880–1914*, London: Routledge.

Lewis, Jane (1981) 'Introduction', Cicely Hamilton, *Marriage as a Trade*, London: The Women's Press.

Lewis, Jane (ed.) (1987) *Before the Vote was Won: Arguments for and against Women's Suffrage 1864–1896*, London: Routledge.

Lewis, Jane (1991) *Women and Social Action in Victorian and Edwardian England*, Aldershot: Edward Elgar.

Lewis, Jane (1995) 'Social Facts, Social Theory and Social Change: The Ideas of Booth in Relation to those of Beatrice Webb, Octavia Hill and Helen Bosanquet', in David Englander and Rosemary O'Day (eds), *Retrieved Riches: Social Investigation in Britain 1830–1914*, Aldershot: Scolar Press.

Lewis, P.W. (1926) *The Art of Being Ruled*, London: Chatto & Windus.

Lewis, P.W. (1950) *Rude Assignment*, London: Hutchinson.

Light, Alison (1991) *Forever England: Femininity, Literature and Conservatism Between the Wars*, London: Routledge.

Linden, Marcel van der and Thorpe, Wayne (eds) (1990) *Revolutionary Syndicalism: An International Perspective*, Aldershot: Scolar Press.

Lindsay, J. (1914) 'The State in Recent Political Theory', *Political Quarterly*, 1(1), February.

Lindsay, J. (1975) *William Morris: His Life and Work*, London: Constable.

Lippincott, B.E. (1938) *Victorian Critics of Democracy: Carlyle, Ruskin, Arnold, Stephen, Maine, Lecky*, Minneapolis: University of Minnesota Press.

Lively, Jack and Lively, Adam (eds) (1994) *Democracy in Britain: A Reader*, Oxford: Blackwell.

London Edinburgh Weekend Return Group (1980) *In and Against the State*, London: Pluto.

Loney, Martin (1986) *The Politics of Greed: The New Right and the Welfare State*, London: Pluto.

Loney, Martin (1987) *The State or the Market*, Oxford: Oxford University Press.

Lovell, Terry (ed.) (1990) *British Feminist Thought: A Reader*, Oxford: Blackwell.

Lovenduski, J. (1988) 'Feminism in the 1980s', *Politics*, 8(1): 32–5.

Lovenduski, Joni and Randall, Vicky (1993) *Contemporary Feminist Politics: Women and Power in Britain*, Oxford: Oxford University Press.

Lovibond, Sabina (1989) 'Feminism and Postmodernism', *New Left Review*, 178, November/December.

Lovibond, Sabina (1992) 'Feminism and Pragmatism: A Reply to Rorty', *New Left Review*, 193, May/June.

Lovibond, Sabina (1994) 'Feminism and the "Crisis of Rationality"', *New Left Review*, 207, September/October.

Lucas, J. (1971) 'Conservatism and Revolution in the 1880s', in J. Lucas (ed.) *Literature and Politics in the Nineteenth Century*, London: Methuen.

Lucas, John (1990) *England and Englishness: Ideas of Englishness in English Poetry, 1688–1900*, London: Hogarth Press.

Lucy, H.W. (ed.) (1885) *Speeches of the Right Hon. Joseph Chamberlain, M.P.*, London: George Routledge & Sons.

Ludlam Steve and Smith, Martin J. (1996) *Contemporary British Conservatism*, London: Macmillan.

Ludovici, A.M. (1921) *The False Assumptions of 'Democracy'*, London: Heath Cranton.

Ludovici, A.M. (1929) [1923] *Woman: A Vindication*, London: Constable.

Ludovici, A.M. (1932) *The Sanctity of Private Property*, London: Heath Cranton.

Ludovici, A.M. (1967) *The Specious Origins of Liberalism: The Genesis of a Delusion*, London: Britons Publishing Co.

McBriar, A.M. (1962) *Fabian Socialism and English Politics 1884–1914*, Cambridge: Cambridge University Press.

McBriar, A.M. (1987) *An Edwardian Mixed Doubles. The Bosanquets versus the Webbs: A Study in British Social Policy 1890–1929*, Oxford: Clarendon Press.

MacCarthy, Fiona (1994) *William Morris: A Life for Our Time*, London: Faber.

McCarthy, John P. (1978) *Hilaire Belloc: Edwardian Radical*, Indianapolis: Liberty Press.

MacCoby, S. (1961) *English Radicalism – the End?*, London: George Allen & Unwin.

MacDonald, J.R. (1900) 'The People in Power', in S. Coit (ed.) *Ethical Democracy*, London: G. Richards.

MacDonald, J.R. (1905) *Socialism and Society*, London: Independent Labour Party.

MacDonald, J.R. (1909) *Socialism and Government*, London: Independent Labour Party.

MacDonald, J.R. (1912) *Syndicalism*, London: Constable.

McDonald, L.C. (1968) *Western Political Theory, from its Origins to the Present Day*, New York: Harcourt Brace Jovanovich.

MacFadyen, D. (1933) *Sir Ebenezer Howard and the Town Planning Movement*, Manchester: Manchester University Press.

Machlup, F. (ed.) (1977) *Essays on Hayek*, London: Routledge & Kegan Paul.

Mackail, J.W. (1899) *The Life of William Morris*, 2 vols, London: Longman, Green & Co.

MacKay, T. (1891) *A Plea for Liberty*, London: John Murray.

MacKechnie, W.S. (1896) *The State and the Individual*, Glasgow: J. MacLehose & Sons.

MacKenzie, N. (ed.) (1958) *Conviction*, London: MacGibbon & Kee.

MacKenzie, N. and J. (1973) *The Time Traveller: The Life of H.G. Wells*, London: Weidenfeld & Nicolson.

MacKenzie, N. and J. (1977) *The First Fabians*, London: Weidenfeld & Nicolson.

MacKenzie, W.J.M. (1975) 'Theories of Local Government', *Explorations in Government*, London: Macmillan.

McKibbin, Ross (1984) 'Why Was There No Marxism in Britain?', *English Historical Review*, 99(391): 299–331.

McLellan, David (ed.) (1991) *Socialism and Democracy*, London: Macmillan.

Macmillan, H. (1966) [1938] *The Middle Way*, London: Macmillan.

McNally, David (1993) *Against the Market*, London: Verso.

McPhee, C. and Fitzgerald, A. (eds) (1987) *The Non-Violent Militant: Selected Writings of Teresa Billington-Greig*, London: Routledge.

Maddox, G. (1986) 'The Christian Democracy of A.D. Lindsay', *Political Studies*, 34: 441–455.

Maine, Sir H. (1885) *Popular Government*, London: John Murray.

Mairet, P. (1936) *A.R. Orage: A Memoir*, London: J.M. Dent.

Maitland, F.W. (1900) 'Introduction', in Otto Gierke, *Political Theories of the Middle Ages*, Cambridge: Cambridge University Press.

Maitland, F.W. (1911) *Collected Papers*, ed. H.A.L. Fisher, Cambridge: Cambridge University Press.

Mallock, W.H. (1878) *The New Republic*, London: Chatto & Windus.

Mallock, W.H. (1886) *The Old Order Changes*, London: Richard Bentley.

Mallock, W.H. (1893) *Labour and the Popular Welfare*, London: Adam & Charles Black.

Mallock, W.H. (1908) *A Critical Examination of Socialism*, London: John Murray.

Mallock, W.H. (1918) *The Limits of Pure Democracy*, London: Chapman & Hall.

Mann, Michael (1995) 'As the Twentieth Century Ages', *New Left Review*, 214, November/December: 104–24.

Mann, T. (1974) [1910–11] *The Industrial Syndicalist*, Nottingham: Spokesman Books.

Mann, Tom (1988) *Tom Mann's Social and Economic Writing: A Pre-Syndicalist Selection*, ed. John Laurent, Nottingham: Spokesman.

Marcus, Jane (1987) *Suffrage and the Pankhursts*, London: Routledge & Kegan Paul.

Marquand, David (1991) *The Progressive Dilemma*, London: Heinemann.

Marr, Andrew (1995) *Ruling Britannia: The Failure and Future of British Democracy*, London: Michael Joseph.

Marshall, P. (1962) 'A British Sensation', in S.E. Bowman (ed.) *Edward Bellamy Abroad*, New York: Twayne Publishers.

Marshall, Peter (1992) *Demanding the Impossible: A History Of Anarchism*, London: HarperCollins.

Martin, K. (1953) *Harold Laski (1893–1950) A Biographical Memoir*, London: Victor Gollancz.

Martin, W. (1967) *'The New Age' Under Orage: Chapters in English Cultural History*, Manchester: Manchester University Press.

Marwick, A. (1964) 'Middle Opinion in the Thirties: Planning, Progress and Political "Agreement"', *English Historical Review*, 79, April.

Massey, Doreen, Segal, Lynne and Wainwright, Hilary (1984) 'And Now for the Good News', in James Curran (ed.) *The Future of the Left*, Cambridge: Polity and *New Socialist*.

Masterman, C.F.G. (1909) *The Condition of England*, London: Methuen.

Matthew, H.C.G. (1973) *The Liberal Imperialists: The Ideas and Politics of a Post-Gladstonian Elite*, Oxford: Oxford University Press.

Meadowcroft, James (ed.) (1994) *L.T. Hobhouse: Liberalism and Other Writings*, Cambridge: Cambridge University Press.

Meadowcroft, James (1995a) *Conceptualizing the State: Innovation and Dispute in British Political Thought 1880–1914*, Oxford: Clarendon.

Meadowcroft, James (1995b) 'State, "Statelessness", and The British Political Tradition', *Contemporary Politics*, 1(2), Summer: 37–56.

Meadowcroft, James (1996) *The Liberal Political Tradition: Contemporary Reappraisals*, Aldershot: Edward Elgar.

Meehan, Elizabeth (1990) 'British Feminism from the 1960s to the 1980s', in Harold L. Smith (ed.) *British Feminism in the Twentieth Century*, Aldershot: Edward Elgar.

Menon, N. (1942) *The Development of W.B. Yeats*, Edinburgh: Oliver & Boyd.

Miliband, David (ed.) (1994) *Reinventing the Left*, Cambridge: Polity.

Miliband, R. (1961) *Parliamentary Socialism*, London: George Allen & Unwin.

Miliband, Ralph (1994) *Socialism for a Sceptical Age*, Oxford: Polity.

Miliband, R., Panitch, L. and Saville, J. (1987) *The Socialist Register 1987*, London: The Merlin Press.

Mill, J.S. (1975a) [1859] 'On Liberty', *Three Essays*, with introduction by R. Wollhein, Oxford: Oxford University Press.

Mill, J.S. (1975b) [1869] 'The Subjection of Women', *Three Essays*, with introduction by R. Wollheim, Oxford: Oxford University Press.

Miller, David (1976) *Social Justice*, Oxford: Clarendon Press.

Miller, David (1989a) 'Why Markets', in Julian LeGrand and Saul Estrin (eds) *Market Socialism*, Oxford: Clarendon.

Miller, David (1989b) *Market, State and Community: Theoretical Foundations of Market Socialism*, Oxford: Clarendon.

Miller, David (1995) 'Citizenship and Pluralism', *Political Studies*, 43(3), September.

Millett, Kate (1971) *Sexual Politics*, London: Rupert Hart-Davis.

Minogue, K.R. (1991) 'Review of Kymlicka, Contemporary Political Philosophy', *Political Studies*, 39(2).

Mitchell, J. (1971) *Woman's Estate*, Harmondsworth: Penguin.

Mitchell, Juliet (1976) 'Women and Equality', in Juliet Mitchell and Ann Oakley (eds) *The Rights and Wrongs of Women*, Harmondsworth: Penguin.

Mitchell, J. (1984a) [1966] 'Women: The Longest Revolution', in *Women: The Longest Revolution: Essays in Feminism and Psychoanalysis*, London: Virago.

Mitchell, Juliet (1984a) *Women: The Longest Revolution: Essays in Feminism and Psychoanalysis*, London: Virago.

Mitchell, Juliet and Oakley, Ann (1976) *The Rights and Wrongs of Women*, Harmondsworth: Penguin.

Mitchell, Juliet and Oakley, Ann (1986) *What is Feminism?*, Oxford: Blackwell.

Montague, F.C. (1885) *The Limits of Individual Liberty*, London: Rivingtons.

Morgan, D. (1975) *Suffragists and Liberals: The Politics of Woman Suffrage in England*, Oxford: Blackwell.

Morgan, K.O. (1975) *Keir Hardie, Radical and Socialist*, London: Weidenfeld & Nicolson.

Morgan, K.O. (1976) 'In Pursuit of Power', *Times Literary Supplement*, 24 December.

Morgan, Kevin (1993) *Harry Pollitt*, Manchester: Manchester University Press.

Morgan, Patricia (1994) 'Double Income, No Kids: The Case for a Family Wage', in Caroline Quest (ed.) *Liberating Women ... From Modern Feminism*, London: IEA.

Morley, David and Chen, Kuan-Hsing (1995) *Stuart Hall: Critical Dialogues*, London: Routledge.

Morley, J. (1896) [1881] *The Life of Richard Cobden*, 2 vols, London: T. Fisher Unwin.

Morris, William (1924) [1890] *News from Nowhere*, London: Longmans, Green & Co.

Morris, William (1973a) [1894] 'How I Became a Socialist', in A.L. Morton (ed.) *Political Writings of William Morris*, London: Lawrence & Wishart.

Morris, William (1973b) [1885] 'Useful Work versus Useless Toil', in A.L.

Morton (ed.) *The Political Writings of William Morris*, London: Lawrence & Wishart.

Morris, W. and Bax, E.B. (1908) [1893] *Socialism, Its Growth and Outcome*, 3rd edn, London: Swan Sonnenschein.

Morton, A.L. (ed.) (1973) *The Political Writings of William Morris*, London: Lawrence & Wishart.

Mosley, O. (1932) *The Greater Britain*, London: British Union of Fascists.

Moss, R. (1975) *The Collapse of Democracy*, London: Temple Smith.

Mouffe, Chantal (1993) *The Return of the Political*, London: Verso.

Mowat, C.L. (1961) *The Charity Organisation Society 1869–1913*, London: Methuen.

Mulgan, Geoff (1994) *Politics in An Antipolitical Age*, Cambridge: Polity.

Mumford, L. (1923) *The Story of Utopias*, London: G.G. Harrap.

Murdoch, I. (1958) 'A House of Theory', in N. MacKenzie (ed.) *Conviction*, London: MacGibbon & Kee.

Murray, R. (1987) 'Ownership, Control, and the Market', *New Left Review*, 164.

Murray, R.H. (1929) *Studies in the English Social and Political Thinkers of the Nineteenth Century, vol. 2: Herbert Spencer to Ramsay MacDonald*, Cambridge: Heffer.

Nairn, Tom (1995) 'Breakwaters of 2000: From Ethnic to Civic Nationalism', *New Left Review*, 214, November/December: 91–103.

Neville, R. (1970) *Play Power*, London: Jonathan Cape.

Newman, Michael (1989) *John Strachey*, Manchester: Manchester University Press.

Newman, Michael (1993) *Harold Laski: A Political Biography*, London: Macmillan.

Newman, Michael (1995) 'The West European Left Today: Crisis, Decline or Renewal?', *Contemporary Politics*, 1(3), Autumn: 134–45.

Nicholls, D. (1962) 'Positive Liberty, 1880–1914', *American Political Science Review*, 56(1).

Nicholls, D. (1975a) *The Pluralist State*, London: Macmillan.

Nicholls, D. (1975b) *Three Varieties of Pluralism*, London: Macmillan.

Nicholls, D. (1989) *Deity and Domination: Images of God and the State in the 19th and 20th Centuries*, London: Routledge.

Nicholls, D. (1994) *The Pluralist State: The Political Ideas of J.N. Figgis and His Contemporaries*, 2nd edn, London: Macmillan.

Nicholson, P.P.N. (1987) 'A Moral View of Politics: T. H. Green and the British Idealists', *Political Studies*, 35(1), March: 116–22.

Nicholson, Peter P. (1990) *The Political Philosophy of the British Idealists: Selected Studies*, Cambridge: Cambridge University Press.

Nisbet, R. (1967) *The Sociological Tradition*, London: Heinemann.

Nisbet, R. (1976) *The Twilight of Authority*, London: Heinemann.

Nisbet, Robert A. (1986) *Conservatism: Dream and Reality*, Milton Keynes: Open University Press.

Normand, Tom (1992) *Wyndham Lewis: Holding the Mirror Up to Politics*, Cambridge: Cambridge University Press.

Norris, Christopher (ed.) (1985) *Inside the Myth: Orwell and the Left*, London: Lawrence & Wishart.

North, Michael (1992) *The Political Aesthetic of Yeats, Eliot and Pound*, Cambridge: Cambridge University Press.

Norton, Philip (1994) 'Conservatism', in Michael Foley (ed.) *Ideas that Shape Politics*, Manchester: Manchester University Press.

Nove, Alec (1983) *The Economics of Feasible Socialism*, London: Allen & Unwin.

Oakeshott, M. (1967) [1962] *Rationalism in Politics and Other Essays*, London: Methuen.

Oakeshott, M. (1975) *On Human Conduct*, Oxford: Clarendon Press.

Oakeshott, Michael (1993) *Morality and Politics in Modern Europe. The Harvard Lectures*, ed. Shirley Robin Letwin, intr. Kenneth Minogue, London: Yale University Press.

Oakley, Ann (1981) *Subject Women*, London: Martin Robertson.

O'Brien, M.D. (1893) *The Natural Right to Freedom*, London: Williams & Norgate.

O'Day, Rosemary (1993) 'Before the Webbs: Beatrice Potter's Early Investigations for Charles Booth's Inquiry', *History*, 78(253), June.

Offer, John (ed.) (1994) *Spencer: Political Writings*, Cambridge: Cambridge University Press.

O'Gorman, F. (1986) *British Conservatism: Conservative Thought from Burke to Thatcher*, London: Longman.

Okin, Susan Moller (1980) *Women in Western Political Thought*, London: Virago.

Okin, Susan Moller (1991) *Justice, Gender and the Family*, London: HarperCollins.

Olivier, S. (1889) 'The Basis of Socialism: Moral', in G.B. Shaw (ed.) *Fabian Essays in Socialism*, London: Allen & Unwin.

Orwell, G. (1938) *Homage to Catalonia*, London: Secker & Warburg.

Orwell, G. (1945) *Animal Farm*, London: Secker & Warburg.

Orwell, G. (1949) *Nineteen Eighty-Four*, London: Secker & Warburg.

Orwell, G. (1962) [1937] *The Road to Wigan Pier*, Harmondsworth: Penguin.

Orwell, G. (1968a) [1941] *The Lion and the Unicorn: Socialism and the English Genius*, Harmondsworth: Penguin.

Orwell, G. (1968b) *The Collected Essays, Journalism and Letters of George Orwell*, ed. Sonia Orwell and Ian Angus, 4 vols, Harmondsworth: Penguin.

Osmond, John (1978) *Creative Conflict: The Politics of Welsh Devolution*, London: Routledge & Kegan Paul.

Ostrogorski, M.Y. (1902) *Democracy and the Organization of Political Parties*, 2 vols, London: Macmillan.

O'Sullivan, N.K. (1972) 'Irrationalism in Politics: A Critique of R.G. Collingwood's New Leviathan', *Political Studies*, 20(2), June.

O'Sullivan, N.K. (1976) *Conservatism*, London: Dent.

Oxford University Socialist Discussion Group (1989) *Out of Apathy: Voices of the New Left 30 Years On*, London: Verso.

Palmer, Bryan D. (1994) *E.P. Thompson: Objections and Oppositions*, London: Verso.

Palmer, T. (1971) *The Trials of Oz*, London: Blond & Briggs.

Pankhurst, Christabel (1913) *The Great Scourge and How to End It*, London: E. Pankhurst.

Parrinder, Patrick (1993) *London Review of Books*, 8 April.

Parrinder, Patrick (1995) *Shadows of the Future: H.G. Wells, Science Fiction and Prophecy*, Liverpool: Liverpool University Press.

Pateman, Carole (1983a) 'Feminist Critiques of the Public/Private Dichotomy', in S. Benn and G. Gaus (eds) *Public and Private in Social Life*, London: Croom Helm.

Pateman, Carole (1983b) 'Feminism and Democracy', in Graeme Duncan (ed.) *Democratic Theory & Practice*, Cambridge: Cambridge University Press.

Pateman, C. (1988) *The Sexual Contract*, Oxford: Polity.

Pateman, Carole (1989) *The Disorder of Women: Democracy, Feminism and Political Theory*, Cambridge: Polity.

Paterson, Lindsay (1994) *The Autonomy of Modern Scotland*, Edinburgh: Edinburgh University Press.

Paul, Ellen Frankel (1988) 'Liberalism, Unintended Order, and Evolutionism', *Political Studies*, 36(2), June.

Paul, Ellen Frankel (1989) 'Herbert Spencer: Second Thoughts – A Response to Michael Taylor', *Political Studies*, 37(3), September.

Peardon, T.P. (1955) 'Two Currents in Contemporary English Political Theory', *American Political Science Review*, 49(2), June.

Pearson, R. and Williams, G. (1984) *Political Thought and Public Policy in the Nineteenth Century: An Introduction*, London: Longmans.

Pedersen, Susan and Mandler, Peter (eds) (1994) *After the Victorians: Private Conscience and Public Duty in Modern Britain*, London: Routledge.

Peel, J.D.Y. (1971) *Herbert Spencer: The Evolution of a Sociologist*, London: Heinemann.

Pelling, H. (ed.) (1954) *The Challenge of Socialism*, London: Adam & Charles Black.

Pelling, H. (1968) *Popular Politics and Society in Late Victorian Britain*, London: Macmillan.

Pembroke, Lord (1885) *Liberty and Socialism*, London: Liberty & Property Defence League.

Penty, A.J. (1906) *The Restoration of the Gild System*, London: Swan Sonnenschein.

Penty, A.J. (1937) *Distributism: A Manifesto*, London: Distributist League.

Percy, E. (1934) *Government in Transition*, London: Methuen.

Peregudov, S. (1980) 'Political Ideas in Modern Britain', *Modern and Contemporary History*, 206–8, Moscow: Academy of Sciences.

Pevsner, N. (1960) *Pioneers of Modern Design: From William Morris to Walter Gropius*, Harmondsworth: Penguin.

Pheby, John (ed.) (1994) *J.A. Hobson after Fifty Years: Freethinker of the Social Sciences*, London: Macmillan.

Phillips, Anne (ed.) (1987a) *Feminism and Equality*, Oxford: Blackwell.

Phillips, Anne (1987b) *Divided Loyalties*, London: Virago.

Phillips, Anne (1991) *Engendering Democracy*, Cambridge: Polity.

Phillips, Anne (1993) *Democracy and Difference*, Cambridge: Polity.

Phillips, Anne (1995) *The Politics of Presence*, Oxford: Oxford University Press.

Pierson, S. (1970) 'Edward Carpenter, Prophet of a Socialist Millenium', *Victorian Studies*, 13(3), March.

Pierson, Stanley (1973) *Marxism and the Origins of British Socialism*, Ithaca and London: Cornell University Press.

Pierson, Stanley (1979) *British Socialists: The Journey from Fantasy to Reality*, Cambridge, Mass.: Harvard University Press.

Pimlott, Ben, Wright, Anthony and Flower, Tony (eds) (1990) *The Alternative: Politics for a Change*, London: W.H. Allen.

Pitkin, H.F. (1974) 'The Roots of Conservatism: Michael Oakeshott and the Denial of Politics', in L.A. Coser and I. Howe (eds), *The New Conservatives: A Critique from the Left*, New York: Quadrangle/New York Times Book Co.

Plant, Raymond (1974) *Community and Ideology: An Essay in Applied Social Philosophy*, London: Routledge & Kegan Paul.

Plant, Raymond (1984) *Equality, Markets and the State*, London: Fabian Society.

Plant, Raymond (1988) *Citizenship, Rights and Socialism*, London: Fabian Society.

Plant, Raymond (1989) 'Socialism, Markets, and End States', in Julian LeGrand and Saul Estrin (eds) *Market Socialism*, Oxford: Clarendon.

Plant, Raymond and Barry, Norman (1990) *Citizenship and Rights in Thatcher's Britain: Two Views*, London: IEA Health and Welfare Unit.

Plowright, John (1987) 'Political Economy and Christian Polity: The Influence of Henry George in England Reassessed', *Victorian Studies, 30*, Winter.

Ponsonby, A. (1909) *The Camel and the Needle's Eye*, London: A.C. Fifield.

Popper, K.R. (1961a) [1945] *The Open Society and its Enemies*, 2 vols, London: Routledge.

Popper, K.R. (1961b) [1957] *The Poverty of Historicism*, 2nd edn, London: Routledge.

Porter, B. (1968) *Critics of Empire: British Radical Attitudes to Colonialism in Africa 1895–1914*, London: Macmillan.

Powell, Enoch J. (1965) *A Nation Not Afraid*, ed. John Wood, London: Hodder & Stoughton.

Powell, Enoch J. (1969) *Freedom and Reality*, Kingswood, Surrey: Elliot Right Way Books.

Pugh, Martin (1988) 'Popular Conservatism in Britain: Continuity and Change, 1880–1987', *The Journal of British Studies*, 27(3).

Pugh, Martin (1992) *Women and the Women's Movement in Britain, 1914–1959*, London: Macmillan.

Pugh, Patricia (1984) *Educate, Agitate, Organize: 100 years of Fabian Socialism*, London: Methuen.

Quail, John (1978) *The Slow Burning Fuse: The Lost History of the British Anarchists*, London: Granada Publishing.

Qualter, Terence H. (1980) *Graham Wallas and the Great Society*, London: Macmillan.

Quest, Caroline (ed.) (1992) *Equal Opportunities: A Feminist Fallacy*, London: IEA.

Quest, Caroline (1994) *Liberating Women ... From Modern Feminism*, London: IEA.

Quinton, Anthony (1978) *The Politics of Imperfection: The Religious Secular Tradition of Conservative thought in England from Hooker to Oakeshott*, London: Faber.

Randall, Vicky (1987) *Women and Politics*, London: Macmillan.

Randle, Michael (1994) *Civil Resistance*, London: Fontana.

Read, H. (1974) [1954] 'Poetry and Anarchism', in *Anarchy and Order, Essays in Politics*, London: Faber.

Réclus, E. and E. (1896) *Renouveau d'une cité*, Paris.

Red-Green Study Group (1995) *What on Earth is to be Done?*, Manchester: Red-Green Study Group.

Reid, F. (1971) 'Keir Hardie's Conversion to Socialism', in A. Briggs and J. Saville (eds) *Essays in Labour History 1886–1923*, London: Macmillan.

Reisman, D. (1982) *State and Welfare: Tawney, Galbraith, and Adam Smith*, London: Macmillan.

Reynolds, S. (1909) *A Poor Man's House*, London: John Lane.

Reynolds, S. (1910) 'What the Poor Want', *Quarterly Review*, 212, January.

Reynolds, S. (1923) *Letters of Stephen Reynolds*, ed. Harold Wright, Richmond: L. & V. Woolf.

Reynolds, S., Wooley, B. and Wooley, T. (1911) *Seems So! A Working Class View of B. & T. Wooley Politics*, London: Macmillan.

Rich, P.B. (1986) *Race and Empire in British Politics*, Cambridge: Cambridge University Press.

Richards, Janet Radcliffe (1980) *The Sceptical Feminist: A Philosophical Enquiry*, London: Routledge & Kegan Paul.

Richter, Melvin (1964) *The Politics of Conscience: T.H. Green and His Age*, London: Weidenfeld & Nicolson.

Ricks, Christopher (1988) *T.S. Eliot and Prejudice*, London: Faber.

Ridley, F.F. (1975) *The Study of Government: Political Science and Public Administration*, London: Allen & Unwin.

Rigby, A. (1974) *Alternative Realities*, London: Routledge & Kegan Paul.

Rigby, L.M. (1950) *John Adam Cramb: Patriot, Historian, Mystic*, London: Adam & Charles Black.

Ring, Jenniffer (1985) 'Mill's The Subjection of Women: The Methodological Limits of Liberal Feminism', *The Review of Politics*, 47(1), January.

Ritchie, D.G. (1895) [1889] *Darwinism and Politics*, 3rd edn, London: Swan Sonnenschein.

Ritchie, D.G. (1891) *The Principles of State Interference*, London: Swan Sonnenschein.

Roach, J. (1957) 'Liberalism and the Victorian Intelligentsia', *Cambridge Historical Journal*, 13(1).

Robbins, K. (1968) 'James Bryce', *Journal of Contemporary History*, 3(4).

Roberts, E. (1973) *Workers' Control*, London: Allen & Unwin.

Robson, W.A. (1928) *Justice and Administrative Law: A Study of the British Constitution*, London: Macmillan.

Robson, W.A. (1976) *Welfare State and Welfare Society: Illusion and Reality*, London: George Allen & Unwin.

Rockow, L. (1925) *Contemporary Political Thought in England*, London: Leonard Parsons.

Rodden, John (1989) *The Politics of Literary Reputation: The Making and Claiming of 'St George' Orwell*, Oxford: Oxford University Press.

Rolph, C.H. (1973) *Kingsley: The Life, Letters, and Diaries of Kingsley Martin*, London: Victor Gollancz.

Roper, J. (1989) *Democracy and its Critics: Anglo-American Democratic Thought in the Nineteenth Century*, London: Unwin Hyman.

Rorty, Richard (1989) *Contingency, Irony and Solidarity*, Cambridge: Cambridge University Press.

Roth, A. (1970) *Enoch Powell: Tory Tribune*, London: Macdonald.

Rover, A. (1967) *Women's Suffrage and Party Politics in Britain 1886–1914*, London: Routledge & Kegan Paul.

Rowbotham, Sheila (1973a) *Hidden From History*, London: Pluto.

Rowbotham, Sheila (1973b) *Women's Consciousness, Man's World*, Harmondsworth: Penguin.

Rowbotham, S. (1977a) 'Edward Carpenter: Prophet of the New Life', in S. Rowbotham and J. Weeks, *Socialism and the New Life: The Personal and Sexual Politics of Edward Carpenter and Havelock Ellis*, London: Pluto.

Rowbotham, S. (1977b) *A New World for Women: Stella Browne – Socialist Feminist*, London: Pluto.

Rowbotham, Sheila and Weeks, Jeffrey (1977) *Socialism and The New Life*, London: Pluto.

Rowbotham, Sheila, Segal, Lynne and Wainwright, Hilary (1979) *Beyond the Fragments*, London: Merlin Press.

Ruddick, Sarah (1990) *Maternal Thinking: Towards a Politics of Peace*, London: The Women's Press.

Russell, B. (1916) *Principles of Social Reconstruction*, London: George Allen & Unwin.

Russell, B. (1918) *Roads to Freedom: Socialism, Anarchism, and Syndicalism*, London: George Allen & Unwin.

Russell, B. (1948) [1920] *The Practice and Theory of Bolshevism*, New York: Simon & Schuster.

Russell, B. and D. (1923) *The Prospects of Industrial Civilization*, London: George Allen & Unwin.

Rustin, Mike (1985) *For A Pluralist Socialism*, London: Verso.

Rustin, Mike (1992) 'Citizenship and Charter 88', *New Left Review*, 191(37–42), January/February.

Ryan, Alan (1984) *Property and Political Theory*, Oxford: Blackwell.

Ryan, A. (1988) *Bertrand Russell: A Political Life*, London: Allen Lane.

Sachs, A. (1976) 'The Myth of Judicial Neutrality', in Pat Carlen (ed.) *The Sociology of Law*, Keele: Sociological Review Monographs 23.

Saville, J. (1976) 'The Twentieth Congress and the British Communist Party', in R. Miliband and J. Saville (eds) *The Socialist Register 1976*, London: The Merlin Press.

Schaffle, A. (1889) *The Quintessence of Socialism*, translated from the 8th German edn under the supervision of Bernard Bosanquet, London: Swan.

Schneer, Jonathan (1990) *George Lansbury*, Manchester: Manchester University Press.

Schreiner, Olive (1978) [1911] *Woman and Labour*, London: Virago.

Scruton, Roger (1984) [1980] *The Meaning of Conservatism*, Harmondsworth: Penguin.

Scruton, Roger (1986) *Sexual Desire*, London: Weidenfeld & Nicolson.

Scruton, Roger (1987) *A Land Held Hostage*, London: The Claridge Press.

Scruton, Roger (ed.) (1991) *Conservative Texts*, London: Macmillan.

Searle, G.R. (1971) *The Quest for National Efficiency: A Study in British Politics and Political Thought 1988–1914*, Oxford: Blackwell.

Segal, Lynne (1986) *Is the Future Female?*, London: Virago.

Selbourne, David (1994) *The Principle of Duty*, London: Sinclair-Stevenson.
Seldon, Arthur (1990) *Capitalism*, Oxford: Blackwell.
Semmel, B. (1960) *Imperialism and Social Reform*, Cambridge: Cambridge University Press.
Sewell, B. (1975) *Cecil Chesterton*, Faversham: Whitefriars.
Sharpe, L.J. (1970) 'Theories and Values of Local Government', *Political Studies*, 18(2), June.
Shaw, G.B. (1887) *An Unsocial Socialist*, London: Swan Sonnenschein.
Shaw, G.B. (1893) *The Impossibilities of Anarchism*, Fabian Tract 45, London: Fabian Society.
Shaw, G.B. (1894) 'Socialism and Superior Brains. A Reply to Mr. Mallock', *Fortnightly Review*, April.
Shaw, G.B. (1921) *Ruskin's Politics*, London: Ruskin Centenary Council.
Shaw, G.B. (1926) [1905] *Major Barbara*, London: Constable.
Shaw, G.B. (1946) [1903] *Man and Superman*, Harmondsworth: Penguin.
Shaw, G.B. (1962) [1889] *Fabian Essays in Socialism*, 6th edn, London: George Allen & Unwin.
Shaw, G.B. (1964) [1919] *Heartbreak House*, Harmondsworth: Penguin.
Shelden, Michael (1991) *Orwell: The Authorised Biography*, London: Heinemann.
Shell, K.L. (1957) 'Industrial Democracy and the British Labour Movement', *Political Science Quarterly*, 72(4), December.
Shils, E. (1955) 'Letter from Milan: The End of Ideology', *Encounter*, 5(5), November.
Shipley, P. (1976) *Revolutionaries in Modern Britain*, London: The Bodley Head.
Sidgwick, H. (1902) *Lectures on the Ethics of T.H. Green, Mr. Herbert Spencer, and J. Martineau*, London: Macmillan.
Simhony, Avital (1991) 'On Forcing Individuals to be Free: T.H. Green's Liberal Theory of Positive Freedom', *Political Studies*, 39(2), June: 303–20.
Sinfield, Alan (1989) *Literature, Politics and Culture in Post-War Britain*, Oxford: Blackwell.
Skidelsky, R. (1975) *Oswald Mosley*, London: Macmillan.
Smith, Adrian (1996) *The New Statesman: Portrait of a Political Weekly, 1913–1931*, London: Frank Cass.
Smith, Anna Marie (1994) *New Right Discourse on Race and Sexuality: Britain, 1968–1990*, Cambridge: Cambridge University Press.
Smith, Harold L. (ed.) (1990) *British Feminism in the Twentieth Century*, Cheltenham: Edward Elgar.
Smith, P. (1967) *Disraelian Conservatism and Social Reform*, London: Routledge & Kegan Paul.
Snowden, P. (1921) *Labour and the New World*, London: Waverley Book Co.
Soffer, Reba N. (1969) 'New Elitism: Social Psychology in Pre-War England', *Journal of British Studies*, 8(2), May.
Soffer, Reba N. (1970) 'The Revolution in English Social Thought, 1880–1914', *American Historical Review*, 75(7).
Soffer, Reba N. (1978) *Ethics and Society in England: The Revolution in the Social Sciences 1870–1914*, Berkeley: University of California Press.
Soffer, Reba N. (1995) *Discipline and Power: The University, History, and the*

Making of an English Elite, 1870–1930, Cambridge: Cambridge University Press.

Sparkes, A.W. (1994) *Talking Politics*, London: Routledge.

Speaight, R. (1957) *The Life of Hilaire Belloc*, Freeport N.Y.: Ayer.

Spencer, H. (1842) *The Proper Sphere of Government*, London: W. Brittain.

Spencer, H. (1851, 1892) *Social Statistics*, 1st and 2nd editions, London: Williams & Norgate.

Spencer, H. (1969) [1884] *The Man versus the State*, Harmondsworth: Penguin.

Spender, Dale (1980) *Man Made Language*, London: Routledge & Kegan Paul.

Spender, Dale (ed.) (1983) *Feminist Theorists: Three Centuries of Women's Intellectual Traditions*, London: The Women's Press.

Spender, S. (1937) *Forward from Liberalism*, London: Victor Gollancz.

Squires, Judith (ed.) (1993) *Principled Positions: Postmodernisms and the Rediscovery of Value*, London: Lawrence & Wishart.

Stacey, Judith (1986) 'Are Feminists Afraid to Leave Home? The Challenge of Conservative Pro-Family Feminism', in Juliet Mitchell and Ann Oakley (eds) *What is Feminism?*, Oxford: Blackwell.

Stafford, D. (1971) 'Anarchists in Britain Today', in David Apter and James Joll (eds) *Anarchism Today*, London: Macmillan.

Stapleton, Julia (1994) *Englishness and the Study of Politics: The Social and Political Thought of Ernest Barker*, Cambridge: Cambridge University Press.

Stead, W.T. (1906) 'The Labour Party and the Books that Helped Make It', *The Review of Reviews*, 33, June.

Steele, Tom (1990) *Alfred Orage and the Leeds Art Club 1893–1923*, Aldershot: Scolar/Gower.

Strachey, J. (1932) *The Coming Struggle for Power*, London: Victor Gollancz.

Strachey, J. (1940) *A Programme for Progress*, London: Victor Gollancz.

Strachey, J. (1956) *Contemporary Capitalism*, London: Victor Gollancz.

Strachey, J. (1959) *The End of Empire*, London: Victor Gollancz.

Strachey, J. (1970) [1952] 'Tasks and Achievements of British Labour', in R.H.S. Crossman (ed.) *New Fabian Essays*, London: Dent.

Strachey, R. (1974) [1928] *The Cause*, Bath: Cedric Chivers.

Sutherland, John (1995) 'Devil Take the Hindmost', *London Review of Books*, vol. 17, no. 24, 14 December: 18–19.

Swindells, Julia and Jardine, Lisa (1990) *What's Left? Women in Culture and the Labour Movement*, London: Routledge.

Tarn, J.N. (1973) *Five Per Cent Philanthropy: An Account of Housing in Urban Areas 1840–1914*, Cambridge: Cambridge University Press.

Tawney, R.H. (1920) *The Sickness of an Acquisitive Society*, London: George Allen & Unwin.

Tawney, R.H. (1921a) *The Acquisitive Society*, London: Fontana.

Tawney, R.H. (1921b) 'Foreword', Carter L. Goodrich, *The Frontier of Control*, London: Pluto.

Tawney, R.H. (1931) *Equality*, London: George Allen & Unwin.

Tawney, R.H. (1943) 'The Abolition of Economic Controls, 1918–1921', *Economic History Review*, 13.

Tawney, R.H. (1953a) *The Webbs in Perspective*, London: Athlone Press.

Tawney, R.H. (1953b) *The Attack and Other Papers*, London: George Allen & Unwin.

Tawney, R.H. (1964) *The Radical Tradition: Twelve Essays on Politics, Education and Literature*, ed. Rita Hinden, London: George Allen & Unwin.

Taylor, A.J. (1972) *Laissez-Faire and State Intervention in Nineteenth Century Britain*, London: Macmillan.

Taylor, Barbara (1983) *Eve and the New Jerusalem*, London: Virago.

Taylor, Joan Kennedy (1994) 'Why Aren't All Women Feminists?', in Caroline Quest (ed.) *Liberating Women ... From Modern Feminism*, London: IEA.

Taylor, L. (1971) 'The Unfinished Sexual Revolution', *Journal of Biosocial Science*, 3.

Taylor, M.W. (1992) *Men Versus The State*, Oxford: Clarendon.

Taylor, Michael (1989) 'The Errors of an Evolutionist: A Reply to Ellen Frankel Paul', *Political Studies*, 37(3).

Terrill, R. (1973) *R.H. Tawney and his Times: Socialism as Fellowship*, Cambridge, Mass: Harvard University Press.

Therborn, Goran (1995) 'The Autobiography of the Twentieth Century', *New Left Review*, 214, November/December.

Thody, Philip (1993) *The Conservative Imagination*, London: Pinter.

Thomas, H. (1973) *John Strachey*, London: Eyre Methuen.

Thomas, Rosamund (1978) *The British Philosophy of Administration*, London: Longman.

Thompson, Dorothy (1996) 'On the Trail of the New Left', *New Left Review*, 215, January/February.

Thompson, E.P. (1974) 'An Open Letter to Leszek Kolakowski', in R. Miliband and J. Saville (eds) *The Socialist Register 1973*, London: The Merlin Press.

Thompson, E.P. (1977) *William Morris, Romantic to Revolutionary*, 2nd edn, London: Merlin Press.

Thompson, E.P. (1960) *Out of Apathy*, London: Stevens and Sons.

Thompson, E.P. (1990) 'The Ends of Cold War', *New Left Review*, 182.

Thompson, F.M.L. (1965) 'Land and Politics in the Nineteenth Century', *Transactions of the Royal Historical Society*, 5th series, 5(15).

Thompson, J.A. and Mejia, A. (1988) *Edwardian Conservatism: Five Studies in Adaption*, London: Routledge.

Thompson, L. (1951) *Portrait of an Englishman: A Life of Robert Blatchford*, London: Victor Gollancz.

Thompson, L. (1971) *The Enthusiasts: A Biography of John and Katharine Bruce Glasier*, London: Victor Gollancz.

Thompson, Noel (1993) *John Strachey: An Intellectual Portrait*, London: Macmillan.

Thompson, P. (1967) *The Work of William Morris*, London: Heinemann.

Thompson, P. (1975) *The Edwardians: The Remaking of British Society*, London: Weidenfeld & Nicolson.

Tindale, Stephen (1994) 'Sustaining Social Democracy: The Politics of the Environment', in David Miliband (ed.) *Reinventing the Left*, Cambridge: Polity.

Titmuss, R.M. (1963) *Essays on 'The Welfare State'*, 2nd edn, London: George Allen & Unwin.

Titmuss, R.M. (1968) *Commitment to Welfare*, London: George Allen & Unwin.

Titmuss, R.M. (1970) *The Gift Relationship: From Human Blood to Social Policy*, Harmondsworth: Penguin.

Tivey, L. and Wright, A. (eds) (1989) *Party Ideology in Britain*, London: Routledge.

Tivey, L.J. and Wright, A.W. (eds) (1992) *Political Thought since 1945: Philosophy, Science, Ideology*, Cheltenham: Edward Elgar.

Tomlinson, Jim (1990) *Hayek and the Market*, London: Pluto.

Townshend, Jules (1991) *J.A. Hobson (Lives of the Left)*, Manchester: Manchester University Press.

Tsuzuki, C. (1961) *H.M. Hyndman and British Socialism*, ed. H. Pelling, Oxford: Oxford University Press.

Tsuzuki, C. (1980) *Edward Carpenter 1844–1929: Prophet of Human Fellowship*, Cambridge: Cambridge University Press.

Tsuzuki, Chushichi (1991) *Tom Mann 1856–1941: The Challenges of Labour*, Oxford: Clarendon.

Tucker, A.V. (1962) 'W.H. Mallock and Late Victorian Conservatism', *University of Toronto Quarterly*, 31(2), January.

Tusscher, Tessa ten (1986) 'Patriarchy, Capitalism and the New Right', in Judy Evans et al. (eds) *Feminism and Political Theory*, London: Sage.

Utley, T.E. (1949) *Essays in Conservatism*, London: Conservative Political Centre.

Utley, T.E. (1968) *Enoch Powell, the Man and his Thinking*, London: Kimber.

Veldman, Meredith (1994) *Fantasy, The Bomb and the Greening of Britain: Romantic Protest, 1945–1980*, Cambridge: Cambridge University Press.

Vernon, James (1993) *Politics and the People: A Study in English Political Culture c. 1815–1867*, Cambridge: Cambridge University Press.

Vincent, A. (ed) (1986) *The Philosophy of T.H. Green*, Aldershot: Gower.

Vincent, Andrew (1992) *Modern Political Ideologies*, Oxford: Blackwell.

Vincent, Andrew (1994) 'British Conservatism and the Problem of Ideology', *Political Studies*, 42(2), June.

Vincent, Andrew and Plant, Raymond (1984) *Philosophy, Politics, and Citizenship: The Life and Thought of the British Idealists*, Oxford: Blackwell.

Vitoux, P. (1969) *Histoire des idées en Grande-Bretagne*, Paris: Libraire Armand Colin.

Vogel, Ursula (1986) 'Rationalism and Romanticism: Two Strategies for Women's Liberation', in Judy Evans et al. (eds) *Feminism and Political Theory*, London: Sage.

Wainwright, H. (1987a) *Labour: A Tale of Two Parties*, London: Hogarth Press.

Wainwright, H. (1987b) 'The Limits of Labourism: 1987 and Beyond', *New Left Review*, 164.

Wainwright, Hilary (1994) *Arguments for a New Left: Answering the Free Market Right*, Oxford: Blackwell.

Wallace, Neil (ed.) (1991) *Thoughts and Fragments about Theatres and Nations*, London: The Guardian.

Wallas, G. (1962) [1889] 'Property under Socialism', in G.B. Shaw (ed.) *Fabian Essays in Socialism*, London: Allen & Unwin.

Wallas, G. (1908) *Human Nature in Politics*, London: Constable.

Wallas, G. (1915) 'Oxford and English Political Thought', *Nation*, 17(7), 15 May.

Wallas, G. (1926) *The Art of Thought*, London: Jonathan Cape.

Wandor, M. (ed.) (1972) *The Body Politic: Writings from the Women's Liberation Movement in Britain 1969–1972*, London: Stage 1.

Ward, C. (ed.) (1987) *A Decade of Anarchy 1961–1970: Selections from the Monthly Journal Anarchy*, London: Freedom Press.

Ward, C. (1973) *Anarchy in Action*, London: George Allen & Unwin.

Ward, C. (1974) *Tenants Take Over*, London: Architectural Press.

Ward, C. (1976) *Housing: An Anarchist Approach*, London: Freedom Press.

Ward, Colin (1989) *Welcome, Thinner City*, London: Bedford Square Press.

Ward, M. (1944) *Gilbert Keith Chesterton*, London: Sheed & Ward.

Warde, Alan (1982) *Consensus and Beyond*, Manchester: Manchester University Press.

Waters, Chris (1990) *British Socialists and the Politics of Popular Culture 1884–1914*, Manchester: Manchester University Press.

Watson, G. (1973) *The English Ideology*, London: Allen Lane.

Watson, George (1977) *Politics and Literature in Modern Britain*, London: Macmillan.

Waylen, Georgina (1986) 'Women and Neo-Liberalism', in Judith Evans et al. (eds) *Feminism and Political Theory*, London: Sage.

Webb, B. (1938) [1926] *My Apprenticeship*, Harmondsworth: Penguin.

Webb, B. (1948) *Our Partnership*, London: Longmans.

Webb, S. (1890) *English Progress Towards Social Democracy*, London: Fabian Society.

Webb, S. (1962) [1889] 'The Basis of Socialism: Historic', in G.B. Shaw (ed.) *Fabian Essays in Socialism*, London: Allen & Unwin.

Webb, S. and B. (1897) *Industrial Democracy*, 2 volumes, London: Longmans.

Webb, S. and B. (1912) 'What Syndicalism Means', *The Crusade Against Destitution*, 3, August.

Webb, S. and B. (1920) *A Constitution for the Socialist Commonwealth of Great Britain*, London: The Authors.

Weedon, Chris (1987) 'Radical and Revolutionary Feminism', in Frankie Ashton and Gill Whitting (eds) *Feminist Theories and Practical Policies*, Bristol: School for Advanced Urban Studies.

Wells, H.G. (1905) *A Modern Utopia*, London: Thomas Nelson.

Wells, H.G. (1906) [1903] *Mankind in the Making*, London: Chapman & Hall.

Wells, H.G. (1911) *The New Machiavelli*, London: John Lane.

Wells, H.G. (1914) [1901] *Anticipations of the Reaction of Mechanical and Scientific Progress upon Human Life and Thought*, London: Chapman & Hall.

Wells, H.G. (1920) *The Outline of History*, London: Newnes.

Wendelken, David (1996) 'Contemporary Conservatism, Human Nature, and Identity: The Philosophy of Roger Scruton', *Politics*, 16(1):17–22.

Wesker, A. (1959a) *Chicken Soup with Barley*, Harmondsworth: Penguin.

Wesker, A. (1959b) *Roots*, Harmondsworth: Penguin.

Wesker, A. (1960) *I'm Talking About Jerusalem*, Harmondsworth: Penguin.

Wesker, A. (1962) *Chips with Everything*, Harmondsworth: Penguin.

White, Joseph (1990) 'Syndicalism in a Mature Industrial Setting: The Case of Britain', in Marcel van der Linden and Wayne Thorpe (eds) *Revolutionary Syndicalism: An International Perspective*, Aldershop: Scolar Press.

White, A. (1894) *The English Democracy, its Promises and Perils*, London: Swan Sonnenschein.

White, A. (1901) *Efficiency and Empire*, London: Methuen.
White, Dan H. (1992) *Lost Comrades: Socialists of the Front Generation 1918–1945*, Cambridge, Mass: Harvard University Press.
White, J. (1991) *Tom Mann*, Manchester: Manchester University Press.
White, R.J. (ed.) (1964) [1950] *The Conservative Tradition*, 2nd edn, London: A. & C. Black.
Wickwar, W.H. (1970) *The Political Theory of Local Government*, Columbia, S. Carol: University of South Carolina Press.
Widgery, D. (ed.) (1975) *The Left in Britain 1956–1968*, Harmondsworth: Penguin.
Wiener, M.J. (1971) *Between Two Worlds: The Political Thought of Graham Wallas*, Oxford: Clarendon Press.
Wilde, O. (1912) [1891] *The Soul of Man under Socialism*, London: Humphreys.
Wilford, R.A. (1976) 'The Federation of Progressive Societies and Individuals', *Journal of Contemporary History*, 11(1), January.
Wilhelm, M.M. (1972) 'The Political Thought of Friederich A. Hayek', *Political Studies*, 20(2), June.
Wilks, Stuart (ed.) (1993) *Talking About Tomorrow: A New Radical Politics*, London: Pluto/New Times.
Willetts, David (1992) *Modern Conservatism*, London: Penguin.
Williams, R. (1961a) [1958] *Culture and Society, 1780–1950*, Harmondsworth: Penguin.
Williams, R. (1961b) *The Long Revolution*, Harmondsworth: Penguin.
Williams, R. (1971) *Orwell*, London: Fontana.
Willis, K. (1977) 'The Introduction and Critical Reception of Marxist Thought in Britain 1850–1900', *The Historical Journal*, 20(2), June.
Wilson, W.L. (1909) *The Menace of Socialism*, London: Grant Richards.
Wiltsher, Anne (1985) *Most Dangerous Women: Feminist Peace Campaigners of the Great War*, London: Pandora.
Wiltshire, David (1978) *The Social & Political Thought of Herbert Spencer*, Oxford: Oxford University Press.
Winch, D. (1969) *Economics and Policy: A Historical Study*, London: Hodder & Stoughton.
Winslow, Barbara (1996) *Sylvia Pankhurst*, London: UCL Press.
Winter, J.M. (1970) 'R.H. Tawney's Early Political Thought', *Past and Present*, 47, May.
Winter, J.M. (1974) *Socialism and the Challenge of War: Ideas and Politics in Britain 1912–18*, London: Routledge & Kegan Paul.
Winter, J.M. and Joslin, D.M. (eds) (1972) *R.H. Tawney's Commonplace Book*, Cambridge: Cambridge University Press.
Wintropp, Norman (1983) *Liberal Democratic Theory and Its Critics*, London: Croom Helm.
Wolfe, Willard (1975) *From Radicalism to Socialism: Men and Ideas in the Formation of Fabian Socialist Doctrines 1881–1889*, London: Yale University Press.
Wolffe, John (1994) *God and Greater Britain: Religion and National Life in Britain and Ireland 1843–1945*, London: Routledge.
Wolin, S. S. (1960) *Politics and Vision: Continuity and Innovation in Western Political Thought*, Boston: Little, Brown.

342 *Bibliography*

Women's Liberation Campaign for Legal and Financial Independence (1975) *The Demand for Independence*, London: WLCLFI.

Wood, J. (ed.) (1970) *Powell and the 1970 General Election*, Kingswood: Elliot Right Way Books.

Wood, N. (1959) *Communism and the British Intellectuals*, London: Victor Gollancz.

Woodcock, G. (1967) *The Crystal Spirit: A Study of George Orwell*, London: Jonathan Cape.

Woodcock, G. (1971) [1963] *Anarchism, Harmondsworth: Penguin.*

Woodcock, G. (1972) *Herbert Read: The Stream and Source*, London: Faber.

Woodcock, George (1992) *Anarchism and Anarchists*, London: Quarry.

Woodcock, G. and Avakumovic, I. (1950) *The Anarchist Prince*, London: T.V. Boardman & Co.

Woolf, L. (1949) 'Political Thought and the Webbs', in M. Cole (ed.) *The Webbs and their Work*, London: Muller.

Woolf, Virginia (1993) [1938] *Three Guineas*, London: Penguin.

Wootton, B. (1934) *Plan or No Plan*, London: Victor Gollancz.

Wootton, B. (1945) *Freedom under Planning*, London: Allen & Unwin.

Wootton, Barbara (1994) *Selected Writings*, 4 vols, ed. Vera Seal and Philip Bean, London: Macmillan.

Wright, A. (1913) *The Unexpurgated Case Against Woman Suffrage*, London: Constable.

Wright, A. (1986) *Socialisms: Theories and Practices*, Oxford: Oxford University Press.

Wright, A. (1987) *R. H. Tawney*, Manchester: Manchester University Press.

Wright, Anthony (1993) *Citizens and Subjects: An Essay on British Politics*, London: Routledge.

Wright, A.W. (1976) 'From Fabianism to Guild Socialism: The Early Political Thought of G.D.H. Cole', *Bulletin of the Society for the Study of Labour History*, 32, Spring.

Wright, A.W. (1979) *G.D.H. Cole and Socialist Democracy*, Oxford: Clarendon Press.

Wright, A.W. (1984) 'Tawneyism Revisited: Equality, Welfare, and Socialism', in Ben Pimlott (ed.) *Fabian Essays in Socialist Thought*, London: Heinemann.

Young, N. (1977) *An Infantile Disorder? The Crisis and Decline of the New Left*, London: Routledge & Kegan Paul.

Zalewski, Marysia (1991) 'The Debauching of Feminist Theory/The Penetration of the Postmodern', *Politics*, 11(1): 30–6.

Zylstra, B. (1968) *From Pluralism to Collectivism: The Development of Harold Laski's Political Thought*, Assen: Van Goreum & Co.

Index

Sachs, Albie 120, 132
Salisbury, 3rd. Marquess 77–8
Salvation Army 18
school meals 28
Schreiner, Olive 127
Schumpeter, Joseph A. 259
science, as a political metaphor 59
Scott, Sir Giles Gilbert 11
Scruton, Roger 225, 234–8
'second wave' of feminism 280
Second World War 135
secular education 34
Segal, Lyn 261, 286–7
Seymour, Henry 67
Shaw, George Bernard 11, 41–5, 53,
    79, 161; *An Unsocial Socialist* 43;
    and Boer War 27; and Hyndman
    36–7; cf. Wells 50–1; *Heartbreak
    House* 44; *Major Barbara* 44; *Man
    and Superman* 43–4; on Chesterton
    & Belloc 93; on democracy 111–2;
    on Soviet Union 171; on
    'tories' 227
Shils, Edward 182
shop tewards' movement 71, 97
Sinn Fein 133
Small Farms and Labourers' Holding
    Company 89
small holdings, Select Committee on
    89
Smiles, Samuel 58
Smith, Toulmin 78, 105
Snowden, Philip 46
social credit 138
social Darwinism 68–70, 74, 78
Social Democratic Federation 34, 82
Social Democratic Party 6
socialism 33–52
socialism and liberalism: Asquith on
    33; Hobhouse on 27, 28, 29;
    Hobson on 31–2; Macdonald on 49
socialism: Belloc on 95–6; Bosanquet
    on 70; end of 2, 4; Haldane and 26;
    Mallock on 73; Morley on 15–6;
    'revisionism' 183–8
Socialist League 83, 88
Socialist Register, The 251
social science 110
Society for the Preservation of
    Ancient Buildings 82

Society of Jesus 39
Solidarity 71
Soviet Union 3, 170–2, 248, 254–5
Spanish Civil War 166
Spectator 208
Spencer, Herbert 24, 59–62, 63, 64,
    65, 66; and Belloc 95; and Cole
    106; cf. Bosanquet 69–70; cf.
    Darwin 59; cf. Hayek 143; cf.
    Hobson 31; on men and women
    120; *The Man versus the State*
    11, 59
Spender, Dale 167, 288
Stalin, Joseph 155
state, growth of 12–13, 15–19; Jones,
    Sir Henry on 17; Spencer on 16;
    Morley on 15–16; Webb on 16–17
Stead, W.T. 18
Stephen, James 111
Strachey, John 137, 168, 196; and
    Mosley 169; and Nazi-Soviet pact
    177; 'revisionism' 184–6; on Soviet
    Union 171; on workers' control
    212–3
Strachey, Ray 123
strikes, and syndicalism 132
Sumption, Jonathan 234
syndicalism 40, 98–100; and strikes
    132; and the servile state 96, 97

Talmon, J.L. 186
Tamworth Manifesto 237
Tanner, John 44
Tarn, Albert 67
Tawney, R.H. 12, 149–154, 189, 214,
    270, 271, 278; accommodation
    with collectivism 139; and Hobson
    153; and workers' control 100; cf.
    Chesterton 92; cf. Chesterton and
    Belloc 153; cf. Crosland 188; cf.
    Hobhouse 153; cf. Mallock &
    Carlyle 151; cf. Morris 153;
    Equality 11, 151ff; on men and
    women 129; puritanism 266–7; on
    Reynolds 72; on Webbs 37–8
taxation, land 28
Tebbitt, Norman 246, 255
Thatcher, Margaret 1, 223
'Thatcherism' 1, 224, 258
Thiers, Adolphe 89